UNDERSTANDING
THE SELF

EDITED BY RICHARD STEVENS

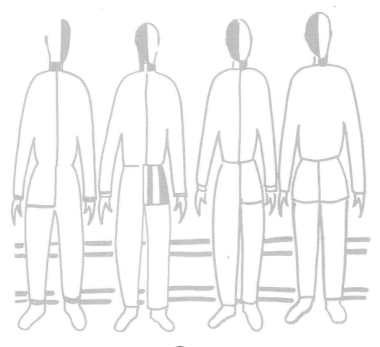

SAGE Publications
London • Thousand Oaks • New Delhi
In association with

The Open
University

Cover illustration: Kasimir Malevich, *Sportsmen*, *c*. 1928–32, oil on canvas, 142×164cm., State Russian Museum, St Petersburg.

The Open University, Walton Hall, Milton Keynes MK7 6AA

SAGE Publications Ltd
6 Bonhill Street
London EC2A 4PU

SAGE Publications Inc
2455 Teller Road
Thousand Oaks
California 91320

Sage Publications India Pvt Ltd
32, M-Block Market
Greater Kailash - I
New Delhi 110 048

British Library Cataloguing in Publication data

A catalogue record for this book is available from the British Library

ISBN 0 7619 5039 7
ISBN 0 7619 5040 0 (pbk)

Library of Congress catalog card number 95-071767

Edited, designed and typeset by the Open University.

Printed in Great Britain by Butler and Tanner Ltd, Frome.

This text forms part of an Open University course D317 *Social Psychology: Personal Lives, Social Worlds*. Details of this and other Open University courses can be obtained from the Course Reservations and Sales Centre, PO Box 724, The Open University, Milton Keynes MK7 6ZS. For availability of other course components, contact Open University Educational Enterprises Ltd, The Open University, Walton Hall, Milton Keynes, MK7 6AA.

16005C/d317b1pi1.2

Contents

Social Psychology: Personal Lives, Social Worlds Course Team

Open University Staff

Dr Dorothy Miell (Course Team Chair, Senior Lecturer in Psychology)

Alison Bannister (Print Buying Co-ordinator)

Penny Bennett (Editor, Social Sciences)

Pam Berry (Compositor)

David Calderwood (Project Control)

Lene Connolly (Print Buying Controller)

Dr Troy Cooper (Staff Tutor)

Dr Rose Croghan (Research Fellow in Psychology)

Sarah Crompton (Graphic Designer)

Dr Rudi Dallos (Staff Tutor)

Jonathan Davies (Graphic Design Co-ordinator)

Jane Elliott (Producer, BBC)

Janis Gilbert (Graphic Artist)

Dr Sue Gregory (Senior Lecturer in Psychology)

Jonathan Hunt (Book Trade Department)

Tom Hunter (Editor, Social Sciences)

Carole Kershaw (Course Secretary)

Vic Lockwood (Senior Producer, BBC)

Dr Janet Maybin (Lecturer, School of Education)

Jeannette Murphy (Senior Lecturer in Health Informatics, University College London Medical School, co-opted on to team during course production)

Lynda Preston (Psychology Secretary)

Dr Roger Sapsford (Senior Lecturer in Research Methods)

Varrie Scott (Course Manager)

Brenda Smith (Staff Tutor)

Paul Smith (Media Librarian)

Richard Stevens (Senior Lecturer in Psychology)

Dr Kerry Thomas (Senior Lecturer in Psychology)

Dr Frederick Toates (Senior Lecturer in Biology)

Pat Vasiliou (Psychology Discipline Secretary)

Dr Diane Watson (Staff Tutor)

Dr Margaret Wetherell (Senior Lecturer in Psychology)

Kathy Wilson (Production Assistant, BBC)

Chris Wooldridge (Editor, Social Sciences)

External authors and tutor consultants

Dr Michael Argyle (Emeritus Reader in Social Psychology, University of Oxford)

Hedy Brown (Retired, Senior Lecturer in Social Psychology, Open University)

Dr David Devalle (OU Social Psychology Tutor)

Professor Robert Hinde (Retired, St John's College, Cambridge)

Dr Mansur Lalljee (University Lecturer in Social Psychology and Fellow of Jesus College)

Jackie Malone (OU Social Psychology Tutor)

Dr Patrick McGhee (Head of Psychology and School Director Teaching and Learning, University of Derby, OU Tutor Consultant)

Helen Morgan (Psychotherapist and Consultant)

Professor Jonathan Potter (Professor of Discourse Analysis, Loughborough University)

Dr Alan Radley (Reader in Health and Social Relations, Loughborough University)

Dr Arthur Still (Part-time Senior Lecturer in Psychology, University of Durham, OU Social Psychology Tutor)

Dr Arlene Vetere (Lecturer in Family Psychology, Reading University)

External assessors

Professor Jerome Bruner (Research Professor of Psychology, New York University, Senior Research Fellow in Law, School of Law, New York University)

Professor Michael Billig (Professor of Social Sciences, Loughborough University)

Professor Steve Duck (Daniel and Amy Starch Distinguished Research Professor of Interpersonal Communication, and Adjunct Professor of Psychology, University of Iowa)

Professor Kenneth J. Gergen (Mustin Professor of Psychology, Swarthmore College, Pennsylvania)

Foreword

Studying social psychology and studying history are akin in one particularly interesting way. For either of them to matter much in your own life, you must end up making what you have learned your own. And the only way to do that is to explore different ways of framing or constructing the subject-matter at hand until you have found *your* way of making sense of it. For just as there is no *the* history, say, of the French Revolution, there is no *the* social psychology of the family. Both 'subjects' gain their meanings through the perspective one brings to bear on them. The French Revolution is a struggle for the rights of man, and it is a chapter in the story of mob tyranny. One studies it differently, even chooses one's facts differently, depending upon which of the two perspectives one has chosen as a focus. And so too the social psychology of the family – whether one wishes to look at family life in terms of 'systems theory', or in terms of the working out of the psychoanalytic Oedipus theme, or from the point of view of the phenomenologies of family members and how they are negotiated in dinner-table conversations.

This Open University social psychology course is a radical departure in teaching social psychology. Rather than insisting that there is a 'right and only' way to look at phenomena social psychologically – *the* social psychology of this or that – it takes the truth of perspective as its starting point. Its aim is to present a variety of perspectives on the standard 'topics' of social psychology, not only to give them depth but also to equip the student with the wherewithal for creating her or his *own* perspective. But it does this in such a way as to recognize not only the relativity of social knowledge, but also to honour the canons of good social science. For the relativity of perspective does not mean that 'anything goes'. Rather, it means that whatever perspective one brings to bear carries with it requirements of method. Has one gained sufficient information on the matter at hand, protected oneself against facile presuppositions, looked with sufficient care at the antecedents of the phenomenon one is studying, and so on? The course attempts to give as clear a view as possible of what constitutes good enquiry as conducted from the vantage-points of several crucial perspectives.

After studying the volumes in this series, the student should be prepared to evaluate different perspectives in social psychology and, as noted, to come up with one of his or her own, one that meets the standards of sound social science. In this sense, these books deliberately merge the conventional categories of teaching and research. The authors have succeeded in resisting the usual 'teacherly' approach of giving standard reviews of the existing literature on some narrow topics, and instead have provided abundant opportunities for the student to try his or her hand at creating original syntheses of several related topics that bear on each other. In doing so, they use the tools of research as a means of teaching in a most creative way.

There is one further feature of the series that needs special mention. Its emphasis upon the place of perspective in the legitimizing of 'facts' and the construction of theories inevitably leads to questions about the philosophy of knowledge – to puzzling issues in epistemology. Rather than simply tabling these and leaving them for some other course to discuss, this course tackles them head on. So in a way, it is a course not only about social psychology, but also, if I may use an odd term, about social epistemology. At times, then, the student will find himself or herself in a dialogue whose other members are not only psychologists and sociologists, but also philosophers and even literary theorists (for in a very deep sense, the 'data' of social psychology are texts of what people said about what they thought or felt, narrative texts at that).

The series crosses many disciplinary boundaries that are often regarded as either taboo or as too forbidding for students to cross. For social psychology is a field of study that grew out of two traditions that have often been regarded as antithetical – even at war with each other. One tradition is primarily societal or cultural, and looks at social interaction from the point of view of the roles and statuses that people occupy within a social structure, specifying the obligations and rights that activate and constrain those who fill these roles and statuses. This is 'sociological' social psychology – and a good part of social psychology as a disciplinary study is situated in sociology departments of universities. The other tradition is psychological, its emphasis squarely on the individual – his or her attitudes, values, reactions, and the like. And as psychological social psychology, this side of the discipline takes its methods from the different approaches that psychology has adopted over the century since its founding. It may emphasize a more strictly experimental approach, a more humanistic one, or one based on what has come to be called 'social constructionism' that sees the data and theories of psychology as situated in or deriving from the discourse of human beings in interaction. The volumes try to make a place for all of these approaches, treating them not as antagonistic to each other, but as complementary.

In tackling social psychology in so multifaceted a way, these books manage something that is rarely tried in the teaching of this subject. They bridge two traditions that rarely meet in the theatre of university instruction – a principally North American 'scientific' tradition based on the positivist ideal of objectivity, and a European tradition that is much more strongly interpretivist in spirit. And they manage to make as good a case as possible for both of them. Some critics of the books will doubtless say, I'm sure, that they give too much credence to one side, some to the other. And this is as it should be.

It is impossible to teach an honest course in social psychology in our times without taking into account the diversity of modern society. There is no such thing as a standard family or a standard work-place about which to make generalizations – whether they be statistical generalizations or interpretative ones. There are indeed families in Britain, for example, that meet the traditional criterion of being 'standard'. They are White, Anglo-Saxon, Protestant, Middle-class. They may fare better on the job market, but they are hardly 'standard' save in some possibly hegemonic sense. What holds for them does not hold for Jamaican families in Spitalfields, for immigrant Pakistani families in Bradford whose children are struggling to find an identity, and so on. So, again almost inevitably, social psychology needs to be sensitive not so much to 'society in general' but to the changing social patterns of our times. And I believe that this series achieves such sensitivity.

During the long preparation of these volumes, I have served in the role of what is called, in Open University terminology, the Course Assessor. Nobody is quite sure what the term means, but one thing is clear: the Course Assessor quickly becomes a partner in dialogue with the course team. I have been such a partner 'from a distance' – geographically if not psychologically. We have been engaged for more than a year in a constant and busy exchange of chapter drafts, memoranda, and conversation – me in New York or in my writing hideaway in West County Cork, they in Milton Keynes. We have used every imaginable form of telecommunication – post, fax, e-mail, telephone. I have found it enormously rewarding, both psychologically and intellectually. For this series has been an adventure for those of us involved in constructing it, not only a scholarly one but, indeed, a moral one. For this is a series designed to teach people not just *about* social psychology, but how to *think* social psychology. And as with any such undertaking, it forced all of us to think hard about what a social psychologist *ought* to be. So I must close this foreword by thanking my friends at the Open University for what I can only describe as a 'consciousness raising trip'. And I rather suspect that the readers of this series will do the same when they're done with it.

Jerome Bruner, New York University

Preface

Understanding the Self is one of three books which form the core of the Open University course D317 *Social Psychology: Personal Lives, Social Worlds.* The others are *Social Interaction and Personal Relationships* (edited by D. Miell and R. Dallos) and *Identity, Groups and Social Issues* (edited by M. Wetherell). Students of the Open University course receive supplementary material, including an opening 'trigger unit' which uses discussion of health and disease to introduce the topics with which the course will be concerned. There is also a book on philosophical and methodological issues in social psychology, a set of projects, four television and eight radio programmes, and three audiocassettes which feature debates around key issues. The three volumes published in this series have been designed to be read independently of this supplementary material.

We recognize that social psychology comes in many forms. Our own particular approach has been developed from the previous social psychology courses which we have offered, and as a result of intensive discussions among members of the course team. We have adopted what might be called a multiple-perspective approach, in that we have included a number of different perspectives on social psychology from social constructionism to experimental social psychology and from psychodynamics to experiential psychology. We believe the essential subject-matter of social psychology to be the meanings through which each of us makes sense of the social world and acts within it. Such meanings are personal and social constructions which need to be understood in the context of both individuals and the interactions and social practices in which they engage. Likewise, any way of investigating or theorizing in social psychology is a construction and needs to be recognized as such. Thus a feature of the course is the explicit attempt to comment on the different perspectives and to discuss the kinds of understanding they represent and the implications of these. This, for example, is the function of the 'Reflections' sections at the end of the chapters in this volume, which I have written in collaboration with each particular author.

While we have not set out to be fully representative, the three volumes in this series contain a wide range of material, including much of the seminal research and theorizing in social psychology; however, this has been reworked in the context of the overall philosophy of the course. We hope the reader/student will take from the books a broad understanding of the different forms that social psychology takes and develop the ability to work in a structured and coherent way with a diversity of ideas and approaches; also that they will stimulate both critical thinking and awareness of some of the wider issues which arise out of studying social psychology. What kind of knowledge, for example, is possible and appropriate in this area? At the same time, each of the books is intended to heighten the reader's capacity for reflection on his or her own life in the light of the concepts and theories presented. We want you to be able to relate the ideas here to your own experience and through this to understand more clearly the social behaviour of yourself and others.

This volume explores five perspectives on understanding the self – biological, cognitive-experimental, experiential (an amalgam of humanistic, phenomenological and existential approaches), social constructionist and psychodynamic. The book is intended not only to deepen understanding of the person in a social world, but to raise key issues and debates about the nature of social psychological enquiry. We hope that it stimulates your understanding both of the self and the nature of psychological enquiry.

I want to thank the people who made unique contributions to this book in different ways. One of the exciting (and at times demanding!) aspects of preparing this book was developing it in the context of an OU course team. Our two superb book assessors, Jerome Bruner and Kenneth Gergen, provided both penetrating feedback and guidance and much food for thought. Several authors contributed useful observations on each other's work: in particular, Margaret Wetherell provided detailed and valuable comments on both chapter content and the structuring of the book. Other members of the team also provided perceptive and helpful feedback in the development of the book, especially Dorothy Miell (the course chair), Jeannette Murphy, Arthur Still, Patrick McGhee, Rudi Dallos, Roger Sapsford, David Devalle and Jackie Malone. Our course editor, Chris Wooldridge, and our course manager, Varrie Scott, provided their calm and assured support throughout production. Finally, my thanks also to Sarah Crompton for her quality design work and to our highly effective secretarial team of Carole Kershaw, Lynda Preston and Pat Vasiliou.

Richard Stevens, for the Course Team

CHAPTER 1

INTRODUCTION: MAKING SENSE OF THE PERSON IN A SOCIAL WORLD

by Richard Stevens

Contents

1 Being a person

Both you and I are aware that we are *persons*. Being a person is not the same as being a machine, a collection of physiological functions or a set of behavioural reflexes. As a person, each of us inhabits a distinctive social world of lived experience. We are conscious of being (and are seen by others as being) a *particular person* with a particular past and with particular expectations of the future. Alex, who lives near me, exists in a world of shadows and sadness. He is fighting cancer, his wife has left him and he is out of work. Only his belief in God has stopped him from trying to end it all. In contrast, for Sally, his next-door neighbour, the future is bright with hope. She has just left school to start work as a hairdresser, which has been her ambition since she worked in her aunt's salon in the school holidays. She lives comfortably with her parents, spends most evenings out enjoying herself with her friends and has just got engaged. Two different persons: two personal worlds which, while they share features in common, are somehow 'owned' by and particular to the people concerned.

The topic of this book is *understanding the self*. As we shall see, the self is a profoundly social phenomenon. And understanding the nature of self or being a person is a necessary basis for comprehending how social life works: for understanding both personal lives and social worlds.

The kinds of question we shall be considering in this book include:

- What does it mean to be a person in a social world?

- What are the different aspects or constituents of selfhood?

- In what ways and to what extent are we as persons created by the social contexts in which we live?

- How do our bodies help to make us the kind of selves we are?

- What is the role of childhood experience?

- How do the ways in which we think relate to who we are as persons?

- How and why is one person different from another?

We shall also be asking questions about how we as psychologists can make sense of persons:

- What kind of knowledge of such a topic is possible and appropriate?

- What kinds of method can be used to help us to investigate and to understand?

- What kinds of understanding of persons in a social world have different approaches in psychology given us? What are their respective strengths and limitations?

Thus, one set of questions focuses on the issue of what a person is and the factors (especially social ones) which influence how we behave and experience. The other set is about forms of knowledge and the process of understanding.

In this Introduction to Book 1, you will first be asked to engage in an exercise designed to prompt your thinking about such questions. This will involve reading and thinking about a set of case studies or 'Windows' which portray three very different people in different ways. This is followed by some discussion of the kinds of questions and issues such accounts raise.

The Introduction will then go on to look more directly at the kinds of understanding involved in making sense of people; in particular, the different forms of theoretical understanding (or perspectives) that you will find in this book (and in social psychology more generally).

The final section sets up and explains the structure of the book to come.

Aims of the Introduction

- To stimulate your thinking about what it is to be a person in a social world.

- To raise issues about the nature of understanding of persons which will be taken up as the book proceeds.

- To present the rationale for the way this book has been conceived.

- To preview the structure and contents of the book.

Because the role of the Introduction is to introduce topics and issues which will become clearer as the book proceeds, it will be worth returning to their discussion here once you have completed the book.

Stop for a moment and reflect on your own experience of being a person. ACTIVITY 1.1
Take about five minutes to jot down whatever comes to your mind when you consider the following questions:

What is involved in being a person? What distinguishes you from being an object, say, or an animal, or another, different person?

Before telling you something of my ideas in response to the kinds of question indicated above, I would like you to begin by reading three rather different accounts of persons and to use these to prompt your own thinking about such issues.

I call these accounts 'windows' because they offer us a glimpse of the persons involved, rather like looking through the windows of a house might do of the occupants within. One or two of the extracts may seem to you somewhat dramatic or literary but they have been selected to stimulate your thinking about the nature, form and variety of being a person in a social world. They present very different people in different worlds and from rather different perspectives.

ACTIVITY 1.2

1   Read each account straight through to try to get a 'feel' of the person involved. What impression do you get? You are not being asked to judge or evaluate the person but to try to imagine what it would be like to be him or her.

2   After reading each account, look back over it and jot down a few notes about the following issues:

• Does reading this account give you any further insights about what it is to be a person?

• What makes people similar to and different from one another and why?

• How do the social worlds of these people differ and what effects might these differences have on them?

• What significance for the self does the body have?

• What is the significance of the capacity for conscious reflection for the self?

• To what extent can we describe or understand another person, how might we try to do this, and what kinds of problem are involved?

You need not spend too long over this. These are not easy questions. Don't worry if you do not come up with too much in the way of answers. The exercise is designed to prompt your thinking about personal being and as a lead-in to the ideas discussed in the next section.

Window 1.1 Liv

The first extract is taken from the autobiographical book *Changing* by the Norwegian film star Liv Ullman. (Linn, whom she mentions, is her daughter.)

My reality this winter consists of many things. Even this: I wake from a doze. My flight is approaching a city. The sun vanishes behind tall mountains. Far below, lights go on in thousands of windows and street advertisements. ... The same women and men will be standing by the same exits and will exclaim the same words of welcome when they see me. People with flowers and kindness, all in a hurry to pack me into a car and drive me to some luxury hotel, where they can abandon me and go home to their own lives. A suite with sitting room and bedroom, deep armchairs upholstered in silk, big windows looking out onto palms and a swimming pool.

Champagne on ice with the compliments of the management. Flowers and baskets of fruit. Hall porters bowing themselves in and out with my luggage and my letters and my telephone messages. Smiles and politeness and the unreality that surrounds it all.

While I smile enthusiastically and thank them.

My reality is also this:

The airplane is circling above a city. There is expectancy in me as I look out into the night. I know it is hot. No need to think of Norwegian homespun and boots for a few days ... air that calls for no more than a thin blouse.

I shall be awake when everyone at home is asleep. ...

It has been a long flight. There has been a film and breakfast and lunch and dinner. Trolleys have been trundled in and out with food and fruit, ice-cold drinks, and a woollen blanket to put round me when I want to sleep.

I try to arrange my hair, glad that Hollywood has accepted my 'natural look'.

At home people will soon be waking up to a dark winter's morning and their feet and bottoms will be freezing, while I am sitting in the shade of a palm, and the feel of the evening air will be sensual, as it never is in Oslo. I shall sleep in a broad, soft bed. Be woken in the morning by a waiter who knows me from earlier visits. He will draw the curtains and let the sun flood into the room, push in a table with breakfast and fresh orange juice. ... Give me a newspaper of a hundred pages and wish me a good day.

It's easy to make me feel secure and happy for a short while. I don't need to be near the man I love. Or Linn. Sometimes the sense of security is within myself.

Source: Ullman, 1976, pp. 9–10

Window 1.2   *Leonard*

The next account is from Oliver Sacks' book *Awakenings* (part of which has been made into a feature film), in which he describes a number of cases of patients who were suffering a special form of Parkinson's disease incurred as a result of having had sleeping-sickness (encephalitis lethargica). Sacks reports on the effects of administering a drug that was new at the time, L-Dopa.

I first saw Leonard L. in the spring of 1966. At this time Mr L. was in his forty-sixth year, completely speechless and completely without voluntary motion except for minute movements of the right hand. With these he could spell out messages on a small letter-board – this had been his only mode of communication for fifteen years ... . Despite his almost incredible degree of immobility and disability, Mr L. was an avid reader (the pages had to be turned by someone else), the librarian at the hospital, and the producer of a stream of brilliant book reviews which appeared in the hospital magazine every month. ...

At the end of my first meeting with Leonard L. I said to him: 'What's it like being the way you are? What would you compare it to?' He spelt out the following answer: 'Caged. Deprived. Like Rilke's "Panther [1]".' And then he swept his eyes around the ward and spelt out: 'This is a human zoo.' Again and again, with his penetrating descriptions, his imaginative metaphors, or his great stock of poetic images, Mr L. would try to evoke the nature of his own being and experience. 'There's an awful presence,' he once tapped out, 'and an awful absence. The presence is a mixture of nagging and pushing and pressure, with being held back and constrained and stopped – I often call it "the goad and halter". The absence is a terrible isolation and coldness and shrinking – more than you can imagine, Dr Sacks, much more than anybody who isn't this way can possibly imagine – a bottomless darkness and unreality.' ...

'At other times,' Mr L. would tap out, 'there's none of this sense of pushing or active taking-away, but a sort of total calmness, a nothingness, which is by no means unpleasant. It's a let-up from the torture. On the other hand, it's something like death. At these times I feel I've been castrated by my illness, and relieved from all the longings other people have.' ...

... Mr L. had shown precocity and withdrawal from his earliest years, and these had become much accentuated with the death of his father when he was six. By the age of ten he would often say: 'I want to spend my life reading and writing. I want to bury myself among books. One can't trust human beings in the least.' In his early adolescent years Leonard L. was indeed continually buried in books, and had few or no friends, and indulged in none of the sexual, social or other activities common to boys of his age. At the age of fifteen his right hand started to become stiff, weak, pale and shrunken: these symptoms – which were the first signs of his post-encephalitic disease – were interpreted by him as a punishment for masturbation and for blasphemous thoughts; ... He was reinforced in these morbid phantasies by the attitude of his mother who also saw his illness as a punishment for sin.

... Despite the gradual spread and progression of his disability, Leonard L. was able to go to Harvard and to graduate with honours, and had almost finished a thesis for his Ph.D. – in his twenty-seventh year – when his disability became so severe as to bring his studies and activities to a total halt. After leaving Harvard, he spent three years at home; and at the age of thirty, almost totally

[1] 'His gaze from going through the bars has grown so weary that it can take in nothing more. For him it is as though there were a thousand bars, and behind the thousand bars no world.'

petrified, he was admitted to Mount Carmel Hospital. On his admission he was at once given charge of the hospital library. He could do little but read, and he *did* nothing but read. He indeed became buried in books from this time on, and thus, in a sense, achieved a dreadful fulfilment of his childhood wish.

... When I asked him how he felt he would usually tap out 'meek', but he would also intimate that he sometimes had a sense of intense violence and power which was 'locked up' inside him, and which he experienced only in dreams. 'I have no exit', he would tap out. 'I am trapped in myself. This stupid body is a prison with windows but no doors.' ...

L-Dopa was started in early March 1969 and raised by degrees to 5.0 gm. a day. Little effect was seen for two weeks, and then a sudden 'conversion' took place. The rigidity vanished from all his limbs, and he felt filled with an access of energy and power; he became able to write and type once again, to rise from his chair, to walk with some assistance and to speak in a loud and clear voice – none of which had been possible since his twenty-fifth year. ... During these two weeks, Mr L. was drunk on reality – on sensations and feelings and relations which had been cut off from him, or distorted, for many decades. He loved going out in the hospital garden: he would touch the flowers and leaves with astonished delight, and sometimes kiss them or press them to his lips. He suddenly desired to see the night-city of New York, which (although so close to) he had not seen, or wanted to see, in twenty years: and on his return from these night-drives he was almost breathless with delight ... .

In April, intimations of trouble appeared. Mr L.'s abundance of health and energy – of 'grace' as he called it – became *too* abundant and started to assume an extravagant, maniacal and grandiose form; at the same time a variety of odd movements and other phenomena made their initial appearance. His sense of harmony and ease and effortless control was replaced by a sense of *too-muchness*, of force and pressure, ... he now became uneasy and dissatisfied, and increasingly filled with painful, unsatisfiable appetites and desires ... which no reality could have met – least of all the grim and confining reality of a Total Institution, an asylum for the dilapidated and dying ... . The most intense and the most thwarted of these yearnings were of a sexual nature, allied with desires for power and possession. No longer satisfied with the pastoral and innocent kissing of flowers, he wanted to touch and kiss all the nurses on the ward – and in his attempts to do so was rebuffed, at first with smiles and jokes and good humour, and then with increasing asperity and anger. Very rapidly, in May, relationships became strained, and Mr L. passed from a gentle amorousness to an enraged and thwarted erotomania. Early in May he asked me if I could arrange for various nurses and nursing aides to 'service' him at night, and suggested – as an alternative – that a brothel-service be set up to meet the needs and hungers of Dopa-charged patients.

By mid-May, Mr L. had become thoroughly 'charged up', in his own words, 'charged and super-charged' with a great surplus, a great *pressure*, of libidinous and aggressive feelings, with an avidity and voracity which could take many forms. In his phantasies, in his notebooks, and in his dreams, his image of himself was no longer that of the meek and mild and melancholy one, but of a burly caveman equipped with an invincible club and an invincible phallus; a Dionysiac god packed with virility and power; a wild, wonderful ravening man-beast who combined kingly, artistic and genital omnipotence. ...

Coinciding with this surge of general excitement, Mr L. ... started to talk with great speed, and to repeat words and phrases again and again (palilalia). ... Tics appeared at this time, and grew more numerous daily: sudden impulsions and tics of the eyes, grimaces, cluckings, and lightning-quick scratchings. Finding himself distracted and decomposed by this increasing furor and fragmentation, Mr L. made his final effort at control, and decided – at the start of June – on an act of supreme coherence and catharsis – the writing of an autobiography: 'It'll bring me together,' he said; 'it'll cast out the devils. It'll bring everything into the full light of day.'

Using his shrunken, dystrophic index-fingers, Mr L. typed out an autobiography 50,000 words in length, in the first three weeks of June. He typed almost ceaselessly – twelve or fifteen hours a day, and *when* he typed he indeed 'came together', and found himself free from his tics and distractions, from the pressures which were driving and shivering his being; ...

The closing scene of this so-mixed summer was precipitated by institutional disapproval of Mr L.'s ravening libido, the threats and condemnations which this brought down on him, and his final, cruel removal to a 'punishment cell' – a tiny three-bedded room containing two dying and dilapidated terminal dements. Deprived of his own room and all his belongings, deprived of his identity and status ... Mr L. fell into suicidal depression and infernal psychosis.

We stopped his L-Dopa towards the end of July. His psychoses and tics continued for another three days, of their own momentum, and then suddenly came to a stop. Mr L. reverted during August to his original motionless state.

Source: Sacks, 1976, pp. 240–51; 255–6

Window 1.3 **Roland**

The final account consists of excerpts from the autobiographical reflections of a French writer and intellectual, Roland Barthes.

This account was selected partly because it adds the new dimension of photographs as a way of expressing aspects of the self.

Again, as with the other two extracts, after reading it, make notes of any further thoughts about what it is to be a person and in response to the points raised at the beginning of this activity.

The childhood photograph is both highly indiscreet (it is my body ... which is presented) and quite discreet (the photograph is not of 'me')

The father's sister: she was alone all her life.

The father, dead very early (in the war), was lodged in no memorial or sacrificial discourse. By maternal intermediary his memory – never an oppressive one – merely touched the surface of childhood with an almost silent bounty.

The family novel

Where do they come from? From a family of notaries in the Haute-Garonne. Thereby endowing me with a race, a class. As the (official) photograph proves. That young man with blue eyes and a pensive elbow will be my father's father. Final stasis of this lineage: my body ...

The mirror stage: 'That's you'

Contemporaries?

I was beginning to walk. Proust was still alive, and finishing *À la Recherche du Temps Perdu.*

As a child, I was often and intensely bored. This evidently began very early, it has continued my whole life, in gusts (increasingly rare, it is true, thanks to work and to friends), and it has always been noticeable to others. A panic boredom, to the point of distress: like the kind I feel in panel discussions, lectures, parties among strangers, group amusements: wherever boredom can *be seen*. Might boredom be my form of hysteria?

Distress: lecturing

Boredom: a panel discussion

'The pleasure of those mornings in U.: the sun, the house, roses, silence, music, coffee, work, sexual quiescence, holiday from aggressions ...'

'Ourselves, always ourselves ...'

... among friends

Where does this expression come from? Nature? Code?

'But I never looked like that!' – How do you know? What is the 'you' you might or might not look like? ... Where is your authentic body? You are the only one who can never see yourself except as an image; you never see your eyes unless they are dulled by the gaze they rest upon the mirror or the lens (I am interested in seeing my eyes only when they look at you): even and especially for your own body, you are condemned to the repertoire of its images.

1942

1970

Gaucher – Left-handed

To be left-handed – what does it mean? You eat contrary to the place assigned to the table setting; you find the grip of the telephone on the wrong side, when someone right-handed has used it before you;

the scissors are not made for your thumb. In school, years ago, you had to struggle to be like the others, you had to normalize your body, sacrifice your good hand to the little society of the *lycée* (I was constrained to draw with my right hand, but I put in the colours with my left: the revenge of impulse); a modest, inconsequential exclusion, socially tolerated, marked adolescent life with a tenuous and persistent crease: you got used to it, adapted to it, and went on …

J'aime, je n'aime pas – I like, I don't like

I like: salad, cinnamon, cheese, pimento, marzipan, the smell of new-cut hay (why doesn't someone with a 'nose' make such a perfume), roses, peonies, lavender, champagne, loosely held political convictions, Glenn Gould, too-cold beer, flat pillows, toast, Havana cigars, Handel, slow walks, pears, white peaches, cherries, colours, watches, all kinds of writing pens, desserts, unrefined salt, realistic novels, the piano, coffee, … etc.

I don't like: … women in slacks, geraniums, strawberries, the harpsichord, Miró, tautologies, animated cartoons, Arthur Rubinstein, villas, the afternoon, Satie, Bartók, Vivaldi, telephoning, children's choruses, Chopin's concertos, … fidelity, spontaneity, evenings with people I don't know, etc.

I like, I don't like: this is of no importance to anyone; this, apparently, has no meaning. And yet all this means: *my body is not the same as yours.* Hence, in this anarchic foam of tastes and distastes … gradually appears the figure of a bodily enigma, requiring complicity or irritation. Here begins the intimidation of the body, which obliges others to endure me *liberally*, to remain silent and polite confronted by pleasures or rejections which they do not share …

Source: Barthes, 1975, pp. 3, 10, 14–15, 19, 21, 23–6, 28–9, 34, 36–7, 42, 98, 116–7

ACTIVITY 1.2
(continued)

Now look back over the notes you have made and draw together your ideas in response to the questions asked at the beginning of this activity:

- What does it mean to be a person?

- What makes people similar to and different from one another and why?

- How do the social worlds of these people differ and what effects might these differences have?

- What parts do the body and conscious reflection (and any other aspects you may have noted) play in constituting who these people are?

- How far can we understand another person and what kinds of problems are involved in attempting to do so?

2 Aspects of the self

What do these extracts suggest about the nature of being a person? What issues do they raise?

What we are doing here is rather like trying to make sense of and compare a series of complex landscapes. There are many features that we can detect, and different kinds of general category which we could use to conceptualize these. (In a landscape these might be, for example, contours of terrain, kind of soil, vegetation, the presence of trees, water, etc.) Any analysis, be it of a physical landscape or a person, is inevitably selective in the features it focuses on and the categories used to classify these: for any account or analysis has to be made from some perspective or other and its form and nature will fundamentally reflect this. (This point will be developed in relation to perspectives in psychology later in this Introduction.) Your responses to the questions will also have been influenced and limited by the particular set of examples used.

So what features should we suggest? I want to draw attention to five aspects of being a person. (However, note that, as we shall see, these are not clear-cut. They constitute *issues to be discussed* rather than clear-cut features which a person 'possesses'.)

1 To be a person involves *embodiment*, or being related to a particular body.

2 To be a person involves *subjective experience*: consciousness, some sense of self, and of agency (the ability to initiate thought and actions). It also involves *cognition*: ways of processing and making sense of that experience.

3 To be a person is to be intrinsically related to others, to exist in a *social medium* of meanings and customs.

4   To be a person may also involve *unconscious feelings*, a sense that some of our experience and our reactions emanate from feelings deep within ourselves of which we may be hardly aware.

5   Finally, to be a person involves some sense of these strands being in complex *interrelation* with each other.

These five broad aspects appear to be fundamental features of what it means to be a person. They seem to apply to all three people in our Windows and to other people as well. While accepting that such an assertion cannot be validated by formal experimental test, it can be checked against your own experience: as you read the discussion of the five aspects below, you might like to consider whether the points made there make sense in terms of your own awareness of yourself and others.

In the subsections that follow, each of these aspects or issues about the self is briefly introduced and illustrated by drawing on the accounts given in the Windows. The aim is to raise some of the questions which will be taken up during the course of the chapters to come.

Look back over the three accounts in the Windows and look for signs of each of these five aspects of the self. Specifically, for each of the three accounts, consider each of the following questions in turn: ACTIVITY 1.3

1   To what extent and in what ways is the sense of being Liv, Leonard or Roland dependent on having the particular *body* which is theirs?

2   How do our subjects *experience* their worlds and *make sense* of that experience?

3   What different ways can you detect in which the sense of self is dependent on present and past *interactions* with other people and participation in a particular society?

4   Can you see any hints of *unconscious feelings* in any of the three accounts?

2.1   The relevance of the body

Embodiment is central to being a person. The body is the vehicle for the exercise of skills, for communicating and relating to others. It is on the body that our very existence as persons depends. The way it functions (or fails to function) can change the basic ground of our experience. Leonard provides the clearest example of this. We see the radical effects of L-Dopa on his emotional landscape, on both his ability to engage with others and his style of responding to the people and environment around him; also on the quality of his sense of self. Often we take the facilitation and influence of the body for granted. One of the effects of temporary disability is that we may realize more fully the body's fundamental importance to our functioning as persons (for a vivid account of this see Sacks, 1986.)

The bodily basis of personal being also locates us at a particular place in a physical world of sensation. The quality of this is a significant characteristic of our personal world. For Liv there is luxury; while Barthes notices the smell of roses, the sound of silence and the taste of coffee.

Our bodily nature also renders us vulnerable – to disease, to pain, even torture or constraint, and to the transience of life.

Note though that our embodiment as persons is very much a social matter too. People usually respond to the person they see. The casual observer, seeing the paralysed figure of Leonard in the cage of his body, might never guess at the richness and complexity of his inner world. Leonard's sexual feelings may emanate from him, but the way others react (or do not react) to them defines the degree to which they can be expressed and what they signify. The ways in which people act towards us may influence the kind of person we think we are. Feeling beautiful or ugly is as much a function of the way others relate to us as it is of the style and character of our physical being. Liv talks about whether Hollywood will accept 'my "natural look"', implying her sense of her body as a certain kind of commodity locked into a 'market of looks'. It is because it is socially unorthodox that Barthes' left-handedness becomes an issue rather than a simple difference between himself and others. Scissors tend to be designed, for example, for right-handed people. Other people give meaning then to our physical characteristics by the way they react to and regard them.

Finally, it is worth noting two curious features of embodiment. In some sense we can transcend it. Because he still communicates to us through his writings, Roland Barthes exists for us as a person even though he is no longer alive. Secondly, the nature of our embodiment is largely given. Although we may attempt to change bodies through dieting and exercise, for example, or even drugs or surgery, we have relatively little control in determining the kind of body we are endowed with, be it female or male, black or white, excitable or calm, or, as with Leonard, 'a prison with windows but no doors'.

2.2   The centrality of experience

Each of us experiences the world through our own particular frame of consciousness. We are conscious not only of a world about us but also of a world within of inner thoughts, feelings and reflections. Much of Leonard's awareness, for example, is made up of imagination and private fantasies.

There is a sense of *multiplicity* in the flow of our conscious experience. We live in many and sometimes unrelated worlds. As Liv says, her reality 'consists of many things'. The rather unreal world of her Hollywood hotel contrasts with the more solid reality of her life in Norway. The very way Barthes presents himself emphasizes the *fragmentation* of being a person. His photographs give us a sample of the different worlds of his consciousness – a holiday beach, lecturing, relaxing with friends. In the course of our daily lives, the 'frame' of conscious awareness is continuously changing. At one time our experience may become fused with, almost part of, the television play we are watching or the book we are reading; they become our conscious reality. At others, it may be immersed in the mechanics of the car as we struggle to renew the brake-linings, or in the flow of the action as we play tennis.

Our capacity to remember endows some sense of continuity to our experience. We look for patterns and consistency, for ways of making sense of our experience. Thus, our conscious awareness is constituted and influenced by our *cognitions*, by our ways of thinking (as well as feeling). So we attribute meanings to events, and responsibility for actions. (See the example cited earlier of Leonard's belief that his illness was retribution for his boyhood masturbation.) This can provide a way of coping with the world, of maintaining some sense of control. Individuals vary in the style and complexity of this cognitive framing. It will be influenced by education, intellect, values, all of which depend in turn, at least in part, on the social contexts in which we live.

Part of the experience of being a person is our sense that we can do things: we can initiate actions and events and carry out personal projects. This is referred to as *agency*. Thus, in an attempt to achieve some sense of coherence in the face of the intense compulsions, pressure and fragmentation eventually brought on by L-Dopa, Leonard decides to type his autobiography. He initiates action to deal with his distress. Even though the account makes clear the enormous bodily and social constraints upon his life, there is still a sense that he has some capacity for autonomous choice. (The degree to which people are capable of autonomous action and what this means is a theme that will be taken up later in the book.) One consequence of our sense of agency is that, as persons, we are likely to hold ourselves and each other *responsible* for the actions we appear to have chosen to do. We accept that we may be called upon (if only in our own mind) to *account* for them – to give reasons for why we acted as we did.

A dominant aspect of conscious awareness is a *sense of self* or identity. We are aware of being a particular person, individual, unique. In part, this is a process of 'I', arising from our sense of engagement and acting within and upon the world, and from our privileged access to the world of our inner thoughts and feelings. In part, also, it derives from an awareness of 'me': an image of the kind of person I am. (This is highlighted in Window 1.3 by Barthes' comments on the photographs of himself.)

One way of thinking of a person's identity is as a fusion of what we might call *personal identity* (i.e. arising from experiences specific to us and our private reflection on these) and of *social identity* (i.e. the characteristics and roles which tend to be attributed to us by others, and the ways in which our social worlds express themselves through us). This double aspect of our sense of self is illustrated in Box 1.1.

BOX 1.1   The double aspect of self

In the extract below, the Argentinian writer Jorge Luis Borges experiences his public image (himself as seen by others) as almost another self, a stranger to the Borges he feels himself to be:

> The other one, the one called Borges, is the one things happen to. ... I know of Borges from the mail and see his name on a list of professors or in a biographical dictionary. I like hourglasses, maps, eighteenth-century typography, the taste of coffee and the prose of Stevenson; he shares these preferences, but in a vain way that turns them into the attributes of an actor. It would be an exaggeration to say that ours is a hostile relationship; I live, let myself go on living, so that Borges may contrive his literature, and this literature justifies me. It is no effort for me to confess that he has achieved some valid pages, but those pages cannot save me, perhaps because what is good belongs to no one, not even to him, but rather to the language and to tradition. Besides, I am destined to perish, definitively, and only some instant of myself can survive in him. Little by little, I am giving over everything to him, though I am quite aware of his perverse custom of falsifying and magnifying things. ... I shall remain in Borges, not in myself (if it is true that I am someone), but I recognize myself less in his books than in many others or in the laborious strumming of a guitar. ...
>
> I do not know which of us has written this page.

(Borges, 1970, pp. 282–3)

Where does the *individuality* of our identity come from? Is it a feature of our genetic inheritance, of the residue of our early emotional experiences as children, or, as was noted in the previous subsection, of construction by the social contexts in which we have grown and live: could it be perhaps a complex function of all three?

Individuality is expressed too through the *values* we place on the different experiences and things which make up our world (as, for example, when a person feels fiercely attached to the kind of music he or she likes). Don't you think that Barthes' list of likes and dislikes tells us quite a lot about the kind of person he is? And, as he points out, his particular tastes may make him seem quite alien to someone else. His comment here draws attention to personal uniqueness and the point that in interacting with others we may experience ourselves as different and apart.

An extraordinary quality of our conscious awareness is our ability to be *reflexive*, to 'stand back' and reflect on our experience. We can even be conscious of being conscious. The quality of reflexiveness comes across in Barthes' account where he deliberately adopts a style of viewing and commenting on himself as if he were another person. Part of this capacity for reflexiveness is the ability to imagine alternatives, that things could be other than as they are. In this sense, we do not experience life as fixed but often believe that there is potential for changing how we are. Thus, we live in the multiple realities not only of actual but of possible worlds.

2.3   The significance of the social

Think for a moment about the role of other people and the social context in the process of creating and sustaining who you are. People form an intrinsic part of the fabric of our personal lives. Even when physically absent, the people of our world may remain with us; as when Liv, circling over California, remembers her friends and daughter in Norway. In Barthes' account we see memories of friends and family held in photographs: or it could be a voice on the telephone, a face in a video.

People are significant for both the opportunities and constraints that they bring. Thus, for Leonard, the nursing staff serve as a source of frustration as well as of vital support and potential gratification. People may also have the power to control us. This may be physical, as when Leonard is eventually shut away. Or it may be a power of 'legitimation', of determining what is legitimate, of what is right and wrong. Thus, the hospital staff exert control over Leonard by making clear their disapproval of his expressions of lust.

As the body provides the medium for our existence as persons, so too does the social. The kind of person we are and can hope to become is grounded in the social practices and the ways of thinking and communicating that we assimilate from the social settings in which we live. Such influences help determine our ways of thinking about and presenting ourselves. Would a male author be as likely as Liv, for example, to arrange his hair and express pleasure 'that Hollywood has accepted my "natural look"'? There is a whole set of attitudes and assumptions around gender (both explicit and implicit): ways in which it is seen as appropriate for men and women to behave and to relate, that are an intrinsic part of particular cultures. And, for almost everyone, being a man or a woman is an intrinsic part of who they are and who they are taken to be.

Look back to Window 1.3. Could you imagine Roland's account having been written by a woman? Give reasons for your answer.   ACTIVITY 1.4

People may respond to others on the basis of stereotyped images and assimilated assumptions about members of a particular group (be this based on class, ethnic background, or some other form of categorization). Such socially derived expectations can also influence the ways in which the members of those groups themselves construct their own sense of personal identity.

The accounts in the Windows show us that one way in which a person's sense of self is constructed by other people is that we are influenced by how others seem to regard and respond to us. That in turn will depend on how they categorize us, the role they place us in, and also sometimes on our access to material and other resources. Liv is given the care and coddling considered appropriate for the film star she is seen to be, while Leonard, for all his brilliance, is subject to the indignities and control that so often go with the status of patient. Knowing the particular kind of person we are or are supposed to be, we know what is expected of us, how we should act and react, even how to think and feel. In this way, interaction becomes a mutual process where outcomes are not simply the product of either participant but of the negotiations between them.

The person we are is also derived from the particular cultural and historical contexts we find ourselves in. There is a sense in which Barthes, for example, is quintessentially French and defined by the family from which he comes. The person we feel ourselves to be is influenced too by the 'moral order' favoured by our culture. This may require us to justify or excuse ourselves or help to explain the kind of person that we are. So Leonard interprets his symptoms as punishment for masturbating.

A key issue to be pursued in this book (and also the series of which it forms a part) is the extent to which being a person is inherently social and the different forms that social construction of the person can take.

2.4   The unconscious basis of being

Our experience of being a person is composed not just of cognitions but of feelings too. Emotions of some kind (e.g. insecurity, pity, surprise, lust, content or just plain boredom) form a constant backdrop for the characters in the Windows. This backdrop may be relatively uniform or, as with Leonard, subject to dramatic change. The emotions may remain as only 'tone' or background or they may become a central, even overwhelming, dynamic in consciousness. Over time, the prevailing emotional tone (e.g. contentedness, depression or anxiety) imparts a distinctive feel to lived experience.

The question arises as to how far we are consciously aware of what we feel and the origins of such feelings. Feelings may not only be confused and conflicting but may seem to originate beyond the borders of conscious apprehension. They may be ineffable or impossible to express. Leonard resorts to metaphors to try to express his feelings of 'awful presence' and 'awful absence', his sense of 'bottomless darkness and unreality'. He talks of the feelings of intense violence and power which he feels are 'locked up' inside him, experienced only in his dreams.

It is not so difficult to detect clues to unconscious feelings in Leonard's case. But what about those who lead more ordered and urbane lives? In a more indirect and subtle way, does Liv hint at underlying unease: for example, in her statement that it is easy to make her feel secure and happy 'for a short while', and her use of the term 'abandon me' in describing how the people assigned to meet her leave her once their job is done? Do we sense here old scripts, perhaps from childhood, lurking beneath present awareness? Just what the place of unconscious feelings is, how pervasive their influence is and the nature of their origins in childhood experience, are issues that will be taken up later in this book.

2.5 Interactions over time

We have noted in the sections above how each aspect is interwoven with the others. Thus, the biological becomes a social matter and the social permeates our sense of self. There is temporal interaction too. Memories of the past, both conscious and unconscious, can affect the present, as can our hopes and fears about the future. Liv's account of the way her plane flight collapses time zones and distance reminds us how even time and space are subject to social construction and are not just personal affairs.

We are dealing then with complex interactions over personally and socially constructed time. It is interesting that each of the accounts forms some kind of narrative – a flow of experiences, actions and events. Situations and moods change. The idea of narrative and changing experience is most clearly in evidence in the account of the administration of L-Dopa to Leonard (with all its subsequent effects) and then its later withdrawal.

For every person, there is an overall sense of personal biographical flow. While there is continuity, in that a person remains in some sense the same across the decades, there is also decided change (if only in that we accumulate experience and that our bodies grow older). Age becomes an important (if often implicit) marker of the person you are. We are reminded of this in Barthes' pictures which depict the child he once was and then the young and, later, older man he was to become. But again, growing older is likely to be as much a social as a biological matter: for people's expectations and attitudes towards both themselves and others may very well be related to assumptions about age.

There is a sense, finally, in which being a person is underpinned existentially by a sense of profound mystery. While, as we have noted earlier, we may have a sense of ourselves as being agents with some capability to self-determine what we do, it is also true that the person we are ultimately derives from factors outside our control. We do not choose our parents, the body we inhabit or the society in which we grow up. The coming into being of each of us and the particular person we are hangs on an infinite chain of chance events – on our parents meeting and their ancestors before them, on the precise moment of our conception, and on one particular sperm reaching the ovum first; events that might have been otherwise and yet were not.

Each aspect of the self introduced here will be taken up and discussed in relation to different perspectives in the subsequent chapters of this book: embodiment in Chapter 2, cognition and subjective experience in Chapters 3 and 4, the significance of the social in Chapter 5 and of the unconscious in Chapter 6. The interrelationship between the aspects will be considered in Chapter 7.

> To what extent do you think that the five aspects of the self distinguished above apply to all people? Would they be meaningful, for example, to someone who had little contact with contemporary Euro-American culture?

3 Psychological understanding

3.1 Understanding persons

So far, what I have been doing is to try to unpack our subject-matter a little and to alert you to some of the questions and issues which arise. Let us now turn our attention to the final question you were asked to consider in your study of the Windows (see Activity 1.2). How far can we understand another person in the social world and what kinds of problem are involved in attempting to do so?

On first thought, this might seem like a fairly straightforward business. There may seem to be a kind of flesh and blood solidity to the persons we know, and perhaps to our own experience of ourselves. (Quite how 'solid' this actually is we shall see later in the book.) So it might just seem therefore a matter of finding the right ways to describe and measure different attributes. However, if you think back to our extracts, you can see that understanding persons is not at all the simple matter that it may at first appear, for being a person is constituted by beliefs and meanings and these can be construed by different people in different ways. Take Leonard, for example. Is he likely to account for himself in quite the same way as do the author (Oliver Sacks), his mother, or the nurses who rebuffed his attempts to kiss and caress them? Which of these four different accounts would represent the 'real Leonard'?

The accounts in the Windows make it clear, in other words, that a person is not a fixed and solid reality. The only way we can conceptualize him or her is from a particular perspective. It will inevitably be a *construction* which reflects as much about the conceptualizer as the person being conceptualized. (This holds for attempts at measurement of persons too. The selection of measurements, and the tests of 'ability' or 'personality' themselves, are just other ways of constructing an impression of the person concerned.)

Note that all the Windows are written from different standpoints. Leonard is described by someone else (Oliver Sacks), Liv's account is autobiograpical. In further contrast, while Barthes' account is autobiographical too, there is a sense in which he tries to distance himself and comment on the picture portrayed. (He actually prefaces his book with the statement that it should be considered 'as if spoken by a character in a novel'.)

The point here is that the person presented, whether it be an autobiographical account or an account by someone else, has to be created or constructed by a narrator of some kind. And the account will reflect this. Part of this is a process of selection – for example, of the information upon which the account is based. Thus, Sacks builds up his impression of Leonard through his own observations and what Leonard and his mother tell him. Accounts are a function too of the form in which they are expressed. All the accounts in the Windows are language-based, though photographs also are used by Barthes.

Look back to Window 1.3 and consider for a moment whether what is conveyed by the photographs about Barthes as a person could have been conveyed by words. What, if anything, was added by the use of photographs (particularly in combination with their sometimes cryptic captions)?

The act of using spoken or written language and the ways in which this is done themselves construct and constrain what we can represent (see Box 1.2). It is interesting in this respect how Leonard resorts to the use of poetry and metaphor to try to express the way he experiences himself; his feelings of being, for example, like a caged panther in a human zoo, of being 'castrated' by his illness, and, under the influence of L-Dopa, of being like a 'wild, wonderful ravening man-beast'.

BOX 1.2   Sign language can express some things better than words

Mark Medoff's play *Children of a Lesser God* (1982) raises the point that sign language may be able to convey some meanings more effectively than the spoken word. Sarah, the central character, was born deaf and refuses to learn any other mode of communication except Ameslan (American sign language), in which she is very proficient. She claims that it has the power to express what vocalization can never do. At one point in the play, she supports this by showing with subtle movements of her two hands the many variations possible in the way that two people can relate to each other, and she does this so vividly that even audiences untutored in Ameslan can understand!

Not only may accounts of persons be influenced by the particular communicative conventions and style adopted by the author, they may also reflect what the narrators wish to convey about themselves (e.g. their use of language, their cleverness, their knowledge of literature). The important point here is that accounts of persons cannot be simply taken at face value as constituting a straightforward portrayal of the person described. They must be regarded as constructions created by someone (even if this is the person him or herself) and as emerging from particular social practices and ways of communicating.

It is important to realize that the way in which an account is constructed is not ancillary but central to any conception of a person. There is no way to avoid it. However, that does not mean that we cannot evaluate such constructions. Some may seem, for example, more self-consistent or consistent with other information than others. Thus, it might be hard to construe as a Don Juan someone who had been been celibate all their life.

The accounts given in the Windows are of real persons. But could you have detected if any of them had been fictional? What does that suggest about the nature of persons and/or the way they can be described?

To what extent then can a person be considered as a being a 'fixed reality' with a true nature? A person can be conceptualized in different ways and this will vary according to context and the perspective of the describer (even when a person is describing him- or herself). Thus, as people grow older, they often view their past life in a new way: they construct a different account of the kind of person they were in the light of their experience of the present.

3.2   The many faces of psychology

The accounts and conceptualizations of persons offered by psychologists can equally be considered to be constructions. By this I mean that studying the person in a social world is not just a question of 'looking at the facts'. For knowledge does not exist 'out there' to be discovered. Psychologists and others create it with the particular concepts, methods and theories they use. It is true that many psychologists, unlike most people in everyday life, have set out to make a *scientific* study of persons. We will need in the course of this book to consider what that means. But even here (as I indicated in the previous subsection in the reference to tests and measurements of personality or ability), the accounts of the person that result are nevertheless still constructions. They will vary depending on the question being asked, the measures and the methods selected to investigate it, and the ways in which the outcomes are presented.

What kinds of understanding then can psychology give us about being a person in a social world? The important point to realize is that psychology does not exist as a homogeneous discipline. Its immediate history may be relatively short but it is extremely varied. Any good review of its history will reveal the way it developed in different fashion at different times and in different places. In the late nineteenth century in Germany, for example, one strong theme was the use of introspection to study systematically the relationship between subjective experience and the physical characteristics of the stimulus. By the early twentieth century in the USA, this had been replaced by behaviourism which deliberately rejected introspection as a valid method. It replaced inward reflection with observation and measurements, often carrying out experiments with animals rather than humans. Running in parallel in Europe was the development of psychoanalysis. Here there were no experiments, no measurements, no systematic research. Instead, ideas and theories emerged from psychotherapists' own self-analyses and their work with neurotic people. In yet further contrast, in France and Britain (and subsequently in the USA), there developed the psychometrics movement, concerned with finding ways for measuring aspects of our psychological make-up, such as tests of intelligence and, later, personality.

Such radical divisions, not just in topic but in method of study and the kind of understanding produced, have characterized psychology throughout its development. Later in the twentieth century, came the emergence of humanistic psychology with its focus on subjective experience and the assumption imported from existentialism that people have some capacity to self-create their own lives. So psychotherapy from this perspective becomes more a matter of facilitating personal growth rather than a question of 'healing illness'. Cognitive psychology used model building and inference from experiments to explore the implicit rules we use to make sense of things and solve problems. Later still, social constructionists were to call into question traditional psychology's focus on the individual studied in isolation from other people, and to emphasize how language and power underpin the social relationships which help to construct who we are. We must remember also that other disciplines such as biology and social anthropology offer psychological insights.

What emerges from a study of the history of psychology is the realization that psychological understanding comes in different forms. In contrast to the natural sciences, psychology is characterized by having a number of coexisting perspectives. Each perspective reflects different assumptions (though these are not often articulated) about the nature of its subject-matter and the way that this should be studied. The belief of the classic behaviourists was that only that which is measurable should form the subject-matter of a scientific psychology. This completely contrasts with the psychoanalytic approach where unconscious meanings (which by definition are not observable directly) are the focus of interest. As another example, the assumption of most experimental psychologists that behaviour is determined contrasts with humanistic psychologists' belief that people have some capacity for agency and choice. Yet again, both the experimentalist and the humanistic preoccupation with the individual contrast with the view of social constructionists that the focus should not be on the individual but on the social medium which, they claim, constructs what we are.

In this discussion of psychology and its perspectives, I have deliberately chosen to widen the focus beyond what is traditionally thought to be social psychology. This is because, although it is true that social psychologists have developed certain traditions of research, the distinctions between what constitutes psychology and what is social psychology are often blurred and the traditions of social psychology draw heavily on broader perspectives in psychology. The perspectives which will be presented in this book to illuminate the person in a social world can, by and large, be found in general psychology too.

Its constructed nature means that the understanding offered by psychologists is positioned within a variety of what we might call particular conventions or 'discourses' (i.e. ways of thinking or talking about things). The theories and ideas which constitute psychological understanding have been generated by particular perspectives – by particular psychologists or groups of psychologists asking particular questions and doing psychology in different contexts. Whether an approach becomes influential and part of the 'literature' of psychology depends on a variety of circumstances, sometimes outside the arena of psychology itself. Does the approach appeal to influential people within the discipline (i.e. is it fashionable)? Is it given legitimation and respect because it conforms with the particular conventions and perspectives which hold sway within the profession of psychology at that particular time? This process may also be strongly influenced by external factors such as funding. The growth of research on attitudes in the 1930s and 1940s, for example, was stimulated both by commercial interest in consumer information and by wartime need for propaganda and for techniques for influencing people's views. Ability and personality testing (and thus the concepts which psychometricians have generated) were stimulated by the search for a more objective basis for educational streaming than the judgement of teachers, and the demand, during two world wars, for effective methods for selecting military personnel.

I do not want to give the impression that the development of social psychological understanding has been *entirely* a matter of individual interest, external influence and fashion. There are clearly criteria, such as consistency, rationality, elegance, which have contributed to the effect and influence of specific theories or pieces of research. We can attempt to evaluate them. Is one theory more consistent with other information, for example? Is it more amenable to formal testing, or is it more likely than another to inspire? But, even here, which particular criteria you choose to select and even how you choose to apply them are open to question and are a matter of construction too.

3.3   Interrelationship between psychological perspectives and aspects of the self

What then is the relationship between the different perspectives which comprise psychology and the different aspects of the self identified in the analysis of the Windows from section 1?

Consciousness (with its different features that were teased out in the earlier discussion in section 2.2) is a good example of a topic that has become a focus for study by a range of contrasting perspectives. Phenomenological analysis (i.e. the direct study of people's subjective experience) has been concerned, for example, to analyse the nature and form of conscious experience. But in terms of the brain processes underlying it, consciousness is also the interest of physiological psychologists. Experimental cognitive psychologists have been interested in modelling the schemas and processing which underpin our consciousness of the world. Philosophers also have theorized about consciousness, and psychoanalysts, while they do not usually focus on conscious experience *per se*, have tried to explore the ways in which it is influenced (for example in our inner worlds of fantasy and dreams) by processes of the unconscious mind. So the different features of conscious experience form a fascinating topic to study precisely because they are at the intersection of so many perspectives. Each perspective can offer its own insights into the nature of a person's experience of the world.

In contrast, some aspects of the self tend to be very much the preserve of one or other perspective and to be excluded or ignored by others. As one example, psychoanalysis, experimental and humanistic approaches have all, in different ways, been criticized for failing to allow for the significance for behaviour of the context of society. Analysis of the way in which the societies in which we live help to construct what we are has been largely the province of sociological and social constructionist forms of social psychology.

An important point to note is that it is difficult for some perspectives to accommodate certain features of being a person because of the very assumptions on which these perspectives are premised. Experimental psychology, for example, works from the assumption that behaviour is determined, and so looks for causes. The idea of people as autonomous agents lies outside the scope of this conception (which is why the idea of will has received, until relatively recently, hardly any attention by academic psychologists since William James wrote about it at the beginning of the century).

Is it then the case that each perspective has its 'focus of convenience' and that the best understanding comes through applying several perspectives and interrelating or contrasting the illumination they provide? Such a 'multiperspective' approach is certainly one way of proceeding. It is the position which would seem to be implied by the preceding discussion, and is the one which will be adopted both in this book and in the series of which it forms a part.

4   The structure of this book

We have seen something of the complex, constructed nature of psychological knowledge: that it is not just a question of carefully examining the 'way people are'. How then will psychological theory and research about the self in a social world be presented in this book?

There are two underlying principles which structure the book. One is to *contrast the contributions made by different perspectives*. The other is to explore in turn some of the *different aspects of being a person* of the kind noted earlier in this chapter. As we might expect from the discussion above of the interrelationship between aspects of the person and perspectives, these two principles are closely interwoven in the structure of the book.

Five contrasting perspectives on the self in a social world have been selected. They are:

A biological perspective (Chapter 2) This places emphasis on the underpinning of social behaviour by physiological and genetic processes. Its most controversial form is represented by sociobiology which argues that much of human social behaviour is based on genetic predispositions which have been selected during the course of evolution.

A cognitive experimentalist perspective (Chapter 3) This is probably the prevailing perpective in academic social psychology in the UK and the USA at the time of writing. It places emphasis on the way we process information and the need to investigate this using measurement and experiments.

An experiential perspective (Chapter 4) This represents an amalgam of the phenomenological, existential and humanistic traditions found in psychology. Their common emphasis is on subjective experience. What form does this experience take and what are its implications for the ways in which we deal with the world?

A social constructionist perspective (Chapter 5) This is the most recent of the perspectives presented and is growing in its influence on social psychology. It argues that persons can only be properly understood in terms of the social practices and ways of thinking and being which constitute their particular society.

A psychodynamic perspective (Chapter 6) This perspective not only draws on the ideas of Freud but also on later developments in psychoanalytic thinking about the person. The emphasis here is on the influence of unconscious thought, the defensive strategies which often underlie this and the lack of unity in personal being.

This set of perspectives presents a broad and varied range of the kinds of methods, approaches and issues which can be found in social psychology. Relatively few traditional textbooks of the subject would present such a wide range of approaches. It is true that in this book some perspectives have been deliberately omitted or played down. There is no use made of a behaviourist perspective, for example; and in both textbooks and journals of social and general psychology much more emphasis would usually be placed on the experimental approach than it will receive here. But, as I have argued, any presentation of social psychology must itself be a construction. A varied set of perspectives has been selected which, it is believed, offers insight and illumination into the process of being a person in a social world and raises issues with which social psychologists should be concerned.

As you will have noted, these perspectives map closely on to the aspects of the self that were discussed in section 2. Each chapter thus not only presents a perspective but also brings a particular aspect into focus as well. So, for example, the *biological perspective* of the second chapter centres on the significance for a person of being embodied (i.e. being in a particular body). The kinds of issue it considers include the complex interrelationship between such 'embodiment' and our experience, actions and ways of relating to other people. It also considers evolution and its implications for human social behaviour, looks at the use of drugs and alcohol and raises questions about the biological basis of consciousness.

The third chapter continues with the methodology of natural science but looks at how it has been applied to help us understand how we make sense of the world. Working largely from the perspective of *experimental studies,* it considers, for example, the processes involved in our categorizations of experiences both within ourselves and in the world around us. It also discusses the ways in which we attribute causality and responsibility and the potential significance of this in terms of how we cope with life.

Chapter 4 retains the focus on the ways in which we experience the world and ourselves but looks at this topic from the contrast of an *experiential perspective*: in other words, it adopts the point of view of a person's own subjective experience rather than the 'outside' view of an objective scientist. How can we differentiate and conceptualize experience? What also are the implications of reflexiveness – our capacity to be aware of ourselves as persons who must eventually face growing older and eventual death, who are confronted with the need to make choices and who can play at least some part in determining who they will become?

Chapter 5 broadens the focus still further by looking at the ways in which we are constructed by the society of which we are a part. It introduces the *social constructionist perspective*. This argues that the boundaries between the personal and the social are blurred. Persons need to be viewed as being a function of fluid and continuously changing patterns of social practices and relationships. Even the most intimate aspects of personal experience such as our emotional feelings, the authors claim, are as much a result of our enmeshment in society as of our biology. This chapter also looks at language and its role, especially during childhood, in the social development of the person.

As the final perspective presented in this book, Chapter 6 takes up the question of the unconscious. It looks at how the *psychodynamic approach* might contribute to social psychology and our understanding of the self. The chapter compares different developments in psychodynamic theorizing which link the experience of self and ways of relating to others to unconscious feelings which have their origins in early life.

(Note that the title of each chapter signifies not only the perspective in question but also its key focus. Thus, the focus is on *embodiment* in the biological perspective of Chapter 2; on the way we *interpret* the world in the experimentalist perspective of Chapter 3; on our capacity for *reflexive awareness* in the experiential perspective of Chapter 4; on the way in which the self is '*distributed*' throughout the social contexts in which we live in the social constructionist perspective of Chapter 5; and on the *defensive* manoeuvres of the unconscious in order to avoid pain in the psychodynamic perspective of Chapter 6.)

The concluding chapter of the book (Chapter 7) will review, contrast and compare the perspectives presented. This will be done in the context of a discussion of issues about the nature of the self in the modern world. This chapter will also return to the kinds of question raised in this Introduction.

4.1   Epistemological reflections

In taking this *multiple perspective approach*, this book (and the series of which it is a part) will present a social psychology which stands at the intersection of different perspectives and is able to interrelate (or at least to present) the many facets of being a person in a social world. It does mean though, of course, that in looking at specific aspects (e.g. the biological basis of social behaviour) the focus will often be on the broad characteristics and implications and not the detail of the processes concerned. It means also that, if this is to be more than a mere juxtaposition of perspectives, we shall have to consider the important issue of *how* such different forms of understanding might interrelate.

To what extent, for example, are the perspectives mutually exclusive? Kuhn (1970) has suggested that the different paradigms found in the natural sciences (e.g. physics) do exclude each other and tend to succeed each other rather than to coexist. But is this true also for psychology, or can perspectives in this discipline be regarded as complementary; as potentially at least fitting together with their different foci, insights and strengths to provide a richer, fuller understanding of psychological life? After all, we are complex creatures; at the same time being biological organisms, using a language and a symbolic world assimilated from our society, and perhaps also ourselves capable of generating novelty and change.

A feature of the approach of this book is that it will strive to be *epistemologically reflexive*. In other words, it will try to reflect on the kind of understanding or knowledge which each perspective represents. The differences between the assumptions made by different perspectives raise, for example, a number of methodological and philosophical issues, some of which have been already touched on in this chapter. At the end of each of the subsequent chapters, there will be a section entitled *Reflections* whose function is to take up issues of this kind raised by the content of that particular chapter.

As we have seen in contrasting them, one key issue between perspectives, for example, is their attitudes to *scientific method*. Is it appropriate to use in social psychology the methods of natural science which have proved so effective in the investigation of the physical world? This debate itself relates to other issues. What, for example, constitutes the *essential subject-matter of social psychology*? Is it social *behaviour* which we can observe and measure; or is it the patterns of *meaning* which make up our experience of our personal and social worlds and help to structure and coordinate our relations with each other? If the latter, does it make sense to try to measure them, or can we only interpret them?

Perspectives differ also in their attitude to *agency*. Should our actions and experiences be considered to be entirely determined or are they in certain respects 'open'? Are they merely the outcome of the confluence of determinants acting upon us, or do we have some scope for autonomy (i.e. for creating actions which are novel and potentially unpredictable)? If we do accept that our actions and ways of making sense are largely determined, what part is played by different kinds of determinants, such as genetics, social context and socialization?

Above all, we shall need to consider what is the *purpose* of a social psychology of persons. Is it to generate objective knowledge about our social behaviour, or to stimulate awareness and reflection about the actions and experience of ourselves and others? Is it to help to emancipate people from oppressive forms of social influence, or even to offer some guidance on how to lead our lives? Or is it perhaps best regarded as some combination of these four?

We shall return to these questions as the book proceeds.

References

Barthes, R. (1977) *Roland Barthes* (trans. by R. Howard), London, Macmillan.

Borges, J.L. (1970) *Labyrinths*, Harmondsworth, Penguin Books.

Kuhn, T. (1970) *The Structure of Scientific Revolutions* (2nd edn), Chicago, University of Chicago Press.

Medoff, M. (1982) *Children of a Lesser God*, Ambergate, Amber Lane Press.

Sacks, O. (1976) *Awakenings*, New York, Vintage Books.

Sacks, O. (1986) *A Leg to Stand On,* London, Picador.

Ullman, L. (1976) *Changing,* New York, Bantam Books.

CHAPTER 2

THE EMBODIED SELF: A BIOLOGICAL PERSPECTIVE

by Frederick Toates

Contents

1   Introduction

This chapter presents a biological perspective, considering insights to be gained in our understanding of the self from the evidence of biology (e.g. by looking at the physical body). It hardly needs saying that our experience of being a person in a social world reflects the fact that we are biological beings, commonly assumed to be the product of a process of evolution. For many who attempt to tackle the diversity of perspectives in psychology, the science of biology has a secure feel to it and forms a logical starting point; all but those adopting a most extreme position would acknowledge that biology must have an important role in understanding the determinants of our behaviour. Behaviour is determined by a nervous system constructed from millions of cells and our behaviour in the world is executed through our nervous system. Thus, the central theme of this chapter will be that, to gain understanding of the self in a social world, we need to address the issue that we are *embodied*.

As one aspect of that embodiment, consider that, rightly or wrongly, we tend to form judgements about others based at least in part upon their physical appearance. Also, by means of mirrors, one is able to assimilate a mental model of one's own appearance, a certain notion of an enduring physical form. Others will judge us in part by our physical appearance. We will have some idea of these judgements and the disparities from ideal forms; this will in turn affect our own experience of being a person, our self-image and reactions towards others.

The chapter will look at various aspects of the interdependence between social and biological factors. Section 2 will introduce some of the basic biological building blocks, such as nerve cells and hormones. It will look at how behaviour is controlled by the activity of the nervous system but will do so from a perspective of interaction. By this is meant that behaviour is controlled by the nervous system but activity within the nervous system is itself dependent upon, amongst other things, the external environment. Therefore, there is a circle of causes. This level of investigation is termed a *causal level* of analysis, and it asks questions about the causes of behaviour in a given individual. Section 3 will show how, in order to understand the determinants of behavioural phenomena, one needs knowledge at the biological level in addition to taking the social matrix into account. The specific example chosen to illustrate this theme is that of alcoholism and drug addiction.

There is another level of looking at biology and behaviour, which is termed the *functional* level. At this level, questions are concerned not with how things work within the individual but with how behaviour has served an *adaptive* value in the history of the species concerned. From even a superficial glance, animals appear to be very well adapted to their environment both in terms of their bodily structure and their behaviour (e.g. building nests in which to shelter and protecting their young). This process of adaptation has taken place over millions of years of evolution.

Behaving in certain ways increased the adaptation of the animal and its offspring. Behaving in other ways decreased their adaptation. Certain adaptive behaviours have therefore emerged. Looking at this process in more detail and considering the special case of humans can sometimes provide answers to the question 'Why do humans tend to do that?' Section 4 will look at the functional level of analysis. It will ask what is the functional significance of social behaviour in terms of its contribution to survival and reproduction. Finally, Section 5 will look at consciousness, asking both causal and functional questions.

Aims of Chapter 2

The aims of this chapter are:

- To demonstrate the reciprocal relationship between biology and social factors.

- To distinguish functional and causal levels of explanation.

- To show how biological ideas can be applied to understanding the self in the context of sociobiology, which will enable such things as sexual jealousy and homosexuality to be seen from a biological perspective.

- To show how alcoholism and drug addiction can be better understood by seeing the underlying biological processes in a social context.

- To show the relevance of biology to consciousness.

- To enable you to extrapolate an understanding of biological phenomena to other areas of social interest.

2 Interacting biological and social factors

2.1 Introduction

The human body is composed of many millions of fundamental building blocks termed cells (e.g. red blood cells that carry oxygen in the blood, cells that constitute the kidneys, and nerve cells that make up the nervous system). Since we are primarily interested in behaviour and this is organized by the nervous system, we shall be concerned mainly with one type of such cell: the neuron or nerve cell. Those neurons in the brain and spinal cord constitute what is termed the central nervous system.

Neurons communicate with each other at junctions termed synapses, where a chemical neurotransmitter is released from one neuron and attaches itself to a second neuron. The second neuron is then excited or inhibited by the arrival of the transmitter (see Figure 2.1a). In a similar way, a neuron can excite a muscle as shown in Figure 2.1b. It was a deficiency in one such neurotransmitter, dopamine, in the brain of Leonard (see Window 1.2 in the Introduction) that was the physical basis of his disorder. Recovery of function depended upon restoration of normal dopamine levels.

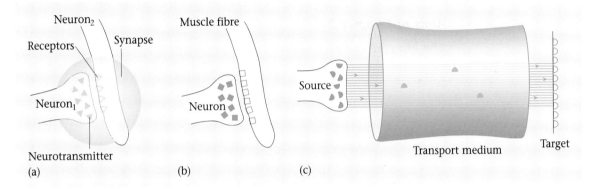

Figure 2.1   *Representation of some biological components: (a) The junction between two neurons, termed a synapse. Note the neurotransmitter substance that is released from neuron$_1$ and fits receptors at neuron$_2$; (b) The junction between a neuron and a muscle; (c) Hormonal transmission. Note that the hormone is transported in the bloodstream and affects a target at some distance in the body*

Through sensory neurons, the nervous system receives information from the external environment and also from the internal environment of the body. Based in large part upon such information, the nervous system organizes behaviour and, amongst other things, causes the secretion of hormones into the bloodstream. A hormone is a chemical messenger that is released at one site, carried around the bloodstream and exerts an action at a distant site (see Figure 2.1c). The distinction between a neurotransmitter and a hormone is therefore in their mode of action, the neurotransmitter having a local action and the hormone being broadcast globally. Hormones have diverse effects, such as to speed up or slow down the beating of the heart, to facilitate digestion or to switch on further hormones concerned with reproduction.

A theme that will be followed throughout the present chapter is summarized in Figure 2.2: there exist dynamic interactions between (a) the central nervous system, (b) the body outside the nervous system, and (c) the external world.

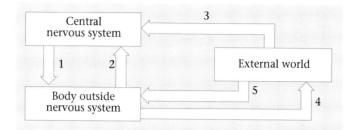

Figure 2.2 *Summary of the interactions between the central nervous system, the remainder of the body and the external world. The nervous system will transmit messages to regions of the body (e.g. heart, stomach, leg muscle) represented by (1). Feedback will convey information from such sites to the central nervous system (2). The central nervous system will be influenced by the external world (3) and via the muscles of the body will influence it (route 1 and 4). The external world can affect other body systems, not just the central nervous system (e.g. through a virus or heat) (5)*

Consider some examples of these interactions. You say something that you wished you had not said. You see signs on the face of another person that you have caused embarrassment. You start to blush. This reaction is caused by the nervous system issuing commands to blood vessels at the skin of your face such that they dilate causing an increased flow of blood at the skin. The other person begins to look even more embarrassed. This makes you still more embarrassed. You perceive the blood flow to your face and you feel even more guilty. Is this a familiar sequence to you? As you can see, it involves a series of interactions within the body (between the central nervous system and peripheral blood vessels) and between two individuals.

As another example, consider the role that the hormone testosterone plays in human behaviour. The hormone seems to sensitize nervous system pathways making the individual more sensitive to, for example, erotic thoughts and stimuli (pathway 2 of Figure 2.2). However, there is also evidence that the level of testosterone itself is affected by the social context (pathway 3 and 1). For example, Mazur et al. (1992) found that winners at chess tournaments showed higher levels of testosterone than losers, and suggested that these high levels encourage participation in further competitive activities. Social context and related expectations appear to influence hormonal activity.

As another example, it is well known that such social factors as divorce, bereavement and unemployment can produce a predisposition to depression. In Figure 2.2 this corresponds to link 3. Changes can be observed in the body as a result of such changes in the nervous system (e.g. there is an increased level of the hormone cortisol in the bloodstream). This corresponds to an effect via link 1 in Figure 2.2: in this case, 'the body system' is the adrenal gland which secretes cortisol in response to a depressed state of the central nervous system. As link 2, there is some evidence that cortisol can exert a bias on the nervous system to incline the organism to further depression (reviewed by Toates, 1995). Certainly, if levels of cortisol are greatly elevated for extended periods, this can cause a decreased number of cortisol receptors in the brain. This biological change might change perceptions of the world and thereby affect social dynamics and lead to a vicious circle of effects.

Our bodies are locked into inextricable complex interactions with other people; we affect and are affected by them. This means that teasing apart simple cause and effect links can often be very difficult if not impossible. It is possible to tease apart *some* of the processes and make *some* assertions in this area, as will be shown below, but the explanations that emerge must be made in the context of complex interactions of the kind represented in Figure 2.2. The remainder of section 2 will look at some examples that illustrate the central theme: in taking a biological perspective the complex interdependence between biology and social factors needs to be central to the discussion.

2.2   The circulatory system and personality

The heart moves blood around the body to meet the needs of the various tissues for a supply of both oxygen and fuel such as glucose. When the metabolic needs of the body increase, as in exercise, the heart pumps more vigorously and increases the supply of these substances. The heart has its own intrinsic rhythm which is a property of the heart muscle itself. However, heart rate can be increased or decreased according to circumstances. One factor that changes heart rate is neural commands from the brain. To use a well-known example cited by William James, on perceiving a bear in the forest, a person's heart rate will tend to increase in preparation for fleeing.

One of the principal hormones involved in the emotion of fear is adrenalin, which is released into the bloodstream from the adrenal gland (situated just above the kidney) at times of high emotion. Another is cortisol, which reinforces the action of adrenalin. Adrenalin has various effects that prepare the body for exertion. For example, fuels are made available from reserves. Heart rate is elevated as a result of adrenalin molecules attaching themselves to receptors at the heart muscle. At such times, the effect of adrenalin serves a vital role.

Of course, a mechanism that is of adaptive value in running from a bear can be maladaptive when stuck in a traffic-jam on the M25 with a crucial business engagement due to commence. However, evolution cannot be expected to provide a solution appropriate under all conditions. In our evolutionary history, times of stress were most usually times of physical exertion, unlike sitting on the M25.

You are doubtless familiar with the dangers to the circulatory system of such things as eating too much saturated fat and smoking, as well as the appeals to take more exercise. The magnitude of the problem of circulatory disorder is enormous. In the United States, the number one fatal disorder is coronary heart disease; all of the cancer deaths combined constitute less than half of the heart disease score. As will now be shown, account must also be taken of the role of social context in trying to understand the circulatory system in health and disease. This issue is a particularly good one for showing the value of a multidisciplinary approach.

There are various theories of exactly what is the relationship between, on the one hand, personality and social interaction and, on the other, the risk of circulatory disorder. One proposal (Wright, 1988) is that the danger lies in having a personality prone to time pressure (e.g. trying to do more than one thing at a time and obsessively concerned with not wasting any of the valuable commodity that is time). Another approach is presented by Williams (1989). The background history to Williams' analysis is found in a pioneering and highly influential study carried out by Meyer Friedman and Ray Rosenman, from which emerged the notion of Type A and Type B personalities. Type As appeared to be the subjects most at risk from coronary heart disease and were characterized by such traits as being in a hurry, ambitiousness and high competitiveness. They were easily aroused to anger. By contrast, their Type B fellow citizens, as the less ambitious and competitive, were found to be at a lower risk. However, subsequent research forced a qualification of this dichotomy in that only certain of the Type A characteristics were associated with increased risk. According to Williams' analysis, the good news is that being competitive, being ambitious and in a hurry, are, *in themselves,* not dangerous. But what for some will be the bad news is, to quote Williams: 'Of all the characteristics grouped under the name Type A, *only those concerned with hostility and related characteristics are toxic to the heart'* (1989, p. 48). As Williams expresses it, 'If yours is a hostile heart, you need to change it into a more trusting heart' (ibid., p. xiii).

Looking at the biological level, the problem is that the blood vessels of the body tend to build up fatty deposits on their walls, which impedes the smooth flow of blood. This build up is in part a function of the amount of fatty substances taken in the diet. So where does social psychology come into the picture in understanding such a process? The explanation is as follows. In our everyday social commerce, we inevitably encounter difficulties and frustration. People don't always do what we would like them to do. Confronted with this situation, the person with a bias towards hostility will tend to react with anger which will activate the hormonal response to threat. Adrenalin and cortisol will be secreted into the bloodstream in large amounts and these will cause fatty acids to be released into the blood from stores in the body. In terms of our biological evolution, these fatty acids would normally be used as fuel for such ends as to fight for our lives or to propel us away from an advancing bear. However, such a reaction is normally inappropriate when, say, confronted with a traffic warden. Regular hostile confrontations lead to a chronic elevation of fatty acid levels in the blood and, since these are not being used as fuel, they are free to roam around forming deposits on blood vessels, which reduces the effectiveness of the circulatory system. The associated increases in blood pressure will make matters still worse. This is the biological background to a heart attack. According to Williams, the message is clear and for once simple – if you are a person easily prone to anger, try to manage the hostility in some constructive way.

Williams refers to a patient, a self-made man 'JS'. JS was used to getting his own way in each situation, largely by bullying and being unpleasant to anyone who crossed him. One day, JS was overtaken by another car, a situation that would normally have provoked the response of speeding to 'pay that bastard back'. Just as he was reaching for the horn to deliver a blast, JS felt as if a red-hot poker was being thrust into his chest. JS had had his first heart attack. Shortly afterwards JS was being injected by a nurse who failed to pierce the right vessel. Just as JS was about to explode in anger with her, again the 'red-hot poker' of a heart attack struck.

Cynicism, a fundamental distrust of others, is particularly toxic to the circulation. This appears to be due to hormonal changes associated with this attitude. As Williams notes, what is prescribed in the teachings of many of the world's religions regarding how to behave towards one's fellow humans accords exactly with current scientific insight: try to see your fellow human beings in a different light. Any reader prone to hostile reactions might like to read Williams' book and follow his advice in this regard. Interestingly, Williams admits that:

> Despite my extensive understanding of how a cynical, mistrusting attitude towards others, anger, and aggressive treatment of others can place one at higher risk of serious health problems, I still find myself harbouring nasty thoughts about the motives of slow people ahead of me in supermarket lines, of drivers who are still sitting there after the traffic light has changed to green, even of unseen folks on some other floor of the building when the elevator doesn't arrive fast enough to suit me.

> *(Williams, 1989, p. 151)*

So what do we do about it? Williams suggests that we should try to distinguish situations in which there really is a threat involved from those that are unimportant and to which we often add a gratuitous element of bad intention, such as thinking that a slow person in a check-out queue really is trying to hold us back. He argues for the use of assertiveness instead of aggression. So, you are in the supposed 'fast lane' check-out at a supermarket and the person in front has too many items for that lane. Rather than exploding or ruminating on the person's evil intentions, you politely point out to them that you are in a hurry whilst actively trying to reject the notion that the other person has the motive of trying to slow you up. You ask that you might go ahead since you have only two items and have an urgent meeting.

Why are some people more hostile than others? Are we born with either a trusting heart or a hostile heart? Williams' conclusion will probably come as little surprise to the reader: the tendencies arise from a complex interaction between genetic and environmental factors (an issue to be discussed in detail later). Thus, genes might exert a bias one way or the other but environmental (e.g. social factors) could then either reinforce or counter the effects of such bias. In forming a trusting heart in children, it is difficult to overemphasize the value of a trusting, nurturing, social environment.

The following section also looks at interactions between peripheral tissues and the central nervous system, and a similar message of the necessity to consider interactions between biological and environmental factors will emerge.

2.3   Interpreting emotional arousal

Emotion is of great interest to psychologists and one aspect of this concerns the nature of the relationship between bodily states (such as hormone levels) and social contexts as determinants of emotion. This section considers a well-known experiment in this area, that of Schachter and Singer (1962). These researchers were interested in the determinants of such emotions as anger, fear and euphoria, reasoning that the determinants might arise from both *cognitive processes* (often stimulated by the social context of the person) and from *peripheral activation*, meaning excitation of the body outside the central nervous system (e.g. a pounding heart or a constricting gut).

Schachter and Singer explored the complex interdependence between (1) the external environment, (2) internal events, in this case, adrenalin level, and (3) subjective feelings. Although most people would find it uncontroversial that factor 1 influences 2 and 3, the lines of causation are probably more complex than that. For instance, does adrenalin level influence subjective feelings? To investigate this, it is necessary to inject subjects with adrenalin and then explore the emotions that they experience. However, life is never simple, particularly in dealing with human subjects, and some elaborate control treatments need to be employed. For a start, one needs subjects injected with a neutral substance to control for the possibility that merely giving any injection would equally well arouse emotion. Thus, some subjects were injected with adrenalin and some were injected with a placebo substance.

Also at the design stage of such an experiment, one needs to ask the question – what do you tell the subjects? Do you tell them the truth about what you are injecting into them or do you lie to them? After all, most people have some idea of the effect of adrenalin on the body and might simply label their emotions according to this knowledge.

BOX 2.1   Schacter and Singer's experiment (1962)

All subjects were told that the study was into the effects on vision of a substance termed Suproxin and that they were being injected with this. Some subjects were correctly informed of the known consequences of injecting adrenalin (e.g. increased heart rate), attributed of course to Suproxin. Other subjects were told nothing of any possible side-effects. A further group was misinformed by being told of side-effects not caused by adrenalin (e.g. numb feet, headache).

Subjects were placed in one of two social contexts, designed to promote either euphoria or anger. Stooges (i.e. actors told to act certain roles) were employed to generate the social contexts. For the euphoria group, the stooge was primed to act in a friendly and extrovert manner, playing various games (e.g. throwing around paper darts). For the anger group, both subject and stooge were asked to fill in a questionnaire, the questions in which gradually became insulting. The stooge reacted negatively to the questions and ultimately tore up the questionnaire and stormed out of the room.

Subsequent to this exposure, subjects were asked how they felt. There was a tendency for adrenalin not to exert an independent effect upon mood but rather to amplify the mood as determined by the stooge in whose presence the subject was placed. In other words, 'adrenalin-injected happy-stooge' subjects became particularly happy and 'adrenalin-injected angry-stooge' subjects became particularly angry (both relative to those subjects who received a saline injection). The result suggested a subtle interaction between bodily state and social context in determining emotion. Mood changes were particularly likely to be reported where the subjects were either not informed or misinformed about the consequences of the injection. Subjects who were truthfully told of the kind of bodily (so-called) side-effects to expect were more likely to attribute these to the injection rather than to the social context.

Nowadays, the issue of experimental ethics would play a bigger role than in the past – is it ethical, in the interests of science, to lie to subjects about what is going into their bodies? What do you think?

To understand mood it seems we need to take both biological factors (e.g. hormone levels) and social factors into account. To understand mental states one needs a knowledge of biology but equally to understand biology one needs to consider the social context. No one discipline has a monopoly over the truth. The result was interpreted in terms of Schachter and Singer's theory of emotion which incorporates the assumption that both peripheral activation and cognitions are essential for the experience of emotion.

In spite of it becoming something of a classic of the psychology literature, subsequent researchers have found some difficulty verifying the result of the experiment. Others have obtained a partial verification. In a review of the literature appearing in the twenty years since the publication of the original report, Reizenzein (1983) concluded that Schachter and Singer's 'strong' position that peripheral activation (e.g. heart-rate elevation) is a *necessary* condition for emotion has not been confirmed.

The kind of experimental evidence leading to this conclusion is that obtained from experimental subjects given beta-blockers. These drugs are sometimes taken by people suffering from anxiety (e.g. a musician with a pounding heart on anticipating crucial performances). Beta-blockers target receptors for adrenalin in the periphery (i.e. the body outside the central nervous system), particularly those involved in the control of the heart and circulation. By blocking the effects of adrenalin, peripheral activation is reduced and yet under laboratory conditions there is no consistent report of a reduction in anxiety. Some subjects do report such a reduction though, and there is the suggestion that these might well be subjects who are attributing considerable weight to the perception of bodily changes. Also, as Plutchik (1980) points out, it would be unlikely that a biological system would evolve such as to be absolutely dependent upon peripheral activation for generating a central nervous system state. Emotions such as anger and fear arise extremely rapidly; meaning that an appropriate response to a foe can be an instantaneous matter of life or death. It would seem unlikely that it should depend absolutely upon a hormone secreted at the adrenal gland and its effect at organs some distance away. However, what might be termed Schachter and Singer's 'weak' position (i.e. that peripheral activation *can play some role* in the generation of emotion) does derive support from subsequent research. Indeed, adrenalin injections have been found to increase anxiety even in a situation where the heart and circulatory system did not respond to them (Plutchik, 1980). This suggests the possibility that adrenalin might have been activating receptors at the brain directly or that it caused some general malaise.

A related experiment carried out by Valins (1970) is of interest here (see Box 2.2). It shows how subtle the effects of peripheral activation can be and that the relationship between peripheral activation and emotion is not necessarily straightforward. Once again, the experiment involved deceiving some experimental subjects.

According to Valins' interpretation, the effect shown here might be described as cognitively rather than biologically mediated. However, the experiment does not refute the existence of pathways from peripheral physiology (e.g. heart, gut) to the brain. In principle, Valins' effect might have been mediated by genuine physiological changes (e.g. changes in actual heart rate following changes in artificial heart rate). Valins argued that this was not so but others have suggested that there exist physiological effects of exposure to an artificially changed heart rate. So the experiment simply alerts us to the possibility that there are a number of different flows of information that can be implicated in these effects.

BOX 2.2 Valins' experiment (1970)

Male subjects were presented with emotion-arousing pictures (nude photographs of women), and at the same time exposed to what they supposed was a recording of their own heart rate. In fact, the 'heart rate' heard was under the control of the experimenter. Is it possible to mask the effect of the true heart rate by such an artificial heart rate? One group heard the sound of an accelerated heart rate at the time of presentation of five photographs and normal heart rate for another five. A second group was exposed to a decelerated heart rate accompanying exposure to five photographs and a normal heart rate to the other five. Subjects were asked to rate the attractiveness of the photographs. As you might well have guessed, pictures corresponding to an accelerated heart rate (relative to a stable baseline) were judged more attractive, but (what might surprise you) so were those corresponding to a deceleration.

Valins argued that subjects were interpreting changes in their supposed heart rate in terms of the emotion-arousing property of the picture and ranking the picture's attraction value accordingly; at some level they were processing information of the kind 'The picture caused my heart rate to *change*, therefore I must find the picture attractive.'

In a study that led to a similar conclusion, Valins examined the reluctance of subjects to approach a snake. The rationale for the study was the possibility that fear might be based in part upon the subject listening to bodily states: 'That thing makes me frightened because it changes my heart rate.' Subjects given false feedback, indicating no acceleration in heart rate, were more willing to approach the snake. This would seem to have potential therapeutic value.

You might feel that such experiments are somewhat contrived (let alone unethical!) but their take-home message is a profound one. It is doubtful whether we could ever fully understand being a person and social life without considering such inextricable interactions of social context and biology. A consideration of biology rapidly dispels any illusions that such issues can be couched in neat and simple terms of 'Is it nature or nurture?' The next section will continue the story-line of emphasizing the relevance of biology to understanding internal mental events and social interactions by looking at the example of pain.

2.4 Pain and the placebo effect

Pain is a somewhat paradoxical phenomenon. On the one hand, it would seem to be something that is universal; surely we all experience pain in much the same way irrespective of our culture? Pain pathways in the nervous system have been well worked out (see Figure 2.3). Without our current understanding of the nervous system, the French philosopher Descartes described specific pathways that mediate painful experience. Compared to, say, human sexuality or fear, pain would seem to be basic, stereotyped and a matter of neural pathways, clearly the business of the physiology department or medical school.

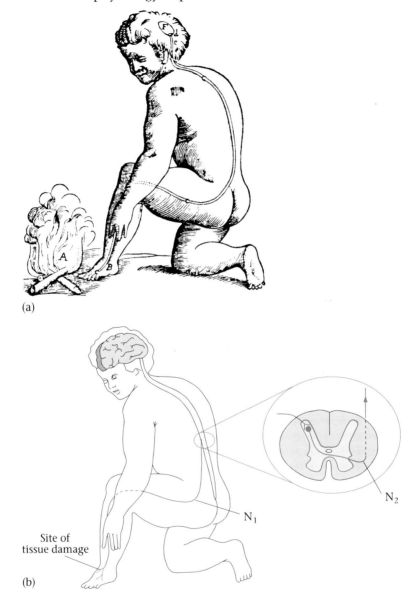

(a)

(b)

Site of tissue damage

N_1

N_2

Figure 2.3 *Representation of pain: (a) Scheme proposed by Descartes, with a pathway carrying information from a peripheral site of tissue damage to the brain; (b) Contemporary understanding of pain, showing a neuron (N_1) carrying information from periphery to spinal cord (shown blown up in cross section) where a synapse (<•) is formed with a second neuron (N_2) that projects to the brain*

On the other hand, pain is subject to a number of influences that are anything but simple. Indeed, social psychology would seem to have a vital role in interpreting some of the data. Thus, whereas the pathways that carry information to the brain are reasonably well understood, the interpretation that the subject places on the information that they carry is dependent upon a number of factors, one of which is social context. A particularly good example to illustrate this is the so-called placebo effect.

The placebo effect can be illustrated by a substance such as morphine (though the effect occurs very widely in different situations). Morphine exerts a pain-reducing (termed analgesic) effect. However, a large number of subjects will obtain a pain-relieving effect if they *believe* that they are getting morphine even if they are injected with a chemically inert substance (Wall, 1993). The context of delivery is important; if the subject is treated by an authority figure in a white coat, this can make a big difference in obtaining analgesia. Wall recalls a doctor who would give the patient placebo tablets with the help of forceps and the remark 'They are too powerful to be touched by hand.' The placebo is not merely some transient quirk that is seen in highly suggestible people but rather a very powerful ubiquitous phenomenon of sometimes long duration. Wall gives the following example.

Angina describes a painful condition that arises at the muscle of the heart wall as a result of an inadequate supply of blood. In the 1950s, a treatment was used consisting of tying other arteries in the body to encourage blood to flow through the heart muscle. The hope was that this would promote sprouting of new vessels at the heart. Large numbers of patients received this operation with general satisfaction. However, in a later analysis, doctors were unable to find any evidence of sprouting of new vessels. Therefore, a controlled study was set up with the control group (unbeknown to them) merely experiencing an incision of the skin. The surprise was that both groups of patients reported a considerable reduction in pain. Perhaps even more surprising is that both groups made progress as indexed by the distance they could walk, their reduction in medication and even the electrical activity of their hearts.

> Think for a while about the ethics of performing such placebo surgery or giving placebo drugs, the so-called 'benevolent lie'. Think also about the implications of such knowledge being generally available. Should information on placebos be kept secret to maintain the mystique of medicine and perhaps some of the efficacy of the effect? You might like to discuss this with your friends, family and other students.

The important message is that something as seemingly basic as pain is dependent upon a complex of psychological factors such as the expectation and goal of the patient, the patient's pain-related behaviour (e.g. the will to get better), as well as the social context. The next section also looks at biology and the social context, developing the argument to include a consideration of the notion of agency.

2.5   Agency

My concept of my fellow beings is centrally coloured by my perception of myself as an agent (i.e. as someone who can effect action on the world and who will be judged responsible for his actions). I feel myself able to make responsible choices and, given a range of possibilities, to enter freely into a certain course of action. For instance, I can choose now to leave my word processor and go to the toilet. In this regard I feel myself to have total freedom. Also, I can choose to divert my thoughts from writing this chapter and start thinking, say, about my dog if I wish. As a scientist, I know that these choices will be embodied in processes within my central nervous system but that does not undermine my feeling of agency. With the privilege of conscious insight, I feel able to account for *why* I did certain things and to be able to do so in a way that no-one else could. I feel myself not only to have agency but, on the basis of its exertion, I feel myself to be capable of acting rationally, and estimate that others will judge me as a rational, goal-oriented person.

My capacity to exercise agency depends upon the integrity of certain brain processes and there are limitations on this ability. For example, I cannot always exercise as much agency over my own thoughts as I would like. In severe cases of painful and disruptive unwanted thoughts (e.g. 'Have I checked the gas-taps the necessary one hundred times?', 'Am I really here?'), medicines can be prescribed which target certain key neurotransmitters in the brain and which cause a relief of symptoms (Toates, 1990). The limitations of movement experienced by sufferers from Parkinson's disease, caused by a disorder of the brain's neurotransmitter dopamine, must severely limit the sense of agency of the sufferer (see the example of Leonard in the Introduction).

I also know that at times I, even as a reasonably healthy individual, will quite explicitly argue that events within my physical body limit my agency. I am sure that I am not unique in this regard. Most of us are perfectly happy to accept the notion of agency in the context of behaviour for which we feel proud and which we judge as acceptable to others (e.g. showing kindness to someone). But most of us are equally willing to attribute responsibility for the behaviour of which we are not so proud to such biologically flavoured causes as genes, bodily fatigue or premenstrual syndrome. Indeed, such an appeal to a biological level of explanation can have some validity in law. For example, evidence of abnormalities in the brain can be used to support a plea of diminished responsibility in a murder trial. Psychiatrists are frequently called into court to give evidence on whether accused people are really responsible for their actions. For example, abnormal levels of the neurotransmitter substance serotonin (also known as 5HT) are related to impulsivity and aggression. Fenwick raises the question: 'Is a person to be held morally responsible for behaviour, however reprehensible, caused by low levels of 5HT?' (1993, p. 118).

You might like now to reflect upon the idea that, as our understanding of the physical basis of behaviour increases as a result of insights on how abnormal brain physiology accompanies abnormal behaviour, so the conviction with which we are able to apply a notion of agency diminishes in parallel. Do you agree? Look back at the account of Leonard given in Window 1.2 in section 1 of the Introduction, and consider to what extent and in what sense he is the agent of his actions and experiences.

ACTIVITY 2.1

It is worth posing the following question: is abnormality of the physical brain synonymous with lack of agency and lack of responsibility for one's actions whereas normal brain functioning is associated with agency and responsibility? This is a question that you might like to hold in mind throughout your reading of this book and the series of which it forms a part. The following section will consider a particular example that illustrates this topic.

Review of section 2

- The nervous system is made up of neurons which communicate at synapses. Chemical neurotransmitter is released at one neuron and attaches itself to another, thereby changing the activity of the second neuron.

- A hormone is a chemical messenger released into the bloodstream at one point, which is carried in the bloodstream and causes an effect at a distant site.

- There are interactions between the nervous system, the remainder of the body and the external environment.

- The circulatory system responds to hormones (e.g. adrenalin and cortisol) released by activity within the central nervous system. Excessive activation as a result of time urgency or hostile social interactions can be harmful.

- The experience of emotion appears to be determined by a complex of physiological factors (e.g. heart rate), social context and cognitive interpretation of the context.

- Pain depends not only upon tissue damage, but also on social context and expectations.

- Agency depends upon the integrity of the central nervous system. Our attribution of personal responsibility can be coloured by our knowledge of the condition of a person's nervous system.

3   Use of drugs and alcohol

3.1   Introduction

This section will use a particular example of behaviour to show in some detail the relevance of a biological perspective to being a person in a social world: people troubled by an excessive consumption of drugs and/or alcohol (termed here 'addicted people'). This topic is used as an example to illustrate the general theme of the chapter: that insight into both being a person and interaction with others requires information derived at the biological level. It is used also to show how the experience of being a person and one's social interactions can be radically transformed by drugs or alcohol.

ACTIVITY 2.2   A quotation from *The First Special Report to the US Congress on Alcohol and Health*, issued in 1973, can help to set the scene. In response to this quotation, try to think how you would explain the phenomena under consideration. What might be the relationship between the mental states described and alcohol ingested?

> The pain the alcoholic person feels is the pain of self-loathing and humiliation … from loss of the respect of his family and friends … from growing isolation and loneliness … from the awareness that he is throwing away much of his unique and creative self and gradually destroying his body and soul. He doesn't usually mean to get drunk, really drunk – he just wants to take the value from alcohol. Getting drunk, really drunk as only an alcoholic person becomes, is a nightmare of lost memories, retching, vertigo, the shakes, and a profound melancholy of regret. Sometimes it becomes a living nightmare of terrifying visions, screaming accusatory voices, and convulsions.
>
> Who would seek such experiences knowingly? …
>
> *(Keller and Rosenberg, 1973)*

Reading this quotation might have stimulated you to think of the kind of explanation that it is valid and useful to offer. For instance, is it helpful to think of the addicted person as *voluntarily* choosing to take alcohol? Alternatively, when applied to an addict, are principles of free-will irrelevant, a 'luxury' viewed from a sober, safe distance of academic discourse? Should we see the alcoholic's behaviour as the result of a disease process? Can the alcoholic really only be understood in terms of his or her social matrix? What are the implications for therapy of these different approaches? Not surprisingly, neat answers to simple questions such as these are elusive. Rather, only highly qualified answers can be tentatively offered. That is not to say that we have only little understanding of the biological bases of addiction. On the contrary, there is an impressive literature on this subject. The real problem comes in putting it all together.

In the case of addictive behaviours, the argument will be developed that biological understanding is imperative; even looking at rats can give us invaluable insights. However, we also need to consider the whole experience of being a person, the uniquely human attributes of consciousness and conscious self-insights, self-image and the like, as well as seeing the individual in a social context.

3.2   The nature of explanation

One point of heated debate in the literature is the validity of the *disease label* or *disease model* to refer to excessive drug and alcohol taking.

Think for a moment about what might be implied by these terms as applied to excessive drug/alcohol taking. What does the word 'disease' mean to you? What might it mean to an addicted person?

The notion of disease derives from within medicine to refer to something such as AIDS or Alzheimer's disease, and the essential features would seem to be: (1) physically identifiable target tissues whose malfunction underlies the disease; (2) clear symptoms of malfunction; and (3) the appropriateness of medical intervention to cure or alleviate the symptoms.

This model has certain features that seem appropriate to drug taking and alcoholism, whereas in other respects it might be misleading. In the case of addictions, the appropriateness of (2) might seem well established but even this assumption needs qualification, as will be argued later in section 3. Some might argue that medical intervention (3) might serve in part to disguise the true causes of malfunction which lie in the domain of social relationships and other external factors. As far as (1) is concerned, it is possible to identify brain regions that play an especially important role in addiction and it is reasonable to speculate that there are abnormalities in these regions. However, it will be shown that use of the term 'disease' in the context of addictive behaviour needs careful qualification and you should note the particular way in which the concept is being used in the following sections.

It is important not to forget that addicts (and their families and friends) read newspapers and watch television just like anyone else. They will be informed about their condition. Alcoholics might well be members of Alcoholics Anonymous and thereby well informed. Models that we develop in psychology tend to diffuse throughout the population. What might be the implication of this?

Rather than simply explaining behaviour, our theoretical models might well also influence it. There is some heated controversy in the literature concerning use of such expressions as 'disease model' of addiction, since these might well influence the addict's own self-image and therefore attitudes towards 'kicking the habit'.

Some have even argued that the disease model encourages irresponsibility and provides an excuse for continued drinking, although others in the treatment process vehemently deny this (discussed by Blum, 1991, p. 241). What is particularly interesting in the context of the present discussion is the advice given by Alcoholics Anonymous to alcoholics seeking help (Blum, 1991, p. 41): 'The urge to denial is so strong that most alcoholics cannot begin the recovery process until they recognize and admit the fact that they are powerless over alcohol.' The slogan 'Let go and let God' epitomizes the philosophy of powerlessness and giving of authority to a higher power. Somewhat paradoxically, by adopting this stance, the way to agency is explicitly to deny agency.

The fact that, in this chapter, we are taking a biological perspective towards such behaviour already says a lot about the type of explanation that it seems reasonable to seek. Until around the beginning of the twentieth century, excess alcohol consumption would have been attributed to a weak will or a sinful nature, in which case it is difficult to see any relevance of biological science. With the development of an understanding of the brain and genetics in the twentieth century, the level of explanation of such aberrant behaviour has shifted towards biology. Neurobiologists have developed models of motivation applicable across species and have applied them to addiction.

3.3   A biological perspective

Rats can be used to provide a 'simple' model of drug addiction. They can first be trained in a Skinner box to press a lever for food. Then the food reward is omitted. In response to a lever press, a small quantity of drug is now injected into the brain or bloodstream through a surgically implanted tube. Whether the behaviour of lever-pressing continues or extinguishes is the criterion of whether the drugs are rewarding. In fact, under these conditions, non-human animals, such as rats, will self-inject opioid drugs. Withdrawal symptoms can be shown when the supply is terminated. This would seem to capture some aspects of human drug taking. In some cases, rats will also readily drink a solution containing alcohol in preference to pure water. Another aspect of the Skinner box might model an important feature of human drug taking. It is known that cues associated with drug reward can come to play a controlling role in the animal's motivation. For example, if the rat has extinguished the lever-pressing habit because the experimenter has not rewarded the bar-presses, the habit can be revived by presenting a cue (e.g. a click or a light flash) that earlier had accompanied reward. Applied to humans, this might capture something of the power of the social context to influence drug craving. Being in a context that in the past was associated with highs (e.g. being with other junkies) can sometimes evoke powerful craving. The placebo effect (discussed earlier) is also appropriate to drug takers; sometimes small highs can be obtained just by being in the appropriate context (e.g. in the presence of others who are injecting) (Stewart et al., 1984).

If an animal, human or otherwise, experiences the positive effects of drugs, they can be subsequently motivated to pursue this. For either rat or human, one could claim that the nervous system retains a memory of past drug effects and the drug seeker is motivated to achieve, and expects to achieve, a similar state. The expectation is of a better state that is to be reached as a result of the behaviour.

At this point, however, you might wonder what the world of a rat in a Skinner box has to do with that of an addict on a city street. Presumably the rat is motivated on a somewhat simpler basis; trigger stimuli such as the lever catch its attention as a result of their past history of associations with the effect of the drug. The rat provides a simple model that gives us some insights. However, such variables as escape from shame and lifting of self-image are perhaps irrelevant concepts for a rat! Humans are able to articulate their expectation of a beneficial change in state as a result of alcohol (e.g. 'I shall feel more optimistic' or 'I shall be less anxious') as compared to non-consumption of alcohol. Perhaps not entirely at odds with lay opinion, scientific results show that the *chemical* action of alcohol is indeed one of mood or 'affective value' increase (Cox and Klinger, 1988). However, in addition, simply the *expectation* of a mood increase can itself effect a change in mood over and above the actual chemical effect. Also, indirect effects of alcohol cause affective changes (e.g. peer acceptance and a lifting of inhibitions placed on other activities, such as talking to members of the opposite sex).

One of the sites of action of drugs such as heroin and alcohol is on parts of the so-called 'old brain' (i.e. regions that have much in common between various species of animal, having appeared early in evolution). There is evidence that, in the case of both rats and humans, there exist individual differences in the susceptibility of these brain regions to the effects of alcohol (Cox and Klinger, 1988). How might such individual differences arise? One possibility to consider is that they might well be genetic in origin (see section 4.2). Selective breeding of rats and studies of human families suggest such a genetic factor. Given the existence of such differences, it is clear that biological science would be relevant to explaining differences in susceptibility to excess alcohol consumption.

Opioid drugs act on receptors that are also located in parts of the old brain. Drugs change the level of neural activity in these brain regions. Genetic differences in tendency to alcoholism might well be reflected in differences in the extent to which mood changes can easily be induced by alcohol (Blum, 1991, p. 66). A variety of different neurotransmitters and hormones, including dopamine, noradrenalin and serotonin, as well as the body's own opiate-like substances, seem to be affected by ingested alcohol (Blum, 1991). This could provide a clue as to the motivational basis of alcohol intake. Since the level of neurotransmitters is affected by alcohol, it is at least possible that their changed level forms the neural base of the rewarding effects of alcohol.

There is the suggestion that in non-addictive people such neurochemical effects are in balance. In the alcohol-prone individual there might be an intrinsic imbalance which is temporarily restored to normal by imbibing alcohol (Blum, 1991). Specifically, Blum suggests that a person predisposed to alcoholism has a deficiency within the opioid system, which is corrected by ingested alcohol.

3.4   Cox and Klinger's model

Cox and Klinger's (1988) model of alcohol consumption '... depicts people as deciding to drink or not to drink on the basis of whether the positive affective consequences that they expect to derive from drinking outweigh those that they expect to derive from not drinking' (p. 170).

Of course, after short-term beneficial effects wear off, the longer-term effects of alcohol consumption can be to increase anxiety and depression.

Cox and Klinger take a holistic view of alcohol consumption, arguing that the decision making underlying the taking of a given drink can only be understood in terms of (a) the current context (e.g. presence of associates drinking) and (b) the subject's expectations of obtaining a better mental state in the near future. Of course, expectations might map with varying degrees of accuracy on to the real events, both as experienced in the past and to be experienced in the future.

A study followed problem drinkers from the time that they made the decision to try to quit drinking (Perri, 1985). It was found that success correlated with the ability of the person to find a successful alternative behaviour pattern with its associated goals and expectations (e.g. a new hobby). Cox and Klinger (1988) conclude: 'In our view, any treatment technique will be doomed to failure if it enables alcoholics to stop drinking but does not provide them with alternative sources of emotional satisfaction' (p. 176).

In such terms, the expression 'disease' might not seem particularly useful. Rather, addictive behaviour might be more usefully viewed in terms of attempts (even if unsuccessful) to come to terms with life.

3.5   Self-image

An interesting experiment in this area was reported by Singer (1993) and involved the relationship between affective states and self-belief discrepancies. Drug taking was shown to be related to attempts by the individual to achieve something, not just in a social context but within the individual's own private world. The conclusions of the study dovetail with those of Cox and Klinger. The idea is that we all have beliefs about ourselves, whether consciously articulated or not. These beliefs might be grouped under such headings as 'actual self' (that is, as accurate a description as one can give of the person that one really is), 'ideal self' (one's image of having achieved one's most ambitious aspiration), and 'ought self' (family or peer expectations of how one ought to be). The term 'dreaded self' would refer to such things as being friendless or impotent.

To get a feel for the value of such terms, you might like to reflect upon these concepts as applied to yourself.

On the basis of such an analysis, it was found that individuals having a large discrepancy between actual self and ideal self were prone to sadness and depression. Subjects showing a large discrepancy between actual self and ought self were more likely to be prone to agitation, anxiety and fear.

Singer and associates theorized that cocaine users might be employing a form of self-medication against a depressed mood and therefore would be expected to show relatively large discrepancies between actual self and ideal self. This was indeed found to be the case.

Do such observations prove that prior discrepancies between actual and ideal self lead these subjects to take cocaine? It doesn't prove it but it suggests this as a possible explanation. However, the causal connection could be in the opposite direction. Cocaine use by certain individuals might be an important cause of the disparate assessments.

Evidence that also tentatively points towards a causal link leading from self-concept to drug taking was obtained by observations made of a given individual. It was found that, on a day-to-day basis, the strength of craving for cocaine correlated with the magnitude of actual–ideal discrepancy. Singer and associates have shown a correlation between the times at which addicts take cocaine and a feeling of low self-esteem. Effective counselling for alcoholism commonly involves an emphasis upon the frame of reference from which the subject's self-esteem and self-condemnation derive. It is found that alcoholics commonly have inflated and unrealistic expectations, with unremitting guilt for not attaining those standards.

3.6   Adaptation or disease?

So is addictive behaviour to be most usefully viewed as a disease or as a life strategy that seems to fail in the long term?

In a somewhat related theory to that of Singer and associates, Alexander (1990) proposes an 'integration failure' explanation of drug taking and argues for an adaptive model, as follows:

The model asserts that sustained integration failure is a grave problem for any person. It may lead to social isolation, depression, and ultimately suicide. Therefore, integration failure creates an urgent need to strive for integration or, failing that, to adopt a 'substitute adaptation' to stave off isolation, depression, and suicidal tendencies.

According to the model, people who do not achieve successful integration *behave adaptively* by choosing one of the substitute adaptations that are available to them. For example, the life of a street addict or a compulsive gambler, with the attendant misery, ill-health, and social stigma, is less painful and provides more hope for survival than the void of no identity at all. Likewise, the banal, mind-numbing addict culture is more bearable than isolation. Chronic intoxication, although unhealthy and boring, can provide distraction from a corrosive pre-occupation with failure.

(Alexander, 1990, p. 39)

Reflect for a moment on the disease model and the adaptive model just described. Are they compatible? What are some of the implications of viewing addiction as a disease or as an adaptation?

Alexander addresses this issue and argues against the disease model. He writes on the adaptive model:

Rather, it portrays addicts as healthy people who have been stymied in their attempt to attain full integration and who have reverted to the most adaptive substitute that they can find. This condition is seen as neither a disease nor a moral failure, but as an unfortunate outcome of the unique interaction of the addict's personal qualities, family, and society.

(ibid., p. 40)

Thus, Alexander's model would go against the not uncommon assumption presented in the popular media that people from a middle-class family background and otherwise of sound mind can somehow *catch* the disease of addiction by a chance encounter.

Alexander's words 'unique interaction of the addict's personal qualities, family, and society' could be modified to something like 'unique interaction of the addict's genes and neural structures, personal qualities, family, and society'.

The language used by the adaptive and disease models tends to be rather different. Thus, the disease model uses expressions like 'out of control' whereas the adaptive model sees the addict as making a choice to take drugs. In terms of the adaptive model, addicts are seen as exerting control by their behaviour. For example, times of reported stress correlate with times of highest tendency to take drugs (though, of course, a correlation on its own does not prove causation). Addicts do sometimes lose their addiction when life circumstances change, without professional help.

The discussion of addiction raised the possibility that there might be a genetic predisposition towards alcoholism. Earlier sections have talked about a genetic bias towards a trusting heart and the evolutionary roots of behaviour. The following section considers the basis for this kind of argument in more detail.

Review of section 3

- In understanding alcoholism or drug addiction, evidence is needed from both biological studies (which can involve comparisons between species) and from the study of peculiarly human aspects such as self-image.

- A term such as 'disease model' has important implications for how we view addiction.

- Environmental context (e.g. social context) can play an important role in the motivation for alcohol ingestion or drug taking.

- Cox and Klinger's model of alcohol ingestion views people as making a decision based upon the anticipated consequences of ingestion.

- There is some evidence that discrepancies between actual and ideal self-images are related to drug taking.

- Alexander argues that drug taking is a form of adaptive behaviour which arises from a failure to obtain integration by other means.

4   Evolution and behaviour

4.1   Introduction

A rich source of insight into human social behaviour might be thought to be available from looking at the evolutionary origins of this behaviour, and section 4 addresses this issue. It looks at the functional level of analysis (i.e. what is the advantage to an animal in behaving in a certain way?). A logical starting point is with Charles Darwin.

Darwin's theory of evolution was a comprehensive attempt to explain the origins of bodily structures and behaviour. Consider the possession of a characteristic such as a bird's wing that is used in flight. It looks as if it has been designed for a purpose, to enable the bird to fly. Prior to Darwin's insight it might indeed have been suggested in academic circles that the wing reveals the intelligence of a designer. However, Darwin argued that such features have evolved by a slow process because they confer a net advantage on their possessor. Given that there is competition for resources such as food and mates, for certain animals (e.g. the giraffe) possession of, say, a longer neck would put them at an advantage compared to an animal of the same species without that attribute; for example, the possessor might be able to reach leaves further from the ground. There will also be a disadvantage, since the longer neck will increase the weight of the animal and will require nutrients, but the assumption is that such costs are outweighed by the benefits. Thus, there is a *net* benefit. Our current understanding is that such characteristics are inherited from one generation to the next (see Figure 2.4).

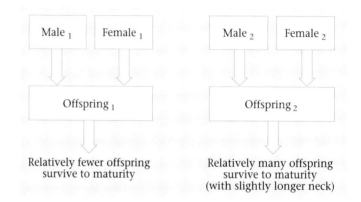

Figure 2.4 *Male$_1$ mates with female$_1$ to produce offspring$_1$ and male$_2$ mates with female$_2$ to produce offspring$_2$. Offspring$_2$ has acquired from either male$_2$ or female$_2$, or a combination of the two, a longer neck than offspring$_1$. This puts 2 at a net advantage and hence the offspring of 2 will be more successful relative to the offspring of 1 in an environment where not all offspring survive to maturity. The characteristic of a slightly longer neck will tend to increase in frequency in the population of this species*

4.2   Genes and inheritance

How is this process of inheritance mediated? Look at Figure 2.5. Genes are structures that code for the proteins that make up the body. For instance, gene$_1$ codes for protein$_1$. The actual structure of the body, including that of the nervous system, will be determined by a complex interaction between genes and the environment (meaning both that within the body and outside). In acquiring genes from the parents, some-times a slight mutation occurs in a gene such that what is acquired is slightly different from the gene possessed by the parent.

Small mutations in the genetic material can be advantageous, disadvan-tageous or neutral. A gene coding for a slightly longer neck might place its possessor at an advantage and such necks would tend to become more frequent in subsequent generations. The gene will become more com-

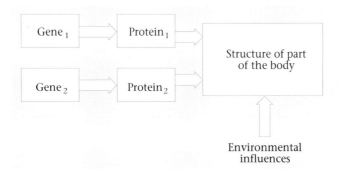

Figure 2.5 *Representation of the role of genes and environment in determining the structure of the body. The figure shows the effect of just two genes, g_1 and g_2, which code for the formation of two proteins (1 and 2). The final structure will be dependent upon a number of proteins as coded by genes and upon environmental influences*

mon because of its own success. Note that many genes might be involved in determining neck length but a slight change in one of them can affect the net result.

A similar logic applies also to nervous systems. Nervous systems acting in combination with the environment determine behaviour. Slight differences in nervous systems can mean the production of slightly different behaviour. Nervous systems are themselves the product of genes that code for the production of proteins. Therefore, slight differences in genes can mean differences in nervous systems and therefore differences in behaviour. Suppose, in a given situation (e.g. meeting a member of the opposite sex), animal$_1$ with nervous system X_1 tends to produce behaviour Y_1 and another animal of the same species (animal$_2$) with a slightly different nervous system X_2 produces behaviour Y_2. Now suppose that behaviour Y_2 is more successful, in that the animal mates more frequently or survives better and produces more offspring. Nervous systems of kind X_2 will therefore tend to become more frequent in a population and those of type X_1 less frequent.

4.3   Sociobiology

Although the story developed so far is relatively uncontroversial in scientific quarters, in recent times one particular development of this line of reasoning termed *sociobiology* has come into prominence and has perhaps generated as much heat as light. The reason why this is so is that sociobiology has claimed that many human behavioural phenomena that previously were thought to be explained in terms of cultural factors can really be explained in biological terms.

Before we go into the details of what sociobiology is claiming, it is important that the reader does not fall into a common fallacy: that of arguing which is the most important – genes or environment, nature or nurture. Genes play a role in determining the structure of the body but so does the environment. Without light, air and nutrients there can be no animal. So, to argue which is the most important is an intellectual cul-de-sac.

Since we can all agree upon this, where is the heat generated by sociobiology? The following example should help to make that clear. Take something like a difference in sexual behaviour (e.g. that males visit prostitutes more than females do and that males are more likely to buy pornography). Clearly, like all else, visiting a prostitute is a matter of both genes *and* environment! The question is whether *differences* between males and females can be explained in terms of *differences* in their genetic make-up. Sociobiologists would tend to argue that they can be explained in this way. The critics of sociobiology would suggest that society makes quite different demands on men and women, rewards their labours differently and gives very different opportunities to them. It is argued that such cultural differences can explain the sex difference. Other critics would argue that the roles of gene and environment are so inextricably linked that even in principle we can never tease them apart.

What then is the logic of sociobiology? Considering the theory of evolution, why should males be more attracted to pornography than females? The logic is as follows. The strategy that will best lead to reproductive success is different between males and females. There is a vastly different reproductive potential between men and women. The woman is limited by the period of pregnancy whereas the male's only limitation is the time of recovery of seminal fluid reserves and motivation. Relatively instant sexual turn-on and promiscuity can serve males well as a strategy of mating since insemination is all that they need to contribute to the reproductive process. The more females that they inseminate, the more offspring they are likely to father. Hence, there is an evolution of such 'instantaneous' processes in males. By contrast, in females, there are greater costs attached to instant turn-on and promiscuity. Once inseminated, the female's reproductive process will be engaged for at least nine months. There is much less to be gained in reproductive terms by changing partners.

In trying to understand behaviour, whether human or non-human, the question always needs to be asked: what are the advantages and disadvantages (in terms of passing on genes) of behaving in this way? For the male, the advantage of multiple partners will be in terms of multiple inseminations. There will be some disadvantages too. There is a lack of security and a failure to invest much in helping any given female during pregnancy and in protecting offspring. However, the sociobiological argument would be that in evolutionary history the advantages have outweighed the disadvantages. In other words, male nervous systems biasing towards a multiple partner strategy have had a net advantage. Thus, this particular characteristic has survived. For the female, there might well be some advantage in a rapid arousal with multiple partners. For instance, one male might be infertile whereas mating with several might allow the fertile male to be found. However, the assumption would be that the disadvantages of this strategy (for example, wasting time and effort and running risks with relatively unproductive sex once already fertilized) have outweighed the advantages. Also, the non-discriminating female risks attaching her genetic material to that of a relatively substandard male, whereas waiting around for longer might allow a more suitable male to appear. He might be able to prove his worth by his behaviour towards the female. Hence, there is a lower tendency for multiple partners and less of an instant arousal in females.

At this point some will protest; surely sexual behaviour has little direct link with reproduction, particularly in this age of contraception and abortion. The point is that no-one is suggesting that males necessarily go out with the conscious *intention* of reproducing. The issue of when in human evolution individuals realized that there is a link between sexual behaviour and reproduction is an interesting one, but it doesn't affect the argument. The sociobiological logic is that the male is simply relentlessly driven by his biological make-up since males so driven have been the ones who have tended to reproduce. Non-human animals also adopt strategies that seem to ensure their genetic perpetuation. Male rats are relatively promiscuous whereas male kingfishers are not. Male rats can afford to be promiscuous since the females take care of rearing the young. By contrast, there is an obvious cost to a promiscuous strategy in kingfishers. Incubation and food-seeking are a joint venture. The genes of a male kingfisher who abandoned the female for long periods would be put at a disadvantage.

To consider another example from the point of view of function, what would one say about the phenomena of alcoholism and drug addiction, discussed earlier? An addiction to alcohol or heroin would clearly seem to be maladaptive; the probability of successful reproduction hardly seems to be increased by such behaviour. So can one make any sense of such behaviour in adaptive terms? Alcohol and the addictive drugs that most concern us these days (e.g. heroin) are, in evolutionary terms, a relatively recent phenomenon. The most devastating use of opiates has only been seen with the development of the hypodermic syringe. Human evolution took place in a world without such means of applying particularly powerful stimuli to the central nervous system, which, in the case of hypodermic injection of opiates, bypasses the conventional reward processes involving sensory neurons (e.g. the taste of food on the tongue stimulating pleasure). It might be said that directly stimulating these processes with drugs cheats the conventional biologically adaptive pleasure processes of eating and copulating, etc.

4.4   The selfish gene debate

A discussion in the area of sociobiology leads logically to the position of Richard Dawkins, as advanced in his best-selling book *The Selfish Gene* (1976). However, a warning is needed with regard to the title of the book. The name is a catchy one – a metaphor, designed to encompass an idea – but it should not be taken to mean that there is something *intrinsically* selfish about genes. Genes are simply chemical structures that code for the production of proteins, the building blocks of the body. Dawkins claims that genes tend to code for nervous systems that produce behaviour of such a kind that the genes will tend (so-called 'selfishly') to be perpetuated.

Suppose that showing a particular behaviour (behaviour 2) serves to increase the reproductive success of $animal_2$ relative to $animal_1$ which shows behaviour 1. For instance, $animal_2$ behaves in a more sexually arousing way to another. This increases $animal_2$'s chances of mating and hence of perpetuating its genes. Hence, $animal_2$'s genes will tend to increase in frequency in the population. The logic of Dawkins' model is that genes can be described as selfish in the sense that, all other things being equal, they will tend to influence nervous system structure in such a way that the behaviour produced will tend to perpetuate the genes. It is important to note that Dawkins is not saying that a single gene controls a single behaviour. Any behaviour will be the product of a nervous system in which numerous genes will play a role. All Dawkins is saying is that changes in any given gene will tend to be favoured by evolution (meaning more likely to be passed to future generations) if its role is such as to influence behaviour in a way that helps this process.

ACTIVITY 2.3   Now stop for a moment and think about the issue of altruism. Altruism is a word used to describe behaviour that serves to help one individual at a cost to the altruist. Can the existence of altruism in nature be explained in Dawkins terms? Can human altruism be understood in these terms?

Suppose that a particular gene g_1 is changed such as to produce a change in structure so that in a given situation the animal behaves more altruistically towards other members of its species. For example, when it observes a completely unrelated member of its own species being attacked, it tends to risk its own life to assist.

In terms of the theoretical model of Dawkins, would you expect such a characteristic to emerge in evolution?

By definition, a gene that exerted a bias towards altruistic behaviour would be one that would be at a disadvantage. Therefore, it would not increase in frequency. Another way of thinking about it is as follows. Suppose the whole population behaved altruistically. This would indeed be to everyone's good. However, suppose that, in such a situation, a gene underwent a change such that it tended to exert a bias towards a strategy of 'not putting yourself out to assist a neighbour in trouble'. The possessor of such a gene would be at an advantage and the gene would increase in frequency.

So, in these terms, how does one explain the appearance of altruistic behaviour? Surely one can find examples of altruism, such as birds feigning injury to lure a predator away from their nests? This would seem to put the adult at risk in the interests of the young – a case of altruism. The answer that theorists in this area give is that the young share genes in common with the parent. By its behaviour the bird is increasing the chances that its young will survive and thereby perpetuate its own genes. No one is suggesting it has a conscious intention of perpetuating the common genes. It is merely that genes will tend to code for their own perpetuation. Birds will not be so altruistic to non-relatives. But there are cases of reciprocal altruism. Indeed, such reciprocity does seem to be the case in examples from nature of apparent altruism between non-relatives.

By now, you might well be protesting that all this might apply to birds but how about humans? Indeed, they can show extreme selfishness but also extreme altruism; for example, Captain Oates walking to his death in the snow or a pilot losing his own life to steer a stricken aircraft away from a village. Even amongst Neanderthals living some 60,000 years ago, there is evidence of altruism. Some remains suggest that severely incapacitated people were kept alive by the charity of others (Eccles, 1992).

The answer that theorists such as Dawkins give to this has two aspects. First, there is the acknowledgement that biology can explain so much but, over and above this, in humans, there exists a social and cultural level which cannot be reduced in any simple way to biology. The second argument is to apply a similar logic to that of the selfish gene but to whole societies; for example, to argue that in-groups who are altruistic to each other but hostile to the out-group will tend to be at an advantage compared with societies that are intrinsically selfish. However, as you might expect, such arguments are highly controversial, with all sorts of social, political and religious implications. For instance, can it be called altruism at all if there is a payoff? Is there always bound to be a payoff even for such worthy souls as Mother Teresa (e.g. spiritual satisfaction or the prospect of a more secure place in the afterlife)? It is beyond the scope of this chapter to go into the details of such arguments for and against. All I can hope to do is to introduce the issues and to give some pointers as to where sociobiology might be relevant to understanding human social interactions. Perhaps a balanced view is to see biological evolution as offering a framework of partial explanation and nothing more. The following two subsections look at where theorists have applied an understanding of biological factors to human social behaviours. They will illustrate the kind of logic that theorists employ and show where illumination might be gained.

4.5   Is there such a thing as a 'gay gene'?

A debate that has gained much momentum recently concerns whether homosexuality is to be understood in terms of genes. We must be careful not to ask a naïve question of the kind 'Which is most important, genes or environment?' Rather, it is reasonable to ask whether *differences* in sexual orientation can be understood at least in part in terms of genetic *differences* between individuals. Of course, homosexuality and heterosexuality are not simple and mutually exclusive categories. There is overlap, so any genetic argument would need careful qualification.

In recent years, the term 'gay genes' has emerged. Some researchers in the USA have argued that the brain contains genetically determined differences that bias certain individuals towards homosexuality.

An interesting book on this topic, *The Sexual Brain,* was written by Simon LeVay (1993). Its central message is one that very much fits the theme being advanced here. In the book, LeVay recalls an earlier statement of his, 'This finding … suggests that sexual orientation has a biological substrate', which LeVay now describes as naïvely implying that there are other aspects of mental life '… that do *not* have a biological substrate – an absurd idea … ' (p. xii).

In other words, LeVay is arguing that any aspect of behaviour and feelings must have a biological aspect since the brain is assumed to be the seat of feelings and the organization of behaviour. LeVay writes:

> People will ask of some trait – homosexuality, for example – 'Is it psychological or is it biological?' By that they generally mean 'Is it some nebulous state of mind resulting from upbringing and social interactions, or is it a matter of genes and brain chemistry?' But this is a false distinction, since even the most nebulous and socially determined states of mind are a matter of genes and brain chemistry too.
>
> *(LeVay, 1993, p. xii)*

So let us accept that all behaviour and feelings are associated in some way with the brain and hence have a biological basis and therefore the genes are inextricably involved. However, this argument does not necessarily lead to the conclusion that differences in sexual orientation can be explained by genetic differences. Scientific investigation is needed to answer this question. Here, as elsewhere, it is logical to suppose that states of mind and behaviour will be complexly determined by interactions between genes and environment. The point that LeVay emphasizes is that traditionally we have tended either to ignore or underestimate the genetic contribution to homosexuality.

So what is the evidence? LeVay cites twin studies in which it has been found that the tendency to either heterosexuality or homosexuality is higher in identical twins than in fraternal twins. Also, looking at the brains of adults at autopsy, differences have been found in the structures of certain regions of the hypothalamus, when comparing gay and straight males. (Interesting differences have also been found when comparing the brain structures of lesbians and heterosexual women, but most research has been directed at males.) Do the differences in brain structure prove a genetic basis to differences in sexual orientation? It is certainly compatible with it and suggestive of it but it does not constitute proof, since environmental factors might be involved. It might be something about life-style (e.g. gays might be less competitive) that contributes to differences in the brain.

As LeVay notes: 'To many people, finding a difference in brain structure between gay and straight men is equivalent to proving that gay men are "born that way". Time and again I have been described as someone who "proved that homosexuality is genetic" or some such thing. I did not' (1993, p. 122).

However, more cautiously, LeVay concludes that the evidence is strongly suggestive of a genetic basis to sexual orientation.

What is interesting in a discussion of the experience of being a person is how certain members of the gay community in the US have used this argument. They have argued for gay rights on the strength that a gay orientation is something (like black skin) that they were born with and therefore cannot constitutionally be discriminated against for revealing.

From the point of view of evolution, try to think about whether there is reason to be dubious about the claim that genes can exert a bias towards homosexuality.

A gay gene would, by definition, be such as to code for biologically unproductive sex and therefore for its own annihilation. How would a gay gene ever spread into the population? It might be linked to a gene that does confer a reproductive advantage, or a so-called gay gene might confer some enormous advantage (creativity?) realized in the occasional heterosexual mating by otherwise gay individuals. In this way, it might offset its inherent disadvantage. There is the possibility that homosexual individuals might make a net contribution to genetic perpetuation by being particularly good at helping heterosexual relatives (LeVay, 1993). It is also conceivable that, for some unknown reason, gay genes might go through repeated cycles of being re-created by mutation and then being eliminated from the population.

4.6   Sexual jealousy

Sexual jealousy is a sadly ubiquitous phenomenon. At worst, it can be a terrifying emotion and (mainly on the part of males) one that is, worldwide, the principal factor underlying spousal violence and homicide (DeKay and Buss, 1992). Extreme sexual jealousy might be understood as an exaggerated and thereby maladaptive reaction to threat; for example, to the threat of a loss of that which is most precious to one. A causal level of analysis would be in terms of such cognitively flavoured things as perceptual processes, representations of the desired state of the world and the threatened actual state of loss. Hormones and brain processes normally serving aggression and fear would presumably also be implicated, in the role of sensitizing this reaction.

At a functional level of analysis, does the theory of evolution offer any insights into the origins of jealousy? If it is to be explained in evolutionary terms, would one expect there to be a sex difference in the trigger stimuli? It is not at all clear from evolutionary considerations that one sex should be *more or less* jealous than the other; each has a great deal to lose from their partner diverting attention elsewhere. However, the contexts and precise trigger stimuli that arouse jealousy might differ between the two sexes. These were questions addressed by Buss et al. (1992) in an experiment described below.

ACTIVITY 2.4   Before reading about the experiment, think about evolutionary arguments for a while and see if you can understand the logic of why there might be a difference between males and females. Think of what each sex has to lose in terms of a reduced probability of their own genetic perpetuation as a result of infidelity by the partner. How could it be a cost to them?

From a functional perspective, the greatest cost to a male would be loss of paternity. Suppose a female is fertilized by a male other than the partner and the partner then invests time and energy in supporting the female during pregnancy and afterwards. Of course, the male is unaware that these are genes other than his own that he is helping to propagate. This would represent a serious cost in terms of his reproductive success. For the female, the situation is different. If a male fertilizes another female, in itself this need have little cost to the first female partner. However, what could prove costly to the female partner is the male's emotional attachment to another female, which could deny her support in bringing up children. Therefore, psychologists adopting an evolutionary perspective suggest that, on a causal level of analysis, the trigger stimuli of jealousy for males will be related to sexual behaviour as such, whereas for females the trigger stimuli will tend to be biased towards cues predictive of loss of commitment and investment in the bond.

So much for the background, but what do the real data show (see Box 2.3)?

BOX 2.3 Investigating sexual jealousy (Buss et al., 1992)

Buss and associates presented the following question to a number of subjects: What would upset or distress you more: (a) imagining your mate having sexual intercourse with someone else, or (b) imagining your mate forming a deep emotional attachment to someone else?

As predicted, most of the women asked this question (85 per cent) opted for (b) whereas most men (60 per cent) opted for (a), a difference that is in the direction predicted by sociobiological theory. Objective physiological indices of emotional arousal such as changes in heart rate and electrical properties of the skin, taken when subjects were asked to envisage their partners in the situations described, fitted with the subjective reports. Of course, although 60 per cent of males opted for (a), there is still the 40 per cent who opted for (b). These tended to be males who had not experienced a committed sexual relationship. Thus, the direction of this result accords with a sex difference that would be predicted on the basis of differences in reproductive strategy and capacity.

Section 4 has discussed evolutionary arguments whereas earlier sections looked mainly at the processes within the nervous system that determine behaviour. The next section of the chapter will draw on both of these sources of insight and address what to many is the last great frontier in psychology. The expression 'last great frontier' should certainly not be taken to mean that all the other frontiers have been crossed. They have not. Rather, it simply means that this one seems to be the most difficult even to approach. However, biological insights might well prove useful in this task.

Review of section 4

- According to Darwin's theory of evolution, physical characteristics and behavioural traits emerged in evolution because they conferred an advantage on their possessor.

- Sociobiology proposes that many aspects of human social behaviour (e.g. sexual jealousy) can be understood in terms of the advantage that they have conferred in evolutionary history.

- The term 'selfish gene' refers to the assumption that, through nervous system structures and behaviour, genes will tend to promote their own perpetuation.

- There is some evidence to suggest that genes might exert a bias towards a heterosexual or homosexual orientation.

5   Consciousness

5.1   Introduction

Consciousness forms the topic of section 5. Its study involves a mixture of objective scientific measurement, theoretical speculation and, inevitably, personal introspective insights. Thus, the bases of section 5 are somewhat different from those of earlier sections.

If you had to nominate any one thing that characterized the essence of self, you might select your *private* state of conscious awareness of the world. (Section 2.2 of the Introduction discussed the centrality of subjective experience.) However, according to evolutionary theory, consciousness must have evolved on the basis of it conferring an advantage on us, and an influential view is that its purpose is to be understood in terms of social interaction. For social psychologists, consciousness is particularly important in the context of the opportunity that self-reflection offers in terms of empathy and developing relationships.

Chapter 4 in this book will deal with consciousness in some detail. It will be considered in the context of theories that link consciousness to the issue of agency and determinism. These are topics for which a biological perspective can prove useful, as will be shown in the remainder of this chapter.

ACTIVITY 2.5

To introduce this topic, stop for a moment and think what is important to you about consciousness and then try to see some ways in which a consideration of biology is relevant to this. You can then compare your thoughts with what I came up with after a short period of rumination.

Consciousness depends upon the integrity of certain brain regions. If their state is altered, as in sleep or under a general anaesthetic, the person's state of consciousness changes profoundly. Brain damage can render a person permanently unconscious. This can then generate difficult ethical and legal questions concerning whether that person's state of self really has ceased to exist (e.g. the decision whether to continue the life of one of the survivors of the Hillsborough football tragedy).

Consideration of consciousness raises the question of *why* in an evolutionary context it should have evolved. Why in terms of biological evolution has a brain evolved that has the complexity necessary to generate consciousness? The answer might be that social interactions with others are crucially dependent upon the assumption that others share the phenomenon of conscious awareness. When they are pinched, they hurt just as we do. They are deserving of sympathy because of what is happening to their state of conscious awareness. Thus, we are able to function more effectively by making reasonable assumptions about conscious states in others. These issues will be addressed later.

My experience of self, my sense of identity and the nature of the contents of my conscious awareness have a lot to do with continuity. I can reflect upon my childhood and recall emotion-laden memories – the pleasant smell of my uncle's pipe in his house in London, the fear on being taken to school for the first time. As I grew up, so my mental state and body changed. Both are considerably different now as compared with then! But in a very real sense, an important aspect of my personal conscious world, my notion of me, of a unique being unlike any other, is intimately tied to a notion of continuity. It is the same me now as it was then. This sense of continuity is critically dependent upon memory – the me of five years of age has ceased to exist but the existence can be reconstructed in memory. These memories clearly have a durable embodiment in some form, commonly assumed to be a physical base in the connections between neurons of the brain. If this memory base is disrupted, as in the case of brain damage by trauma or disease (e.g. Alzheimer's disease), then the personal world must surely be radically changed. Some people, on learning about the effects of brain damage on loss of consciousness and memory, feel a sense of the fragility of the personal world. It depends critically upon brain processes that can be vulnerable and, in spite of the wisdom of nature and the medical profession, are not totally protected against disease and decay.

Now, after a speculative flow of thinking, let's turn to the details of a biological approach to consciousness.

5.2   The nature and function of consciousness

There is something so peculiarly *you* about your conscious state, involving at its core your awareness of yourself. Our inner thoughts can provide us with a free, private and apparently uncensored movie screen that can entertain us when all else fails. Yet, although it seems idiosyncratic and is unobservable to others, to many investigators conscious awareness is a viable target for scientific scrutiny. Presumably, consciousness emerged in evolution not just because it provides us with an idiosyncratic free movie screen but because it gave animals that possessed it an advantage in reproductive terms. Hence, researchers ask the same combination of questions of consciousness as of other aspects of brain and behaviour – how does it work and what is its evolutionary significance? Attempting to answer these questions from a scientific perspective means considering features common to any possessor of human consciousness. However, it might also be able to help us to understand the more idiosyncratic aspects of conscious awareness, seen as a key aspect of our personal world.

How people view the physical basis of their own minds is an interesting topic that you might like to explore with your friends. Presumably, how we feel about our personal world could have something to do with the kind of explanatory model we employ to think about the embodiment of our own mind. For instance, some people envisage a fundamentally different kind of substance that permeates the brain and constitutes the mind. This substance is assumed to obey rather different physical principles from those applicable to the physical substances that make up the brain (e.g. it might survive brain disintegration and be able to pass through otherwise impermeable physical barriers). You might feel that such an assumption is more appropriate to wet Sunday afternoons spent in darkened Victorian seance rooms rather than to a modern scientific view of the mind, and such an opinion would be shared by the majority of neuroscientists. However, it is revealing to examine recent discussions that try to illuminate the physical base of consciousness (e.g. Bock and Marsh, 1993). These show clearly that, after 2,000 or more years of consideration of such questions as the nature of the relationship between mind and body, we are still groping in the dark and, more than anything else, a reasonable dose of modesty is needed.

What then, from the viewpoint of biological science, is the nature of the problem to be explained? One useful way of approaching this might be to compare and contrast conscious and unconscious information processing, and such a line of argument will be addressed in section 5.4. Although unconscious processing is complex, in principle its explanation raises no insuperable conceptual hurdle. In terms of the amount of information that can be held at a point in time, conscious processing of information is very focused compared with unconscious processing. Some investigators (e.g. Baars, 1988) would claim that we can only hold one item at a time in conscious awareness. A new item will displace the old. In unconscious processing, many separate parallel operations can be carried out.

5.3   Consciousness and the physical brain

In so far as there exists a consensus within behavioural science, it is that consciousness is a complex property of the physical brain. But how the activity of neurons translates into the phenomenon of consciousness escapes our imagination. In causal terms, one can do little more than to claim that when a very large number of neurons are connected together in a certain way and such a brain has a history of interaction within a social context, the property of consciousness occurs. How? What is the nature of the translation process? I feel you would be disappointed in a search for an explanation of consciousness in the physical working of the brain. As fantastic as the brain is, perhaps evolution has not provided us with one capable of understanding its own product, conscious awareness.

On close examination, scientists can ascertain that brains are composed of such things as neurons and their associated neurotransmitters, together with other cells and hormones that communicate between cells. Reducing these components still further, we find complex molecules. Clearly, the study of all this is the business of neurobiology and nothing is found suggestive of any special property that might contribute to consciousness. Therefore, when we come to try to relate such biological processes to the 'inner screen' of self-awareness, the flow of consciousness, we encounter a profound difficulty: nothing in the bits gives the slightest clue as to how the properties of the whole can arise. For instance, the neurotransmitters dopamine and noradrenalin seem to be particularly active in the brain on occasions that we describe as emotionally arousing (e.g. when lust, fear or anger are experienced). But, on examining their chemical structures, these neurotransmitters seem rather like any other chemical. In principle, a whole host of chemicals might do the job just as well. Looking at whole neurons gives us no clue either, and the circuits of which they form a part can often be modelled well using techniques developed for computers and engineering control systems, neither of which presumably would we want to term conscious. So we look in vain at the components if we seek there something that contributes to the peculiar quality of consciousness.

It is possible to make some intelligent speculations on what the processes corresponding to consciousness are doing in terms of behaviour. The kind of information processing that is performed at a conscious level as opposed to an unconscious level is not difficult to describe, as will be shown shortly. The problem is to understand the subjective personal quality ('private world' quality) of consciousness. An example will illustrate the point. It is clear that evolution should equip animals with processes that help to move them away from damaging stimuli (e.g. heat, cold or sharp objects). These processes need to be quite complex and sophisticated, with a capacity to facilitate learning. Why though, we might ask, does the underlying process take on the *peculiar subjective character* that is described by the human sufferer with such expressions as 'a relentless evil', 'drives you suicidal' and 'so horrendous you can't imagine'? Scientists can build complex robots that put the avoidance of damaging stimuli at the top of their priorities and learn by their mistakes, but I guess most of us would not suppose them to experience sensations that we would describe as 'evil' or, conversely, as 'pleasurable'. Would you? Would you want to sympathize emotionally with a robot?

5.4   Evolution and consciousness

The issue is often raised as to whether animals other than humans possess consciousness. Are rats conscious? Are chimpanzees? If so, do we need to suggest that fish are? Do dogs have selves? They certainly have social interactions. Do answers to such questions affect the way that the British, as a nation of pet lovers, treat animals as opposed to humans? One possible solution is to suggest that consciousness is a gradually appearing property of brains as they become more complex. Thus, we might suggest some kind of consciousness in rats (for example, the capacity for a conscious sensation of pain with aversive qualities), but we might argue that rats do not self-reflect. Alternatively, we might suggest a sudden appearance of consciousness at a certain level of brain complexity. This might be at the human level. Frankly, so much is speculation, but considerations of function served might prove useful.

The approach adopted here is to ask two closely related questions, as follows. What is the kind of information processing that is implicated in possessing consciousness, and what advantage does it confer on an animal to have this capacity? Opinion is divided on this issue, and the two broad classes of opinion will be presented here. In considering such questions, it can be useful first to fill in the background to the story and to think of the most basic mechanisms that would allow an animal to survive. Then we can ask how evolution might have improved upon such processes in a way that leads ultimately to the emergence of consciousness.

Consider problems that are common to any animal: (1) for its own physical survival, it must obtain nutrients and avoid tissue damage; and (2) genetic perpetuation must be achieved by some kind of reproduction. For example, a simple animal might just react to high or low temperatures by being programmed automatically to move away until an intermediate temperature is reached. Nutrient deficiency could programme the animal to suck in certain nutrient-yielding chemicals. It might reproduce simply by splitting in two. Such processes are to be understood mainly as *reactions to* events in the environment in which the animal is located. Imagine now a slightly more sophisticated animal, one that is able to anticipate events; evolution has equipped it with a learning capacity. Rather than simply responding to excess heat by moving away, the animal can learn associations predictive of excess heat. For instance, a particularly hot environment might be surrounded by a characteristic chemical. By associating the adverse temperature with the chemical, the animal can escape from the region and thereby completely avoid contact with the adverse environment. Such an animal might then be at an advantage relative to the one that can only react to adverse environments. Imagine now a still more sophisticated process in which the animal is able to form within its nervous system a representation of its environment. This is normally termed a *cognition* or *cognitive map*. Within this representation are located sites of potential food but also danger regions. Now the animal's foraging can be better organized and the advantage to its genetic perpetuation is not difficult to appreciate. It can set out on a foraging task directed towards certain sites and taking cognizance of places to be avoided. At this stage, we would say that the animal's nervous system has encoded a *representation* of its environment. Animals such as rats show clear evidence of forming such representations of their environment. Representations allow the facility for flexibility in the animal's commerce with its environment.

There are broadly two theories that attempt to explain consciousness and these will now be outlined.

> While reading the following discussion of the two theories, ask yourself whether they need be mutually exclusive or whether both might be correct.

It is in the context of the flexibility of behaviour that one group of theorists (e.g. Dawkins, 1993; Oatley, 1992) postulates the emergence of consciousness. They note that cognition gives enormous scope for flexibility (i.e. devising novel solutions to problems on the basis of extrapolation from the past and into the future, and taking unexpected circumstances into account). However, in a constant environment much of our (and presumably other animals') day-to-day predictable behaviour does not call upon novel solutions to be found. It is carried out in a repetitive, rather stereotyped way. In humans, we would say that it is carried out at a level below that of conscious awareness. This was noted by the philosopher and psychologist William James: '… very absent-minded persons in going to their bedroom to dress for dinner have been known to take off one garment after another and finally to get into bed, merely because that was the habitual issue of the first few movements when performed at a later hour' (James, 1890).

You might well have experience of riding a bicycle perfectly well, whilst consciously attending to something very different. That well-practised behaviour such as riding a bicycle can become automatic and thereby not take up the capacity of conscious awareness is clearly advantageous to our coping with a rich and complex environment. The inevitable price that we pay for such a shift to 'autopilot' is, for example, occasionally getting into bed at the wrong time. Indeed, we are able to perform many of the things that we do much better unconsciously than consciously. Typing, cycling, aerobics, walking, etc. are often best done automatically and thereby do not tie up our very limited conscious processing capacity. Skill-acquisition corresponds to a shift towards automatization and thereby rapidity. Most of us can very effectively walk and chew gum simultaneously, with no interference between the two activities. By contrast, conscious awareness seems to be focused on only one thing at a time. A distraction will switch us away from what were the previous contents of consciousness.

So, considering just how limited is our conscious capacity for handling information compared with the seemingly infinite capacity of our unconscious and its ability to do several things at a time, why on earth did consciousness ever evolve? The answer, according to the first group of theorists, is that, effective as the automatic mode of operation is, it cannot by definition cope with novel situations. If an automatic sequence should fail (e.g. if the brakes on our bicycle fail on a down-hill slope), what then? We clearly need a monitor of our actions that alerts us when things go in an unexpected direction and switches us out of autopilot mode and into a more cognitive, flexible, reasoning mode. These theorists argue that consciousness evolved along with emotional reactivity. For instance, the brakes failing gives rise to an emotion of fear such that keeping control occupies all of our attention. Thus, consciousness needs to be able to take an overview, to see everything going on, as one purposive, goal-directed system.

Such processes of monitoring the world and spotting the unexpected are much more complex than those postulated at the beginning of this subsection, and certain researchers would describe them as conscious, even in rats. However, the rat which we have endowed with such processes does not necessarily thereby acquire a sense of self. Our rat can certainly make some extrapolations in time and space and can switch from auto-pilot to cognitive control when things go wrong. Some theorists would endow it with conscious awareness, but we have still not given it the quality of self-reflection.

Now consider a still more sophisticated brain, this time one that forms a complex cognitive representation not only of the physical features of the external environment but also of psychological features of the self and others. Such cognitive processes can represent the whole animal, its past feelings and anticipated future states. Personality traits of other animals can also be represented, such that, for instance, animal X is labelled as reliable and animal Y as devious. Information on these more abstract states can then be exploited in given specific instances of future social interaction. The possessor of such a brain can reflect upon his or her own qualities and compare these with the qualities of others. Interactions with others can benefit from the information held in the form of a representation of the *whole* animal, a representation of the anticipated states of others minds, and even representations of what the animal thinks other animals are thinking of it. An animal having experienced pain can extrapolate on the basis of another animal seen to be in a state that might be characterized as pain. The other animal's future moves (e.g. attack, flee, scream or retire) can be predicted on the basis of what, from personal experience, it feels like to be in pain. It is only at this level of evolutionary development that the second group of theorists (e.g. Humphrey, 1976) would postulate the emergence of consciousness. It is appropriate for advanced social primates. In such terms, consciousness *is* synonymous with a representation of self and a capacity for complex social cognition. It is commonly supposed that, in complex social interactions, such a rich source of information being available to a social animal would prove invaluable in both cooperation and competition and thereby in perpetuating genes. Consciousness might thereby be seen as intrinsically a social phenomenon that has evolved in social animals.

Whether one sees consciousness as a monitor of behaviour that spots discrepancies in the state of the world or as a means of advancing social contact, a certain logic follows. In terms of a contemporary understanding of biology, consciousness would have to be extremely valuable in its role to justify its emergence in evolution, since it is clear that there is a cost attached. The sophistication of the human brain necessary to generate consciousness is expensive in such terms. In proportion to its weight, the brain takes a large amount of the body's daily energy consumption, all the more so in the case of, for example, university students struggling with a difficult intellectual task. Also, the size that the human head needs to be in order to house such a brain makes birth relatively difficult for human females. (Such things have caused some, such as the physicist, mathematician and science-fiction writer Sir Fred Hoyle, to doubt whether random and purposeless evolutionary processes alone can explain the emergence of consciousness. What else might be involved, I will leave you to imagine!)

When dealing with a complex system such as the brain and consciousness, insight can be gained by looking at malfunction. In this case, brain damage or surgical intervention in the brain can sometimes give insight into the nature and function of consciousness.

5.5   Brain function and malfunction

5.5.1   Split brains

Looking at the anatomy of the human brain, is there any clue as to how the sense of a unified whole self can emerge from its structure? Perhaps the first thing that strikes us on looking at a brain is the division of most of it into two halves along the midline (see Figure 2.6 overleaf).

This also struck the philosophers of old. The French philosopher Descartes suggested that the pineal gland (the brain structure that was undivided and closest to the top of the head) held the key to much of our sense of unity. It was through this structure that our indivisible and immaterial soul was said to interact with our physical and all too easily destructible body. Perhaps not many in the behavioural sciences would subscribe to this view today, but as the eminent neuroscientist and theologian, Donald MacKay, aptly remarked, 'what to put in its place is far from clear' (1987, p. 5).

The way that the brain and nerve pathways in the body are organized is such that information from the left half of our body is projected predominantly to the right side of the brain and information from the right is projected predominantly to the left side. The control of the left hand and leg resides in the right hemisphere and that of the right arm and leg in the left. A giant bundle of fibres, termed the corpus callosum, conveys information from one side of the brain to the other (see Figure 2.6). In spite of this profound division in the brain, the world outside normally has a quality of unity about it. Furthermore, we normally feel ourselves to be executing a unified plan of action on the world.

Given the complexity of the brain and considering analogies with other systems, you might have supposed that any destruction or cutting of parts of the brain would have a devastating effect on consciousness. After all, removal of a substantial part of a TV set or aircraft might be expected to have a profoundly deleterious effect on performance. What is surprising about consciousness is its invulnerability to extensive brain damage.

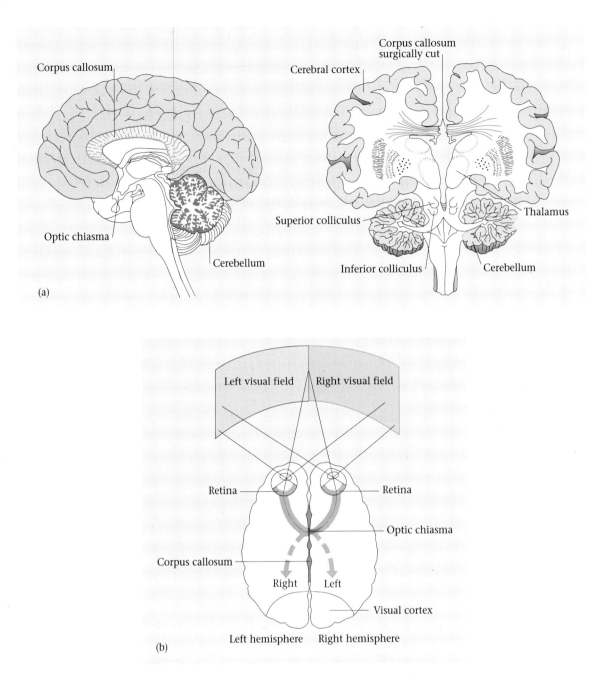

Figure 2.6 *Views of the brain: (a) Two sections of the brain, that to the left being a cross-section and showing only one half; (b) A view of a brain from above as a person looks at a spot immediately ahead. Note the pathways that carry visual information from the retina to the visual cortex of the brain. As the person stares at a spot, information from the right visual field is projected to the left half of each retina and then to the left hemisphere. Information from the left visual field is projected to the right half of each retina and then to the right hemisphere*

Sometimes a deficit can only be detected after testing on sophisticated equipment and using subtle probes. Surgical removal of one of the brain's hemispheres does not destroy consciousness. Consciousness appears therefore to be a property of both hemispheres such that if one is lacking in some way the other is able to compensate.

Sometimes the corpus callosum is cut by a surgeon in an attempt to alleviate a condition of epilepsy, a technique investigated by Roger Sperry (1967). Using tests on such patients, it is possible to create conflict between bits of information, each of which is organized in only one hemisphere and maps on to an action effected by only one half of the body. Speech is organized in the left half of the brain, where motor activity controlling the right side of the body is also organized. By projecting images to the left visual field, the information arrives in the right hemisphere. Researchers found that such subjects were commonly unable to verbalize what they were seeing but could select with the left hand an object corresponding to that projected on to the screen (e.g. a comb or a pen).

In one case, a subject was trained to use each half system of the brain to perform a task specific to that half. Two levers were available. Each half brain was given the task of aligning visually a stimulus with a reference point by means of one lever that moved one visual stimulus. Each half was trained to execute the task via the hand over which it exerts control. That is to say, the left half brain had the right hand at its disposal for acting, via a lever, upon visual information arriving at the left visual cortex. The right half brain had the left hand available for acting, via another lever, upon information arriving at the right visual cortex. Two different moving visual stimuli demanding two different patterns of tracking could then be presented simultaneously, one to each hemisphere. After the subject obtained some proficiency at such parallel processing, the two control levers were surreptitiously clamped together creating a conflict situation between the commands of the two hemispheres. A strong physical conflict between the two hands was observed, rather than one hand simply dominating.

Consider the split-brain patient for a moment and reflect on whether you would be troubled by a notion of two selves in one brain. Then read the following quotation from Donald MacKay and reflect on what MacKay calls the 'cash-value' of such a claim. By this he means the useful insight and actual practical help in understanding which might be gained by the description of 'two persons'.

ACTIVITY 2.6

What cash-value would we normally attach to talk of 'two persons'? Each would have, at a minimum, to be a centre of conscious aware-ness and, at least in principle, a terminal of dialogue – someone who could be met, interrogated, informed, argued with and so forth. Moreover, each must be not just a receiver of sensory information and

> a generator of bodily movements but an evaluator of both. Evaluation is a crucial ingredient of personal agency. ... Persons ... are autonomous and conscious evaluators, in the sense that at least to some extent they are able to set and readjust their own norms and criteria according to changing circumstances, in the light of long-range plans. Most significantly for our purpose, talk of 'two persons' implies the possibility in principle of *dialogue between them* ...
>
> *(MacKay, 1987, p. 8)*

So, given this logic, Sperry, MacKay and their associates set about testing split-brain subjects, in an attempt to introduce one half person to the other. Would it be possible, they wondered, to stimulate a dialogue between them? Some evidence was found to show that one hemisphere could pose a question of another and then wait to get the answer back. Although, as before, evidence was found for different sensory and motor coordinations and even different evaluations of a given stimulus in the two hemispheres, MacKay reported: '... despite all encouragements we found no sign at all of recognition of the other "half" as a separate person, nor of independence at the normative level where priorities and criteria of evaluation are themselves evaluated – the characteristic human activity with which we associate the term "will" ' (1987, p. 9).

Indeed, one subject's spontaneous question to the experimenters might seem to be the most revealing evidence of all: 'Are you guys trying to make two people out of me?' (MacKay, 1987, p. 13).

The essence of MacKay's argument is that evidence of independent performance of two different mathematical operations and independent sensory-motor action and even independent goal pursuit between the two hemispheres does not amount to two conscious beings. In support of this interpretation, he notes that, as we have discussed, in intact humans there are many complex sensory-motor actions that can be performed at an unconscious level. Thus, in a broad sense, MacKay's conclusions would fit the premise most closely associated with Descartes: that of an indivisible mind. This is a sort of super executive, planner and conscience feeler which would normally work in collaboration with some processes that can function unconsciously.

5.5.2 Damaged brains

The Oxford psychologist Larry Weiskrantz (1987) has made a study of patients with certain types of brain damage; for example, that induced by chronic alcoholism. Such patients can learn certain skilled motor tasks (e.g. tracking a moving target) involving sensory-motor coordination. If intact subjects were exhibiting the same degree of skill, they would be able to articulate to others the nature of the task they were performing, consciously recalling the experience of one trial at the start of another day's trial. However, the kind of brain-damaged patients studied by Weiskrantz seem to have no awareness of the skill they are showing. As you have seen already, there is nothing inherently implausible about performing skills in the absence of conscious awareness. Indeed, our survival depends upon this capacity. What is surprising about these subjects is, in contrast to intact controls, their inability to tap into and articulate verbally their skill on request. The skill is apparent to all but the subject exhibiting the skill.

In some such cases, the patient might show normal intelligence and perceptual ability but a frightening deficit in memory. For instance, a psychologist might see a patient and test him or her repeatedly, leave the room for a minute and, on returning, the patient will deny having met the psychologist before.

You might like to think about the subjective world of such a patient. Could the sense of continuity that earlier was argued to be a feature of the self (see section 5.1) be said to exist?

A phenomenon termed 'blindsight' has also been investigated by Weiskrantz and is relevant to the present discussion. This condition is caused by damage to the visual system, specifically the visual cortex (see Figure 2.6b). It was long believed that such patients were totally blind in the region of their visual field corresponding to the damaged cortex, and only some rather special experimentation enabled their visual capacity to be revealed. In fact, they have a good capacity to detect events and their onset and offset in this 'blind' part of the field and to perform some basic discriminations. But the subjects do not acknowledge their ability. Rather, they report that they could not see anything and were simply guessing ('playing the experimenter's game'). Patients express surprise at being told of their success.

Both the amnesic syndrome and blindsight patients show abilities without awareness of these abilities. What are the implications of these phenomena for our area of interest? Weiskrantz argues:

The person can process information if it leads to a straightforward and unambiguous route from stimulus to response, in the absence of 'thought'. What I think has become disconnected is a monitoring system, one that is not part of a serial information-processing chain itself, but which can monitor what is going on. I think that is the kind of neural organization one is looking for in order to explain awareness.

(Weiskrantz, 1987, p. 316)

In such terms then, our integrated sense of self has evolved as a kind of overall monitor.

A similar logic to this was developed by Gray (1993). Gray suggests that much of the trouble encountered in trying to understand consciousness is generated by falling into the trap of thinking that consciousness is mainly about detecting stimuli and executing responses. Conscious awareness is often too slow for this. Furthermore, except in novel situations, stimulus processing and response execution can be organized at an unconscious level. Much of what consciousness is doing is therefore monitoring *after the event*. It is concerned with modifying future reactions based upon past experiences.

Review of section 5

- Conscious experience is commonly assumed to be a property of the physical brain and depends upon the integrity of the brain. The question of what exactly is the relationship between consciousness and the physical brain represents a daunting intellectual challenge.

- It is generally assumed that consciousness emerged in evolution because it conferred an advantage on its possessor.

- Some believe that consciousness emerged as a means of giving flexibility to behaviour. Other theorists suggest that consciousness evolved as a facilitator of social relations. These two ideas need not be mutually incompatible.

- Information on the nature of consciousness can be derived from the study of damaged brains.

- In the so-called split brain, the pathways that carry information from one hemisphere to the other are cut. It is interesting to speculate as to whether conscious experience is thereby split.

- Some brain-damaged patients can perform complex sensory-motor skills without awareness that they are performing them. This suggests that consciousness serves a monitoring·role and is not necessarily involved in individual motor acts.

6 Overview

What this chapter has tried to do is to show the relevance of a biological approach to gaining insight into the self in a social world. The view presented is an interactive one, in which the biology of the body is seen in interaction with the environment. Behaviour depends upon the nervous system, but the state of the nervous system depends in part upon the environmental context, including social factors. Thus, to understand, say, pain or emotion, information is needed at both the level of biological processes (e.g. activity in neurons detecting tissue damage) and the social matrix (e.g. the presence of doctors in white coats). In seeking to explain behaviour, the chapter has argued for the necessity of looking at both causal explanations (e.g. how behaviour is caused by neurons, hormones, etc.) and evolutionary explanations (the functions served by behaviour as expressed in terms of evolutionary theory).

The chapter has placed considerable emphasis upon two issues: addictive behaviour and consciousness. Clearly, both phenomena have aspects that are peculiarly personal and not open to inspection from outside. However, a biological perspective is clearly necessary to gain insight into how the brain can support the phenomenon of consciousness and how the processes of motivation can support a habit of addiction. Both phenomena also come into the public domain in terms of social interaction. Consciousness, it is argued, has emerged through evolution since it confers an advantage on its possessor. This might well be a social effect: the possessor of consciousness is able to anticipate the moves of another possessor based upon introspection and extrapolation to the other individual. In the case of addiction, the social matrix of the addict is also crucial in gaining an understanding. However, that social matrix can really only be fully understood, it is argued here, with the help of a biological understanding.

Acknowledgement

I am most grateful to Alastair Ewing and Heather McLannahan for their comments on this chapter.

Further reading

This chapter can only give a sample of the available material that serves to bring together biology and social psychology. A few suggested further reading topics are as follows:

For a strong argument that researchers need to integrate biological and social psychological inputs in order to understand feeding, see Booth, D.A. (1994) *Psychology of Nutrition*, London, Taylor and Francis. For an introduction to the topic, see Logue, A.W. (1991) *The Psychology of Eating and Drinking*, San Francisco, W.H. Freeman.

For a study of stress addressing both biological and psychological issues, see Williams, R. (1989) *The Trusting Heart*, New York, The Free Press, or Sapolsky, R. (1992) *Why Zebras Don't Get Ulcers*, San Francisco, W.H. Freeman.

For pain, see Melzack, R. and Wall, P. (1984) *The Challenge of Pain*, Harmondsworth, Penguin Books.

For a study of emotion, see Frijda, N.H. (1986) *The Emotions*, Cambridge, Cambridge University Press.

For sociobiology, see Buss, D.M. (1989) 'Sex differences in human mate preferences: evolutionary hypotheses tested in 37 cultures', *Behavioural and Brain Sciences*, vol. 12, pp. 1–49; Buss, D.M. (1994) *The Evolution of Desire – Strategies of Human Mating*, New York, Basic Books; Ridley, M. (1994) *The Red Queen*, Harmondsworth, Penguin Books.

For consciousness, see Baars, B.J. (1988) *A Cognitive Theory of Consciousness*, Cambridge, Cambridge University Press; Bock, G.R. and Marsh, J. (eds) (1993) *Experimental and Theoretical Studies of Consciousness – Ciba Foundation Symposium 174*, Chichester, John Wiley; and an excellent new journal started in 1994, *Journal of Consciousness Studies*.

References

Alexander, B.K. (1990) 'The empirical and theoretical bases for an adaptive model of addiction', *The Journal of Drug Issues,* vol. 20, pp. 37–65.

Baars, B.J. (1988) *A Cognitive Theory of Consciousness,* Cambridge, Cambridge University Press.

Blum, K. (1991) *Alcohol and the Addictive Brain: New Hope for Alcoholics from Biogenetic Research,* New York, The Free Press.

Bock, G.R. and Marsh, J. (eds) (1993) *Experimental and Theoretical Studies of Consciousness – Ciba Foundation Symposium 174,* Chichester, John Wiley.

Buss, D.M., Larsen, R.J., Weston, D. and Semmelroth, J. (1992) 'Sex differences in jealousy: evolution, physiology and psychology', *Psychological Science,* vol. 3, pp. 251–5.

Cox, W.M. and Klinger, E. (1988) 'A motivational model of alcohol use', *Journal of Abnormal Psychology,* 97, pp. 168–80.

Dawkins, M. (1993) *Through Our Eyes Only? The Search For Animal Consciousness,* Oxford, W.H. Freeman.

Dawkins, R. (1976) *The Selfish Gene,* Oxford, Oxford University Press.

DeKay, W.T. and Buss, D.M. (1992) 'Human nature, individual differences, and the importance of context: perspectives from evolutionary psychology', *Current Directions in Psychological Science,* vol. 1, pp. 184–9.

Eccles, J.C. (1992) *The Human Psyche,* London, Routledge.

Fenwick, P. (1993) 'Discussion', in Bock, G.R. and Marsh, J. (eds) (1993).

Humphrey, N. (1976) 'The social function of intelligence', in Bateson, P.P.G. and Hinde, R.A. (eds) *Growing Points in Ethology,* Cambridge, Cambridge University Press.

Gray, J. (1993) 'Discussion', in Bock, G.R. and Marsh, J. (eds) (1993).

James, W. (1890) *The Principles of Psychology,* New York, Holt.

Keller, M. and Rosenberg, S.S. (eds) (1973) *Alcohol and Health: Report from the Secretary of Health, Education and Welfare*, Scribner, New York (first published in 1972 under the title *First Special Report to the US Congress on Alcohol and Health*).

LeVay, S. (1993) *The Sexual Brain,* Cambridge, Mass., MIT Press.

Mazur, A., Booth, A. and Dabbs, J. (1992) 'Testosterone and chess competition', *Social Psychology Quarterly,* vol. 5, pp. 70–7.

MacKay, D. (1987) 'Divided brains – divided minds?', in Blakemore, C. and Greenfield, S. (eds) *Mindwaves – Thoughts on Intelligence, Identity and Consciousness*, Oxford, Basil Blackwell.

Oatley, K. (1992) *Best Laid Schemes: The Psychology of Emotions*, Cambridge, Cambridge University Press.

Pcrri, M.G. (1985) 'Self-change strategies for the control of smoking, obesity and problem drinking', in Shiffman, S. and Wills, T.A. (eds) *Coping and Substance Abuse*, Orlando, Academic Press.

Plutchik, R. (1980) *Emotion – A Psychoevolutionary Synthesis*, New York, Harper and Row.

Reizenzein, R. (1983) 'The Schachter theory of emotion: two decades later', *Psychological Bulletin,* vol. 94, pp. 239–64.

Schachter, S. and Singer, J.E. (1962) 'Cognitive, social and physiological determinants of emotional state', *Psychological Review,* vol. 69, pp. 379–99.

Singer, J.L. (1993) 'Experimental studies of ongoing conscious experience', in Bock, G.R. and Marsh, J. (eds) (1993).

Sperry, R. (1967) 'The great cerebral commissure', in McGaugh, J.L., Weinberger, N.M. and Whalen, R.E. (eds) *Psychobiology – The Biological Bases of Behaviour,* San Francisco, W.H. Freeman (reprinted from *Scientific American* of January 1964).

Stewart, J., de Wit, H. and Eikelboom, R. (1984) 'Role of unconditioned and conditioned drug effects in the self-administration of opiates and stimulants', *Psychological Review,* vol. 91, pp. 251–68.

Toates, F. (1990) *Obsessional Thoughts and Behaviour,* Wellingborough, Thorsons (reprinted in 1992 as *Obsessive Compulsive Disorder,* London, Thorsons).

Toates, F. (1995) *Stress: Conceptual and Biological Aspects*, Chichester, John Wiley.

Valins, S. (1970) 'The perception and labeling of bodily changes as determinants of emotional behaviour', in Black, P. (ed.) *Physiological Correlates of Emotion,* New York, Academic Press.

Wall, P. (1993) 'Pain and the placebo response,' in Bock, G.R. and Marsh, J. (eds) (1993).

Weiskrantz, L. (1987) 'Neuropsychology and the nature of consciousness', in Blackmore, C. and Greenfield, S. (eds) *Mindwaves – Thoughts on Intelligence, Identity and Consciousness,* Oxford, Basil Blackwell.

Williams, R. (1989) *The Trusting Heart,* New York, The Free Press.

Wright, L. (1988) 'The Type A behaviour pattern and coronary artery disease', *American Psychologist,* vol. 43, pp. 2–14.

Reflections

This chapter has taken one perspective on the self in a social world, the biological one, though it has done this in a way that has acknowledged the role of other perspectives. As we saw in the Introduction, psychology is not a unified body of knowledge and the line presented here is but one amongst different approaches which may conflict in their way of understanding aspects of the person. For instance, the approach to unconscious information processing taken here is rather different from that you will meet in Chapter 6 in the context of a psychodynamic approach. Whether such different approaches are compatible or not, or whether at the end of the day you will have to decide between them, is an interesting key issue to hold in mind.

Complex interactions

A strong theme running through this chapter has been that the dynamic nature of the interactions between an individual and his or her social and physical environment is crucial to an understanding of social psychology. The issue has raised itself in the context of the role of biological factors. For instance, a gene might give a bias towards height. This affects how we behave. It will affect how others behave towards us and it will affect how we feel others feel about us. The example of alcoholism and addictive behaviours given in the chapter brings out rather well the complex interdependence of factors involved. Genetics might yield a nervous system with a certain bias towards vulnerability to alcoholism. However, whether the person becomes an alcoholic will depend also upon a host of other factors such as self-image and sources of gratification. How others behave towards the alcoholic will affect his or her behaviour and self-image.

The interaction of the social with the biological is also well brought out in those theories that relate the evolution of consciousness to its usefulness in promoting social interactions.

The potential impact of psychological theories

An interesting related issue here is the potential of psychological theories to influence (and therefore change) the very people who are their subject-matter and whom they are seeking to understand. Where explanations of alcoholism are made public, they may come to the attention of alcoholics themselves and their families and friends. So such explanations not only serve to describe and explain alcoholics but may also influence their mind and behaviour. Alcoholics are likely to be differently affected, for example, by learning that they have highly sensitive neural pathways that can bias towards pathology as opposed to being told they are evil or of weak will. Such considerations raise questions about the degree to which some psychological theories have a moral dimension as well as offering a way of understanding the subject-matter in question. It also means that such theories can sometimes become self-fulfilling prophecies in that they may serve to generate the pattern of behaviour or experience which they purport to describe.

Autonomy and determinism

The discussion of alcoholism also raises questions about the degree to which people have the autonomy to choose how they behave (or 'free-will'). The issue of determinism raises itself in a particular context in the present chapter – that of genetic determinism. Is it all in the genes? Just what is, and what is not, 'in the genes' remains debatable, but we can certainly say that any naïve assumption that everything is determined by genes is wrong. Perhaps we should see the gene as offering a bias towards certain ways of behaving, reacting and feeling. This was discussed, for instance, in the context of sexual jealousy. As it is only a bias, there is still room for other factors to act. Perhaps we should see the gene as helping to code for a nervous system with which agency or autonomous action may be exercised. As such it will constrain, or make possible, or make more likely, certain courses of action rather than others.

We shall come back to the issue of autonomy and determinism later in the book, particularly in Chapter 4 where a theoretical model will be offered which attempts to reconcile the ideas of determinism and auton-omy and argues that we do not necessarily have to see them as opposed.

The relevance of scientific method

The chapter is a mixture of 'hard-nosed' scientific evidence, theoretical speculation and personal anecdote. It is worth noting that scientific method takes different forms. There is *causal* investigation using careful observation, measurement and often experimentation. But there is also *functional* analysis like much of the application of evolutionary theory to social behaviour. As we saw with the discussion of sociobiology and its exploration of the implications of Darwinian theory for social behaviour, this moves us into more analytic and speculative approaches. Even here, however, there is often some attempt to test the idea being presented (see Buss's work on jealousy, for example).

It is difficult to imagine anything more hard-nosed and 'respectable' than observing the activity of neurons and hormones, and such evidence sometimes sits uncomfortably with the speculation and anecdote. But what is the status of these different sources of evidence? Should we always defer to the scientific over the anecdotal and thereby hope to enhance the status of psychology? It must be remembered, as we can see in this chapter, that science rarely if ever produces unquestionable facts. They need to be interpreted. Questions arise in relation to scientific studies which are not always easy to deal with by scientific method. And as we shall see in the other chapters, because of the nature of its subject-matter, social psychology contains a mixture of methods, many of which go outside the format of natural science methodology. That is not to say they are necessarily any the less valuable for that. The point in common between all the methods used is that they all involve some kind of rational and systematic attempt to investigate the person in a social world. Maybe psychology is, of its very essence, a hybrid subject, part science and part involving other forms of analysis and theorizing. The present chapter is specifically *not* promoting a message of the kind 'We bet you thought understanding social behaviour was all about such vague terms as "mental states" and "feelings", but what we can show is that it is really all about neurotransmitters and hormones.' Nothing that we have discussed encourages us to relinquish control to the biology department. Biology is one perspective that must take its place with the rest.

The next chapter, in adopting an *experimentalist* perspective, retains the emphasis on scientific method which we have seen here but, in this case, applies it not to the biological factors relating to the self in a social world but directly to the ways we interpret and make sense of social behaviour, situations and ourselves.

CHAPTER 3

THE INTERPRETING SELF: AN EXPERIMENTALIST PERSPECTIVE

by Mansur Lalljee

Contents

1   Introduction

Let's begin at the beginning: for instance, at square 1 in a game of snakes and ladders. It's your throw. On square 7 is a ladder. A great big ladder that will take you up to square 54. So you need to throw a six. You take the dice in your hand, look at it intently, and blow on it. You then shake the dice vigorously, and let it roll proudly on to the board!

This pattern of behaviour will be familiar to anyone who has played the game. You go through a particular sequence of activities or throw the dice in a particular way if you need to get a six; and a different way if you need to get a one. And you know it works, sometimes! Does this show that you seriously think you can control the roll of the dice? Or at least influence its outcome to some extent? Surely not! You only play snakes and ladders with young children. It is a rather boring game of chance, and one which has no element of skill. Maybe the rituals engaged in to try to throw a six are simply a way of making the game a bit more fun. Even if that is so, you might wonder what signals you are sending to the child you are playing with! And if you received similar signals as a child, might there be some residual vestige of that belief?

This chapter deals with some of the processes involved in making sense of our social worlds. The outcome of our game of snakes and ladders is clearly a matter of chance, but for the important events which people really wish to explain – a success or failure at an important task, the breakup of a relationship, an accident or an illness – the explanation is never so clear. 'Was it just luck? Or was it something I did? Was it my fault or the other person's?' This chapter on the 'interpreting self' will examine some of the processes involved in making sense, at some of the ways in which people interpret their own outcomes and the outcomes of others.

After a brief look at 'luck', the chapter will move on to consider the processes involved in categorization – one of the building blocks of understanding. The integral connection between the act and the actor and the importance of our conception of the actor in making sense of what he or she is doing will be stressed. The sense we make of an event will inevitably depend upon our knowledge and beliefs about that event and about events like it. One cognitive model of how people put information together to come to an explanation will be examined and its major limitations considered. Here the importance of the social context of explanation-giving will be emphasized. We will then move on to examine the importance of feelings of control for effective psychological functioning, and the relationship between helplessness and depression. Finally, we will remind ourselves that most of the research described has been carried out in the West and consider some of the relevant research in non-western countries.

Before we return to the question of luck and chance, we should consider two preliminary questions. The first concerns the general orientation of this chapter, and the second concerns its implicit concept of self.

1.1   The perspective of the chapter

The perspective of this chapter, like that of the previous one, draws its general orientation from the natural sciences. This orientation is widespread, not only in psychology but also in other social sciences such as economics. Its main goal is to establish causal relationships. Working from this perspective, the investigator proceeds from hypotheses to test them in a systematic way. Of course, these hypotheses may come from a variety of sources including informal observations, qualitative explorations or case studies, but the goal would be to form hypotheses about the processes and to test them. There are also ideas about what constitutes appropriate data. Reports which are made about an event at a later date are seldom regarded as good evidence because memory is notoriously fallible and we know about the reconstructive processes whereby memory works. Similarly, a person's own explanation of the processes underlying his or her thoughts, feelings and behaviour would not be regarded as evidence for the validity of that explanation. This is not to say that these explanations are unimportant, because a person's own thoughts, feelings and behaviour may be guided by such explanations. So they are treated not as accurate reports about the relevant psychological processes, but as a person's own interpretations of what is going on.

For much psychological research, the experiment is the favoured method of investigation. Experiments enable us to investigate systematically what variable is causing what effects. They can do this by controlling for other variables, and by manipulating variables systematically in order to examine their effects. Most experiments are performed in laboratories, and while the lab enables us to have control over variables, it also raises questions about the generality of the processes investigated. Field experiments (i.e. those carried out in natural settings) are more powerful, but raise enormous problems about their practicability. Besides experiments, the other favoured technique of investigators adopting a scientific orientation is the questionnaire. Questionnaire studies enable us to study a wider range of phenomena, but it is often more difficult to establish relationships of cause and effect. However, this is possible through the use of longitudinal designs and complex statistical analyses of the data. In this chapter you will come across examples of laboratory and field experiments, and longitudinal studies as well.

While the range of methods used is wider than the experiment, the term 'an experimentalist perspective' applies easily enough to the contents of this chapter. The introduction of experiments in psychology as a whole (including social psychology) marked a move towards a scientific analysis of psychological processes. The emphasis of the experimental approach is on measurement, on reliability and on objectivity. As in the other sciences, the goals include establishing generalizations and making predictions.

The prediction is about something measurable, usually some aspect of a person's behaviour. But the 'behaviour' studied is very wide indeed. It includes what people say, the marks they make on a questionnaire, and the time they take to respond to items on computer screens. The approach is neither positivist nor behaviourist, while having been influenced by both. Positivism was a philosophical movement which hinged on a verificationist theory about the nature of truth and of meaning. The orientation adopted here does not involve any such theory. Behaviourists are generally interested in the relationships between stimuli and responses. The mainstream of social psychology has never been behaviourist, and the work described in this chapter will be concerned with people's thoughts and feelings as well as with what they do.

1.2   Levels of analysis and the concept of self

This methodological perspective involves a commitment to certain goals and to finding out things in a particular way. However, there is no *one* concept of self that is necessarily linked to this orientation. Over the past few decades, the idea of the self as continuously concerned with making sense of what is going on – the interpreting self – has been one of the central themes in social psychology. The concept of self that I will out-line briefly is a reflection of the current state of the development of the subject, and with time this will undoubtedly change.

As a preliminary to considering the concept of self implicit in this research, it may be helpful to draw a distinction between three levels in the analysis of social psychological processes. One level is the *intraper-sonal level*. Here the focus is on what goes on within the person. This includes cognitive processes (such as memory, categorization, thinking and feeling) and motivational processes (such as the need for control and for self-esteem). Another level of analysis is the *interpersonal level*. This focuses on what goes on between people, and includes a consideration of the importance of self-presentation, and of the nature of relationships and social interaction. The third level of analysis is the *societal level*. Here the focus is on understanding cultural processes and their implications for the processes already mentioned.

All three levels of analysis are relevant to our understanding of social psychology generally, and all are relevant to our understanding of the 'interpreting self'. Most of the research in the area has focused upon intrapersonal, primarily cognitive, factors. At times this emphasis on cog-nitive information processing has been so marked that it seems that the implicit model of the person is of some kind of 'cognitive hermit' – a person who does not have any desires, who does not communicate with anyone else, and who lives outside society! But this would be a caricature. While this chapter will discuss some of the cognitive processes involved, it will also be considering motivational processes, and interpersonal and cultural ones as well.

Aims of Chapter 3

The aims of this chapter are:

- To introduce the reader to the scientific analysis of social behaviour.

- To illustrate this with reference to a wide range of different types of empirical study.

- To illustrate the wide range of processes involved in the analysis of the interpreting self.

1.3 Was it just luck?

Let us return to throwing dice. Games of chance involving dice occur in many contexts of serious gambling. Take, for instance, the game of 'craps'. It's a game where people make bets on the throw of dice. As it is quite a complicated game, I will not attempt to describe the rules! Henslin (1967) observed the 'craps shooting' activities of a group of taxi drivers in the USA and reported that they have sets of practices to influence the roll of the dice. Henslin inferred these strategies from the behaviour of the participants and from what they said, including the advice that they gave to the novice in their midst. Real money was at stake, and winning was clearly important to the participants. Henslin writes:

> One does not simply listlessly throw out the dice, check the combination they form and quickly throw them out again, continuing until there is a significant result … This is what I did the first night I played, and an experienced player reacted to this by saying, 'Take your time! Don't throw 'em out so fast! Take your time and work on it!' A short while later, this player instructed me more fully by saying, 'Talk to 'em! Talk to 'em when ya shoot!'
>
> *(1967, p. 319)*

You shouldn't just pick up the dice, throw them and then see what you've got – you should talk to the dice, take your time and work it out, work out what number you want! It seemed as if the cab drivers believed that a hard throw produces a large number and a gentle throw a low number. Effort is required and confidence is the key whereby the 'shooter' can establish and maintain control over the dice.

Maybe all these are still essentially part of the ritual of the game – a more serious version of the rituals in the game of snakes and ladders; and taken about as seriously when it comes to beliefs about control. In order to disentangle the processes involved, we can turn to some studies carried out in psychologists' laboratories.

BOX 3.1   Fate and control in the laboratory

One of the earliest studies was carried out by Strickland et al. (1966), who instructed the participants in their experiment to bet on dice either before or after throwing their dice. (They could not see the outcome of their throw from where they stood.) In the 'normal' sequence, participants first bet on a particular number and then threw the dice. In the 'fate' sequence, the participants first threw the dice, and *then* bet on having thrown a particular number. Strickland et al. found that the participants adopted more conservative betting strategies, and tended to bet less money, in the 'fate' sequence than in the 'normal' sequence. Maybe people do feel that they have more control over the throw of the dice when they know what outcome they want!

These ideas have been elaborated and the processes clarified through a number of further experiments. Langer (1983) suggests that, for most events, whether we achieve the outcomes we desire is partly a matter of our own skill, effort and factors over which we have control. However, outcomes are also influenced by factors outside our control and have an element of chance. The more a task is 'skill-like' the more we are likely to believe that we have control over it. If you choose to perform a task, if you are familiar with it and highly involved, you are more likely to believe that you have some degree of control over the outcome. This sensible and adaptive strategy has the unexpected consequence of our behaving as if we had control over some of the few events over which we know we do not. The generally positive consequences of believing that we are in control over our outcomes will form a major part of our discussion later in the chapter.

The reasons why we seem to prefer not to attribute events to chance can be found at several levels. Perhaps at its most elementary, saying that something was due to chance is not to have an explanation for it. Explaining events gives us an *understanding* of what has happened, which makes us feel that the world is a comprehensible place. Not all explanations make *predictions* about what is likely to occur in the future, but some do. If they do, then besides making sense of the past, an explanation can give us a handle on what to expect in the future, and enable us to adjust our actions accordingly. If I can predict that it is going to rain, then I can take an umbrella, or change the date of a picnic. Some explanations also enable us to exercise some degree of *control* over events. If I know that I failed an examination because I did not work hard, then I can work harder in the future; and if I know what food will make my cholesterol level worse, I can do something about it. So providing us with a sense of understanding, prediction and control are three vital functions that explanations fulfil.

Review of section 1

- The perspective of this chapter is that of experimental social psychology. This perspective is similar in its methodological approach to the biological perspective of Chapter 2.

- The focus of the chapter is on how people interpret events. Interpretations serve to provide a person with a sense of understanding, prediction and control.

- The processes of interpretation will be considered at three levels of analysis: the intrapersonal, the interpersonal and the societal.

2 The psychology of categorization

2.1 Interpreting social behaviour

Understanding involves putting things into categories. This is true about every domain of human activity. If we know what something is, we know what it is related to and how to respond to it. Social behaviour is potentially ambiguous, and the meaning of an act has to be constructed by the perceiver. If a batsman leaves the field shaking his head, is he expressing dissent with the umpire's decision to give him out, or is he expressing disappointment? Is putting a hand on the shoulder of another person an expression of sympathy, paternalism or harassment? If you are told about the shortcomings of your essay, is the person telling you being rude, or simply frank, or giving you helpful feedback? And if the person says it is excellent, is that 'being honest' or 'being obsequious'? A description of an event already makes some decisions about what sort of event it is.

One central feature which will make a difference to how an event is classified is the person performing the act. Let me illustrate this through a study by Duncan (1976) described in Box 3.2.

BOX 3.2 Interpreting ambiguous behaviour

Duncan's subjects, who were white American college students, observed what they thought was a real interaction between two participants. The participants were discussing a case study, and as it went along, the discussion got somewhat heated and one of the participants gave the other what the author of the paper describes as 'an ambiguous shove'. Though the subjects were led to believe they were viewing an ongoing interaction, in fact the material was a videotape which had been previously prepared by the experimenter. The subjects were instructed to rate various aspects of the interaction. Of special interest for present purposes is the way in which the subjects classified the 'ambiguous shove'. A number of different videotapes had been constructed, varying the ethnic group membership of the partners interacting. The participants were either both white, both black or consisted of pairs of one black and one white person. As can be seen from Table 3.1, when the shove was given by a black person, 35 of the 48 white subjects who watched the scene classified it as 'violent behaviour', while when the shove was given by a white person only 6 of the 48 subjects classified it as violent.

Table 3.1   Categorization of 'ambiguous shove' as a function of race of harm-doer

Categorization	Black harm-doer	White harm-doer
Playing around	1*	11*
Dramatizes	3	19
Aggressive behaviour	9	12
Violent behaviour	35	6

* Number of subjects using the categorization

Source: adapted from Duncan, 1976, Table 1, p. 595

How should we understand these results? Is it essentially a case of racism amongst a small group of American students at a particular historical period? It is difficult to think of it simply as racism, since Duncan later obtained comparable results with a group of black subjects watching the same videotaped behaviour (Duncan, 1979). That implies that both groups shared some of the same stereotypes of black people. But of course the views of either group might change. Would this in some important sense invalidate the results that Duncan obtained? I think not. The general point being made here is that the interpretation of social behaviour is dependent upon a range of factors, including, as in the present case, beliefs about the nature of the person who is performing the act. If the subjects in the experiment had different beliefs, they would still draw upon them to make sense of the behaviour in question.

Other experimental evidence has illustrated the ways in which labels such as gender, ethnicity, and class all influence the interpretation and evaluation of what people do.

2.2 Categorization and prototypes

What then are some of the processes involved in categorization? One early answer to this question saw category membership as a function of possessing the relevant criteria for membership of that category. If a figure consists of four equal sides and has angles of 90 degrees, then it is a square, and all squares are alike in their squareness. If a figure has three sides joined together, then its a triangle. For mathematical shapes like these, you can specify the attributes, the set of necessary and sufficient conditions, that determine class membership; and it was thought that the same principles applied to the categorization of objects. This view also implied that all members of the category were equally qualified as members of the category, since they possessed these attributes, and that differences between categories were clear and distinct. They depended on the possession or otherwise of these attributes (a four-sided figure with all its angles right angles is either a square or a rectangle – there is nothing in between).

ACTIVITY 3.1   Think of the concept of 'bird', and quickly write down a list of seven birds. (You might want to ask other people around you to do the same, and see if there is any overlap in your lists.)

The traditional view of categorization was challenged by the philosopher Ludwig Wittgenstein (1953), and gave way to a view of categorization based on the idea of family resemblance. In the psychological literature, it was Eleanor Rosch who made this particular position influential (see, for instance, Rosch, 1975, 1978). Rosch showed that members of a category vary in terms of their typicality and that the boundaries between classes are often unclear. In your list of birds, you probably had examples such as sparrows and robins, but not ostriches or penguins or even chickens and turkeys. This is because certain instances are better exemplars of a particular category than others. For example, a sparrow is a more typical instance of the category 'bird' than is a turkey, and a chair is a more typical instance of the category 'furniture' than is a rug. How then do we decide whether a particular case is a bird or that something is a piece of furniture? Categorization is dependent upon comparing the particular instance with the typical instances or prototype of that category. There is a wide range of evidence for the psychological reality of prototypes. For instance, more typical instances are categorized faster, and are more likely to be produced when people are asked to list instances of a particular category.

Views differ about the precise nature of prototypes. Some are more inclined to see the prototype as consisting of separate descriptions of some of the exemplars of the category, while others see it as some sort of summary representation of a probabilistic kind. More importantly, a number of studies have shown that similarity by itself is not an adequate account of categorization. Concepts have an underlying coherence. Thus, in the case of the concept 'bird', the attributes 'having wings', 'flies', 'having feathers' and 'living in trees' are not independent, nor are they simply arbitrarily correlated. There is a functional interrelationship between these attributes, a coherence underlying them. Furthermore, our categories are flexible and are adapted to the function they are required to serve, and so unusual instances may not be categorized solely on the basis of their similarity to a prototype. But, for our present purposes, the basic point that categorization proceeds on some basis like prototype matching, particularly for standard cases of a class, must not be lost sight of. Moreover, since categorization is no longer seen as the ascription of necessary and sufficient conditions, it is sufficiently open-ended to permit disagreement about whether a particular case is or is not an instance of a particular category. For many events, these disagreements can be seen in the arguments that people have about such assignments. (The question of where our prototypes come from will be considered briefly at the end of the next section.)

2.3   Illness prototypes

Let us now consider how the concept of *prototype* might help us understand categorization in the social world.

Before you go on, please read the following description, and answer the question which follows it:

ACTIVITY 3.2

> 'P. is 50 years old. He has a high-powered job which gives him little time for exercise or relaxation. P. tends to over-indulge in rich gourmet food. Consequently he has been overweight for some time. P. does not seem to have any stamina any more. Nowadays he becomes breathless and sometimes has chest pains after a small amount of physical exertion.'

Please indicate which illness, from the list below, you think the person is suffering from. If you think that none of the diagnoses listed is appropriate, but would like to specify some other, please do so:

AIDS	Arthritis	Heart disease	Influenza	Leukaemia
Mumps	Pneumonia	Typhoid	Other	

My guess is that you diagnosed the illness as heart disease. But how did you come to that conclusion? Did you do it essentially by reading off the symptoms of heart disease – like lack of stamina, breathlessness and chest pains? Is it a bit like deciding that a particular figure is a square – by counting the four sides and checking the right-angles? Or is the concept of prototype of some help here? The 'prototype view' would imply that we have a coherent set of beliefs about an illness which may well include symptoms, but includes a lot more besides. For instance, it includes beliefs about the sort of person who typically gets that illness, its typical cause, how serious it is, and its typical effects. The process of diagnosis does not simply rest on an analysis of the symptoms, but on a process of matching the particular case with the prototype of that illness.

The example you considered in Activity 3.2 comes from a study by Lalljee et al. (1993). They presented first-year students at a polytechnic with a number of written descriptions. These consisted partly of symptom information and partly of information about the person, and possible explanations for the illness. In the example cited in Activity 3.2, 95.8 per cent of people said that the person described was suffering from heart disease. That's just what we would expect, because the description matched the prototype of the illness. But what would happen if the same symptoms were ascribed to someone else – a child perhaps, or a teenager, or someone from the 'third world'. If the subjects were basing their diagnosis solely on the symptoms, then the diagnosis of heart disease should be equally frequent in all cases. If, however, the judgements were being made on the basis of prototypes, then the proportion should be considerably lower. This is in fact what happens. The diagnoses of heart disease fell to around 35 per cent when the symptoms were ascribed to a child or young person, and to 5 per cent when ascribed to someone from the 'third world'! Similar results were also found for other illnesses. In fact, in this study the nature of the person was more important than the symptoms (though not statistically significantly so) when making diagnoses!

This study was carried out with people without medical training or background, and it would be interesting and important to know whether similar tendencies were shown by doctors, nurses and other members of the medical profession. With regard to heart disease, it does seem that 'being male' is an important part of the prototype held by the medical profession, and there is some concern that doctors are less likely to diagnose heart disease in the case of women. Another important question concerns whether illness prototypes apply to a person's interpretations of their *own* symptoms. For instance, would a man who saw himself as middle-aged be more likely to interpret his breathlessness as a heart condition than someone who did not think of himself in those terms? It has been shown that delay in interpreting a particular set of changes as symptoms of, for instance, myocardial infarction (heart attack), may make the difference between life and death (see Matthews et al., 1983). The ideas also need to be extended cross-culturally. Is the importance given to the person in the diagnosis prevalent in all cultures, or is it a particular feature of individualistic societies? The importance attached to the person as an independent entity will be addressed in section 6 of this chapter.

The concept of prototype may also be helpful in understanding why an illness becomes classified as a particular sort of illness. Perhaps the best recent example of this is the case of Acquired Immune Deficiency Syndrome or AIDS (Seale, 1985). AIDS was first classified as a sexually transmitted disease, and was readily dubbed the 'gay plague' because of its prevalence in the homosexual community. Classifying it as *sexually* transmitted quickly led to its being seen as transmitted through *immoral* sexual practices. This in turn elicited moral condemnation. Compare the connotations implicit in describing something as a *sexually transmitted* disease to those of transmission by *an airborne* or *a water-borne virus*. Seale also suggests that classifying AIDS as a sexually transmitted disease may have influenced the attempts made to understand how the disease is transmitted and how it could be controlled. The cause attributed to the illness seems to be part of a package of other beliefs about the illness, including the sort of person who typically gets the illness and how to prevent it. These are the sorts of features that we consider relevant to prototypes of illness.

Make a list of where you think your prototype of heart disease comes from.   ACTIVITY 3.3
Make another list about where you think your prototype of AIDS comes from.
Examine the similarities and differences between the two lists, and try and
work out why they might be different. Do you think your prototypes would be
the same as a doctor's? What might explain their differences?

The sources of our prototypes are all around us. In many cases we form prototypes of events for which we have no direct knowledge. The sources for such prototypes include the early stories that we may have had read to us and then the ones that we ourselves read. They also include the wide range of media sources, television, radio, newspapers, that constantly bombard us, and whose messages may sometimes be implicit rather than explicit. In other cases these may be elaborated through interactions with family and friends and through our own direct experiences. Categorization enables us to act upon the world, and the refinement and complexity of our category systems in a particular domain crucially depend upon what we need to do with them.

So to sum up, categorization is a fundamental part of understanding, and the concept of prototypes is invaluable in helping us to understand that process. A prototype consists of a set of features, including an explanation of why the event occurred, and the categorization of a particular instance involves matching the features of that instance with those of the prototype.

2.4   Knowing how I feel

The material used in Lalljee et al.'s study described in the previous section consisted of written descriptions of hypothetical other people. The present section will consider how we make sense of *our own* internal states. Pennebaker (1984) argues that people are not very accurate in identifying physiological changes and Pennebaker and Skelton (1981) showed that a person's expectations about changes in internal sensations influence the changes they report. Our emotions and our actions are guided by our interpretations of bodily sensations and such interpretations can, as noted in the previous section, be a matter of life and death. In this section, these issues will be illustrated with reference to normal and to clinically disturbed behaviour.

2.4.1   Interpreting arousal

Chapter 2 has already explored the idea that subjective feelings are not simply a function of internal states. Many emotional states cannot be distinguished purely in terms of changes in the autonomic nervous system, and emotions as experientially different as anger and happiness are marked by similar changes in heart rate and blood flow. Schachter and Singer's study (discussed in section 2.3 of Chapter 2) showed that the external environment – or rather the interpretation placed on the external environment – played a crucial role in interpreting the emotion felt.

The interpretation of our internal states can influence our perceptions of other people and our behaviour towards them. Zillman and his colleagues have carried out a series of experiments that show this (Zillman et al., 1974; Cantor et al., 1975). In one of them (see Box 3.3), they show the effects of unexplained arousal on hostile behaviour.

It is important to point out that the results reported in Box 3.3 cannot be explained as a *direct* result of arousal, without any intervening process of attribution (at some implicit level). If increased arousal led directly to increased hostility then we would expect that the participants who were most highly aroused – those who had just performed the exercises – would be most hostile. But they were not – presumably because they attributed their arousal to the exercise rather than to feelings of hostility.

So it seems that we interpret our internal states in terms of the context or situation in which we are and that this influences what we do. Of course, normally we have a clear and evident explanation for our arousal. If you see someone walking towards you with a knife in a dark alley, it is the perception of danger which causes the arousal, and you know that. But there are other cases where some form of interpretation is necessary. Imagine that you are very tired, and you know that being tired makes you irritable. A friend comes into the room, and says something rather irritating. Since you know that you are tired, you make allowances for that, and realize that you may be being touchy. To use the jargon that will be used later on, you *attribute the cause* of your reaction not so much

---

BOX 3.3   Effects of unexplained arousal

Each participant in this study by Zillman et al. (1974) was asked to have a session on an exercise bicycle. Measures of blood pressure and heart rate made it clear that they had become highly aroused, and at the end of the session they were clearly aware of their arousal. Over time the arousal decays, but self-ratings by the participants showed that they thought this decay occurred faster than it does. So for some time they were actually aroused but did not realize that they were. Their behaviour in this experimental condition is of particular interest here. The participants were given the opportunity to be aggressive towards someone who had insulted them. When this opportunity was given immediately after the ride (when the person was aroused, and knew it), or when the arousal had in fact decayed, there was little difference in the degree of hostility that the person showed. However, the participants showed greater hostility in the intermediate condition; that is, the condition where they were aroused, but did not realize it. Rather than attribute their emotional state to the effects of exercise, they attributed it instead to their own feelings of hostility, and behaved accordingly.

---

to the other person's remark, but to your own tiredness. But what if you are somewhat tired but don't realize it? In such cases you may be unclear about the causes of your irritation and may well attribute your irritability not to your own tiredness, but to the remark of the other person. Since you think that the person is behaving in an irritating way, then surely you are justified in snapping at him or her!

2.4.2   Panic attacks

The importance of comparable processes which involve the interpretation of internal states has been recently implicated in panic attacks. 'A panic attack consists of an intense feeling of apprehension or impending doom which is of sudden onset and is associated with a wide range of distressing physical sensations' (Clark, 1989, p. 52). According to the diagnostic manual of the American Psychiatric Association, for an episode to be classified as a panic attack the episode should include at least four of the following symptoms: shortness of breath, dizziness, palpitations or accelerated heart rate, trembling or shaking, sweating, choking, nausea, depersonalization, numbness or tingling sensations, hot flushes, chest pain or discomfort, fear of dying, fear of going crazy or doing something uncontrolled. There are further criteria about the frequency of the attacks and the lack of any clear organic cause which are also involved in the diagnosis of panic disorder. Note that the attacks are not associated with a particular set of circumstances (i.e. they are not phobic reactions to particular stimuli), but occur in a wide range of circumstances. However, the person who suffers from panic attacks may gradually become so concerned about the possibility of fainting or engaging in uncontrolled behaviour that they might end up simply staying at home. Agoraphobia is a frequent accompaniment to panic disorder.

Panic disorder has been frequently alleviated through the use of drugs, and was generally thought to have biological origins. However, recently the importance of cognitive explanations to supplement, not necessarily to supplant, the biological explanations, has been recognized. The model presented by Clark (1986) in his influential paper 'A cognitive approach to panic' is shown in Figure 3.1. The start of the sequence is the 'trigger stimulus' which may be an external event (such as a wide open space for an agoraphobic) or internal stimuli (such as thoughts, images or sensations). This leads to apprehension, which quite naturally gives rise to a range of bodily sensations which are associated with anxiety. These sensations are then interpreted as 'catastrophic'. The person believes that the racing pulse is a sign of imminent heart attack; or that breathlessness will lead to a failure to breathe; or that the dizziness could lead to fainting. Having interpreted this racing pulse as a sign of impending heart attack, the person engages in what is considered to be 'preventative' behaviour. For instance, this could be lying down to rest. Not having the heart attack is then interpreted as a consequence of this 'preventative' action. Note that the initial stimuli could be the result of all sorts of relatively mundane factors (such as sudden exertion). But it is the particular interpretation of these bodily sensations which leads to panic attacks.

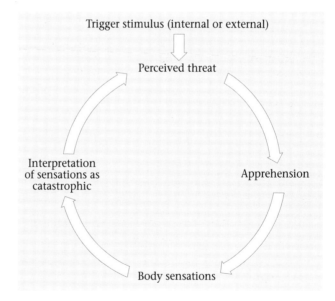

Figure 3.1 *The suggested sequence of events in a panic attack (Source: based on Clark, 1986, p. 463)*

What evidence is there to support this theory, and what are its consequences for treatment? Clark and his colleagues have carried out a series of studies which show that panic patients show a greater tendency to interpret bodily sensations in catastrophic terms than do control groups of patients with generalized anxiety disorder and people with no medical problems. They have also showed that such catastrophic interpretations are likely to increase the degree of anxiety and panic felt by panic disorder patients.

If it is the catastrophic interpretation of bodily sensations that leads to panic attacks, then influencing these interpretations, enabling people to interpret these sensations in other ways, should lead to a decrease in such episodes. How might one accomplish that? The cognitive-behaviour therapy that Clark and others advocate involves various strategies. The beliefs of the patient that these bodily sensations presage impending calamity must be treated as hypotheses that the patient holds. Their inadequacy is then exposed through discussion as well as through specific exercises. Thus, the person can be made to realize that turning attention inwards upon bodily sensations can lead to greater anxiety; that similar symptoms can be produced by hyperventilation and can be controlled; that if the person does not engage in the preventative or avoidant behaviour, the catastrophic consequences do not occur. There are various case studies that do support the effectiveness of such therapy for panic disorders. Most recently, Clark et al. (1994) have reported a systematic comparison between cognitive therapy, relaxation training, and the use of the drug imipramine. All three treatments were better than no treatment; but when the treatments were compared, the cognitive therapy emerged as more effective than the other two groups, both shortly after the therapy was concluded and fifteen months later.

To sum up: the two examples presented here (panic attacks and interpreting arousal) are intended to show that even when it comes to those aspects of ourselves that are most intimate and immediate, where knowledge of ourselves seems most direct, the importance of interpreting what is going on is also central.

Review of section 2

- Categorization is one of the building blocks of understanding.

- Categorization of standard cases involves the matching of a particular instance with a prototype.

- Interpretation is a vital process, even in understanding our own internal states.

3   Persons as the origins of actions

In the Introductory chapter and again in Chapter 2, reference was made to the importance of agency with regard to one's feelings about oneself. People experience themselves as agents, acting upon the world, having goals and desires that they try to fulfil. We experience ourselves as the initiators of actions, and agency may be a central component of what it is to be a person. (This is discussed further in Chapter 4.) Of course, we also attribute agency to other people, seeing them as having their own goals and desires, and as initiators of their own actions. Perhaps it is because we think of persons as originators of action that we tend to underestimate the importance of chance when explaining events. The tendency to interpret the act in terms of the actor, shown by Duncan's study of the categorization of the 'ambiguous shove' described in Box 3.2, and the interpretation of the symptoms of illness in terms of the nature of the person showing those symptoms, also emphasizes the psychological unity between the actor and the event.

It was Heider, in his seminal work *The Psychology of Interpersonal Relations* (1958), who pioneered the social psychology of how the layperson makes sense of the world. It is a rich and varied work, calling upon material from a wide range of different sources (including philosophy, sociology, and experimental psychology). Many of his insights were later systematized and developed, and referred to as 'attribution theory'. I prefer not to use that term, since there is no one 'theory' of how people attribute causes to events, but several different hypotheses and models about what may be going on.

This section will consider two related issues, both stemming directly from Heider. The first follows from the notion of persons as origins, and concerns the claim that we overestimate the importance of the person in causing behaviour, and underestimate the importance of situational causes. The second concerns the differences in explanation provided by the person performing an act and someone observing the act. Here the claim is that, while observers provide explanations in terms of the characteristics of the actor, the actor provides explanations more in terms of the situation. Note that in the two cases we are making different comparisons. In the second case, the comparison is between the explanations provided by actors and observers; while in the first the comparison is between the explanation provided by a particular person and the true or correct explanation for that event.

3.1   The fundamental attribution error?

People frequently see outcomes as caused by the person rather than the context or situation in which they occur. Consider some of the classic studies in social psychology like Milgram's studies of obedience. The act of giving another person powerful electric shocks when you have been instructed to do so is often explained by people in terms of being the action of a sadistic personality. That view seems to stem from a failure to appreciate the importance of contextual factors in causing behaviour. Milgram's studies showed just how important these are. But his experiments were not set up to examine the question of how the layperson explains events.

In order to find a systematic exploration of that issue, we must look to an extensive series of studies carried out by Jones and his colleagues (see Jones, 1979 for an overview). They found that even when experimental subjects were told quite clearly that the views espoused by a target person were solely a function of the experimenter's instructions, they still inferred that the person had attitudes congruent with the views espoused. A typical experiment of theirs is described in Box 3.4.

BOX 3.4   Inferring another person's attitudes from his or her behaviour

The subjects ('observers') in a typical study by Jones and his colleagues (1979) would read an essay or listen to a tape-recording of a speech ostensibly written by another student. In one early study, the essay and speech expressed views about racial segregation. The experimenters varied two factors. One concerned whether the speeches adopted an attitude in favour of or against racial segregation. The other concerned the degree of choice that the speech maker (the hypothetical target person) had about what attitude to adopt. In the 'choice' condition, subjects were told that the target person had chosen whether to write a pro- or an anti-essay. In the 'no choice' condition, subjects were told that the target person had had no choice about what attitude to adopt. He had been assigned to a particular condition as part of his course work. (In fact, all the essays in this study had been written by the experimenters.) The subjects were asked, amongst other things, to estimate the attitudes of the speech maker to racial integration. For subjects in the 'choice' condition, the issue was clear enough. If the target person chose which attitude to adopt, and the speech was pro-segregation, then the person had a pro-segregation attitude; and if it was anti-segregation, then the person had an anti-segregation attitude. But what of subjects in the 'no choice' condition? Since the subjects knew (and this was checked out by the experimenters later) that the speech was delivered under instructions to adopt a particular stance, they should say that the speech was uninformative about the attitude of the writer. In fact, even in the 'no choice' condition, the subjects inferred attitudes congruent with the speech. This seems a good demonstration of the tendency to attribute events to the person, and to underestimate the importance of contextual variables in causing behaviour.

Jones's studies are powerful demonstrations of the tendency to explain behaviour in terms of the characteristics of the actor. Can you think of important examples of this tendency in everyday life?

The tendency to see persons as origins may be partly reflected in the tendency for people to blame victims for their fate, and even for victims of illnesses and disasters to blame themselves. This has been found for a wide range of outcomes including rape, AIDS and other illnesses, accidents, and bereavement. But it is not the case that everyone always explains outcomes in terms of the actor. The tendency towards victim blaming is moderated by a wide range of individual and group factors. For instance, the attitudes held by men towards women are related to the degree of victim blame found in rape cases; and general political attitudes are related to different explanations for unemployment and poverty. The process should be seen not as an invariant, but as a powerful tendency which underlies our understanding of human action.

Before turning to the question of why this effect occurs, we must spend a moment on what it is to be called. In an influential paper, Lee Ross (1977) referred to this as the 'fundamental attribution error'. Is it an 'error'? It makes sense to refer to something as an error if there is a right answer and we know what that is. In the case of Jones's studies, the term 'error' sits uneasily, since the studies were never set up to measure the attitudes of the essay writers. On the other hand, it is certainly unnecessary to explain an act in terms of the person's attitudes when you have an entirely adequate situational explanation. Other writers prefer to refer to it as a 'bias' – a strong preference in a particular direction. Jones himself uses the term 'overattribution'. I am unhappy with all of these terms. They all smack of the implication that there is a 'correct' answer, and an 'unbiased' way of processing information or making attributions; and that the layperson is inadequate in this regard. I think it makes perfectly good sense to refer to it as a 'powerful tendency'. Whether that tendency leads to the 'correct' attribution on any particular occasion might depend on the particular circumstances. No doubt in some cases the explanation in terms of the actor may well be right, just as in other cases it might well be wrong. While it is important to realize that these tendencies can indeed lead us to error, it is more important for us to examine the processes underlying the tendencies and the functions they serve.

Heider (1944) himself offered a range of explanations for this tendency, based on cognitive and social processes. In some sense it is 'simpler' to explain outcomes in terms of the actor than to engage in an analysis of the relative contribution of person and situation to the act. Heider also draws on findings from developmental psychology, such as Piaget's work on animistic thinking in young children. For the young child, the agency that they themselves show in making things happen may be the origins of their understanding of the causes of action. These experiences of agency may be powerfully reinforced by others round the young child, who attribute intentionality to him or her. Other people's behaviour is explained in similar terms, and goals and intentions are also used to explain events in the physical world. This is related to ideas about responsibility, also mentioned by Heider. There is an integral relationship between the ideas of cause and responsibility, and people are generally held responsible for the consequences they have caused. Of course, there are various excuses that we can use to claim that we are not responsible for consequences that we have caused (such as 'It was an accident', or 'I could not have reasonably foreseen it'); but you are responsible for your acts and their consequences until shown otherwise. Surely it must work this way. I find it difficult to imagine everyday life in an ordered society where the rule was the other way round – that you are not responsible for your acts or their consequences until shown otherwise. Thus, the roots of our belief concerning 'persons as origins' may lie partly in the attribution of responsibility and the creation of social order.

BOX 3.5   Value of the experimental method

One of the great strengths of the experimental method is that it enables a systematic exploration of an effect and of what its cause might be. The studies of Jones and his colleagues used the 'attitude-attribution' paradigm to explore, in greater detail, the robustness of the tendency to attribute events to the person. For example, they investigated the following factors:

1   It is possible that the results of the study reported in Box 3.4 were a function of some unspecified feature of the *topic* used in the study. In order to rule this out, a range of topics was used in other studies. These included attitudes towards taking marijuana, attitudes towards medical care, and attitudes towards an amnesty for draft evaders. The fact that comparable results were obtained using different topics ensures that the results obtained were not simply due to the nature of the topic.

2   Another possible problem concerns the *information contained in the essays and speeches* that were presented to the subjects. In the initial studies, the essays were written by Professor Jones and his colleagues. Perhaps they knew a great deal about the topic and wrote highly sophisticated material. When reading or listening to the material, the observers may have thought that no ordinary student was likely to have such knowledge. They may have attributed the material to the attitude of the author because they assumed that only someone holding that particular attitude would have such specialized knowledge. To rule out this possibility, in later studies the material was prepared by other students. Again, similar results were obtained. So the effect was not due to any esoteric knowledge being used.

3   In order to explain why someone might have written an essay counter to their own attitudes, observers were told a plausible cover story. For instance, in one study they were told that the target person had been asked to defend that particular position as

part of an examination answer; in another study that it was material for a debate; in a third that it was material for an experiment. But perhaps the *observers did not fully accept what the experimenter told them.* After all, the persons defending the position did have a choice. They could have refused to do what was asked of them. It is difficult to establish whether or not the observers were thinking like this. However, if they were, they certainly underestimated the effects of situational factors on people's behaviour. We can say this because when the experimenter did ask a group of students to write essays (some of which were counter-attitudinal), none of the students refused.

4   Jones and his colleagues also systematically manipulated the *quality, strength* and *persuasiveness* of the essays. These manipulations made little difference to the observers' attributions.

5   In yet another study, the observers watched and listened to videotapes where the target person was apparently *reading out arguments that had been compiled by someone else.* Even here there was a significant effect of the attitude position taken, in spite of the 'no choice' instructions. Where the stimulus material consisted only of *audiotapes,* the effect was still obtained. However, there was one condition in which the effect was not obtained. This was where the observer was told that the target person had simply copied the essay from someone else!

The series of experiments show that the effect observed is a robust one. There seems to be a strong association of actor and act, even when one is told that the act was carried out for reasons unconnected with the actor's attitudes. The experimental method enables us to see *if the same processes occur in other contexts and conditions.*

I will conclude this section with two quotations from Jones (1979) to remind you of the general issue we are dealing with, and its implications:

[making] inferences from behaviour about personality, is a ubiquitous activity of paramount significance for all of us. Understanding how people make inferences about others' stable characteristics from observations of their behaviour in various contexts is also one of the most fundamental problems in social and clinical psychology.

Later Jones goes on to say:

[the] fundamental attribution error may create havoc in the courts, the schoolroom, and the family to say nothing of the special arenas of counselling and diagnosis. Greater concessions to situational pressure and greater ambiguity tolerance may be the ultimate beneficiaries of the sustained analysis of the fundamental attribution error and its determinants.

(1979, pp. 107, 108)

3.2   Divergent perspectives in explanation: actors and observers

Consider the following scenario. Imagine you have just seen a cyclist riding dangerously across a red traffic light. From the previous discussion of persons as origins, we would expect the observer to explain the act in terms of the characteristics of the actor. Thus, as the observer you might say, 'What a careless person!' But what of the cyclist? Is the cyclist likely to explain the act in the same way? Or is the cyclist more likely to explain it in terms of being late for an appointment and so being in a hurry? To take another example, suppose you see a person walking along loaded with shopping which then gets tipped on to the pavement? Another person stops and helps the shopper collect the strewn objects and put them safely back. You might think, 'What a helpful person!' But what of the person – the 'helper'? How do you suppose the helper might explain his or her own behaviour? The idea that different people explain events in different ways may not be news, but surely it is news if we can characterize these differences in a systematic way. The claim is that while the observer is more likely to explain the act in terms of the characteristics of the actor, the person performing the act is more likely to explain the act in terms of the situation.

Now let us turn to an experimental demonstration of this. The subjects in a study by Nisbett et al. (1973) had agreed to participate in an experiment to do with decision making. They met in the lab in pairs, and were assigned to roles – one as the person 'making the decisions' (the 'actor'), the other observing the actor from the other side of a one-way mirror (the 'observer'). The actor was then approached by a third party – ostensibly nothing to do with the study – and asked if she would volunteer for a good cause (showing people round the university campus as part of an effort to raise money for a centre concerned with education amongst underprivileged groups). The actor, making this decision, was watched by the observer. After the decision had been made, the actor and the observer were asked to fill in a questionnaire. Amongst the questions asked of the observer was how likely the actor would be to volunteer for another good cause. And the comparable question was asked of the actor ('How likely are you … ?'). The logic underlying this is as follows: if the decision to volunteer was attributed largely to the actor's personality, then you would assume that she would volunteer for another good cause (because she is a helpful person). If it is attributed more to the situation, then you would not expect her to volunteer for the other cause. The results show that there was a stronger tendency for the observer to attribute the act to the disposition of the actor than for the actor to attribute the act to her own disposition.

How would you account for these differences in attribution by actors and observers? How would you test whether these hypotheses were correct?

Several different processes may be involved in this effect, and we do not have to choose between them since they are all relevant.

1 Perceptual focus

Perhaps the divergence in attribution is literally a function of difference in perspective. The observer is looking at the actor. It is normally the actor's behaviour that shows more movement and is more attention-gaining than the situation, which is relatively static. The actor, on the other hand, is not looking at him/herself, but at the context. There have been various tests of this perceptual hypothesis, some involving the use of mirrors to focus attention on self, others which have presented subjects with videotapes of social interactions taken from different perspectives and examined the effects of these on attribution. Sure enough, they find effects of perceptual orientation on attribution. I think this is of enormous importance in everyday life. In all our interactions we are literally looking at each other from different perspectives. As lovers, parent and child, interviewer and interviewee, professional and client, teacher and pupil – we are likely to have different understandings of what is going on partly because of our visual perspective. There must therefore be a deep-seated underlying tendency to explain each other's behaviour in different ways, simply as a function of the fact that we have different perspectives. These differences are likely to be implicit, and taken for granted, and so seldom realized or explored. And if our explanations do differ in a systematic way, then it is hardly surprising that we have difficulty communicating with each other.

2 Informational variables

Another process contributing to actor–observer differences lies in the different information available to the people involved. The observer only has information from one event and he or she tends to generalize from that. The actor has information about his or her own behaviour over longer periods of time. For instance, the actor knows that on some occasions he or she behaves in a helpful way and at other times not. This does assume that the actor's behaviour is quite variable, and it is likely that this assumption is correct. Work on the validity of personality traits has shown that people are far less stable in their behaviour than many psychologists and laypersons might expect.

3 Motivational variables

It was mentioned earlier (see section 1.3) that one of the main functions of attribution is to satisfy the need to control and predict one's environment. Explaining a person's behaviour in terms of their personality enables us to anticipate their future behaviour, and to organize our own behaviour accordingly. Actors, on the other hand, want to maintain their freedom to behave in different ways to meet the demands of each new situation, and so prefer to see their behaviour as a flexible response to the situation, rather than the function of the same behaviour pattern.

From our discussion of these perceptual, informational and motivational processes, it should be clear that the actor–observer differences described need not always occur. In fact, by understanding the underlying processes it is possible to predict when they will and when they will not. Take for instance the case of a quarrel between two partners, where one blames the other, and explains what is going on in terms of his or her underlying personality. Our understanding of the perceptual processes involved in attribution would lead us to expect that if they saw a film of the quarrel from each other's physical perspective, this should change their attributions. Similar effects may be obtained by encouraging them to process information more carefully and thoroughly – for instance, by reminding them of instances where the other person behaved in a positive and sensitive way. And if one partner is motivated not simply to predict the other's behaviour in order to cope with it, but is motivated to maintain the relationship, and to change the other's behaviour, then attributions to the situation may be more likely.

Review of section 3

- There is a powerful tendency to explain a person's behaviour in terms of his or her own characteristics, rather than in terms of the situation.

- Compared with observers, however, actors are more likely to explain their behaviour in terms of the situation.

4 Informational and conversational processes

Let's start this section with a puzzle.   ACTIVITY 3.5

Here is some information about John:

1 John usually fails his history examinations.

2 Hardly anyone else failed their history examination.

3 John failed most of his other examinations.

Please write down your answer to this question: Why did John fail his history examination?

Before we consider your explanation, I should provide some context. In the previous section, where we considered actor–observer differences in explanation, I mentioned the importance of informational and motivational processes in arriving at an explanation. The present section begins by considering some of the informational processes; while motivation will be considered when we return to the importance of control in section 5.

4.1   Mainly about information processing

Now, let us return to your explanation of why John failed his history exam. Did you conclude that it was something about John, probably that he was not very bright or that he was chronically lazy? That is what one influential model of how a person arrives at an attribution of causality would predict (Kelley, 1967, 1973). We generally think of the cause of an event as that which produces it or makes it occur. In more formal terms it is that which is present when the effect is present and absent when the effect is absent. The cause and the effect covary. In the present example, the effect we are seeking to explain is that of the *failure* in the history examination. Let's see where we can get to by analysing what covaries with this failure.

Proposition 1 tells us that the effect (failure) covaries with both John and with history exams. Such information about the responses of the person to the target (here, a history exam) on other occasions is called consistency information.

Proposition 2 tells us that the effect (failure) does not occur in the absence of John. It does not covary with the history exam. Such information about the responses of other people in the same situation is called consensus information.

Proposition 3 tells us that the effect (failure) always occurs in the presence of John (i.e. it covaries with John). Such information about the responses of the person in other similar contexts is called distinctiveness information.

Hence the effect is present when John is present, and absent when John is absent. So this analysis of covariation suggests that the failure was caused by John.

This is a rough sketch of Kelley's model. He adopted the analogy of a scientist to model the layperson's thinking and suggested that laypersons carry out a kind of analysis of variance on the data they have and use that to arrive at causal attributions – just as psychologists might carry out an analysis of variance on their data and come to their conclusions about what causes what. The general idea is that people arrive at an attribution of causality as a function of their analysis of covariation, and that this covariation is coded along the dimensions of consistency, consensus and distinctiveness (CCD). The pattern of CCD information presented in the example above leads to an attribution in terms of the person; but other patterns of covariation lead to other attributions (for instance, to the 'stimulus' (the history exam), to the circumstances (e.g. a noisy examination hall), or to the interactions between the person, the stimulus and the circumstances (see Jaspars, 1983)).

Is this an accurate description of the processes involved in arriving at an attribution? Many studies have done more or less what we have just done. They present people with an event, present them with varying combinations of CCD information, and ask them to explain why the event took place. These studies have shown some support for the covariational model (e.g McArthur, 1972). Such studies show that people *can* process information in that way. But is that what people *normally* do? Studies using more open-ended formats have suggested that people are not particularly concerned about CCD information, and that they adopt a variety of shortcuts rather than engage in a broad general information search (see, for instance, Garland et al., 1975; Lalljee et al., 1984; Hewstone, 1989).

Let us consider two major objections to the covariational model. First, the idea of a general information search assumes that we have little prior knowledge to go on. Earlier in the chapter, I showed how event prototypes influence categorization, the building block of understanding. Since explanation is a feature of event prototypes, categorization is related to explanation. If the episode of receiving negative comments on your assignment is categorized as 'being rude', then one set of explanations is likely to be invoked. People are rude because they want to put you down, or because they are rude people, or because they are in foul moods, or because they think too much of themselves. Alternatively, if the episode is categorized as 'being frank', then another set of explanations may be invoked (such as wanting to help, being honest and straightforward, etc.) There is evidence to support the idea that such processes do operate (Lalljee et al., 1992). Our explanations then do not involve a *general* information search, but call upon our prototypes and the stock of beliefs we have about the world and the way it works.

Besides having a great deal of prior knowledge, much of it derived from general cultural sources, to guide our explanations, the general character of our explanations is predisposed through our language.

Here are brief descriptions of two events followed by two possible explanations for each. In each case, please indicate which explanation is the more likely. Please reply to this rapidly without a great deal of analysis.

ACTIVITY 3.6

Event A: Ted helps Paul. Why?

Explanation 1: It is mainly to do with Ted.

Explanation 2: It is mainly to do with Paul.

Event B: John likes Peter. Why?

Explanation 1: It is mainly to do with John.

Explanation 2: It is mainly to do with Peter.

It is likely that you explained Event A more in terms of Ted, and Event B more in terms of Peter. This would be consistent with the findings of Brown and Fish (1983). They showed that different kinds of verbs seem to imply different patterns of causality, and that this is frequently signalled by the availability of adjectival forms. From 'help', we can get 'helpful' for someone who helps most other people, but there is no corresponding word to describe someone who is helped by most other people. In contrast, from 'like' we get 'likeable' for someone who most people like; but there is no equivalent for someone who goes round liking most people. Of course, this does not mean that helping is always explained in terms of the person helping, or liking in terms of the person liked. We can easily say 'He's so helpless that everyone helps him' or 'That's John, he likes most people'. While there is something in 'helps' that directs our explanation towards the helper and something in 'likes' that directs our explanation towards the person liked, other processes are also at work when we explain any act of helping. The point here is that language carries with it some of the burden of explanation.

The second major objection to the covariational approach lies in its assumption that there is 'an explanation' for an event. In fact, there are several conditions which contribute to a particular outcome. John may have failed his history test because he is not very bright and very lazy, and he may also have gone to a school that does not encourage pupils who are not very academically able, and his parents may have paid little attention to his work. Rather than thinking of 'the' cause, we can think of these conditions as a 'causal field' (Mackie, 1974). How do we decide what are the constituents of the causal field? No doubt we start with ideas that are 'given', we draw on the stock of ideas that we have about events like that and why they occur; and check if they operate in this particular case (Lalljee et al., 1984; Pyszcznski and Greenberg, 1987). As we shall see in section 4.2, such an approach makes possible the flexibility with which explanations can be used in conversation.

In spite of its shortcomings, Kelley's analysis of variance model has played a crucial role in the development of work in this area. In the 1950s, much of the research on the processes involved in forming impressions of other people flowed from the idea that people are constantly distorting their views of others as a result of their own wishes, desires and motives. Rather than seeing people as distorters of information, the analysis of variance model saw the person as a seeker after truth who came to conclusions on the basis of a careful and systematic weighing of the evidence. Kelley's work on attribution processes (of which the analysis of variance model is just one part) resulted in an enormous increase in interest in the cognitive processes which underlie the ways in which we experience events.

4.2   Mainly about conversation

Given that there are a variety of conditions that lead to a particular effect, do we come out with the entire list of conditions when asked why John failed his history test? This seems unlikely. The explanations we give to others are usually brief and to the point. What principles guide causal selection? In order to answer the question in a systematic way, we should turn to a branch of linguistics called pragmatics, which is concerned with the way in which language is used in communication.

Notice we have now changed focus and our level of analysis. Unlike Kelley, and the 'scientist' model of explanation, where explanation is seen as an intrapsychic process, we are now considering it in its familiar interactional context as a communicative act. Following Leech (1983) we can think of language use in interpersonal encounters as being guided by two major principles: the *cooperative principle* and the *politeness principle*. These conversational postulates enable the resolution of a number of problems of understanding the meanings of utterances, but it is beyond the scope of this chapter to follow through with those issues. However, we will examine their implication for causal selection.

---

1   Assuming that the following explanations of why John failed his history test are both true, under what circumstances do you think each of them might be mentioned?

Explanation 1: Because he is lazy.

Explanation 2: Because the school is not very good.

2   Here is a brief extract from a possible dialogue between two people, A and B:

A: 'What caused the fire?'

B: 'The oxygen in the atmosphere.'

Under what conditions would B's answer be appropriate?

ACTIVITY 3.7

4.2.1   The cooperative principle

At first glance, B's answer in the second example in Activity 3.7 seems absurd: not because it may not be true, but because it violates the cooperative principle – it tells the other person what he or she already knows. There is normally oxygen in the atmosphere, we take that for granted, and want to know what made the difference in this particular case. If, however, the fire took place in a scientific laboratory which was supposed to be free of oxygen, it would make perfectly good sense to answer 'Because of the oxygen in the atmosphere'.

The cooperative principle enjoins speakers to say things that are true, and not say things for which they lack evidence; to be informative, giving the listener the right amount of information; to be relevant; and to avoid obscurity and ambiguity (Grice, 1975). The cooperative principle enjoins us to be as informative *as required*. So you would probably not list all the conditions that led to the effect (e.g. to the fire), because they would mostly be unnecessary to the interactional purposes.

The importance of the cooperative principle for the selection of explanations was demonstrated by Slugoski et al. (1993). In one of their studies, subjects were presented with information about a person ('Jack') who had done well in his Chemistry A levels. They were given a sheet of background information, part of which described the excellence of the school, its science staff, laboratories and equipment, etc. Part of it described Jack as very intelligent, well prepared, calm, etc. The subjects took part in two different experimental conversations – with a laboratory task in between. Both conversations were supposedly with educational researchers, but while in one case the researcher was apparently familiar with the school (but not with Jack), in the other case the researcher was apparently familiar with Jack but not with the school. What the subjects said in each conversation was tape-recorded, and then coded for the degree to which it explained Jack's success in terms of him and in terms of the school. There is a strong effect of the shared information on the information presented. If the interlocutor (i.e. the supposed educational researcher) knows about Jack (but not the school), the attributions give more weight to the school; where the interlocutor knows about the school (but not Jack), the attributions give more weight to Jack. I wonder if interlocutors take into account the fact that the speaker is tailoring the explanation of an event to meet what she or he sees as the knowledge that the other person has. If not, they could emerge with an incorrect view of what the speaker thinks about the causes of the event. That would be another source of misunderstanding and miscommunication between people. I know of no empirical evidence that addresses this issue.

4.2.2   The politeness principle

The politeness principle is concerned with the 'face' of the participants. In social interaction we are concerned not simply with our own 'face', but also with the 'faces' of the other participants. The politeness principle is concerned with such issues as tact, modesty, and generosity. We would expect these principles to be relevant to the question of causal selection. There are a number of experiments that show that the explanation one adopts may vary as a function of the audience to which it is presented. For instance, Schlenker et al. (1990) showed that people are likely to engage in more cautious and less boastful explanations if they anticipate a critical audience than if they anticipate a supportive one. Studies concerned with attribution and self-presentation or impression management show how explanations are tailored to save the face of the person providing the explanation. And it is worth noting that explanations do make a difference to the way one is seen by other people. For instance, the competence and likeability of a teacher whose student has just failed is, in part, dependent upon the explanation that the teacher offers. Those who explain the failure in terms of themselves are likely to be rated more positively on both these dimensions than those who explain the failure in terms of the student (Tetlock, 1980). Note that this research is focused on the face-needs of the explainer. There seems to be no attention paid to how explanations are used to protect and maintain the faces of the other participants.

We began this section by outlining a covariational model which described the processes involved in explanation as a search for information along a small number of general dimensions culminating in 'an explanation' for that event. Our final description involved thinking about explanations as communicative acts which draw upon intrapsychic, interpersonal and societal processes. For most events we have socially given explanations for why they occur, and apply these to particular cases. Little information processing may be involved. Sometimes we have to search from available explanations to find out what suits the particular case we are explaining. We generally recognize that a range of conditions must be satisfied in order for an event to occur, and have to select what to say on a particular occasion. The process whereby we select which explanation to provide on a particular occasion may be largely governed by the principles of cooperativeness and politeness.

In section 1 of this chapter, the functions ascribed to making sense of or explaining events included those of understanding, prediction and control. By incorporating the principles of cooperativeness and politeness into our discussion, we have begun to consider interpersonal functions as well. However, explanations are related not only to 'face' but also to identity. Thus, explaining poverty in terms of the lack of effort of the poor or in terms of the greed and avarice of the rich also involves a claim by the speaker to belong to a particular sort of group, which holds certain attitudes and values important. While cooperativeness and politeness help us to make a systematic start in understanding the interpersonal functions of explanation, they will not be adequate to do full justice to the range of functions that explanations fulfil.

Review of section 4

- The process of covariation cannot adequately account for how people interpret events.

- Conversational processes such as cooperativeness and politeness are central to an analysis of explanations.

5 Control and helplessness

This chapter began by considering the inadequacy of explanations in terms of chance, and describing how people seem to import considerations of skill into what are actually affairs of chance. The importance of control as a central motive in our understanding of events was stressed. Although control played no part in the discussion of informational and conversational processes in the previous section, the need for control may well underlie a person's search for information, and a person may well prefer an explanation that implies control over an outcome to one that implies none. In the present section, the focus returns to the importance of control. First, we shall look at the importance of control for elderly people; and then we shall examine in more detail the psychological consequences of helplessness.

5.1   Control and ageing

Stereotypes of ageing in western culture today are generally negative. Elderly people are frequently seen as helpless and passive, with failing memory, mental incompetence, and an inability to learn new things or to make any sort of worthwhile contribution to society. Research has addressed the question of the effects of such stereotypes on elderly people themselves, asking whether they might become, for example, more passive, if they are treated as passive and lacking in control. What are the psychological consequences of being looked after? Whilst homes for elderly people may well be run for the residents, the residents themselves may have little choice or control over what is going on. Might not the consequences of such a regime be passivity and helplessness, rather than control? But even if these are the consequences, does it really matter? Perhaps if people are well-looked after, that may be what they want and need – particularly at that time of life. Talking about control and so on is all very well, but might it disrupt the smooth running of the establishment? If the residents had control, would each inevitably want to do different things? The result could be chaos. Is there no way in which the residents' needs for control can be reconciled with the planning and uniformity that inevitably form part of an institution? Is the clash inevitable?

Perhaps we are already jumping the gun. Before we get into the question just raised, it would be sensible to see if control does make a difference to people in residences for the elderly. One of the most important studies to show systematic effects was carried out by Langer and Rodin (1976). Their study was conducted in a nursing home in the state of Connecticut that was well known for the quality of its care. The nursing home was on four floors and the residents on each of the floors had little contact with the residents on the other floors. So the investigators selected two of the floors (where the patients were comparable on a number of relevant indices) for their study. Data from 52 subjects formed the main results. The administrator called the residents of each floor together for a meeting. To one group he stressed the importance of their taking responsibility for what was happening in the establishment; to the other he emphasized how concerned the staff were about the well-being of the residents. The best way to give you an idea about how these two talks varied is to reprint them in detail (see Extract 3.1).

Extract 3.1

[*Responsibility induced group.*] I brought you together today to give you some information about Arden House. I was surprised to learn that many of you don't know about the things that are available to you and, more important, that many of you don't realize the influence you have over your own lives here. Take a minute to think of the decisions you can and should be making. For example, you have the responsibility of caring for yourselves, of deciding whether or not you want to make this a home you can be proud of and happy in. You should be deciding how you want your rooms to be arranged – whether you want it to be as it is or whether you want the staff to help you rearrange the furniture. You should be deciding how you want to spend your time, for example, whether you want to be visiting your friends who live on this floor or on other floors, whether you want to visit in your room or your friends' room, in the lounge, the dining room, etc., or whether you want to be watching television, listening to the radio, writing, reading, or planning social events. In other words, it's your life and you can make of it whatever you want.

This brings me to another point. If you are unsatisfied with anything here, you have the influence to change it. It's your responsibility to make your complaints known, to tell us what you would like to change, to tell us what you would like. These are just a few of the things you could and should be deciding and thinking about now and from time to time everyday. You made these decisions before you came here and you can and should be making them now.

We're thinking of instituting some way for airing complaints, suggestions, etc. Let [nurse's name] know if you think this is a good idea and how you think we should go about doing it. In any case let her know what your complaints or suggestions are.

Also, I want to take this opportunity to give you each a present from the Arden House. [A box of small plants was passed around, and patients were given two decisions to make: first, whether or not they wanted a plant at all, and second, to choose which one they wanted. All residents did select a plant.] The plants are yours to keep and take care of as you'd like.

One last thing, I wanted to tell you that we're showing a movie two nights next week, Thursday and Friday. You should decide which night you'd like to go, if you choose to see it at all.

[*Comparison group.*] I brought you together today to give you some information about the Arden House. I was surprised to learn that many of you don't know about the things that are available to you; that many of you don't realize all you're allowed to do here. Take a minute to think of all the options that we've provided for you in order for your life to be fuller and more interesting. For example, you're permitted to visit people on the other floors and to use the lounge on this floor for visiting as well as the dining room or your own rooms. We want your rooms to be as nice as they can be, and we've tried to make them that way for you. We want you to be happy here. We feel that it's our responsibility to make this a home you can be proud of and happy in, and we want to do all we can to help you.

This brings me to another point. If you have any complaints or suggestions about anything, let [nurse's name] know what they are. Let us know how we can best help you. You should feel that you have free access to anyone on the staff, and we will do the best we can to provide individualized attention and time for you.

Also, I wanted to take this opportunity to give you each a present from the Arden House. [The nurse walked around with a box of plants and each patient was handed one.] The plants are yours to keep. The nurses will water and care for them for you.

One last thing, I wanted to tell you that we're showing a movie next week on Thursday and Friday. We'll let you know later which day you're scheduled to see it.

Source: Langer and Rodin, 1976, pp. 193–4

When I first read these sets of statements, I was very surprised that they would be expected to make any difference to the residents. They do, and I am still surprised. The investigators used a range of indices including self-reports by the residents, ratings by an interviewer, and ratings by nurses who did not know about the study. Three weeks after the talk, the residents in the responsibility induced group gave themselves higher scores on ratings of happiness and activity. The interviewer rated them higher on alertness than the comparison group; and a wider range of ratings made by the nurses, some to do with overall improvement, others to do with more specific behaviour (such as the amount of time spent visiting other patients), also showed that the responsibility group came off better. What is even more impressive is that, in a follow-up study eighteen months later, these differences were largely maintained, and there was also a difference in mortality rates between the two groups. Those in the responsibility group showed a higher probability of being alive than those in the comparison group (Rodin and Langer, 1977). This field experiment clearly shows that enhanced control can make a critical difference to the well-being and longevity of elderly people. Now let us look at the implications of lack of control more generally.

5.2   Helplessness and depression

The opposite of feeling in control is feeling helpless, and it is to a theory of depression that emphasizes helplessness that we now turn. This theory of *learned helplessness* originated through a series of studies carried out by Seligman and his colleagues on learning in dogs (see Seligman, 1975).

They found that after dogs placed in a shuttle box had been exposed to electric shocks from which they could not escape, they became apathetic and simply accepted the shock. They seemed to show a range of behaviour that is generally associated with depression in humans. Further, when they were subsequently put in a new environment where they *could* escape from shock, they simply failed to learn that they could escape. Once they had learned that what they did had no effect on outcomes, they simply withdrew and made no further effort. Their behaviour was no longer a function of the particular context in which they were, but a function of a learned predisposition. As a result of repeated experiences of non-contingency between responses and outcomes, the animals seemed to have learned to be helpless. Seligman's dogs, when they had repeatedly experienced lack of contingency between their responses and their outcomes, showed many of the signs that seemed similar to those shown by depressed humans. So Seligman and his colleagues speculated that learned helplessness may be a cause of depression in humans.

Few of us will not have experienced a period of depression as a result of loss, failure and disappointment. The diagnostic criteria for a clinically significant episode of depression offered by the American Psychiatric Association involve the following: depressed mood most of the day, nearly everyday and/or markedly diminished interest or pleasure in all, or almost all, activities most of the day, nearly every day. Other symptoms of depression include significant changes in appetite and weight, insomnia or hypersomnia, fatigue or loss of energy, feelings of worthlessness, diminished ability to think or concentrate, and recurrent thoughts of death.

But a description of clinical symptoms does not do justice to the experience of depressed people. Depressed individuals feel worthless, that they cannot do anything, that life is not worth living. They generally have no interest in things around them, and even activities that previously gave them pleasure hold no joy. Between 9 per cent and 20 per cent of the population of the USA has significant symptoms of depression, a substantial number of people will have a clinically definable episode of depression in their lives, and the proportion of the population suffering from depression is increasing (Gotlib and Hammen, 1992).

There are two main types of depression: manic-depression and unipolar depression. The former is marked by great changes in mood from hyperactivity to apathy and is thought to have a different aetiology from unipolar depression. Our focus here is on unipolar depression. Chapter 2 has emphasized the importance of our biological make-up for understanding human behaviour, and a wide range of processes including genetic and physiological ones are probably implicated in the cause of depression. Even within unipolar depression, there may be different subtypes with different causes. Our purpose here is not to review the literature on depression, but to explore the part played by control and by explanatory style in our understanding of depression.

When Seligman and his colleagues applied the ideas of learned helpless-ness to humans, they realized that people responded to the situations studied in a variety of different ways and there were also marked differ-ences in the extent to which people generalized from one situation to the next. Their reformulation of the original theory emphasized the explanations that people gave for events as a crucial variable influencing people's behaviour, and consequently their proneness to depression. *Attributional style* (later called *explanatory style*), a person's tendency to invoke certain kinds of explanation rather than others, became the cen-tral intervening construct to account for these differences.

Let us look more closely at explanatory style and its measurement. There has been a great deal of research into attribution processes that shows that most people explain their successes in terms of themselves and their failures in terms of the situation (see Ross and Fletcher, 1985). We are already familiar (from section 3) with this *internal–external* dimension. But we need two more dimensions for our present analysis: *stability* and *globality*. A *stable* cause is one that is likely to continue over time; an *unstable* one is likely to change. Thinking 'They didn't like me because I am an irritable person' is providing a *stable* cause; while 'They did not like me because I was in a bad mood' invokes an *unstable* cause. An explanation for failing a statistics test like 'because I am bad at maths' is an explanation in terms of a cause that is *specific;* while an explanation like 'because I am not clever' is more *global*.

One of the main ways of measuring a person's explanatory style is the Attributional Style Questionnaire. Box 3.6 contains a description of the ASQ. There is evidence that there are stable differences between people in explanatory style. Broadly two main styles have been distinguished. Some people tend to explain positive outcomes in terms of internal, stable and global factors, and explain negative outcomes in terms of external, unstable and specific ones. Other people tend to explain nega-tive outcomes in terms of internal, stable and global factors and positive ones in terms of external, unstable and specific ones. While I have referred to these as 'two main styles', explanatory style is more appropri-ately thought of as a continuum rather than in terms of discrete categories.

BOX 3.6   The Attributional Style Questionnaire (ASQ)

Respondents to the ASQ are given the following instructions:

> Please try to vividly imagine yourself in the situations that follow. If such a situation happened to you, what would you feel would have caused it? While events may have many causes, we want you to pick only one – the cause if this event happened to *you*. Please write this cause in the blank provided after each event. Next we want to ask you some questions about the cause. To summarize, we want you to:
>
> 1   Read each situation and imagine it happening to you.
>
> 2   Decide what you feel would be the *major* cause of the situation if it happened to you.
>
> 3   Write one cause in the blank provided.
>
> 4   Answer three questions about the cause.

The ASQ presents subjects with six bad events (e.g. you meet a friend who acts with hostility towards you; you can't get all the work done that others expect of you) and six good events (e.g. you do a project that is highly praised; your boyfriend or girlfriend is treating you more lovingly). The subjects are asked to rate the cause of each event on 7-point scales according to its internality versus externality, stability versus instability, and globality versus specificity.

So, for each cause, subjects answer the following questions:

> Is this cause due to something about you or something about other people or circumstances?
>
> In the future will this cause again be present?
>
> Is the cause something that influences this situation or does it also influence other areas of your life?

Ratings are made in the direction of increasing internality, stability, and globality, and they are averaged across the good and bad events separately. A composite explanatory-style score is sometimes formed by combining scores from the three dimensions.

Source: adapted from Peterson et al., 1993, p. 156

Returning to our discussion of depression, Seligman and his colleagues suggested that explaining negative events in terms of internal, stable, and global causes was a factor in the aetiology of depression. If a failure is explained in terms of oneself, then this has negative consequences for one's self-esteem. If it is explained in terms of a stable cause, then little can be done to change it. If it is due to a global cause, then there are no other comparable domains in which one might influence outcomes. It would not be surprising then if experiencing a series of negative events, together with a tendency to explain the events in terms of internal, stable and global causes, were related to depression.

But is it? Three separate questions need to be addressed. The first is whether it is true that the explanatory style of depressed people is different from that of non-depressed people in the way predicted. The second question concerns whether any difference in explanatory style (if it exists) is not just a correlate but also a cause of depression rather than a symptom. Finally we may ask whether changes in a person's explanatory style during therapy lead to change in depression. The answer to all these questions seems to be 'yes', but with differing levels of certainty.

Analysing over a hundred studies which compared the explanatory styles of depressed and non-depressed people, Sweeney et al. (1986) showed that there is a clear relationship between depression and explanatory style. Further, studies have shown that the explanatory style is specific to depressed people, and not for instance simply a function of any form of mental illness (e.g. schizophrenia) or the result of hospitalization for other medical or surgical reasons (Raps et al., 1982).

The causal question is harder to answer. Not only are there fewer longitudinal studies, but their design and analysis need to be more complex. We have already seen that there is an association between depression and explanatory style. It is also the case that depression can be quite stable, such that depression scores at one point in time can predict depression scores at a later point. So both these factors, explanatory style at time T1 and depression at time T1 must be considered in the prediction of depression at time T2. It is only if explanatory style has an independent effect, after taking into account the importance of the earlier depression, that we can we make causal claims. Two studies of children aged about 10 years did find such effects (Nolen-Hoeksema, 1986; Seligman et al., 1984). Explanatory style predicted scores on a depression inventory 3 to 6 months later, even when initial depression scores were taken into account. Another study looking at how university students felt after failure on an examination found that explanatory style measured at the beginning of term did predict depression after failure (Metalsky et al., 1987). So the evidence seems to be in the right direction, but it is not unequivocal. While it seems clear that explanatory style has a causal influence on what we might think of as 'normal' depression (i.e. depressed feelings etc., but not of the intensity and duration to be considered a clinically significant episode), the evidence for adult depressed patients is less clear (see Gotlib and Hammen, 1992).

Finally, a number of studies have shown that explanatory style predicts recovery from depression (see Brewin, 1985). People who are depressed, but have relatively 'healthy' attributional styles, are likely to recover from depression more rapidly than people who do not – even when the initial level of depression is taken into account. Peterson et al. (1993) report some studies that show that therapeutic interventions which change explanatory style may also be an effective treatment for depression. Focusing exclusively on explanatory style is a rather narrow therapeutic focus. More generally, changes in ways in which people think about themselves and their explanations for their outcomes form part of cognitive therapy, and that has frequently been shown to be an effective treatment for depression, though not necessarily the only one.

5.3   More about explanatory style

In fact, the theory of learned helplessness, particularly the importance of explanatory style, has been applied to a wide range of social problems. These include achievement at work, in school, and in athletics, as well as interpersonal behaviour including shyness, loneliness and domestic violence. While in many of these studies the ideas of learned helplessness have been incompletely applied, and in many cases the evidence is equivocal, there are certainly some important successes. Physical health is a good example. Peterson (1988) investigated the relationship between explanatory style and two measures of physical health. Each respondent was asked to complete a version of the Attributional Style Questionnaire (see Box 3.6), as a measure of explanatory style. A month later, respondents were asked to list all the illnesses they had experienced during the past 30 days. They were followed up again a year later and asked to indicate the number of times they had visited the doctor during the past year. Respondents who tended to give stable and global explanations for negative events reported twice as many days ill (8.56 vs. 3.70) and almost four times as many visits to the doctor (3.56 vs. 0.95) as respondents who preferred unstable and specific explanations.

The processes that link explanatory style with illness are not clear. After reporting some further, exploratory, work, Peterson tentatively suggests that explanatory style may be related to a person's health-related life-style and their beliefs in their ability to change unhealthy life-style habits. His study was carried out with relatively healthy young adults, and the illnesses they reported were mainly minor infectious diseases like colds, sore throats and flu. Peterson reminds us that it is possible that the same relationships may not hold for more serious illnesses.

Peterson et al. (1988) looked at the influence of explanatory style on health decades later. As part of a longitudinal study based at Harvard University after the Second World War, a group of students was administered a large number of psychological and physical tests, and then followed up with medical checks at various time intervals. Some of the material collected when these young men were 25 years old involved recounting their experiences during the war. Peterson and colleagues extracted an index of attributional style from this interview material – and also tried to ensure that the differences in attributional style (which was analysed several decades after the interviews had been carried out) were not due to different wartime experiences. They found a relationship between explanatory style at 25 and health in early middle age (35–50)! In later middle-age the relationship dropped off. The authors speculate that health in later life may be more clearly a function of constitutional or life-style factors. While we must always remember that the effects obtained could be a function of other variables associated with explanatory style, the studies do form powerful evidence for the importance of explanatory style.

Peterson, Maier and Seligman have moved on from focusing on 'learned helplessness' and 'depression' to studying and promoting 'optimism', calling, in avowedly utopian moments, for the opening of 'optimism institutes' where research on control can be applied to schools, work settings and to society as a whole. But they also caution that optimism may not always be good for you. In the laboratory, the degree of control that a person has over an outcome can be systematically varied from 0 to 100 per cent, but outside the lab we do not know how much control we do actually have. Peterson et al. accept that, where one does not have control, perseverance may be a futile waste of energy, and it may be better to lie low, conserve one's energies, and wait until something changes. But they claim that, on balance, it is preferable for a person's well-being to be optimistic, even if this might involve estimating a degree of control that is illusory.

In this section we have shown that control is an important part of effective psychological functioning and that ways of making sense of the world that undermine a person's sense of control are related to psychological disturbance. Feelings of helplessness are frequently a function of repeated events over which one feels one has no control. Interpreting such events in terms of stable, global and internal causes leads to lower expectations, less persistence and feelings of shame and guilt (Weiner, 1992). What then are the origins of the differences in explanatory style? Dweck et al. (1978) have shown that the way in which a child explains his or her success or failure in school is related to the ways in which the teacher explains these. Seligman et al. (1984) suggest that the explanatory styles of children of both sexes are similar to those of their mothers. If the mothers spent more time with the children than the fathers, this would make perfectly good sense. In any case, imitation of parents and the treatment of the child by important people in his or her environment are two important processes involved in socialization. The way that others treat you is likely to be crucial to the development of your explanatory style, as it is for your self-concept generally.

In fact, the discussion has focused too single-mindedly on control. I did mention earlier that explaining negative outcomes in terms of self, and positive outcomes in terms of external causes has consequences for self-esteem. Depression is also related to feelings of lack of self-worth, and our self-esteem too may be partly anchored in our explanatory style. Further, the discussion has also focused exclusively on intrapersonal variables. Lack of social support has also been shown to be implicated in the causality of depression. No doubt social support is important in all kinds of practical ways, but undoubtedly one of the key features of social networks is talk. I would be most surprised if talk with potentially depressed friends did not include discussions about the explanations for events ('No, it was not your fault' or 'It was just bad luck, and I'm sure you can do it next time', etc.), as well as implicit and explicit statements about their worth. While it is not within the scope of this chapter to examine more generally the processes involved in the development of the self-concept, I now want to move on to consider cultural differences in the concept of the person and the ways in which these are related to how people interpret events.

Review of section 5

- Feelings of control over one's environment are important for a person's well-being.

- Explanatory style is related to depression and to physical health, though the processes through which they are linked are not entirely clear.

6   Culture and explanation

Psychology is still a predominantly American discipline, and most of the studies discussed so far, and the conclusions drawn from them, have been based on research carried out in the USA. While we often refer to North America and Western Europe as 'the West', there are clearly wide variations in the cultures of people living in these areas. Still, most of the participants in the studies described in this chapter came from groups whose roots lie in the Judaic-Christian tradition and the culture of ancient Greece. Inevitably, important questions arise as to the generality of these results. Are we studying processes that are general, or are we studying processes that are only relevant to a particular culture at a particular point in time? While there have been a considerable number of studies carried out in various other parts of the world, it is only relatively recently that cross-cultural studies are beginning to form an important part of social psychology (see, for instance, Smith and Bond, 1993). One reason for the current interest is the development of a potential framework for understanding the differences between societies, so studies are not left with the potentially lame conclusion that the psychological processes in some other cultures are somewhat different from 'the West'. In this section I want to examine some of the work in this burgeoning area. It is a recently developing area and, though the issues are of central importance, the comparisons I shall attempt to make will be incomplete. (Further discussion of psychology and culture will be found in Chapter 5 on the 'distributed' self.)

In 1980, Hofstede reported an analysis of questionnaire data collected from over 100,000 employees in over 50 countries who were employed by a multinational corporation which he refers to as 'Hermes'. Hermes had offices all over the non-communist world of the time, including America,

Asia, Africa, Australia, and Europe. The questions were primarily concerned with work-related issues, and aspects of the employees' work experiences. As a result of factor analysing the data from these questionnaires, he concluded that the differences between countries could be thought of as lying across four factors. These were power distance, uncertainty avoidance, individualism–collectivism, and masculinity–femininity (see Table 3.2 for examples of items that illustrate these factors). Of these, the individualism–collectivism dimension has received most attention. This distinction has been an important one in western thought for some time.

Table 3.2 Hofstede's four dimensions of culture-related values

Value	Questionnaire item	Response for high score
Power distance	How frequently, in your experience, does the following problem occur: employees being afraid to express their disagreement with their managers?	(Frequently)
Uncertainty avoidance	Company rules should not be broken, even if the employee thinks it is in the company's best interest	(Strongly agree)
	How long do you think you will continue working for this company?	(Until I retire)
Individualism	How important is it to you to have a job which leaves you sufficient time for your personal or family life?	(Very)
	How important is it to you to have considerable freedom to adapt your own approach to the job?	(Very)
Femininity	How important is it to you to have a good working relationship with your manager?	(Very)
	How important is it to you to work with other people who cooperate well with one another?	(Very)
Masculinity	How important is it to you to have an opportunity for higher earnings?	(Very)
	How important is it to you to get recognition you deserve when you do a good job?	(Very)

Source: adapted from Smith and Bond, 1993, p. 39

Before going on to the next section, please could you write down twenty different statements about yourself in answer to the question 'Who am I?' Answer as if you are giving the answers to yourself, not to somebody else. Write down your answers in the order in which they occur to you. Don't worry about logic or importance. Do it fairly quickly.

When you finish doing that, please return to the chapter. Your replies to the task will be considered shortly.

ACTIVITY 3.8

6.1   Individualism–collectivism and the concept of the person

In his discussion of the concept of individualism, Lukes (1973) distinguishes between what he refers to as the 'doctrines' of individualism, and its 'unit ideas'. The former consist of political, social, religious and ethical policies and practices; while the latter focus on views concerning the nature of the person. For individualists, like the philosophers John Locke or Thomas Hobbes, individuals are pictured abstractly, as given, with given interests, wants, needs, etc. Society and the state are seen as arrangements that are developed out of these prior needs and are justified by satisfying them. Hobbes, for instance, compared the development of people to that of mushrooms which, he went on to say, 'come to full maturity without all kind of engagement to each other' (quoted in Lukes, 1973, p. 77). This *abstract* conception of the person is central to individualism, and is also associated with other unit ideas such as the importance of autonomy, privacy and self-development. Marx, on the other hand, is severely critical of this idea of the isolated individual, which he sees as a fiction. Marx held that 'man is not an abstract being squatting outside the world. Man is the human world, the state, society' (quoted in Lukes, 1973, p. 75).

This suggests that the concept of self in a society which is dominated by individualistic ideas might be very different from one which is more collectivist in its orientation. While several studies have obtained broadly similar results, we shall consider one study that has compared the self-descriptions of people from Japan and from the USA, and then examine some research on explanations.

The psychological test that has generally been used to look at people's self-concepts is the Twenty Statements Test (TST). It is the test you completed before beginning this section. Cousins (1989) administered the TST to university students in Japan and in the USA in order to look at such differences.

He coded the responses into several categories. One central category for our present purposes is that of the 'pure psychological attribute'. Responses such as 'I am honest' or 'I am happy-go-lucky' would fall into this category. They are general, abstract descriptions of the person, usually personality traits. Contrast these with responses which specify the context of the behaviour, such as 'I am talkative in class' (which specifies where the behaviour takes place), or 'I am helpful to my family' (which specifies the other people in whose presence the behaviour occurs). These are examples of the category 'qualified psychological attribute' because they specify the context, rather than imply that the attribute is a general category of the person. 'Pure psychological attributes' are more decontextualized than 'qualified psychological attributes'.

Another important category was that of 'social role', which includes familiar role concepts such as 'a college student', 'a father', 'an accountant'.

ACTIVITY 3.9

Try to code your own responses to Activity 3.8 using three main categories: social role, pure psychological attribute, and qualified psychological attribute. Use a fourth 'miscellaneous' category for those responses that do not fit readily into any of these three (e.g. references to your likes, preferences and activities, etc.). This may not be so easy, since using such categories and performing such a 'content analysis' requires the use of a coding scheme which discusses the categories in much more detail and provides many more examples than you have. In order to check that the scheme is used reliably, at least two people code the data independently and their agreement is checked. Only then does the statistical analysis of the data proceed. Check if the proportions of your responses in the three main categories are similar to those found amongst the American students studied by Cousins presented below. If they are very different, how would you explain the differences?

There was a substantial difference between the American and the Japanese subjects in their use of 'pure psychological attributes'. 58 per cent of the responses provided by the American subjects fell into this category. The figure for the Japanese was 19 per cent. The difference in the use of the 'social role' category was in the other direction. While only 9 per cent of the American responses fell into this category, 27 per cent of the Japanese ones did. There was no difference in their use of 'qualified psychological attributes' – about 9 per cent in each case.

These results clearly show that the Americans tend to describe themselves in more abstract and general ways, and the Japanese describe themselves more in terms of social roles. This is what one might expect given that one is a far more individualistic culture than the other. The three categories we have focused upon comprise only part of the system used by Cousins. Other differences between the two groups in terms of less frequent categories, like 'activities' and 'preferences', also support the view that the Japanese descriptions are more concrete than those of the Americans.

How are these differences to be explained? Children develop from concrete contextualized thinking to abstract thinking, and it has been suggested that societies too develop in this way. This argument was first put forward to explain differences in modes of thinking between western industrial societies and simpler non-industrialized ones. It is unlikely that this explanation will serve even to explain the differences between industrial and non-industrialized societies, and it seems even more far-fetched to explain differences between the USA and contemporary Japan in this way.

The currently favoured explanation is that different societies have different 'concepts of the person'. In the West, the person is thought of as an autonomous unit, consisting of a set of core attributes, that are carried with the person through time and context. It is the sort of idea that is very much in harmony with the ideas of Locke and Hobbes mentioned earlier. In Japan, India and most parts of the world other than 'the West', people are seen in terms of their roles and relationships, in terms of their activities and interests, because of the interconnected networks in those societies. For people living in such societies, the self integrally includes social relationships and social context. Societies that are organized in particular ways – and this organization includes philosophical and religious beliefs as well as social organization – also have certain ways of looking at the person congruent with those ways. The roots of the individualistic western concept of the self have been sought in its Christian foundations (see Dumont, 1985), and over the centuries there have been a wide range of historical and social influences at work which have resulted in the particular concept that is dominant in the West.

Though most of the studies in this area have attempted to explore the concept of the person through written descriptions of one sort or another, an ingenious study by Semin and Rubini (1990) examined the insults that people employ. The study was carried out in Italy, and the investigators compared the frequency of types of insult in northern Italy, which is more individualistic, with those in southern Italy, which is more collectivist. Individualistic insults were those that focused on the person. They included references to the person's physical (e.g. ugly, fat) or psychological (e.g stupid, imbecile) characteristics; references using the names of animals (e.g. pig, swine); and references to excreta/dirtiness and sexual insults. Relational insults included those expressing incestuous relationships, sexual and other insults directed at the target person's relatives; and curses directed at other members of the person family. Partial support was found for the hypothesis that in the North there would be more individualistic insults than in the South. This is more vivid and closer to what happens in everyday life than written self-descriptions. Note too that the comparisons were made between two different parts of a Western European country. While our general characterization of 'the West' as individualistic may be a reasonable and an accurate one, it is clearly an oversimplification. There are important differences along this dimension within a country, and besides there are also likely to be differences as a function of context. Working in an organization and at a job that encourages individualism, a person may well show individualistic modes of thinking; but the same person may well adopt more collectivist modes when with their family or their local club.

6.2   Individualism–collectivism and explanation

We have noted that the concept of the person is culturally relative. Let us turn now to how this might be related to the explanations that are provided for what people do. Miller (1984) compared the explanations provided by Americans in Chicago and by Hindu Indians in Mysore for the positive and negative behaviour of other people, classifying these explanations into those that referred to general dispositions and those that referred to the context of the event. The participants were of four different age groups (8, 11, 15 and adults). There were no differences in the explanations offered by the youngest children: the Indian and the American 8-year-olds explained behaviour in the same way. However, there was a marked difference in the explanations provided by the adults. The American adults provided explanations primarily in terms of the general dispositions of the actor, while the Indians provided explanations more in terms of the context. This fits nicely with the idea, suggested by Shweder and Bourne (1982), that the Hindu Indians tend to describe themselves in more contextual ways than the Americans. However, there are methodological problems with both these studies. In particular, there was no control for the degree of acquaintance between the respondents and the people they were describing (or whose behaviour they were explaining). In the earlier section on actor–observer differences in attribution (see section 3.2), it was implied that if you have more information about a person, you are more likely to make situational attributions for their behaviour. So if the Indian respondents knew their target persons better than the respondents from the USA, this difference could account for the results obtained.

In a more recent study comparing Moroccan and Dutch children in Amsterdam, Van den Heuvel (1992) found that there were differences on a self-description task, but not on an attribution task. Van den Heuvel thought that, since the Moroccan children were from a more collectivist culture than the native Dutch children, they should show more collectivist styles of description and explanation. Sure enough, the native Dutch children did present more self-descriptors in terms of psychological traits and attitudes, while the Moroccan children offered more self-descriptors in terms of social characteristics like group membership. Since these Moroccan children were living in Amsterdam, and were about 10–11 years old, these results are very striking. However, there were no consistent differences on the attribution task. This may not be so surprising, since Miller too found no difference in explanation at that age. It does seem, then, that there may be no straightforward relationship between the concept of the person and the way in which behaviour is explained.

I am sure that in due course it will be shown that not only are there systematic differences between the concept of the person in individualistic and in collectivist cultures, but that there are also systematic differences in ways of explaining events. Let us consider the implications of such results for our notion of persons as origins of actions. Earlier in the chapter, I suggested that this tendency was a product of the association of person and action and a function of developmental, cognitive and social processes (see section 3.1). However, a range of individual and group differences were also mentioned. The cross-cultural research could show that very general cultural theories are also at work in our explanations. This theme will be explored in much more detail in Chapter 5.

The principles underlying the attribution of blame and of self-blame in different cultures and the consequences of such attributions for the psychological well-being of the persons concerned are also issues which need further investigation. Self-blame played an important part in the earlier discussion of depression. The general argument of Seligman and his colleagues was that depressed people explain their negative outcomes in terms of internal, stable and global causes; while non-depressed people tend to explain them more in terms of external, unstable and specific causes. Explanatory style has been shown to be an important predictor of a wide range of positive outcomes in the realms of mental and physical health. No comparable research seems to have been carried out in non-western cultures. However, there has been some work done on people's explanations for success and failure. There is some suggestion that the Japanese may show a 'modesty' bias rather than a 'self-enhancing' one, but the results are not entirely clear. Understanding differences of this sort becomes even more complex in cross-cultural studies because the meanings of terms like 'ability' and 'effort' may be different in different cultures. For instance, one group may see 'ability' as more stable than another; or 'effort' as less controllable. The reformulated learned helplessness model rests on certain relationships between explanatory style and other variables such as expectations, persistence, control and self-esteem. These relationships too are in need of cross-cultural validation.

Finally, a brief word about control. While there are social class and cultural differences in the beliefs that people have about the amount of control they can exercise over their environments, the importance of satisfying the need for control has been discussed by many anthropologists and historians (see, for instance, Malinowski, 1948; Thomas, 1971). The research considered in this chapter has focused its attention on controlling outside events – the environment. This emphasis follows the frequently enunciated goals of science – to understand the world in order to change it. In a collectivist society, however, where the happiness of the individual is expressed in part through the harmony of the group, an alternative goal might be to understand the world in order to change oneself.

7 Conclusions

This chapter has discussed some of the processes involved in interpreting events. The main focus has been directed towards intrapersonal processes. We looked at the cognitive processes involved in categorization through the use of prototypes; and perceptual and cognitive processes figured in the explanation of the 'fundamental attribution error' and of actor–observer differences. Cognitive factors again played a part in the discussion of the informational processes involved in explanation; and cognitive individual differences such as differences in explanatory style were shown to have important consequences for a person's physical and psychological health.

But while understanding may be one of the functions of explanation, the importance of motivational processes has been another central theme. The need to predict the behaviour of other people may be another process that accounts for actor–observer differences in explanation; and feelings of control – and, conversely, of helplessness – have been shown to be important factors in a person's well-being.

Less attention has been paid to interactional processes. They featured explicitly when we considered the conversational processes involved in explanation. However, the importance of interactional processes has been hinted at various other points in the chapter. It was mentioned that the prototype approach to categorization readily lends itself to disagreement about the categorization of unusual instances, and these may well be discussed in conversation. Interactions with adults were drawn upon to understand the origins of our prototypes and of a person's explanatory style; and the importance of social support for the development of depression was also mentioned.

Finally, we moved to the societal level, and looked at the relationship between different cultures, the ways in which these were related to differing concepts of the person, and this in turn related to the ways in which people explained events. But while for the purpose of this chapter the societal level was discussed last, it has implications for the other levels. Our explanations cannot be properly understood without taking into account cultural factors – not just informational and conversational ones. Individualistic cultures highlight the decontextualized self, and abstract characteristics of the person may as a result be the preferred explanatory form. Many of our prototypes are derived from cultural sources such as folk-tales and the media; and our category systems develop as tools to aid us in accomplishing the tasks that our particular environment sets us.

Further reading

Most of the research in this area is published in academic journals, and one profitable next step would be to read some of the articles that have been referred to in this chapter. Reading the original articles will give you a much clearer idea of the details of the methods used by experimental social psychologists. And the articles will also convey far more about the theories being explored than I have been able to do in this chapter. One central journal for the discipline is the *Journal of Personality and Social Psychology*.

Here is a list of books that you might find helpful.

Langer, E.J. (1983) *The Psychology of Control*, Beverly Hills, Sage. (This consists of a number of articles by Langer and her colleagues which deal with 'illusions of control', 'control in everyday situations', and 'loss of control and remedial treatments'.)

Peterson, C., Maier, S.F. and Seligman, M.E.P. (1993) *Learned Helplessness: A Theory for the Age of Personal Control*, New York, Oxford University Press. (An extensive review of the ideas of learned helplessness and their development; as well as their application to a wide variety of phenomena.)

Hewstone, M. (1989) *Causal Attribution*, Oxford, Blackwell. (An exhaustive review of much of the work on attribution theory.)

Smith, P.B. and Bond, M.H. (1993) *Social Psychology Across Cultures: Analysis and Perspectives*, Hemel Hempstead, Harvester Wheatsheaf. (One of the growing range of books on culture and social psychology. Chapter 3, 'Culture: the neglected concept', and Chapter 6, 'Social cognition', are specially relevant to the present chapter.)

References

Brewin, C.R. (1985) 'Depression and causal attributions: what is their relation?', *Psychological Bulletin*, vol. 98, pp. 297–309.

Brown, R. and Fish, D. (1983) 'The psychological causality implicit in language', *Cognition*, vol. 14, pp. 237–86.

Cantor, J.R., Zillman, D. and Bryant, J. (1975) 'Enhancement of experienced sexual arousal in response to erotic stimuli through misattribution of unrelated residual excitation', *Journal of Personality and Social Psychology*, vol. 32, pp. 69–75.

Clark, D.M. (1986) 'A cognitive approach to panic', *Behaviour Research and Therapy*, vol. 24, pp. 461–70.

Clark, D.M. (1989) 'Anxiety states: panic and generalized anxiety', in Hawton, K., Salkovskis, P., Kirk, J. et al. (eds) *Cognitive Behaviour Therapy for Psychiatric Problems: A Practical Guide*, Oxford, Oxford University Press.

Clark, D.M., Salkovskis, P.M., Hackmann, A., Middleton, H., Anastasiades, P. and Gelder, M. (1994) 'A comparison of cognitive therapy, applied relaxation and imipramine in the treatment of panic disorder', *British Journal of Psychiatry*, vol. 164, pp. 759–69.

Cousins, S.D. (1989) 'Culture and self-perception in Japan and the United States', *Journal of Personality and Social Psychology*, vol. 56, pp. 124–31.

Dumont, L. (1985) 'A modified view of our origins: the Christian beginnings of modern individualism', in Carrithers, M., Collins, S. and Lukes, S. (eds) *The Category of the Person: Anthropology, Philosophy, History*, Cambridge, Cambridge University Press.

Duncan, B.L. (1976) 'Differential social perception and attribution of intergroup violence: testing the lower limits of stereotyping of blacks', *Journal of Personality and Social Psychology*, vol. 34, pp. 590–8.

Duncan, B.L. (1979) 'The effects of race of harm-doer and victim on social perception and the attributional behaviour', *Journal of Psychology*, vol. 101, pp. 103–5.

Dweck, C.S., Davidson, W., Nelson, S. and Enna, B. (1978) 'Sex differences in learned helplessness: II The contingencies of evaluative feedback in the classroom. III an experimental analysis', *Developmental Psychology*, vol. 14, pp. 268–76.

Garland, H., Hardy, A. and Stephenson, L. (1975) 'Information research as affected by attribution type and response category', *Personality and Social Psychology Bulletin*, vol. 4, pp. 612–15.

Gotlib, I.H. and Hammen, C.L. (1992) *Psychological Aspects of Depression: Towards a Cognitive-Interpersonal Integration*, Chichester, John Wiley.

Grice, H.P. (1975) 'Meaning', *Philosophical Review*, vol. 66, pp. 377–88.

Heider, F. (1944) 'Social perception and phenomenal causality', *Psychological Review*, vol. 51, pp. 358–74.

Heider, F. (1958) *The Psychology of Interpersonal Relations*, New York, John Wiley.

Henslin, J.M. (1967) 'Craps and magic', *American Journal of Sociology*, vol. 73, pp. 316–30.

Hewstone, M. (1989) *Causal Attribution: From Cognitive Processes to Collective Beliefs*, Oxford, Blackwell.

Hofstede, G. (1980) *Culture's Consequences: International Differences in Work-related Values*, Beverly Hills, Sage.

Jaspars, J. (1983) 'The process of causal attribution in common sense', in Hewstone, M. (ed.) *Attribution Theory: Social and Functional Extensions*, Oxford, Blackwell.

Jones, E.E. (1979) 'The rocky road from acts to dispositions', *American Psychologist*, vol. 34, pp. 107–17.

Kelley, H.H. (1967) 'Attribution theory in social psychology', in Levine, D. (ed.) *Nebraska Symposium on Motivation*, Lincoln, University of Nebraska Press.

Kelley, H.H. (1973) 'The process of causal attribution', *American Psychologist*, vol. 28, pp. 107–28.

Lalljee, M., Lamb, R. and Abelson, R.P. (1992) 'The role of event prototypes in categorization and explanation', in Stroebe, W. and Hewstone, M. (eds) *European Review of Social Psychology*, vol. 3, pp. 153–82.

Lalljee, M., Lamb, R. and Carnibella, G. (1993) 'Lay prototypes of illness: their content use', *Psychology and Health*, vol. 8, pp. 33–49.

Lalljee, M., Lamb, R., Furnham, A. and Jaspars, J.M.F. (1984) 'Explanations and information search: inductive and hypothesis testing approaches arriving at an explanation', *British Journal of Social Psychology*, vol. 23, pp. 201–12.

Langer, E.J. (1983) *The Psychology of Control*, Beverly Hills, Sage.

Langer, E.J. and Rodin, J. (1976) 'The effects of choice and enhanced personal responsibility for the aged: a field experiment in an institutional setting', *Journal of Personality and Social Psychology*, vol. 34, pp. 191–8.

Leech, G. (1983) *Principles of Pragmatics*, Longman, London.

Lukes, S. (1973) *Individualism*, Oxford, Blackwell.

Mackie, J.L. (1974) *The Cement of the Universe: A Study of Causation*, Oxford, Clarendon.

Malinowski, B. (1948) *Magic, Science and Religion and Other Essays*, London, Souvenir Press.

Matthews, K.A., Siegel, J.M., Kullar, L.H., Thompson, M. and Varat, M. (1983) 'Determinants of decision to seek medical treatment by patients with acute myocardial infarction symptoms', *Journal of Personality and Social Psychology*, vol. 44, pp. 1144–56.

McArthur, L.A. (1972) 'The how and what of why: some determinants and consequences of causal attribution', *Journal of Personality and Social Psychology*, vol. 22, pp. 171–93.

Metalsky, G.I., Halberstadt, L.J., and Abramson, L.Y. (1987) 'Vulnerability to depressive mood reactions: toward a more powerful test of the diathesis-stress and causal mediation components of the reformulated theory of depression', *Journal of Personality and Social Psychology*, vol. 52, pp. 386–93.

Miller, J.G. (1984) 'Culture and the development of everyday social explanation', *Journal of Personality and Social Psychology*, vol. 46, pp. 961–78.

Nisbett, R.E., Caputo, C., Legant, P. and Maracek, J. (1973) 'Behaviour as seen by the actor and as seen by the observer', *Journal of Personality and Social Psychology*, vol. 27, pp. 154–64.

Nolen-Hoeksema, S. (1986) *Developmental studies of Explanatory Style and Learned Helplessness in Children*, Ph.D. thesis, University of Pennsylvania.

Pennebaker, J.W. (1984) 'Accuracy of symptom perception', in Baum, A., Taylor, S.E. and Singers, J.E. (eds) *Handbook of Psychology and Health, 4, Social Psychology Aspects of Health*, Hillsdale, Lawrence Erlbaum.

Pennebaker, J.W. and Skelton, J. A. (1981) 'Selective monitoring of bodily sensations', *Journal of Personality and Social Psychology*, vol. 41, pp. 213–23.

Peterson, C. (1988) 'Explanatory style as a risk factor for illness', *Cognitive Therapy and Research,* vol. 12, pp. 117–30.

Peterson, C., Maier, S.F. and Seligman, M.E.P. (1993) *Learned Helplessness: A Theory for the Age of Personal Control,* New York, Oxford University Press.

Peterson, C., Seligman, M.E.P. and Vaillant, G.E. (1988) 'Pessimistic explanatory style is a risk factor for physical illness: a thirty-five year longitudinal study', *Journal of Personality and Social Psychology,* vol. 55, pp. 23–7.

Pyszcznski, T.A. and Greenberg, J. (1987) 'Toward an integration of cognitive and motivational perspectives on social inference: a biased hypothesis-testing model', in Berkowitz, L. (ed.) *Advances in Experimental Social Psychology,* vol. 20, San Diego, Academic Press.

Raps, C.S., Peterson, C., Reinhard, K.E., Abramson, L.Y. and Seligman, M.E.P. (1982) 'Attributional style among depressed patients', *Journal of Abnormal Psychology,* vol. 91, pp. 102–8.

Rodin, J. and Langer, E.J. (1977) 'Long-term effects of a control-relevant intervention with the institutionalized aged', *Journal of Personality and Social Psychology,* vol. 35, pp. 897–902.

Rosch, E. (1975) 'Cognitive representations of sematic categories', *Journal of Experimental Psychology: General,* vol. 104, pp. 192–233.

Rosch, E. (1978) 'Principles of categorization', in Rosch, E. and Lloyds, B. (eds) *Cognition and Categorization,* Hillsdale, Lawrence Erlbaum.

Ross, L. (1977) 'The intuitive psychologist and his shortcomings: distortions in the attribution process', in Berkowitz, L. (ed.) *Advances in Experimental Social Psychology,* vol. 10, New York, Academic Press.

Ross, M. and Fletcher, G.J.O. (1985) 'Attribution and social perception', in Lindzey, G. and Aronson, E. (eds) *The Handbook of Social Psychology* (3rd edn, vol. 2), Reading, Mass., Addison Wesley.

Schlenker, B.R., Weigold, M.F. and Hallam, J.R. (1990) 'Self-serving attributions in social context: effects of self-esteem and social pressure', *Journal of Personality and Social Psychology,* vol. 58, pp. 855–63.

Seale, J. (1985) 'How to turn a disease into VD', *New Scientist,* June, pp. 38–41.

Seligman, M.E.P. (1975) *Helplessness: On Depression, Development and Death,* San Francisco, W.H. Freeman.

Seligman, M.E.P., Peterson, C., Kaslow, N.J., Tannenbaum, R.J., Alloy, L.B. and Abramson, L.Y. (1984) 'Attribution style and depressive symptoms among children', *Journal of Abnormal Psychology,* vol. 83, pp. 235-8.

Semin, G.R. and Rubini, M. (1990) 'Unfolding the concept of person by verbal abuse', *European Journal of Social Psychology,* vol. 20, pp. 463–74.

Shweder, R.A. and Bourne, E.J. (1982) 'Does the concept of the person vary cross-culturally?', in Marsella, A.J. and White, G.M. (eds) *Cultural Conceptions of Mental Health and Therapy,* Dordrecht, Holland, D. Reidel.

Slugoski, B.R., Lalljee, M., Lamb, R. and Ginsburg, G.P. (1993) 'Attribution in conversational context: effect of mental knowledge on explanation-giving', *European Journal of Social Psychology,* vol. 23, no. 3, pp. 219–38.

Smith, P.B. and Bond, M.H. (1993) *Social Psychology Across Cultures: Analysis and Perspectives*, Hemel Hempstead, Harvester Wheatsheaf.

Strickland, L.H., Lewicki, R.J. and Katz, A.M. (1966) 'Temporal orientation and perceived control as determinants of risk-taking', *Journal of Experimental Social Psychology*, vol. 2, pp. 143–51.

Sweeney, P.D., Anderson, K. and Bailey, S. (1986) 'Attributional style in depression: a meta-analytic review', *Journal of Personality and Social Psychology*, vol. 46, pp. 974–91.

Tetlock, P.E. (1980) 'Explaining teacher explanations of pupil performance: a self-presentational interpretation', *Social Psychology Quarterly*, vol. 43, pp. 283–90.

Thomas, K. (1971) *Religion and the Decline of Magic*, London, Weidenfeld and Nicolson.

Van den Heuvel, H. (1992) *Us and Them: The Influence of Ethnicity and Gender on Stereotypes, Attitudes and Explanations of Behaviour*, Amsterdam, University of Amsterdam.

Weiner, B. (1992) *Human Motivation: Metaphors, Theories and Research*, Newbury Park, Sage.

Wittgenstein, L. (1953) *Philosophical Investigations*, Oxford, Blackwell.

Zillman, D., Johnson, R.C. and Day, K.D. (1974) 'Attribution of apparent arousal and proficiency of recovery from sympathetic activation affecting excitation transfer to aggressive behaviour', *Journal of Experimental Social Psychology*, vol. 10, pp. 503–15.

Reflections

This chapter has focused on the ways in which we interpret or make sense of social behaviour in relation to both ourselves and others.

The theme of the interpreting self was explored at three levels of analysis – the intrapersonal, the interpersonal and the societal. Thus, some studies were seen to focus on processes 'within' the individual: the processes underlying the way we categorize, for example. Other studies demonstrated the influence of principles such as those for cooperation and politeness in communication between one person and another. Yet others pointed out that not only our conceptions of ourselves but also the ways in which we interpret the behaviour of others seem to be related to the culture in which we live.

Complex interactions

In the previous chapter, a strong theme was the complex interactions between different aspects of being, biological and social for example. Here again in this chapter, albeit from a different angle, we encounter the idea of complex interactions: that we must consider different levels of explanation and the ways in which these interact; that to understand individual processes, for example, we must also take into account the cultural context and vice versa. Another kind of interaction highlighted by this chapter is the way in which cognition and emotion are intrinsically interlinked. For example, studies on attribution style and depression would seem to indicate that the ways in which we make sense of events and attribute causality are linked with feelings, with our tendency to be sad or happy.

Autonomy and control

Chapter 2 also raised the question of determinism and autonomy. Just how much of our behaviour can be ascribed to our own intentions as opposed to being entirely determined? A strong theme in Chapter 3 has been the significance of a sense of personal control. Making sense of the behaviour of others and of ourselves, it has been argued, is part of the process of trying to deal with the world, a way of assuming control over events. Some sense of control in our lives, the work of Langer and Rodin and of Seligman et al. would suggest, is even necessary for people to remain mentally and physically healthy. The import of these studies then is to suggest that a sense of agency is a crucial feature in our experience of ourselves. We have to bear in mind, however, that Langer and Seligman's research was carried out in the USA. Given the findings of the cross-cultural studies also described in Chapter 3, how far would you expect their findings to hold for other cultural groups, for example in countries like India and Japan?

The studies of Langer and Rodin and of Seligman et al., which appear to show the importance of a sense of control, also illustrate another theme mentioned in the Reflections section of Chapter 2 – the self-fulfilling potential of much of psychological work. If one is alerted to these findings that emphasize the importance of a sense of control in our lives, perhaps this is likely to encourage a more autonomous style. If I believe that the expression of agency is an important aspect of who I am, then I may well be more likely to assert this in my life.

Practical implications

An interesting feature of this chapter is the reference to several ways in which the kind of research discussed here can have practical value. Langer and Rodin's research, for example, shows us how residential environments can be structured to allow for individual choice which, in itself, is likely to lead to the greater well-being of residents. Attribution style studies have useful implications for the clinical treatment of depression, panic and possibly other kinds of anxiety state too. Although the studies are not discussed in detail in Chapter 3, it has also been claimed that attributional style relates to children's performance in school (Weiner, 1979). If children think that their poor performance on a test, say, was due to some temporary situational cause like feeling ill on the day, then they cope better with the next test. But, if they attribute failure to long-lasting, internal and unalterable dispositional causes, then they do not expect to do well in the next test and their performance drops to meet their expectations. Training programmes designed to change the attributional style of pupils seem to produce good effects (e.g. Dweck, 1975).

There is practical relevance also for everyday life. Knowing something about the ways in which we attribute the sources of action (that as observers, for example, we are more likely to attribute the source of an action to the person doing it) can help us to be alert to such effects in our own perception of events.

The value and limitations of the experimental method

This chapter represents an experimentalist perspective in psychology which attempts to apply the approach of natural science to psychological phenomena. The methods of natural science also underpinned much of the work discussed in Chapter 2, on the biological perspective. The scientific approach, as presented in both chapters, has at its core the need to measure and observe in as precise a way as possible. However, there are some differences between the use of scientific method by the two perspectives. Chapter 2 distinguished between causal and functional analysis (the latter being seen, for example, in the approach of sociobiology). The emphasis in Chapter 3, though, has been solely on the search for causal connections. The best way to establish causal relationships is to test hypotheses by means of experiment, and this is the primary method featured in this chapter.

The illustrations and discussion in the chapter provide a useful way of becoming more fully aware of the characteristics of the experimental approach and its values and limitations. As we have seen, experimentation involves the careful manipulation of certain variables, while holding others as constant as possible, to see what effects that manipulation has. It has the ultimate aim of establishing cause-effect links.

Experimentation applied to issues in social psychology would seem to have much to recommend it. As the studies discussed in the chapter illustrate, this approach enables psychologists to penetrate and begin to understand processes (of which we would normally be unaware) which underlie our ways of making sense. And even if many findings might be discovered by simple reflection, experimentation can establish more firmly the existence of such effects and explore how they operate. As the series of experiments by Jones and his colleagues described in Boxes 3.4 and 3.5 demonstrates very nicely, our understanding of a phenomenon can be refined by variations in the way an experiment is performed. So, in order to understand more about why we tend to attribute attitudes to speakers (even when we know they did not choose to express the view in question), factors such as topic, form of presentation and context can all be manipulated to assess the particular effects they may have.

Because of the promise it holds, experimentation has been the chosen method of psychology since its beginnings in the late nineteenth century, when the methods of physiology (i.e. those of natural science) first began to be applied to the problems of philosophy. And, at the time of writing, it would be fair to say that the experimental approach is currently the most dominant approach in academic social psychology in the UK and the USA.

By no means all psychologists, however, have been convinced of its value. The discussion in this chapter has indicated some of the problems involved. The original assumption underlying experimental psychology was that there are universal processes which are true for all people and that these can be discovered by the use of experimentation. But, in social psychological research, we often find problems of generalization. An effect may apply for the subjects investigated but how far is this true for subjects of a different type or from a different culture? As we have seen, whereas American subjects have a strong tendency to see actors as the origins of their actions, Indian subjects may be more inclined to make situational attributions. Thus, the 'laws' of social psychology tend to be local rather than universal. It may also be asked how far the typical experiments we find in social psychology really explain, or how far they are essentially merely descriptive. For instance, the first example of a laboratory experiment you encountered in the chapter (Strickland et al., 1966) tells that participants bet more on dice before rather than after throwing the dice, but in itself it does not tell us *why* they did this. You might like to consider how many of the other experiments discussed in this chapter serve, in this way, to describe rather than explain.

Another problem with experiments can be artificiality. In order to control for random effects, it is necessary to set up conditions in a laboratory which may be somewhat remote from everyday-life situations. And sometimes the way experimenters set up an experiment can produce results which, although they may seem valid at the time, are off track. (As an example of this, consider the eventually-discarded covariance approach of Kelley as an explanation of how we make attributions; as the chapter points out, people *can* process information in the way that Kelley's model suggests, but this not what they *normally* do.)

More profound and problematic questions can also be raised. How far can the subtleties of social meaning be measured? To what extent is it appropriate to regard social behaviour and experience as causally determined? If the answer to either of these questions is in doubt, then this raises questions about the adequacy of experimentation as a method for research in this area.

The succeeding chapters in this book pick up on some of the issues discussed in Chapter 3. Chapter 4 will also focus on how we experience the world and ourselves; Chapter 5 will explore further the ways in which culture constructs our conceptions of ourselves and others; and Chapter 6 will explore how influences of which we are unaware (the 'unconscious') can shape the ways in which we think and feel. However, none of these chapters adopts an experimental approach. Of course, there are different limitations when we leave the seeming security of the experimental approach and we will need to consider them. It is worth being alert to these methodological contrasts at this stage, but we shall return for a fuller discussion of them later in the book.

We go on now to Chapter 4, which also explores the ways in which people experience their worlds, and where the significance of autonomy and choice is also a theme. These are looked at, however, in a phenomenological and experiential way.

References

Dweck, C.S. (1975) 'The role of expectations and attributions in the alleviation of learned helplessness', *Journal of Personality and Social Psychology,* vol. 31, pp. 674–85.

Weiner, B. (1979) 'A motivational theory for some classroom experiences', *Journal of Educational Psychology,* vol. 71, pp. 3–25.

CHAPTER 4
THE REFLEXIVE SELF: AN EXPERIENTIAL PERSPECTIVE

by Richard Stevens

Contents

1   Introduction: an experiential perspective

The central theme of this book is the different ways in which psychology can help us make sense of the self. In the analysis of the case studies (Windows) presented in Chapter 1, it was suggested that one feature of being a person was the centrality of experience, that 'each of us experiences the world through our own particular frame of consciousness'. Various features of the subjective experience of self were discussed, including a sense of agency and reflexiveness (or self-awareness). Chapter 2 took up the topics of both consciousness and agency (among others). But it was concerned to examine these from the standpoint of the light which biological studies might throw on them: for example, by considering the evolution of consciousness, and the relation between consciousness and the brain.

Chapter 3 shifted the focus from biology to mind and behaviour. But the approach, as in Chapter 2, was to use the methodological style of natural science. As we saw, this means observation, measurement and, where possible, experiments. So a person's experience is viewed, as it were, from the 'outside', usually being inferred from his or her responses and behaviour. The emphasis there was largely on the cognitive aspect – the person as problem solver.

This chapter will look more generally at the topic of *subjective experience* itself, especially from the standpoint of the experiencing person. It is difficult to give a precise definition of subjective experience but, in effect, it refers to 'first person experience' (i.e. what you, I, or any other person is aware of) and the process of being aware. The terms *subjective experience* and *conscious awareness* are largely interchangeable. But subjective experience tends to be used more broadly to refer to the totality of a person's experience, even where that is subtle and elusive; while consciousness (and conscious awareness) tends to refer to the focus of our awareness. We can also distinguish between awareness (i.e being aware of something) and reflexive awareness (being aware of being aware). Some of the different facets of subjective experience will be distinguished and discussed in the course of the chapter.

> Imagine yourself as a person without subjective experience or consciousness. In what ways would you be different? What would you be unable to do that you can do now? To what extent do you think that such an individual could be regarded as being a person?

This question directs your attention to how crucial subjective experience is. Our very sense of being depends on it. Without it we would have no conscious memories of the past or anticipations of the future; no feelings of love, compassion, tenderness or rage; we would have no awareness of ourselves, nor could we read, learn or connect with the subjectivity of others.

In spite of its centrality, twentieth-century psychology has, until relatively recently, tended to avoid subjective experience as a topic. The reason for this has largely been methodological. Although we may be able to express what we experience to some extent through language, our world of consciousness is largely a private affair, open only to our own introspections. The nature of such experience makes it difficult to apply the usual procedures of natural science, for to study subjective experience is to concern yourself with *meanings* (i.e. beliefs, feelings, ways of making sense and evaluating the world as perceived). Such a subject-matter, it might be argued, is essentially qualitative not quantitative: for while we may be able to describe our subjective experience, we cannot measure it, at least not without losing its richness and the *quality* which gives it its authentic feel. Nor is it usually relevant to set up experiments to test hypotheses which try to explain actions in terms of cause-effect laws. Although antecedent meanings may help to determine subsequent actions and ways of making sense, it is the overall pattern of meaning that is significant. The reductionist approach of experimental psychology which requires isolating specific, measurable causes or effects and examining the relationship between them is unlikely to yield much insight into this process.

Because of its subject-matter, this chapter marks a shift both in methodological approach and in the style of this book. It will draw on theoretical analysis and qualitative accounts rather than experimental research. This will also be the case with the perspectives presented in the remaining chapters of the book. This chapter, however, is also distinctive in the direct appeal it makes to personal experience. As it will focus on subjective experience itself rather than on its outward and observable manifestations, you will often be asked to consider the issues discussed in relation to your own experience. How do *you* experience the phenomenon in question? How far does a particular account make sense in terms of *your* experience? The activities and in-text questions often play this role of relating the discussion to your own life, and it is therefore recommended that you try each one as you encounter it, before reading on.

The title of this chapter refers to an *experiential* perspective. This means that it focuses on the experiencing person and the lived realities of existence. In fact, I have created this as a perspective by drawing on three related theoretical perspectives – phenomenological, existential and humanistic.

To adopt a *phenomenological* approach is essentially to try to study human awareness as we experience it. (It is called 'phenomenological' because it deals directly with phenomena, i.e. 'that which we are aware of'.) The fundamental questions we are concerned with here are: What is the nature of subjective experience and how can we conceptualize it? What constitutes particular experiences: what do they feel like?

BOX 4.1

The importance of taking a phenomenological approach is emphasized by Rollo May (1983). He recalls a time when he spent a year and a half in bed in a tuberculosis hospital. He read two key books on anxiety, one by Freud and the other by the Danish philosopher Kierkegaard:

> What powerfully struck me then was that Kierkegaard was writing about exactly what my fellow patients and I were going through. Freud was not; he was writing on a different level, giving formulations of the psychic mechanisms by which anxiety comes about. Kierkegaard was portraying what is immediately experienced by human beings in crisis ... Freud was writing on the technical level ... he *knew about* anxiety. Kierkegaard ... *knew anxiety.*

(pp. 14–15)

The assumption here is that, when we are studying the person in a social world, the most significant information is what people are feeling and experiencing. So we need to introspect on our own experience. Or we can ask others to do so and get them to give us accounts of this so that we can construct some understanding of the ways in which they make sense of some aspect of their world. Phenomenological accounts are often in the first person – the writer reports on his or her own experiences. But they can be third-person as well. This happens in novels, autobiographies and clinical reports. (We saw an example in Chapter 1 in the account of Leonard by Oliver Sacks.) But because subjective experience is essentially personal and private, phenomenological accounts inevitably involve some appeal to the experience of the reader. Although we may not have had the same particular experiences as those in the account, we can understand them by analogy with, or extrapolation from, our own experience.

The phenomenological perspective had its origins in German philosophy with thinkers such as Husserl. Subsequently, others such as the French psychologist Merleau-Ponty adopted a phenomenological approach to psychological issues. While different phenomenologists vary in the specifics of their approach, they all focus upon experience: their concern is with what is experientially real rather than abstractly true.

Today, direct phenomenological analysis of experience in itself is a relatively small and specialized area of psychology. Such studies typically require participants in the research (and often the researcher too) to reflect on and provide detailed accounts of some aspect of their experience (e.g. anger (Giorgi et al., 1971), being burgled (Fischer and Wertz, 1979), close friendship (Becker, 1987), intimacy (Register and Henley, 1992), authenticity (Rahilly,1993)). There are various methods for analysing such accounts. These may involve, for example, identifying key narratives, themes and statements and using the accounts to extract the constituents of an experience and its structural characteristics.

Phenomenological analysis is more likely to be coupled with other methods. Early in the history of psychology, William James attempted to relate reflection on his own experience to data from psychological experiments and what was known about the functioning of the brain. This 'mixed-method' approach is now being adopted in contemporary studies of consciousness which seek understanding by interrelating philosophical analyses with the results of cognitive experiments, people's reports of their own experience, and neurophysiological information about the brain (e.g. Flanagan, 1992). Many social psychologists, such as Goffman and Berger, have also been influenced by phenomenological approaches and incorporate the analysis of experiences into their accounts.

Existentialism also adopts the standpoint of subjective experience, but the focus is on the dynamic quality of human existence. Existentialism conceives of persons as being always in the process of 'becoming'. Its focus is on awareness of the human condition and what arises from the human capacity to reflect on our own experience of being a person. We have a sense of being able to choose our thoughts and actions, for example, and, in so doing, to help to create who we are. We are aware of being mortal and facing eventual non-being. We may also search to find some meaning and engagement with life.

Like phenomenology, existentialism also has its origins in philosophy. In the nineteenth century, Kierkegaard wrote of the need to face the fact of the finiteness of life. Later, Nietzsche stressed the power of individuals to choose and their capacity to create who they will become. In the twentieth century, Martin Heidegger extended the phenomenological approach to analyse the experience of being, or personal existence. Heidegger's ideas were taken up and made more widely known by French philosophers and writers like Sartre and Camus. They emphasized, for example, the notion of 'authenticity' to signify actions in accordance with existential realities such as our ability to choose. Psychiatrists such as Binswanger also began to adopt an existential approach in psychotherapy.

The third related perspective which has influenced the approach of this chapter is *humanistic psychology*. This originated in the USA during the late 1950s and the 1960s as an explicit reaction to the dominance of both the scientific abstraction of behaviourism and the emphasis on the unconscious of psychoanalysis. These perspectives, it was considered, left out of account much of the real stuff of human experience. The founders of humanistic psychology were strongly influenced by phenomenological and existential thinking. The central thrust of much of Carl Rogers' theoretical and therapeutic work, for instance, was to find ways of becoming more intensely aware of one's feelings and experience. Another influential figure in the humanistic psychology movement, Abraham Maslow, was concerned, not only with optimal personal development or 'self-actualization', but also with heightened consciousness in the form of 'peak experiences'. (For more detailed discussion of humanistic psychology, see Stevens, 1990.)

The experiential perspective of this chapter, then, draws its inspiration from an amalgam of phenomenological, existential and humanistic approaches. As a perspective, it is wide-ranging and, while it is not represented by a coherent body of interrelated research in the same way as (say) the experimental study of social cognition, it does encompass a lot of important work and ideas which have great relevance to understanding the self. We shall look at a variety of studies and approaches which are in the spirit rather than the letter of these specific traditions. My aim is not to focus on standard phenomenological or existential analyses but to refer to psychological studies and ideas which may serve to stimulate your thinking about your awareness of your own life. A particular model of the person emerges from the phenomenological-existential-humanistic traditions and it is this that guides the themes and approach of this chapter. Different aspects of this model will be discussed more specifically as the chapter proceeds, but its three dominant features are worth flagging here. (If you find the accounts below a little difficult to grasp fully at first reading, remember that these features will become more apparent later.)

- *To be a person is to experience oneself as existing in the world.* Subjective experience is always from the perspective of a particular person. We experience ourselves as body-mind unities, in that our bodies seem to be an integral part of who we are. The meanings which constitute a person's experience of the world emerge from the relationships between the experiencer and the objects and people which populate his or her world. In this sense, the world of experience is not confined to 'within the head'.

- *To be a person is to be an active, intentional agent* who engages with, and can influence, the world. Our lives are goal-directed. Such goals may be reflected upon – as purposes experienced as part of our lives (perhaps, for example, we may want to get a degree, become a psychologist or get married). Or they may be (in Merleau-Ponty's term) 'pre-reflective' – intentions evident from our actions, though we may have no conscious awareness of having intended to do the action in question. (These differ, however, from Freudian unconscious goals (see Chapter 6) in that they are usually fairly readily accessible to conscious post-reflection.) However, we are born into a world not of our choosing, with significant aspects which make us what we are (e.g. cultural and historical contexts, gender, particular parents) decided for us (Heidegger, 1962, has called this 'thrown-ness'). Our capacity for intentional action is therefore qualified – it does not constitute total freedom but rather what has been termed 'situated' freedom.

- *To be a person is to possess reflexive awareness.* An extraordinary feature of being human is our potential capacity for self-awareness – to be aware of our thoughts, feelings and ourselves. An extension of this is the imagination to conceive of possibilities, of alternative ways in which things might be. Such reflexive awareness is not only intrinsic to our experience of the world but can also provide an important basis for ways in which we act and live our lives. The capacity for self-awareness and for envisioning possibilities, when applied to reflecting on the conditions of human existence, may also confront with existential dilemmas.

Part 1 this chapter focuses on *studying subjective experience*. It begins with a ple of studies which serve to differentiate consciousness. It moves on look at theories which help us to conceptualize and gain access to th ays in which people experience their worlds. It concludes with discussi of a way (the use of metaphor) of conceptualizing consciousness itse nd of the role of imagination and fantasy in subjective experience. A c theme will be that conscious awareness not only enables us to repre r model the world about and within us but can also be a means o

Part 2 takes up more spe our reflexive awareness of being a person by discussing three issues – the experience of time (and finiteness), the capacity to cho e need for meaningfulness.

Aims of Chapter 4

The aims of this chapter are:

- To demonstrate that studying subjective experience is important for psychology and for understanding the person in a social world, and to indicate the problems involved in such study.

- To deepen your awareness of the nature of subjective experience.

- To present contrasting analyses of aspects of subjective experience, specifically the stream of consciousness, flow experience, modes of consciousness and personal construct theory.

- To consider the usefulness of metaphor as a way of conceptualizing consciousness.

- To demonstrate the varied roles of imagination and fantasy in our lives.

- To explore existential issues, specifically time and awareness of our mortality, our capacity for choice, and our need for meaningfulness.

- To stimulate your own reflection and thinking about the experience of life.

PART 1:   STUDYING CONSCIOUS EXPERIENCE

2   Differentiating consciousness: four studies

This section introduces four very different studies of consciousness. We begin with the seminal ideas of James on stream of consciousness. Then we move on to more modern work, by Csikszentmihalyi, on 'flow' experiences, Donaldson on 'modes of mind', and finally to Kelly and his personal construct theory. Each study comes at subjective experience in a somewhat different way. They thus provide a set of varied insights which help us to become more aware of aspects of our own and other people's experience (and the problems involved in conceptualizing these).

2.1   James: the stream of consciousness

At the end of the last century, William James provided probably the best systematic, phenomenological description of consciousness by a psychologist. His *Principles of Psychology* (first published in 1890) seems fresh and makes interesting reading, full of insights, even today. He was not so much interested in specific content – the particular thoughts or feelings a person might have – but in the universal features of consciousness (i.e. the general aspects which it possesses for all of us). So you can test James's analysis against what consciousness feels like for you.

James noted how conscious awareness is characterized by *continual change*:

> Our state of mind is never precisely the same. Every thought we have of a given fact is, strictly speaking, unique, and only bears a resemblance of kind with our other thoughts of the same fact. ... Experience is remoulding us every moment, and our mental reaction on every given thing is really a resultant of our experience of the whole world up to that date.
>
> *(James, 1950, pp. 233–4)*

He also stressed its *continuity* and flow – the *stream-like* nature of consciousness: 'It *feels* unbroken; a waking day of it is sensibly a unit as long as that day lasts, in the sense in which the hours themselves are units, as having all their parts next to each other, with no intrusive alien substance between' (ibid., p. 238).

James recognized, nevertheless, that subjective experience does not come in a homogeneous web. He distinguished *sub-worlds of experience*, like those of the senses, science, philosophical and abstract beliefs, the super-natural and myths, etc., each with 'its own special and separate style of existence'. There are contrasts also in both the *quality* and *pace* of consciousness: 'Like a bird's life, it seems to be an alternation of flights and perchings' (ibid., p. 243).

He worked towards a definition of consciousness:

> ... the mind is at every stage a theatre of simultaneous possibilities. Consciousness consists in the comparison of these with each other, the selection of some, and the suppression of the rest by the reinforcing and inhibiting agency of attention. ... The mind, in short, works on the data it receives very much as a sculptor works on his block of stone. In a sense the statue stood there from eternity. But there were a thousand different ones beside it, and the sculptor alone is to thank for having extricated this one from the rest.
>
> (ibid., p. 288)

You may have noticed some similarities here to the discussion of subjective experience in section 2.2 of Chapter 1. The significance of the flow of time which was noted there is implicit in James's notions of change and continuity. James's concepts of sub-worlds of experience and of the mind as a 'theatre of simultaneous possibilities' (with awareness at any one point being a particular selection and construction from these possibilities) also relate to the ideas discussed there of the *multiplicity* of personal worlds and the *reflexiveness* which enables us to adopt different perspectives to our experience.

This notion of the mind as a 'theatre of simultaneous possibilities' emphasizes that selection and attention play a central role in consciousness. James distinguishes between different kinds of attention, such as active or deliberate attention, on the one hand, and passive or effortless attention, where the directing of attention is purely reflex and responsive to other events, on the other. James also discussed the 'fringe' or 'penumbra' of consciousness around the central focus. This context or edge of consciousness gives a particular feel to what we are conscious of, may be the source of vague apprehensions or anticipations, and may serve to direct the focus of our awareness.

Another feature of consciousness in James's analysis worth noting here is that consciousness is always located in a person: 'The only states of consciousness that we naturally deal with are found in personal consciousnesses, minds, selves, concrete particular I's and you's' (ibid., p. 226). Consciousness in his view is always personal and therefore essentially private. (To what extent this is true is a question you may wish to return to after reading the next chapter.) James also discusses our *sense of self* and *will* (the ability to direct both thought and action) which he sees as core aspects of conscious experience.

Observing the stream of consciousness   ACTIVITY 4.1

As we have seen, James describes consciousness as characterized by the following features. It is continuous, constantly changing, always located in a person. It contains sub-worlds and differences in quality and pace. It involves selection from possibilities and attention applied in either a responsive or deliberate way. There is a less clearly perceived 'fringe' around a central focus.

If possible, find a quiet place to relax. Make yourself comfortable (e.g. take off your shoes if you like). Spend about five minutes quietly reflecting on the flow of your own experience. Then try to capture on paper what strikes you as the central features of your consciousness. Compare this with James's general features as summarized above. Do these now make sense in relation to your own experience?

Can you see any problems in constructing a 'scientific' psychology on the basis of this kind of analysis?

2.2   Csikszentmihalyi: flow experience

This American psychologist with a tongue-twisting Hungarian name (pronounce it like 'chikshentmeehai') follows in many ways in the tradition of the kind of phenomenological analysis which interested James. But whereas James's analysis ranged broadly over several facets of consciousness, Csikszentmihalyi's work, which is much more recent (1988, 1992), focuses on a specific aspect which he calls 'flow experience'. This notion has emerged from a number of studies of situations which people find either enjoyable or boring. In particular, Csikszentmihalyi has been interested in how people feel when they most enjoy themselves. He regards being conscious as meaning that 'certain specific conscious events (sensations, feelings, thoughts, intentions) are occurring, and that we are able to direct their course. ... Thus we might think of consciousness as *intentionally ordered information*' (1992, p. 26). In this statement, Csikszentmihalyi is emphasizing the capacity of consciousness not just to represent but to direct. Such direction (or intentionality) keeps 'information in consciousness ordered' (ibid., p. 27). Csikszentmihalyi equates the focusing of attention with 'psychic energy'. He regards the ability to be in control of this resource (i.e. being able to focus attention at will rather than letting it be focused for you by the flow of events) as being an invaluable skill in living one's life. He contrasts what he calls 'entropy', where intrusive events or thoughts 'disorder' consciousness and disrupt intentionality, with 'flow'. Flow is where incoming information is congruent with goals, facilitating the effortless flow of psychic energy. Csikszentmihalyi refers to this as 'optimal experience'. It is where 'attention can be freely invested' (ibid., p. 40). It is 'when all a person's relevant skills are needed to cope with the challenges of a situation [and] that person's attention is completely absorbed by the activity' (ibid., p. 53) (see Box 4.2).

BOX 4.2 The flow experience

Below are several examples from the numerous illustrations of flow experience which Csikszentmihalyi provides:

> A dancer describes how it feels when a performance is going well: 'Your concentration is very complete. Your mind isn't wandering, you are not thinking of something else; you are totally involved in what you are doing ... Your energy is flowing very smoothly. You feel relaxed, comfortable, and energetic.'

> A rock climber explains how it feels when he is scaling a mountain: 'You are so involved in what you are doing [that] you aren't thinking of yourself as separate from the immediate activity ... You don't see yourself as separate from what you are doing.'

> A mother who enjoys the time spent with her small daughter: 'Her reading is the one thing that she's really into, and we read together. She reads to me, and I read to her, and that's a time when I sort of lose touch with the rest of the world, I'm totally absorbed in what I'm doing.'

> A chess player tells of playing in a tournament: '... the concentration is like breathing – you never think of it. The roof could fall in and, if it missed you, you would be unaware of it.'

> *(Csikszentmihalyi, 1992, pp. 53–4)*

Flow, then, involves the concentration of consciousness directed to some end. This could take the form of mountaineering, studying for a degree or reading this chapter. But it could also come about when cleaning the kitchen or working on an assembly line. It depends on how the activity is performed as much as on the nature of the activity itself. Csikszentmihalyi emphasizes that a core characteristic of a flow experience is that it is 'autotelic' or an end in itself.

Is the idea of 'flow' meaningful in terms of your own experience? If so, in what kind of situations have you experienced flow?

How far do you think this experience is likely to be unique to people who live in modern western society?

Csikszentmihalyi claims that such flow experiences are the most enjoyable that we can have and that they are essential to a feeling of well-being. When individuals can organize what they do so that flow experiences occur regularly, the quality of their lives will inevitably improve. He argues that people often feel discontented because much of modern entertainment (such as watching sport and TV) is essentially passive spectating and hence cannot offer the involvement of flow experience: 'Collectively we are wasting each year the equivalent of millions of years of human consciousness. The energy that could be used to focus on complex goals, to provide for enjoyable growth, is squandered on patterns of stimulation that only mimic reality' (ibid., pp. 162–3).

2.3   Donaldson: modes of mind

Margaret Donaldson is a developmental psychologist whose previous work has been empirically rather than phenomenologically oriented. (Readers may be familiar with her extensions and qualifications of Piaget's ideas.) In a more recent contribution (1992), however, she has offered an analysis of the development of what she terms 'modes of mind'. Although this depends only partially on direct accounts of experiences, it does very usefully serve to extend our discussion of the differentiation of kinds of awareness.

Drawing on her own observations as a child psychologist and on a range of research studies, she claims that there are different 'modes of mind' which emerge during the course of individual development. Each mode is based on a different sense of space–time. She distinguishes four – point, line, construct and transcendent modes. The *point mode* refers to immediate, here-and-now experience. *Line mode* is where it becomes possible to remember the past and anticipate the future. *Construct mode* is the capacity to construct concepts (e.g. dog) which are independent of specific instances. The *transcendent mode* is where the mind is able to function in the abstract – to go beyond the concept of seven fishes, say, and conceive of the idea of seven itself.

Can you imagine what a world of experience would be like if it was confined to a point mode? (To help you answer this question, you may want to recall or refer back to section 5.5.2 on damaged brains in Chapter 2.)

As implied above, Donaldson sees these modes as gradually emerging during the course of development. Initially, the consciousness of the infant is confined to the *point mode*:

> To get some sense of what this early point-mode experience might feel like, think of listening to a concerto which is familiar but not well known. When and where did you hear it before? You don't know. You must have heard it somewhere, though, or your present experience would be quite different. At the start of the first movement you cannot anticipate the second movement at all; but as the first movement closes the opening bars of the next one arise in your mind. Much infant experience is probably like this except that the question: 'When did I hear that before?' cannot be asked – and not just for lack of words but for lack of an appropriate conception of structured time.
>
> *(Donaldson, 1992, p. 42)*

The first signs of *line mode* thought begin to appear at about 8 to 10 months, she claims, when there is some evidence of awareness of a personal past and future possibilities. With the appearance of the line mode, Donaldson considers, there is differentiation of consciousness into four forms – *thought* (in the sense of knowing, understanding and solving problems), *emotion* (which, for her, signifies 'that which matters'), *perception* and directed *action*.

Intimations of the *construct mode* (i.e. the capacity to construct concepts independent of specific instances) begin at around the age of 3 or 4 years. In this third mode 'we are no longer restricted to a consideration of episodes in our own experience – or even those we have heard about from others. We start to be actively and consciously concerned about the general nature of things' (ibid., p. 80). This is not an easy stage to achieve and its early phase of development may involve the confusion of point and construct modes. Donaldson gives a nice example of this in a 4-year-old boy:

Callum: Is God everywhere?

Mother: Yes, dear.

Callum: Is he in this room?

Mother: Yes, he is.

Callum: Is he in my mug?

Mother (growing uneasy): Er – yes.

Callum (clapping his hand over his mug): Got him!

(ibid., p. 80)

Donaldson distinguishes three different kinds of *construct mode*. There is the *intellectual construct mode* where intellect and cognition dominate, and what she terms the *value-sensing construct mode* which is characterized by feelings and values. A third kind, the *core construct mode*, as she calls it, refers to those central constructs in which thought and feeling are intermingled (as they typically are when constructs first start to develop). So 'as we grow up, we all develop beliefs about the nature of the universe, about our own social group, about other social groups – and about ourselves. Typically, these beliefs are passionately held. They matter to us'. They comprise the most intimate part of ourselves – the core of 'the emotional belief systems that constitute what we call our "character" and our "attitudes"' (ibid., p. 83). Here, she considers, is the first source of a reflective notion of self.

The *transcendent mode* represents a further shift to abstraction. Although the construct modes are less bound to specific referents and contexts than the line mode, they are still linked to the known. The transcendent mode is about the purely abstract. While many people never fully attain this mode, Donaldson believes, on the basis of her observations of children in Scotland and the USA, that the rudiments of the transcendent mode generally make their appearance around the age of 9.

The most thought-provoking aspect of her analysis is Donaldson's assertion that the transcendent mode comes not only in intellectual form but in emotional form as well. The *intellectual transcendent mode* is, of course, the realm of abstract thought such as mathematics and logic. The *value-sensing transcendent mode*, in contrast, she sees manifest in certain types of religious or spiritual experience and also in some responses to poetry and music. One example she quotes is from a poem by Wordsworth (*The Prelude*) expressing the transcendent, mystic wonder inspired in him by nature and which she sees as 'a passionate account of his own experiences of the value-sensing modes – especially the transcendent mode' (ibid., p. 182):

> ... and I would stand,
> If the night blackened with a coming storm,
> Beneath some rock, listening to notes that are
> The ghostly language of the ancient earth,
> Or make their dim abode in distant winds.
> Thence did I drink the visionary power ...

Donaldson tries to plot not only the way these different modes unfold in individual development but also how they manifest themselves and have emerged in western history. In particular, she points to the relative lack of development of the value-sensing modes in contemporary society. She suggests that much of current interest in 'new age' activities is an attempt to fill the existential vacuum that results from this.

Donaldson's ideas are not that easy to grasp (particularly when presented in summary form as here), and she fully acknowledges that they are speculative. But they do offer, in Erik Erikson's phrase, a useful 'tool to think with' by drawing our attention to the different forms of subjective experience in which we can engage. Although Donaldson prefers to use the word 'mind', it would seem reasonable to view her analysis as an account of different kinds of consciousness. She is claiming that consciousness comes in different forms (i.e. perception, thought, emotion and action) and in different modes (i.e. point, line, construct and transcendent). Her analysis would suggest that a person may engage, at separate times, in quite different modes of consciousness. It also implies that there are differences in the range and quality of conscious experience of different individuals. The degree of individual ability to experience the transcendent, in particular, varies enormously, and only a few of us, she accepts, will ever manage to cope with, for example, the more abstruse realms of mathematics and pure logic. Access to both the intellectual transcendent mode (e.g. the worlds of pure maths and logic) and the value-sensing transcendent mode (e.g. the worlds of spiritual and artistic inspiration) are certainly likely to require time and effort, as well as a modicum of personal potential. It is worth noting that this analysis would seem to imply that one form of personal development lies in extending our ability (in so far as we can) to engage in modes which hitherto we have not experienced (which is, of course, what a lot of education is about).

Can you think of specific examples from your own experience of ways in which your capacity to engage in the transcendent modes (either the intellectual or the value-sensing varieties, or both) has been extended?

2.4 Kelly: personal construct theory

Although, as we have seen, Donaldson touches on individual differences in subjective experience, her account, like those of James and Csikzsentmihalyi, is primarily focused on general differentiations which apply (at least potentially) to all people. But what about more specific differences in the ways in which people experience and attribute meanings to their world: how can these be conceptualized and discovered?

George Kelly was an American psychologist and psychotherapist and one of the founders in the 1950s of the Association for Humanistic Psychology. It is probably true to say that his influence has been greater in the UK than in his own country, largely because of the enthusiasm of two British clinical psychologists, Don Bannister and Fay Fransella, for his ideas. Kelly's work has had a particular appeal to clinical psychologists in the UK where training has tended to be experimental and research-oriented. Qualified clinicians often encounter difficulty in applying this approach when confronted with the messy and complex problems of their clients. It is hard then to focus only on what is observable (as their training encouraged) and not get drawn into trying to make sense of their clients' experience. Kelly's approach provides them with a solution to the tension between the two worlds of their training and of their clients in the forms of a theory (personal construct theory) and, in particular, a method (the repertory grid) which promises to do justice to them both. Kelly's approach makes it possible to chart the nature of each person's world as she or he experiences it: but it makes it possible to elicit this from each person individually, rather than by imposing pre-set categories upon their experience.

Part of Kelly's particular appeal is that he spans the divide between cognitive and phenomenological psychology. On the one hand, he offers an 'outside', general way of understanding the way people make sense of the world. On the other, he provides a means of understanding and gaining access to the standpoint of a particular experiencer.

The main concept in Kelly's theory, as its name suggests, is *personal constructs*. These are the bipolar dimensions which constitute the discriminations we make in our experience of the world. So one way in which a particular person may classify a specific experience, for example, is as 'pleasant' as opposed to 'unpleasant'; or an ageing hippie may think of it as 'groovy' as opposed to 'square'. A construct has a focus and range of convenience. This means it may apply especially to some aspects of our world, be peripheral to others, and to yet others (which are outside its range of convenience) it may not apply at all. 'Tame–savage' might be used by a person to classify dogs, for example, but it is less likely to be applied when distinguishing between theories in psychology (though it might be by some people!). It is important to realize that Kelly is not talking about the concepts a person has but rather the key dimensions of discrimination which underlie his or her experience of the world. Most people will not be consciously aware of what constructs they are using to make sense of their experience. A construct is best thought of, Kelly suggests, as a 'reference axis devised ... for establishing a personal orientation toward the various events (encountered)'. A person can use this 'portable device for ordering symbols along scales, for placing events into categories, or for defining classes in the various familiar ways that suit his [*sic*] needs ... the construct is much more clearly a psychological guidance than it is either a limited collection of things or a common essence distilled out of them' (Kelly, 1979, p. 11).

The idea of constructs becomes clearer if we consider one of the main methods which Kelly devised to find out what constructs a person is using – the *repertory grid technique*. You might like to try a limited version of this.

Repertory grid technique

Think of five people you know who are (for the purpose of this exercise) fairly different kinds of people and write down their names. These are 'elements'. (By elements Kelly refers to any object, person or aspect of your personal world.) Now take three of these people (or elements) and think of a way in which two of them are alike and the other one is different. (For example, Ted and Jane might be seen as 'good fun' but Peter as the opposite, as a 'wet blanket'). Then continue with another combination of three elements (taken from your sample of five) and find a way in which two of these are alike and the third one is different. Keep on going until you have exhausted all possible combinations of three elements from your set of five. In the example I give above, the first bipolar construct is 'good fun–wet blanket'. You may well manage to extract ten or more bipolar constructs of your own, for there are ten possible combinations of three elements from a set of five, and you may want to generate more than one construct in the case of some triads.

Note that these constructs are *individual* to you. No-one suggested which particular constructs you should use. They were generated by the ways in which you distinguished between the people in your set. They provide a sample of the kinds of construct which you typically use when construing people. We would of course need to elicit quite a few more in order to get a proper idea of the way you see others.

What would also be interesting to add to an activity like this would be to work out the ways in which your constructs interrelate with each other. It might be the case, for example, that whenever you use the construct 'physically attractive–unattractive' you also tend to apply the construct 'arrogant–sensitive'. If so, this might indicate that you tend to see attractive people as arrogant. Before doing the grid, you may not have been aware of this association in the ways you construe. Generating constructs and analysing a construct grid (i.e. of the repertory of constructs that you use) can often bring surprises. It can also open up understanding of your own or someone else's behaviour. Knowing how constructs are related may help us understand why a person persists in a particular kind of behaviour. For example, suppose Sarah is constantly criticized for being unreliable. If we were to investigate her construct system, we might find that the construct 'unreliable–reliable' was strongly related to the constructs 'spontaneous–predictable' and 'interesting–boring'. Although she may want to become more reliable, she may find it difficult because such a change implicitly carries with it the danger that she will become boringly predictable.

As you can see from these examples, Kelly did not think of constructs as operating in isolation but as being *organized* or interrelated. One way to explore the organization of the constructs a person uses is to follow the strategy above and see how they are interrelated in the ways in which they are used.

Some constructs are more *central* than others. There is a technique for finding out which are the more central ones called 'laddering' (developed by Hinkle, 1965), which is illustrated in the following activity.

ACTIVITY 4.3   **Laddering**

Select one of the constructs you elicited in the previous activity. Ask yourself on which side of the bipolar construct you would prefer to be (e.g. if it was 'organized–disorganized', perhaps you might prefer 'organized'). Then decide why you prefer this, eliciting a higher order construct in the process (e.g. perhaps you prefer 'organized' because it means being efficient, so 'being inefficient–being efficient' becomes your higher order construct). Repeat this process with the new construct and so on until you can go no further.

The higher up the hierarchy a construct is, the more central it is for that person's functioning. Kelly considered that if central constructs come under threat of invalidation this arouses a strong emotional reaction. So if one of the central characteristics of the person I see myself to be is 'tolerance', and someone accuses me of 'intolerance', I will feel as if my whole identity is under attack and may try desperately to justify myself.

Another way in which constructs vary is in their degree of *permeability*. This refers to the degree to which a construct is open to change and development through experience.

Think for a moment whether your construct 'educated–uneducated' has changed as a result of your studies.

Before a person embarks upon higher-level study, for example, he or she may often think that education is a matter of acquiring facts and knowledge. Later there may be realization that a more significant feature is a style of critical and analytic thinking.

Although, as we have seen, the pattern of constructs a person uses is essentially individual, there will, of course, be considerable overlap with the constructs which other people use. And it is on such *communality*, as Kelly terms it, that communication depends. There is a considerable amount of evidence (see Duck, 1973) that we like people who construe things in much the same way as we do. This is probably because the fact that they do so helps us to validate our model of the world and, as our construction of the world to a large extent constitutes our identity, the latter also receives support. It may also, of course, be easier to communicate with them. (For the use of personal construct theory in understanding relationships, see Dallos, 1996.)

In this brief overview, I have indicated some of the key ideas in Kelly's theory of personal constructs. In fact, he published this in two volumes in which (perhaps reflecting his background in mathematics) he presented the theory in a formal fashion with a fundamental postulate and a set of corollaries developing from that. The fundamental postulate he expressed as 'a person's processes are psychologically channelized by the ways in which he [sic] anticipates events' (1955, p. 46). (In other words, a person comes to process information about the world in terms of how he or she anticipates events will occur.) The corollaries each encapsulate the kinds of feature we have already considered, such as the dichotomous or bipolar nature of constructs, individuality, organization, communality, and the extension and modulation of constructs through experience.

Kelly's approach not only offers a way of understanding and getting access to the way in which a person understands the world, but also emphasizes the active, constructive nature of experience. A premise underlying his theory is the idea of *constructive alternativism*. He assumes that people have considerable autonomy in the ways in which they can construe: there are usually alternative ways of construing open to us and, in this way, we have a part to play in ourselves determining the nature of our experience. As Kelly expresses it: 'Man [sic] creates his own ways of seeing the world in which he lives; the world does not create them for him' (1955, p. 12). Events 'are subject to as great a variety of constructions as our wits will enable us to contrive. ... all our present perceptions are open to question and reconsideration ... even the most obvious occurrences of everyday life might appear utterly transformed if we were inventive enough to construe them differently' (1970, p. 1). Kelly sees the person as developing constructs through active exploration, questioning and testing of the world. In this respect, the approach of the person is analogous to that of the scientist, for '... Both seek to anticipate events. Both have their theories, in terms of which they attempt to structure the current occurrences. Both hypothesize. Both observe. Both reluctantly revise their predictions in the light of what they observe ...' (1980, p. 24).

You may remember, from the discussion in the previous chapter of the covariance model of attribution, that the metaphor of the person as scientist was also used by Harold Kelley. It is worth noting (particularly perhaps in view of the similarity of their names) that the two psychologists used this metaphor quite independently of each other's work.

The notion of 'constructs' holds the promise of providing a relatively precise way of conceptualizing and assessing the ways in which a person attributes meanings to the world. The danger is that constructs are easily reified (or made a thing of) and it is arguable as to how far eliciting constructs can reveal the complex interrelated fabric and fluid richness of subjective experience. But at least constructs are based on the distinctions an individual actually makes, rather than being (as is the case with personality inventories and attitude scales) measures imposed on a person as a result of whatever particular test happens to be used.

Kelly also makes the point that emotion arises from the ways in which we construe. So, as we noted earlier, anxiety may be aroused when central constructs are under threat. (If you think back to the previous chapter, you will recall that, in linking attribution style with feelings of depression, attribution theory, like personal construct theory, also regards emotional feelings as being intrinsically related to the ways in which we think about the world and ourselves.) Personal construct therapy focuses on modifying the way a client construes the world. Kelly found that a typical problem for many of his patients was that their constructs had become too fixed and rigid. The therapist's job, according to Kelly, is to encourage new ways of construing which may 'work better'.

2.5   Some food for thought

ACTIVITY 4.4

Look back over the four accounts presented in sections 2.1 to 2.4 and answer the following questions:

1   In what ways are these four accounts different?

2   Are they in some sense fundamentally different or alternative accounts (i.e. where one is right and the others are wrong)? Or are they better regarded as complementary, illuminating different aspects of conscious experience?

3   What is the value of accounts of this kind? What can they do?

2.5.1   Phenomenological differentiation

Each of the four accounts would seem quite different. They use different concepts and approach subjective experience from very different angles. Nevertheless, they do not contradict each other and I think that they are best regarded as complementary. James provides a very general account of different facets of experienced consciousness. In contrast, Csikszentmihalyi focuses on the very specific aspect of 'flow' experience. Donaldson approaches mind or experience from a developmental angle. But the modes she suggests are quite consistent with the different features which James refers to (e.g. point and line modes would seem to relate to the stream of consciousness; transcendent modes could be related to James's notions of special sub-worlds of consciousness such as philosophical and abstract beliefs). The account which is most distinct from the others, perhaps, is Kelly's construct theory and this is because he does not focus on the phenomenology of conscious experience so much as on what underpins the meaning distinctions that help to constitute it. In this way, the four accounts provide a range of different but potentially complementary ways of understanding more about subjective experience.

What these phenomenologically-oriented accounts have served to do, then, I would suggest, is broadly to differentiate aspects of our conscious experience. Because we have direct access only to our own consciousness, you might like to consider what criteria we can use for assessing them. The most direct test of such differentiations is against our own experience (and that of other people). Do they make sense and fit with your experience? One problem you may find here is that of labelling, in that similar experiences may be conceptualized in different ways. For example, if you are familiar with Maslow's idea of 'peak experience', you may feel that there are similarities between that and Csikszentmihalyi's account of 'flow experience'. There are some similarities too between the notion of peak experience and the kind of experiences which Donaldson would include in her value-sensing transcendental mode. While it should not be surprising that different accounts come up with similar concepts, it does emphasize the difficulty of establishing an agreed taxonomy of subjective experience.

What is being suggested here is that accounts such as the ones presented in section 2 sensitize us to aspects of our experience through articulating these at a verbal level. However, a different approach might be to argue that accounts such as these serve to *construct* the very experience they claim to describe. It is only once we know about 'flow experience' that we can experience it. It is the constructs themselves that make the experience an experienced 'reality'. On the basis of your reading of these accounts, what do you think? Are they helping us to differentiate and become more aware of qualities which exist in experience? Or are such accounts serving to create something which otherwise would not be there?

2.5.2   Universality?

A key issue which will be taken up in this book is: how far do qualities of subjective experience apply to all people (i.e. are they 'universal') and how far do they apply merely to people from a particular kind of culture, or even just to specific individuals?

As far as personal constructs are concerned, it would seem reasonable to suppose that many of the ones we use are specific to particular social contexts and that we assimilate them from the people we encounter, the television and radio programmes we watch and listen to, and the books, newspapers, and magazines we read. Some psychologists have argued that some constructs at least are developed mutually, in that they emerge directly from our interactions with others. They claim that there will be constructs which are common to particular couples (Duck, 1982) or to families (Dallos, 1991).

But what about other more general qualities of our experience? How far is the flow experience, for example, merely a feature of our particular society? The analyses of James, Csikszentmihalyi and Donaldson are clearly intended to apply universally to all people. Certainly, Csikszentmihalyi is in no doubt about the matter: he is adamant that flow experiences are a universal affair:

> With the help of this theoretical model my research team at the University of Chicago and, afterward, colleagues around the world interviewed thousands of individuals from many different walks of life. These studies suggested that optimal experiences were described in the same way by men and women, by young people and old, regardless of cultural differences. The flow experience was not just a peculiarity of affluent, industrialized élites. It was reported in essentially the same words by old women from Korea, by adults in Thailand and India, by teenagers in Tokyo, by Navajo shepherds, by farmers in the Italian Alps, and by workers on the assembly line in Chicago.
>
> *(Csikszentmihalyi, 1992, p. 4)*

Donaldson clearly regards societies as fostering particular kinds of modes as opposed to others. In modern technological society, for example, intellectual modes are encouraged more than value-sensing ones. She also acknowledges, as we have seen, that there are individual differences and that these may be in part dependent on the social contexts and relationships a person experiences, particularly as a child. However, she does not regard it as inevitable that children internalize the particular reality of their care-givers or society. As she puts it: 'their conversations are so full of doubts and wonderings – and, often, of an ability to "take on" adults and confound them' (1992, p. 86). She cites an example of a father asking his 3-year-old son about gender identity:

Father: Stephen, are you a little boy or a little girl?

Stephen: I'm a doggie.

Father: Come on now, Stephen! Be sensible. Are you a little boy or a little girl?

Stephen: Gr-rrr! Woof!

(ibid., p.86)

She concludes: 'the attempt at testing ended in helpless laughter. Who may be said to have set the rules of the game?' (ibid., p. 86). Donaldson is emphasizing that children develop their understanding through active involvement – questioning, watching and listening, playing, reading. They are not simply influenced by either parents or social context. This implies agreement (albeit from a different angle) with Csikszentmihalyi's position that the qualities of subjective experience cannot be regarded merely as a product of culture. (This topic of social construction will be taken up in the next chapter and you may wish to reconsider this issue then.)

2.5.3 Intersubjectivity

Although the accounts in this section confirm how consciousness is personal and private and one cannot directly experience another's consciousness, a fundamental basis for distinguishing between people and objects is that we assume other people to have a consciousness similar to our own. In effect, I can communicate with you only by assuming a consciousness in you. In writing this, for example, I assume that you the reader possess consciousness (and this means that you will understand what I type in here in a way that my computer's printer cannot, even though it 'reads' this when it prints a draft). This assumption of consciousness, understanding and self in others we refer to as *intersubjectivity*. It forms the fundamental premise on which our social life, interactions and relationships intrinsically depend. For some phenomenological psychologists, such as Merleau-Ponty, our awareness of the subjectivities of others forms an important and intrinsic part of our subjective experience. We become aware of ourselves through our awareness of others being aware of us.

Review of section 2

- James's account emphasizes how consciousness has continuity and flow and how it relates to a sense of self and will. He distinguishes sub-worlds of experience, and describes consciousness as a 'theatre of simultaneous possibilities', controlled by attention (both responsive and deliberate), and possessing a focus and a fringe.

- Csikszentmihalyi's account, based on interviews as well as introspection, centres on 'flow experience'. It emphasizes the importance of absorbing activity and the focusing of attention for psychological well-being.

- Donaldson suggests a differentiation of consciousness (or mind) into thought, emotion, perception, and action. In particular, she distinguishes point, line, construct, and transcendent modes of mind (the latter two taking both intellectual and feeling forms). She claims that these emerge in the course of individual development.

- Kelly's personal construct theory focuses on differences between individuals in predicting events and making sense of their experience. Constructs are organized in hierarchies, and differ in permeability, centrality and communality. The primary technique used for eliciting constructs is the repertory grid. Other key concepts are constructive alternativism and the model of the person as 'scientist'.

- Two questions to be considered are: Are these accounts to be regarded as articulating and differentiating the nature of subjective experience or as constructing it? Are the experiences described to be regarded as universal or as products of a particular culture?

3 Metaphor as a basis for understanding consciousness

ACTIVITY 4.5

1 For about three minutes, try to be consciously aware of what you are conscious of.

2 Then, reflect for a few minutes on what goes on in your consciousness. Try to describe in a few words what consciousness is like.

These are not easy activities.

It is interesting that Kelly uses a metaphor (the 'person as scientist') in his conceptualization of personal experience. Indeed, in all of the studies we looked at earlier we see metaphor used generally as a way of describing the differentiations concerned. Thus, for James, consciousness is a 'stream', a sculptor working a stone, and (following Descartes) a 'theatre'. For Csikzsentmihalyi, some kinds of experience are in 'flow', and Donaldson talks of 'point' and 'line' modes.

This is not surprising, for the use of metaphor is one of the most important means we have of extending our understanding. What a metaphor does is to place a concept in the context of another concept and, by so doing, alter its meaning and implications. In this way, the juxtaposition or fusion of the two concepts involved often creates an emergent third meaning which is more than just the sum of the other two. For example, the metaphorical idea that 'time is money' generates a whole set of related ideas (borrowing, investing and wasting time, etc.). It changes our way of thinking about time.

In this section, I want to explore the idea that the use of metaphor provides a very useful analogy for conscious experience. By understanding what a metaphor does, we may gain further insights into the properties of conscious experience and what that can do.

That language fundamentally depends on metaphor to extend its capacity to describe things is obvious. Our speech is stuffed with metaphors both dead and alive. We talk of pop 'stars', of being 'stumped' and 'undermined', of 'going downhill' or 'climbing the ladder of success'. It is not easy to write a standard sentence without a metaphor lurking somewhere in the background, and any creative user of language is likely to coin his or her own. But the use of metaphor is more than a literary device. It is fundamental to our capacity to give meaning to and deal with the world about us. Not only is it, as Rumelhart (1979) has pointed out, the essential ingredient of language acquisition, but it is also a key means of developing new concepts and gaining new ways of understanding.

The usefulness of metaphor for deepening our understanding is particularly apparent when we try to make sense of psychological life (see Box 4.3)

BOX 4.3   The use of metaphor to make sense of love

Love is a physical force (electromagnetic, gravitational, etc.)

I could feel the *electricity* between us. There were *sparks*. I was *magnetically drawn* to her. They are uncontrollably *attracted* to each other. They *gravitated* to each other immediately. His whole life *revolves* around her. The *atmosphere* around them is always *charged*. There is incredible *energy* in their relationship. They lost their *momentum*.

Love is a patient

This is a *sick* relationship. They have a *strong, healthy* marriage. The marriage is *dead* – it can't be *revived*. Their marriage is on *the mend*. We're getting *back on our feet*. Their relationship is in *really good shape*. They've got a *listless* marriage. Their marriage is *on its last legs*. It's a *tired* affair.

Love is madness

I'm *crazy* about her. She *drives me out of my mind*. He constantly *raves* about her. He's gone *mad* over her. I'm just *wild* about Harry. I'm *insane* about her.

Love is magic

She *cast her spell* over me. The *magic* is gone. I was *spellbound*. She had me *hypnotized*. He has me *in a trance*. I was *entranced* by him. I'm *charmed* by her. She is *bewitching*.

Love is war

He is known for his many rapid *conquests*. She *fought for* him, but his mistress *won out*. He *fled from* her *advances*. She *pursued* him relentlessly. He is slowly *gaining ground* with her. He *won* her hand in marriage. He *overpowered* her. She is *besieged* by suitors. He has to *fend* them *off*. He *enlisted the aid* of her friends. He *made an ally* of her mother. Theirs is a *misalliance* if I've ever seen one.

Source: Lakoff and Johnson, 1980, p. 49

Metaphor serves to deepen one's experience by imbuing it with the connotations and implications of the concept it is related to. So to talk of snow being a 'blanket' is not just to view it as a cover but is also to infuse it with associated feelings of warmth, softness and cosiness. Let me give another example taken from Tennessee Williams's play *Orpheus*

Descending. Val Xavier, the young wanderer who is the central character in the play, at one point talks of himself as a tiny, transparent bird that flies so high that it cannot be seen, and sleeps on the wind so that it never returns to earth.

The way metaphor is described here is broadly in line with what has been perhaps the most widely accepted account of metaphor – the interaction model of Black (1979). The thorny issues surrounding the problem of precisely defining what a metaphor is, however, are outside the scope of this chapter. If you are interested in a more detailed exploration of this issue, see the Ortony (1979) volume in which Black's paper appears.

The examples in Box 4.3 make clear how widely used metaphors are in making sense of psychological life. (You may also remember, from Window 1.2 in Chapter 1, how Leonard used poetry and metaphor to express his feelings and situation.) The next question we need to go on to consider is: can we find a metaphor or metaphors which might help us to conceptualize effectively the nature of consciousness itself?

Julian Jaynes (1990) has pointed out that, in everyday speech, perhaps the most common metaphors used for consciousness are taken from our experience of vision and three-dimensional space:

We 'see' solutions to problems, the best of which may be 'brilliant', and the person 'brighter' and 'clear-headed' as opposed to 'dull', 'fuzzy-minded', or 'obscure' solutions. …

… we can be 'broad-minded', 'deep', 'open', or 'narrow-minded'; we can be 'occupied'; we can 'get something off our minds', 'put something out of mind', or we can 'get it', let something 'penetrate', or 'hold' it in mind.

As with a real space, something can be at the 'back' of our mind, in its 'inner recesses', or 'beyond' our mind, or 'out' of our mind. In argument we try to 'get things through' to someone, to 'reach' their 'understanding' or find a 'common ground', or 'point out', etc.,

(Jaynes, 1990, pp. 55–6)

It is not just our ordinary ways of describing and making sense of the world and personal experience which rest on metaphor but theorizing by psychologists too. Like any other theorizing, this is based on metaphors drawn from our experience and thus it is rooted in the historical and social context in which the theorist lives (but see Box 4.4). If we take theorizing about mind and brain for example, the conceptions of the seventeenth-century philosophers, and later the early psychologists, drew on the molecular theorizing of physics and chemistry after the invention of the microscope. This is reflected in the idea of the mind as associations of elements of sensations. With the advance of technology, we see continual updating of the concepts which are applied. The ideas of electricity and magnetism were applied to 'make sense' of hypnotism and animal magnetism. Later, as the concept of 'force fields' made its appearance in physics, so it was taken up by *Gestalt* psychologists. (Interestingly, the concepts borrowed from other disciplines are very often themselves metaphors. Thus, understanding is extended by the propagation of metaphors themselves.) Today, it is fashionable in much of psychology to draw on images taken from *computer science*. Conscious experience is regarded as a product of the computer-like operations of the brain (e.g. Johnson-Laird, 1988; Dennett, 1991). Such metaphors are best seen as 'root metaphors', in that they carry with them a whole set of associated ways of looking at and making sense of the phenomenon in question.

BOX 4.4   Constructivist and realist positions

The position presented here (in keeping with the view presented in this book and series) is a constructivist view of scientific and theoretical understanding. There are other perspectives (such as, for example, the school of thought broadly referred to as positivism) which have taken a non-constructivist (or realist) approach. This assumes a 'world out there' (realism) and that the task of science is to pare down its conceptualizations to best represent that reality. From this view metaphors would be regarded, because of their essential fuzziness and lack of precision, as something to be avoided. Nevertheless, the history of scientific and psychological theorizing makes clear the central role that metaphor has played. Indeed, Boyd (1979) has argued that metaphors are often essential for the development of new scientific ideas.

The problem is that, although the right metaphor can illuminate a phenomenon by alerting you to its critical features, the wrong metaphor can actually serve to obscure these. For all its usefulness in everyday communication, thinking of consciousness as three-dimensional space is only of limited value as a metaphor. Subjective experience does not have the tangible properties associated with 'mind-space': it is by no means a 'copy' or picture of the world. Nor is it equivalent to a computer operation. Jaynes's argument is, in fact, that no metaphor taken from the physical world is adequate when applied to consciousness. For 'it should be immediately apparent that there is not and cannot be anything in our immediate experience that is like immediate experience itself. There is therefore a sense in which we shall never be able to understand consciousness in the same way that we can understand things we are conscious of' (1990, p. 53).

Two key points emerge then from the preceding discussion. One is the assertion that the way to make sense of any aspect of our experience is to find an appropriate metaphor. Another is the difficulty of finding a metaphor which is effective in conceptualizing the nature of subjective experience.

Jaynes's solution to this dilemma is to suggest that the most effective metaphor to use for making sense of subjective experience is metaphor itself. He argues that subjective consciousness is itself grounded in, and generated by, processes of comparison and conjunction similar to those of metaphor. The nub of his conception is expressed in the following paragraph:

> Subjective conscious mind is an analogue of what is called the real world. It is built up with a vocabulary or lexical field whose terms are all metaphors or analogues of behaviour in the physical world. Its reality is of the same order as mathematics. It allows us to shortcut behavioural processes and arrive at more adequate decisions. Like mathematics, it is an operator rather than a thing or repository. And it is intimately bound up with volition and decision.
>
> *(Jaynes, 1990, p. 55)*

ACTIVITY 4.6   This is not an easy statement to digest. Read it through carefully again and note down what you think are the key ideas it expresses.

Let me try to unpack this rather difficult statement and clarify the main ideas which underlie it.

1   By the term *analogue*, Jaynes is suggesting that consciousness, rather like a map, is a *metaphorical representation*, not a direct copy, of the world as experienced. It is a metaphorical representation of the world which is itself built up with metaphors.

2   Jaynes describes consciousness as an *operator* 'intimately bound up with volition and decision'. An operator in mathematics is a process such as squaring, multiplying or taking a root which serves to transform the numbers it is applied to. The point here is that consciousness is not just a representation of our experience of the world but can act on that experience and transform it. For although a metaphor may be generated by the interaction of two concepts (and by thus attaching the connotations and implications of one to the other), once created, it has itself the power to transform our awareness of the experiences on which it is based. This, as we have already noted, is one way in which scientific theorizing proceeds. To take a further example from everyday life, one way of conceptualizing relationships with other people is to draw on metaphors based on the skin and physical contact. So we think of a person as 'thick-skinned' or as someone who has to be 'handled' carefully in case we 'rub her up the wrong way' etc. Once such a way of looking at people has been generated (either by the metaphors provided in the conventions of our language and culture or by our personal capacity to generate our own), then this acts upon our experience and makes it more likely that we will make sense of relationships in this kind of way and be particularly sensitive to features which relate to this conception.

Think back to Kelly's notion of 'personal construct'. Is this concept similar to that of metaphor as described above? Do constructs serve similar functions to metaphors?

The point is then that conceiving of consciousness as being both metaphor-like and constituted by metaphors is appropriate for (and draws attention to) not only the capacity of consciousness to represent the world we experience but also its generative power to create new experiences. As it is possible to create entirely novel metaphors from further conjunctions of existing ones, Jaynes's conception of consciousness as metaphor allows both for the *openness* of consciousness (i.e. its power to generate ever-new ways of framing experience) and its capacity to create abstract conceptions which are not directly related to specific perceptions or feelings (as we saw was the case with Donaldson's construct and transcendent modes).

What do you think of Jaynes's idea that the most useful model for consciousness is metaphor? How could one go about assessing it? What criteria would you want to use?

If, as was asserted earlier, metaphors can both illuminate and obscure, how do we know whether this one is an enlightening one or one that will set us on the wrong track? The first question is – what criteria can we employ to assess it? Jaynes provides no experimental evidence in support of his ideas. Nor is it obvious that evidence of that kind would be relevant. One way of evaluating them is to try the method suggested in the previous section in assessing the accounts of different aspects of experience: that is, to see whether they make sense when you reflect on your own conscious experience. Another way is to consider whether his model helps us to make better or more satisfying sense of otherwise confusing aspects of a phenomenon. This is also inevitably a fairly subjective judgement, but it seems to me that a reasonable case could be made that it does, for the model accounts for the stability of consciousness, and its predictability and effectiveness in dealing with the world while, at the same time, allowing for its intangibility and elusiveness and its power to actively construct what we experience. For the metaphors which make up consciousness are, at the same time, both *analogues* of the world of experience and *operators* upon it.

Finally, we might ask what the practical implications are of using a model of this kind. Although Jaynes's scheme is, like consciousness itself, somewhat elusive and intangible, its end-product is to provide us with a way of thinking about consciousness which is quite different, for example, from physically-based notions like 'mind-space' or computers. One of the effects of mechanistic models of mind in the history of psychology has been to rule out (or at least to render peripheral) ideas such as agency and autonomy. The model presented here acknowledges that consciousness may be open and not fixed and also the idea that it is potentially generative (capable of creating the new) and not merely a vehicle of monitoring or representation. It means that we look at (here we go again with a mind-space metaphor!) and think about consciousness quite differently from how we do if our model is based, for example, on a machine.

Let me make two final points to relate this conception to ideas from elsewhere in this chapter and book. I think that there is some similarity in effect between Jaynes's idea of consciousness as being constituted by metaphors and Kelly's idea of personal constructs. For, with ideas such as 'constructive alternativism', Kelly's emphasis is on how our ways of construing can serve actively to create our experience as well as representing it.

Although neither Jaynes nor Kelly make this point, their ideas could also be regarded as throwing light on the way personal consciousness emerges from the interactions and negotiations between an individual and the people and symbolic meanings (i.e. language and culture) which form his or her social world. For the metaphors which constitute our consciousness are generated not only by comparisons we make ourselves but also by the metaphors embedded in the language we use, other people's utterances and the social contexts in which we grow up and live. By assimilating such metaphors, we may come to see the world as others do. (The issue of the social construction of personal experience and the self will be taken up in the next chapter.)

I want, in the concluding section of Part 1, to develop this last point by looking at a pervasive feature of our subjective experience – the use of fantasy and imagination in our inner world of reflection. It will be argued that this too can be generative and can serve to change the ways in which we feel, think and act.

Review of section 3

- Metaphor provides an important basis for the extension and development of new ways of experiencing and making sense.

- A useful model for consciousness would be to see it as possessing similar qualities to metaphor, in that it not only represents our experience but is also generative – capable of creating something different or new.

4   Imagination and fantasy

By imagination and fantasy, I refer to our ability to create in our mind and reflect upon images and events with their associated feelings: what we might call, if you like, the process of inner dialogue.

Stop for a moment and reflect on the significance of imagination and fantasy in your own personal experience.

ACTIVITY 4.7

How much of your time do you spend in some kind of day-dreaming or inner reflection?

Have there been particular times in your life when you engaged in a lot of this?

What kinds of reflection or fantasizing do you engage in?

What purpose, if any, do they serve?

Even in the brief glimpses into personal experience afforded by the Windows in Chapter 1, we saw the part played by imagination and fantasy. Liv Ullman in the plane circling over Hollywood, for example, imagines life back in Norway and the people she loves there. For Leonard, fantasy seems at times even to dominate his consciousness. The capacity for imagination also underlies some of the features of subjective experience that were discussed in Chapter 1. Our sense of living in *time,* for instance, rests not only on remembered images of past events but also on the ability to think of ourselves in the future. Imagined scenarios contribute to the *multiple* nature of our conscious experience, and *reflexiveness* includes the ability to see in one's mind how one appears to be for others.

For children, imagination and fantasy clearly play an explicit and important role: in their play they try out adult behaviours, create stories and scenes and attribute personalities and life to dolls and teddy bears. As Erikson and others have pointed out, this is not just a question of amusement, for it is through play that children learn about the world, develop abilities and explore their needs and anxieties: in other words, help to develop and transform themselves. To illustrate this, Erikson quotes a delightful sequence from Mark Twain's *Tom Sawyer* in which Tom's friend Ben Rogers 'hove in sight ... personating the *Missouri* ...' and being 'boat and captain and engine-bells combined ...'. In such ways, growing children explore, synthesize different aspects of themselves and their experiences and learn to become masters of themselves both in body and mind, while assimilating the metaphors of their culture:

> One 'meaning' of Ben's play could be that it affords his ego a temporary victory over his gangling body and self by making a well-functioning whole out of brain (captain), the nerves and muscles of will (signal system and engine), and the whole bulk of the body (boat). It permits him to be an entity within which he is his own boss,

because he obeys himself. At the same time, he chooses his metaphors from the tool world of the young machine age, and antici- pates the identity of the machine god of his day: the captain of the *Big Missouri*.

(Erikson, 1950, p. 190)

With the onset of adolescence, fantasy is expressed more through inner thought than explicit play. At such a critical time for identity formation, one would expect a preoccupation with fantasy (both realistic and other- wise) about the multiple possibilities now opening up in personal development, relationships and work. (As Singer, 1981, has commented, given the likelihood that any request or remark by a parent is likely to interrupt an absorbing fantasy, this may be one reason at least for the reputed touchiness of adolescents.)

Most surveys have found that the majority of adults also seem to engage in some form of 'day-dreaming' every day (Singer, 1981). Most people say that they enjoy their day-dreaming and it is not surprising that a com- mon use of fantasy is as a diversion; as, for example, when we replay in our minds memories of pleasurable or significant events. Closely related to this are those 'what it would be like' sequences in which we rehearse in fantasy the scripts of desire – winning a marathon or the pools, for example, or becoming a politician, or marrying the person of our dreams. There are also what we might call substitute fantasies where the sequence is focused on a desired person who is absent or unobtainable. Thus, someone whose partner or spouse has died or is absent might pic- ture their loved-one sitting in a familiar chair or cuddling up to them through the night. Note that while fantasy may take 'free-flow' form, it does not have to, because we can deliberately choose to focus on some areas rather than others. In this sense, we can *to some degree direct and control what we experience.* One way in which we might do this is to use inner reflection to try to change or come to terms with the way we feel about some aspect of our lives (perhaps, in particular, those which arouse shame and guilt). These are what I would call *working-through reflections.* They may involve 'replaying' the scene to try to digest and conceptualize in different ways what has happened; or they may entail musing on what might have been but was not done.

(Of course, there are some fantasies or thought sequences, particularly negative or frightening ones, that may intrude into consciousness unasked and undesired. We may want to avoid thinking about them but be unable to do so. Such intrusive fantasies are best considered in rela- tion to the discussion of the unconscious (see Chapter 6).)

Fantasy also often accompanies ongoing experiences. This may be no more than those momentary anticipations as when the doorbell rings and a repertoire of possibilities as to whom it might be flashes through our mind as we go to answer it. Or it could be the inner, running commentary with themselves (or perhaps with God or with an imagined loved-one) which some people engage in as a way of coping with anxiety-provoking or difficult situations ('Now come on, old man, just three more miles to go!'). There are *accompaniment fantasies* also whose effect is to make mundane situations more exciting:

> While driving through Huddersfield recently a friend of mine was stopped by the police. 'Do you know how fast you were going?' he was asked. 'As a matter of fact I know exactly how fast I was driving,' replied my friend. 'I was doing precisely 38 mph, in third gear at 2,850 revs per minute.'
>
> Suspecting a smart ass the police officer asked him how he could be so sure. 'Because I was pretending to take part in the Monte Carlo Rally,' said my friend, who will not see fifty again.
>
> … In order to make his journey through the Pennines more tolerable he had invented a game for himself, complete with bizarre hazards like forest fires, Alpine avalanches, nubile Parisienne hitch-hikers, amphetamine-fired Tour de France cyclists and surly OAS-type gendarmerie.
>
> *(Connolly, 1982, p. 7)*

We see, in this extract, how such accompaniment fantasies could be regarded as being a form of sustained or 'root' metaphor, reflecting through the events which are happening and serving to transform them into a new and more exciting experience. Also included in this subcategory of *enhancing* fantasies is the use of imagination to intensify sexual feelings. In a study of women's sexual fantasies, Hariton and Singer (1974) found that 65 per cent of their 'normal' subjects engaged in 'moderate to high levels' of fantasy during sex. Such fantasies involved, for example, other lovers, multiple partners, different contexts such as being on the beach, or imagining resisting and being overcome (see also Friday, 1976). There is no reason, of course, to suppose that fantasy plays any less a part for men.

Fantasy then is a constant part of subjective experience, serving to please and pain us, helping us to clarify what we have done and plan to do, arousing hopes and anticipations, occasionally becoming a burden and sometimes a vital resource (see Box 4.5 overleaf).

One important use of imagination can be to *energize* and to stimulate action; fantasies, in other words, can 'get us going'. As Yeats put it, the 'imagination has some way of lighting on the truth which reason has not, and … its commandments … are the most binding we can ever know' (Yeats, 1961, p. 65). It is through imagination that we are inspired to create our futures. This is not just a matter of exploring alternatives, but of finding images which can precipitate us into movement, as when we suddenly see (and feel) how life could be. Like metaphors, such images serve to transform experience and, in so doing, direct and sustain our movement into the future. As suggested earlier, one way of regarding the role of fantasy in our lives (particularly in its enhancing and energizing forms) is as a type of root metaphor. It allows a new pattern of meaning and action to emerge because of the new context (with its connotations and implications) which it provides. Some people's lives are centred on some 'personal myth', seen by them, for example, as a way to salvation,

BOX 4.5   The power of fantasy

The powerful role which fantasy plays for those who are captive is well-documented in the accounts of hostages, held often in conditions of extreme deprivation for months, even years. Brian Keenan in his book *An Evil Cradling* (1992) provides a particularly vivid account of his own experience as a hostage in Beirut. While he was imprisoned alone, fantasy came to dominate his life, becoming both a source of concern and a resource for survival:

> ... my imagination gave me images, some beautiful, some disturbing and unendurably ever-present. The vast landscape of the mind unfolds on its own. At times I felt the compensation of this gift and at other times cursed my imagination that it could bring me sensations so contorted, so strange and so incoherent that I screamed ...

> ... I begin again to plot and plan and try to find a direction for my thinking. There are strange occasions when I find myself thinking of two different and completely unrelated things simultaneously. ... I can ask and answer questions on each of these very different subjects at one and the same moment.

> ... I began to dread my freedom, if it should come. ... I returned to an old strategy of thinking through all the books that I had read as a child, and which I remembered so clearly now. And began again to recall films and make them different or simply use them as a stepping stone, to direct the mind away from this desire to remain captive.

> ... I decided to become my own self-observer ... I allowed myself to do and be and say and think and feel all the things that were in me, but at the same time could stand outside observing and attempting to understand.

> *(Keenan, 1992, pp. 32, 69, 73 and 78)*

or as a hero's journey against adversity. Fantasy may be used to energize more limited sectors of one's life. In writing this section of this chapter, for example, I see it at the moment as fighting a battle to gain command of a rather wild and difficult hump of ground.

The mythology of a culture provides a rich source of personal myths and metaphors. Almost all cultures provide tales of the exploits of legendary figures, stories of gods and goddesses and saints and about the creation of the world. Our culture is no exception. Not only have we inherited a wealth of contemporary mythology from other times but, it might be argued, mythical characters and themes are continuously being both revamped and created anew in television, cinema and popular books. Comedy and drama are the shared and structured public forms of the private fantasies already discussed.

In particular, culture can equip a person with energizing symbols and images which carry the power to guide and generate our actions. Their power (e.g. the power of the flag, the cross, the heroic theme) cannot be overestimated. They inspired the building of the Pyramids and the cathedrals of the Middle Ages, they lead Hindus to die from starvation rather than slaughter the cattle around them, members of terrorist groups to plant bombs that maim and kill, and young Muslims to seek glorious death in battle as martyrs. (For an excellent discussion of this in relation to Armenian terrorism, see Tololyan, 1989.)

Campbell (1973) sees myths as serving important functions, including providing a symbolic basis for morality and guidance towards spiritual enrichment. For Campbell, though, the problem is that many of the energizing myths we have in Euro-American culture today have been inherited from another time and culture. They fail to take account of or easily fit within a western, rational, science-based understanding of the world. What we need, he argues, are new forms appropriate to our time and understanding.

ACTIVITY 4.8

This section has stressed the potential role of imagination in directing what and how we experience as well as providing a basis for our actions. You may remember that in Chapter 3 there was also a focus on changing ways of thought in order to produce changes in feelings and behaviour. Can you remember references there to therapeutic techniques for deliberately shifting the kind of attributions that people make or their ways of thinking about a particular action or event?

Two examples you might come up with are Clark et al.'s work with patients suffering from panic attacks (section 2.4.2) and the work on depression and attribution style by Seligman and others (section 5.2). These are consistent with the idea put forward here that people can be encouraged to use their ability to select the thoughts they focus on in order deliberately to change their mental state. This is a technique that can more generally be used to produce personal change (for a good example of similar techniques used for self-development, see Robbins, 1992).

1   You might like to try in your daily life the deliberate use of imagination to foster the kinds of way in which you want to feel. As a general strategy, deliberately reduce the amount of time you spend on depressing or disempowering thoughts (i.e. ones which do not make you feel good). Deliberately increase the time you spend on enjoyable fantasies and especially those that are energizing (e.g. the positive features of your present situation and the goals you are reaching for). Note any effects that this strategy has on you.

2   You may also like to set up a situation with friends where, together, you are able to share, compare and explore the kinds of inner world of fantasy that you tend to engage in.

Review of section 4

- The process of inner reflection and fantasy is a significant component of subjective experience and provides further demonstration of its generative power.

- Imagination and fantasy are important means of personal development: through the medium of play in younger children and through inner reflection as we grow older.

- Different types of fantasy may be identified: inner replays of past or future experiences, substitute fantasies, intrusive fantasies, working-through fantasies, accompaniment fantasies (which include enhancing fantasies).

- A particularly important kind of inner reflection is energizing fantasies. These may draw from cultural myths and metaphors.

PART 2:   REFLEXIVE AWARENESS AND EXISTENTIAL ISSUES

5   Introduction: the existential position

One of the extraordinary properties of consciousness is our ability to reflect on the act of experiencing (i.e. to be conscious of being conscious). We might call this the capacity for *reflexive awareness* or 'reflexivity'. We are capable not only of feeling happy or sad, for example, but of being aware that we are feeling that way. We can 'monitor' our own actions as well as our thoughts and feelings; in other words, be aware of what we are doing. We can do this either retrospectively or actually as we are doing it (though this is usually more difficult).

---

1   Stop what you are doing for a moment and just be aware of being aware.

2   Later, when you are moving around engaged in your normal activities, try for a time, while doing them, to be aware as far as you can of your actions, sensations, feelings and thoughts. This is sometimes called 'being mindful'.

ACTIVITY 4.9

A significant aspect of this reflexive awareness is the ability of each of us to be *aware of ourselves as experiencing, existing persons*. This has important implications. For there are distinctive issues which arise from the experience of being a self-aware and existing human individual which we might call *existential concerns*. For example, we are aware of our *finiteness*: because we are aware of existing in a flow of time, we know that we will not live for ever (at least not in terms of our physical body and the kind of existence we experience now). Our power of reflexiveness also makes it possible for us to question the *meaningfulness* of our life experience, to review the values which we ourselves hold, and to search for new and more satisfactory forms. Our ability to imagine alternative, future courses of action and our awareness of our agency (i.e. that we can initiate action) mean that we have to confront the issue of *choice*.

It can be seen that, in adopting this existential perspective, we are making an assumption of autonomy: that is, that reflexiveness itself can play a part in generating what we think and do. Hence our thoughts and actions have a quality of openness and are not entirely predictable by others, even if they had full knowledge of antecedent conditions.

This, as you will have noticed, is in line with the discussion in Part 1. Csikszentmihalyi's idea that consciousness directs as well as represents, Kelly's concept of constructive alternativism, the notion of subjective experience as analogous to metaphor, and the uses of fantasy and imagination, all imply the power of conscious thought to generate novelty.

Not only does taking an existential perspective necessarily involve making the assumption of autonomy, but existential awareness also confronts us with issues which we have to come to terms with in some way. We have to form some kind of response to the awareness that we are finite, that we have the ability to choose to act in different ways, that we play a part in creating who we are; even if our response is only to seek to ignore such awareness. Facing the fact of the ever-changing nature of our being and our own eventual non-existence is, from an existential point of view, to respond *authentically*. (The alternative might be, for example, to attempt inauthentically to circumvent anxiety by seeking or assuming a false sense of permanence.) Again, we act authentically if we acknowledge our freedom to make choices and 'own' (i.e. take responsibility for) our decisions and actions, rather than assuming that these are (or allowing them to be) determined for us.

You might like to think about this notion of authenticity in relation to the models of the person suggested by the biological and the cognitive-experimental perspectives presented in Chapters 2 and 3. Contrast the idea of acting authentically with the ways in which they account for the basis for our actions.

Note that the existential position is *not* that all people are concerned with these issues every day: there are clearly notable differences between both individuals and cultures in how salient such concerns are and in the kind of response they elicit. But it is to argue that such issues are intrinsic to the human condition, whether we acknowledge them or not.

Existential psychotherapists work from the assumption that one of the primary sources of neurotic problems lies in the blocks and defences which we erect against the anxiety which our experience of existing may create. Thus, one person may try to repress awareness of the fact of his eventual death; another may avoid all opportunity for making choices which could affect his or her life.

In the sections which follow, three existential concerns will be discussed in turn – *time*, *choice* and *meaningfulness*. Such issues have been of particular interest both to existential psychotherapists (see, for example, May, 1958, and Yalom, 1980) and to existential philosophers and thinkers such as Nietzsche, Kierkegaard, Sartre and Camus. And they are certainly relevant to any attempt to understand the grounds for personal being and social life.

These sections are in the form of essays which bring together theoretical ideas, reflections, activities and even poetry. They are partly phenomenological (in that they are concerned to differentiate aspects of experience), partly theoretical (in that they discuss the basis, context and implications of such experience), but they are primarily existential. For they are intended, in the spirit of the existential position, to stimulate your thinking about these issues in relation to your own life experience. In studying them, your task is twofold. Try to note the main theoretical ideas and issues and consider their implications for understanding the self. But also see whether they make sense *to you* and prompt feelings about *your* experience of being.

6   Time

'... Life can only be understood backwards. But ... it must be lived forwards.' (Kierkegaard)

6.1   The experience of time

The centrality of time as a dimension of our personal worlds was clearly revealed in the Windows in Chapter 1. Each is set in a narrative of events, and involves memories of past experiences and anticipation of future ones.

We are not here concerned with the concept of time in physics and philosophy. From a phenomenological point of view the word 'time' is an abstraction used to refer to the *flux* – the ongoing flow-like nature of our experience, coupled with our capacity to remember fragments of the past and to envision possibilities in the future. This flow seems to be not so much a continuity but a succession of phases or cycles, each with its distinctive qualities and marked out by our involvement in the ecological and social contexts in which we live. So wintery days follow autumnal ones; Monday morning for many people has a decidedly different feel from Saturday night.

Another feature of the flow of time is its sense of being 'the continuous creation of unforeseeable novelty' (Bergson, 1965). We may know what to expect, but when it happens it is never *precisely* as we predict.

Although we are located in an ever-changing present, this contains within it both our awareness of the past and anticipations of the future. As St Augustine pointed out in his *Confessions,* there are 'three times: a present of past things, a present of present things, and a present of future things' (1961, p. 269). Awareness of the past is sustained not just by present memory but by objects in our present experience which are associated with earlier times. Photographs often provide particularly powerful links (see Box 4.6). Nevertheless, phenomenologically, it may be a misconception to regard the past as immutable. For although it cannot be regained, it can be reconceptualized in the present and seen as something other than it appeared to be at the time. Anticipations of the future may also influence our awareness of the past as well as the present. As May has expressed it, 'What an individual seeks to *become* determines what he remembers of his *has been'* (1958, p. 69).

BOX 4.6   Photographs as present encapsulations of the past

In their book *The Meaning of Things* (1981) Csikszentmihalyi and Rochberg-Halton discuss how objects can form a link with a past which we may not even have experienced ourselves. The following account was given by a woman who was born and raised in Chicago:

> Photographs … That is the link with the past, the pictures of people that I never knew, and whom my children will certainly never know. I'm the kind of person who looks up relatives. It's a link with the past, the knowledge that these people are a part of our lives. I consider the loss of an irreplaceable photo a terrible, terrible loss. … But the ones my mother has from Europe are just irreplaceable. The people are all dead. All of their belongings were confiscated. There's nothing left.

> … All of my mother's five brothers and sisters, their husbands and wives, their children, her cousins, all of her childhood friends, everybody was slaughtered. Some died in the concentration camps, starvation and torture. Some were killed, pulled right out of their homes, and murdered, not just by the Nazis. … Butchered by the local townspeople, who were given free rein by the Nazis to kill the Jews.

> … But I have the pictures and I see them.

(Csikszentmihalyi and Rochberg-Halton, 1981, p. 223)

The experience of time is set in a series of widening perspectives: our personal biography, awareness of how this meshes with the lives of significant others such as grandparents, broader historical perspectives and, for some people, superordinate frameworks of unimaginable scale – the evolution of our species, of life and our planet.

6.2   Factors underlying variations in the experience of time

The flow of experience seems highly variable: sometimes it flies by, on other occasions it drags.

What kinds of factor do you think influence your experience of time?

Sections 6.2.1 and 6.2.2 contain some of my thoughts on this.

6.2.1   Personal factors

Awareness of time seems intrinsically bound up with the kind of *activities and experiences we are engaged in,* and how pleasurable and how involving these are. Our awareness of how much time has elapsed seems dependent on *perspective* too. Have you found, as I have, that while you are involved in varied and interesting activities, time seems to pass rapidly, but in retrospect it always seems as though a long time has elapsed? On the other hand, when life is more humdrum, time seems to flow more slowly, but in retrospect it seems difficult to believe a week, say, has gone by. (William James observed this too, and there are several studies which have found it to be a common experience (see Friedman, 1990).)

The pace of our experience of time is not just bound up with activities but also with *mood states,* for example of excitement and depression (which in turn relate to physiological functioning). If you look back at the account of Leonard in Chapter 1 and compare the various phases of his experience of taking L-Dopa, there are qualitative differences in the flow of his experiential time – periods of mad rush and impulsion, others of quiet emptiness. He is clearly aware of such differences, and later reported having had more experiences during his time on L-Dopa than in all the previous years of his life combined.

Perhaps you have noticed that the years seem to be getting shorter as you grow older. One reason for this may be that the length of any particular unit of time taken as a proportion of the span of life we have lived does become progressively smaller. There is certainly evidence that the way we experience time is related to the *stage of life* we have reached (Cottle and Klineberg, 1974), and that the older we get the more quickly it seems to pass. This seems to hold for people in their twenties through to those beyond retirement (Joubert, 1983). For children, time seems to have a more expansive feel, in the sense that what for us are short periods are long ones for them: and the younger the child the less ability he or she seems to have to conceive of the future. The increase in cognitive capacity which comes with the attainment of what Piaget has called formal operational thinking opens up time perspective for adolescents. But while there may be preoccupation with thoughts and plans for the future, adolescence is also often characterized by a sense of interminable waiting for it all to begin:

> So much of adolescence is an ill-defined dying,
> An intolerable waiting,
> A longing for another place and time ...
>
> *(Roethke, 1968, p. 162)*

The experience of time also depends on the *context* we are in. It is particularly when a person is cut-off from the normal flow of everyday life that the differences possible in the experience of time are brought home forcibly. Brian Keenan (1992), who was quoted in section 4, noted changes in his awareness of time when imprisoned as a hostage. Serge has also written powerfully about the experience of time in prison:

So as not to lose track of the date, you have to count the days attentively, mark each one with a cross. One morning you discover that there are forty-seven days – or one hundred and twenty, or three hundred and forty-seven! – and that it is a straight path leading backwards without the slightest break: colourless, insipid, senseless. Not a single landmark is visible. Months have passed like so many days; entire days pass like minutes. Future time is terrifying. The present is heavy with torpor.

Each minute may be marvellously – or horribly – profound. That depends to a certain extent on yourself. There are swift hours and very long seconds. Past time is void. There is no chronology of events to mark it; external duration no longer exists.

(Serge, 1970, pp. 56–7)

6.2.2   Societal factors

The constant time checks we use today – the radio signals and the bleep of digital watches in workplace and at home – are, of course, of relatively recent origin. In traditional societies, where time is marked only by natural events such as dawn or dusk or the changing seasons, there is hardly likely to be a time crisis. Mbiti has argued that in traditional African consciousness the concept of a future, apart from events which inevitably will occur as natural cycles, is virtually absent. There is an almost exclusive focus on 'what is present and what is past' (Mbiti, 1969).

Fromm (1960) has linked the increasing importance of clock time to the growth of capitalism: '… in Nurnberg the clocks have been striking the quarter hours since the sixteenth century. Too many holidays began to appear as a misfortune. Time was so valuable that one felt one should never spend it for any purpose which was not useful' (Fromm, 1960, p. 49).

With the development of a technological society time became a commodity, equivalent to money, a scarce resource. The rate of social and technological change has now accelerated and, with the elaboration of theories of evolution and the origins of the universe, the contextual time-scale in which we set ourselves has vastly expanded.

For most students and workers in contemporary western society, time dominates much of our life (as no doubt you will be only too aware!). We plan ahead, marking dates of events, meetings and deadlines in calendars and diaries, and struggle to complete work on time. Time can too easily seem to be harrying and hurrying us into the future. Our attention can become distracted from the here-and-now by our concern with the present of things to come.

A striking feature of contemporary life is the multiplicity of different settings which we experience: for example, the worlds of work, home and different leisure activities. Time has to be budgeted and activities synchronized to make possible such multiple involvements. Another aspect of living in modern society is the sense it fosters that there are numerous opportunities and possibilities open to us. As this encourages us to plan our future with the aim of maximizing these, any free time is likely to be quickly absorbed.

The imposition of time structures, however, should not necessarily be regarded in a negative light. There is evidence, for example, that one of the major disadvantages of becoming unemployed is the loss of the time structuring which goes with work (Jahoda, 1982). And when Fryer and Payne (1984) studied a sample of people identified as coping with their unemployment in a creative and positive way, they found that one of their distinguishing characteristics was the ability to generate their own personal structuring of time.

Stopping time

ACTIVITY 4.10

Payne (1974) has suggested the following exercises as a way to help break the feeling of being imposed on by the flow of events, to help bring us back to experiencing the present. You might like to try them sometime:

1   Stop reading for a minute or two and try to be here – now. Quiet your breathing and increase the pauses before and after exhalation. Take in as much of what is going on as you can – the sounds, the motions of things, the flow of feelings within you, the positions and tensions of your body, your thoughts. Especially attend to any other persons, and your own sense of yourself as being present, right here, right now. As you do this, *stop time*. Be aware that everything happening or existing is just as it should be, was to be, will be, is. There is no time, there is only now, this moment.

2   Gather together a few friends who are familiar with the notion of being here-now and have practised a bit. Pick a relaxed and pleasant spot away from distractions of noise or other persons and sit closely together so that you can easily see and touch each other. Take a few minutes to attend to what is present – the sensory environment, your own internal states and the presence of those around you. Then concentrate your attention primarily on being with each other. Talk or not as you wish. But help one another not to stray into reveries or away from the group. Try to be fully here – now with each other. Maintain eye contact by looking into the eyes of the others and as you look, feel, and sense what is going on, *reflect on the timelessness of it. Make the effort to stop time.* Be aware, understand that *there is no time within you*, that here the past and the future flow together into the now and now is forever. This moment is eternal.

(Payne, 1974, pp. 123–4)

ACTIVITY 4.11   To make a small exploration of your dependence on artificial means for structuring time, you might like to try going for half or even a whole day without wearing a watch and deliberately avoiding any form of time check (including listening to the radio). Later, reflect on your experience. What did it feel like? How important did it become for you to know what the time was? Why?

6.3   Finiteness

Time inevitably implies change – the sense that things future will become things present, that that which is now will never be again. For many people, for much of their lives, this may be experienced as a sense of *progression* – of moving towards potentially brighter, richer, more developed horizons. But as we grow older, perhaps, the future may become more circumscribed, more definitive. Under some circumstances, such as unemployment, the flow may be experienced as *deterioration*. Taylor notes this also in his study (with Cohen) of long-term prisoners:

> … for these long-term prisoners there was a continuous anxiety about psychic degeneration. … monitoring their own psychic state therefore assumed a special importance. And as a further stimulus to such self-monitoring and the concomitant anxiety it induced, there were all around them in the wing, frightening examples of men who appeared to have lost all contact with reality.
>
> *(The Open University, 1976, pp. 13–14)*

The sense of time as fleeting and irrevocable is a theme that recurs in the literature of many cultures. The Persian poet Omar Khayyám wrote in *The Rubáiyát* many centuries ago:

> The Moving Finger writes; and, having writ,
> Moves on; Nor all thy Piety nor Wit
> Shall lure it back to cancel half a Line,
> Nor all thy Tears wash out a Word of it.

Time becomes an existential issue because we are aware that it cannot be turned back (i.e. it is irrevocable): deeds done cannot be undone, possibilities unrealized never will be. Also, the allotment of time to each of us, although variable, is finite: so each of us has to confront in some way the fact that at some stage we shall physically cease to be.

The gradual movement through our lives towards non-being is perhaps the most profound conflict which underlies human existence. As Yalom asserts: 'The fear of death plays a major role in our internal experience; it haunts as does nothing else; it rumbles continuously under the surface; it is a dark, unsettling presence at the rim of consciousness' (Yalom,

1980, p. 27). Uncertainty about the actual time when we shall die may help to make it more tolerable to bear but does not subtract from the certainty that it will come someday.

We deal with it in different ways. We may react with anger at our impotence in the face of it. As Dylan Thomas exhorted his father:

> Do not go gentle into that good night,
> Old Age should burn and rave at close of day:
> Rage, rage against the dying of the light.

> *(Thomas, 1952, p. 159)*

We are more likely though to erect defences against full awareness of its inevitability – an implicit feeling perhaps that somehow we are 'special' and that 'it cannot happen to us'. For most of us, such defences are fragile at best. They are easily disturbed, particularly as we grow older, by reminders of ageing or mortality – the death of a friend, retirement, a bout of illness, or even annual rituals such as birthdays or New Year's Eve which mark the passing of the years. Entering a new phase in our lives, through divorce, for example, or even by commitment to a new relationship, may also remind us that we are one stage nearer to the end. And, of course, existence is full of 'little deaths' where friendships fade, children grow up and houses are lived in no more.

Society tends to support (indeed may actively encourage) our attempts to shield ourselves from the prospect of non-being. A widespread reaction, particularly by many religions, has been in effect to *deny* it. Thus it is asserted that, while our physical bodies may die, the important essence of ourselves or soul continues to exist in some form of 'afterlife'. A rather different approach which is common in present-day secular societies is to *ignore* it – staving off the awareness of eventual death by involvement in a continuous round of projects and activities. As each one is completed so a new one is taken up in its place.

Perhaps the most realistic way to cope, in that it does not seek to ignore or deny the reality of death, is to attempt to *transcend* it. This may be done by seeking some form of 'immortality' in this world: for example, by having children, by creating products which will live on after you have gone, by influencing other people's lives in some way, or by being remembered for some achievement. Many of the most strenuous activities we engage in are fuelled by this underlying need. Joyce Smith, the first woman to finish in the 1982 London Marathon seemed to indicate this when asked why she had entered: 'It would be nice to be remembered as an outstanding marathon runner. A lot of athletes achieve a lot, but in the end they're forgotten. Deep down I just want to be remembered' *(Daily Mail,* 11 May, 1982). Another way of transcending it comes with the exuberant emotional release on festivals and occasions when we break free of normal restraints of time and responsibility to celebrate existence here and now with song, dance, drink and laughter.

Another strategy of coping is to reframe death, much as Buddhism does; to see it not as an ending but as a fusion with universal and continuing life. Related to this, perhaps, is the attitude of *acceptance* of eventual non-being suggested by T.S. Eliot's lines from 'East Coker':

> Houses live and die; there is a time for building
> And a time for living and for generation
> And a time for the wind to break the loosened pane ...

(Eliot, 1974, p. 196)

This seems to be echoed in Erikson's idea that out of the final phase of life, and emerging from the interplay of opposing feelings of 'ego integrity' (acceptance of one's life for what it has been) and despair, comes the virtue of *wisdom* – 'the detached yet active concern with life itself in the face of death itself' (Erikson, 1980, p. 23).

Whatever resolution of this existential issue is attempted, the awareness that we shall eventually die and that the end could come unexpectedly through accident or illness or even as a consequence of our own or another's action generates an underlying sense of *vulnerability* in our personal world. There are times in the experience of many people when this insecurity of existence surfaces. In *The Varieties of Religious Experience* (first published in 1892), William James provides an example which, although in the book he attributes to an anonymous 'French correspondent', he later admitted to be autobiographical (see James, 1920, p. 145):

> I went one evening into a dressing-room in the twilight to procure some article that was there; when suddenly there fell upon me without any warning, just as if it came out of the darkness, a horrible fear of my own existence ... it was like a revelation; and although the immediate feelings passed away, the experience has made me sympathetic with morbid feelings of others ever since ... I dreaded to be left alone. I remember wondering how other people could live, how I myself had ever lived, so unconscious of that pit of insecurity beneath the surface of life.

(James, 1960, pp. 166–7)

There have been those, from the Greek Stoics and the Romans Cicero and Seneca, who have argued that awareness of our vulnerability and the prospect of death can enrich rather than impoverish our zest for life. When Gulliver in Jonathan Swift's book visits the Island of Luggnag, the most miserable beings he meets there are the Struldbuggs who have a spot on their foreheads which signifies that they will be alive forever, though their bodies continue to age and their minds to deteriorate. Several existential philosophers and humanistic psychologists in particular have emphasized that, paradoxically, far from casting a pall of gloom, awareness of the inevitability of one's own eventual death can intensify the vitality of our experience of living. Martin Heidegger (1962), for example, has asserted that, for 'authentic' existence, we need to live with *mindfulness of being* rather than with the forgetfulness which is so characteristic of our ordinary everyday experience. It is the need to confront unavoidable 'urgent experiences' like the fact of death that can jolt one into mindfulness. This effect has been clearly documented in several studies where people who have confronted the likelihood of death have been asked about the subsequent influence of this on their lives (e.g. Schmitt, 1976; Noyes, 1981). A common occurrence is that it changes their experience of living. One patient had come close to death through kidney failure. After a length of time on renal dialysis she had received a successful kidney transplant:

> Actually the only way I can describe myself is that I think of myself as having lived two lives. I even call them the first and the second Kathy. The first Kathy died during dialysis. She could not make it long in the face of death. A second Kathy had to be born. This is the Kathy that was born in the midst of death ... The first Kathy was a frivolous kid. She lived only one minute at a time. She quibbled about cold food in the cafeteria, about the boredom of surgical nursing lectures, about the unfairness of her parents. Her goal in life was to have fun on the weekends ... The future was far away and of little concern. She lived for trivia only.
>
> But the second Kathy – that's me now. I am infatuated with life. Look at the beauty in the sky! It's gorgeously blue! I go into a flower garden, and every flower takes on such fabulous colours that I am dazzled by their beauty ... One thing I do know, had I remained my first Kathy, I would have played away my whole life, and I would never have known what the real joy of living was all about. I had to face death eyeball to eyeball before I could live. I had to die in order to live.
>
> *(Schmitt, 1976, p. 54)*

Becoming more fully aware of our finiteness can intensify the delight we have in the time that is left to us. It can serve to turn our attention from trivialities and encourage us to live in a richer and more authentic way.

---

1   *Life-line:* Draw a line. At one end represent the moment of your birth: at the other the likely point of your death. Estimate and mark in where you are now in your life on the scale of this line. Meditate on this for a few moments.

ACTIVITY 4.12

Some other activities which you might like to try at some time:

2   *Lifetime:* Working on the basis of likely correlates, such as the average age of death of people closely related to you, whether you smoke or are overweight, your state of health, etc., estimate roughly the year when you think you might die. Then work out (i) how many years and (ii) convert that into the number of weeks that there are between then and now.

3   *Time budgeting:* This section has been concerned with the way we experience time. But awareness of the finiteness of existence may make it important to us to think about how we *use* time as well. You might like to

keep a diary of how you spend your time, breaking up the days into 24 one-hour periods and noting what you do during each. At the end of each week, analyse the pattern, breaking it down into appropriate subcategories and noting how much time you spend overall on each kind of activity. Reflect on whether this is how you *want* to use your time and, if necessary, on ways in which you can modify your schedule to bring the pattern more into line with what you would like.

(If you are interested in improving your time-management skills, you might also like to look (when you have the time!) at the following books: particularly recommended is Servan-Schreiber (1989); also Lakein (1984) and Fontana (1993).)

Review of section 6

- *The experience of time:* Time is an ongoing flow, segmented into phases, involving continuous novelty, where awareness of the past and future can only be experienced in the present. There are different temporal contexts (e.g. personal, that of known others, historical, evolutionary, cosmic).

- *Factors underlying time variation:* Factors which influence the way time is experienced include the nature of the experience engaged in, whether the perspective from which time is viewed is ongoing or retrospective, prevailing mood, stage of life, immediate context. Societal context (e.g. traditional vs. modern) is also a significant factor.

- *Finiteness:* Time can be experienced as open-ended, a progression, as circumscribed, or even as deterioration. Irrevocability and finiteness make time an existential issue.

- *Defences* against finiteness include denying, ignoring, transcending and accepting it.

- *Mindfulness of being:* Awareness of the vulnerability and finiteness of life can enrich life experience rather than undermine it, as effects of near-death experiences demonstrate.

7   Choice

Time as an existential problem is not just a question of coming to terms with the prospect of change and eventual non-being. It is compounded by our power of *agency* – the capacity to initiate change through our own action. As was noted in the previous section, we are aware that our actions have consequences, often irrevocable ones. How we choose (or do not choose) to act and feel may well determine what will or will not happen, or what we will become. Because of this, we have a sense of playing a part in the creation of our own futures.

7.1   Autonomy and determinism

We certainly *experience* some capacity for self-direction, for choosing what we do – these are attributes which (to borrow a phrase) no self-respecting person would be caught without. As we have seen, however (and will see in subsequent chapters of this book), there are many factors on which our actions and experience clearly depend. Chapter 2, for example, discussed how our agency is constrained and influenced by bio-logical processes. In the two chapters which follow this one, you will consider the impact of the social contexts in which we live (Chapter 5) and of unconscious feelings laid down in the early years of childhood (Chapter 6) on who we are and what we do. So, though we may experience being free to choose, what sort of freedom can this be?

One problem with discussion of this issue is that too often determinism is posited as an irreconcilable alternative to something called 'free-will'. Another difficulty is the failure to make clear what this 'free-will' is actu-ally supposed to mean. Once you have accounted for the influence of factors of the kind we have noted above, what else is there which could be said to generate experience and behaviour?

One way of breaking through this impasse is to think of our actions as analogous to language. It is clear that we are radically dependent on both biological inheritance and social context. Had you inherited the genes of a frog you would not be anything like the person you are now. But had you grown up as a member of a Chinese family, this also would have been a radically different life experience from the one you have had. These kinds of statement are true also for the language you speak. That too is totally dependent on vocal apparatus and brain centres of a specific kind, and also on the opportunity to assimilate from society a particular set of language conventions.

Stop reading and speak or write down a sentence which you are pretty sure   ACTIVITY 4.13
no-one has ever uttered before.

The interesting point about what you have just done is that you have created something completely original by means of an ability which itself might be regarded as totally dependent on factors outside your control. So, although the form of the language we speak may be determined for us, can we say that this is always true also for the outcomes we produce in using it? The critical factor here is that language is a *rule-generated* system. The capacity to use the rules and the particular conventions which govern them may be laid down by biology and society, but they can (though not necessarily) be used to generate utterances which are totally novel. This is what we call the 'openness' of language. It could be argued that the ways in which we frame our experience, interact with each other and plan and execute our actions are also generated by implicit rules. So this analogy would seem an appropriate one to enable us to conceptualize how, even given the biological and social construction of our personal worlds, we are still able to generate new and personal forms of what we think and do. A better term than 'free-will' for this ability is perhaps 'autonomy'.

The point of drawing on this analogy with language is not to suggest that this is sufficient to account for what autonomy is, but rather to demonstrate that accepting that biology and society shape behaviour need not rule out the idea of autonomy. Indeed, it can be argued that determinism and autonomy are inherently linked. As Rollo May has put it, 'a person moves *toward* freedom and responsibility in his living as he becomes more conscious of the *deterministic* experiences in his life ... *Freedom* is thus not the opposite to determinism' (1967, p.175).

Another way of looking at this matter is to appreciate that perspectives construct the realities with which they deal. This is to say that much of the traditional confusion here and difficulty in reconciling the notions of autonomy (or· 'freedom') and determinism (or 'nature/nurture') has arisen because these have emerged from different perspectives rooted in different contexts: in the former case our 'first-person' subjective experience of living, in the latter our 'third-person' observation of the natural world. The critical issue is the impact that such perspectives may have on us and the ways we conduct our lives, depending on whether they encourage a view of people as entirely determined or as capable of at least some degree of autonomy.

If we view the world from a phenomenological perspective, it is quite apparent that we have choice. And, as was suggested in Part 1, we are able to influence both our actions and what we experience by the ways in which we focus our attention, imagination and reflection. (In terms of Jaynes's analogy with metaphor, subjective experience acts both as an analogue and an operator: it both represents and directs.) We are capable thus of generating alternative ways of constructing experience. It is an open and fluid rather than a closed and fixed process.

It is important to recognize, however, that even existentialists acknowledge that there are very real constraints on our autonomy. As noted earlier, Heidegger (1962) has written of 'thrownness' (*Geworfenheit*) to refer to the fact that we were born at at particular time to particular people in a particular cultural and historical context. The phenomenological position is that freedom is 'situated'. We make choices within situations with material and under conditions which are not (at least originally) of our own choosing. (Paradoxically, even the need to choose is thrust upon us by the fact of existence. As Sartre expressed it 'people are condemned to be free!')

ACTIVITY 4.14

1   Reflect for a moment on the degree to which you consider yourself able to choose what you experience and do.

2   Note three examples where you feel you have exercised choice. How far and in what sense were you autonomous? What was involved?

3   Do you enjoy exercising such autonomy (i.e. deciding yourself what you will do and experience)?

4   Do you sometimes seek to avoid the responsibility of choice? If so, in what ways do you do this?

7.2   The experience of autonomy

The exercise of autonomy is a personal act of creation. Experientially, it would seem to have two facets. It involves *reflection* on what alternatives we feel are open to us; and also the *commitment* to one or other of them in thought, word or action. (The emphasis on reflection is not to deny that spontaneous, undeliberated action may also be experienced as autonomous, but, for it to be considered so, we do need at some level to be aware of what we are doing and to accept that this is what we choose to do.)

Exercising autonomy involves taking *responsibility* for or 'owning' one's own actions. As noted in the discussion of agency in Chapter 1, section 2.2, in everyday life people do hold both themselves and others responsible for what they do, provided (as is usually the case) that their actions are assumed to have been freely chosen.

Being responsible means being *accountable*; that is, we may be called upon to account for (if only to ourselves) *why* we chose to do what we did. Some existentialists (such as Sartre in his early writings) have taken the extreme position of regarding people as responsible for *all* that they experience and do, including actions which they choose not to carry out. (There is not the space here to go into the detail of existentialist philosophy but it might be worth noting in passing that one basis for this position is the idea of *intentionality*: that our perception and awareness are 'directed at' objects and the world, and that our experience is therefore constituted by our own consciousness as well as by the nature of the objects themselves. A useful example offered by Rollo May (1969,

p. 224) to illustrate intentionality is to imagine a house as seen by an estate agent, an artist, a person looking for a house to rent, or someone coming to visit friends. In each case it is the same house but, because of their different needs, it is likely to be constituted very differently in the consciousness of each of the people mentioned. In this sense, we 'own' and are responsible for the way we experience the world as well as for the actions we take.)

7.3 Fear of freedom

Although it seems difficult to envisage human existence without some implicit sense of personal autonomy, some writers have questioned how far the experience of autonomy is a socially constructed one, dependent on historical and cultural context. Erich Fromm (1960) has suggested that personal autonomy assumed significance only fairly recently in human history, coming into prominence with the advent of capitalism and the rise of secularism. For, with the weakening of cultural and religious belief systems which traditionally provided firm guidance for action (both in terms of moral precepts and the inner sense that God would provide direction), autonomy becomes a problem. People are aware of their power to choose. But they do not always know *what* to choose – at least not when they try to act with a reflective eye for the nature and potential consequences of what they do.

A basic problem here, as existentialists see it, is that autonomy is yours and yours alone. There are no real guidelines and there is no-one else to tell you what to do, for that would be to relinquish your autonomy. Such *groundlessness is* a fundamental source of existential anxiety, deeper, some believe, than the fear of death (as Kierkegaard put it (1957, p. 139), 'dread is the possibility of freedom'). By taking responsibility for our actions and attitudes we acknowledge that they are a part of what we are. Choosing how to act, think and feel is thus an act of self-creation. To choose also means, of course, to exclude the rejected alternatives – to know that these events will not happen, and that they are experiences we may never know.

Confronted with such onerous responsibility, people often seek to escape. In his book *Existential Psychotherapy* (1980), strongly recommended to readers interested in this area, Irvin Yalom has described some of the defences against autonomy which he typically finds among his clients. They may attempt to *displace responsibility* for their lives on to other people – the therapist, for example, or their spouse, or a friend, or astrology. They may avoid it by *refusing to take decisions,* by *behaving impulsively* without thought, by *compulsive behaviour,* or even by *going 'crazy',* acting in a way which can be assumed to be beyond their control.

Fromm also asserts that people find it difficult to accept their freedom to choose. They shirk the responsibility it demands and fear the isolation it may bring. The mechanisms of escape which he describes focus on the ways in which individuals relate to society. One way, for example, is by submission to the orthodoxy of a political ideology or a religious belief system. One reason why authoritarian regimes (and perhaps some contemporary cults) may appeal to some people is that they offer the means to escape from their freedom. Another escape route common, according to Fromm, in contemporary 'marketing' societies is to allow our choices to be dictated by fashion. The changing tastes and reactions of other people become a key arbiter in determining what we do and how we are to be.

But, the existentialist would argue, there is no escape. To try to avoid the existential reality of choice is equally to choose. To live authentically, it is necessary, they assert, to accept our responsibility, to 'own' what we do (and what we do not do) and to acknowledge this as *our* personal choice. For an existentialist, guilt does not derive from transgressions against a particular moral code but from failing to live in an authentic way.

7.4   Cultivating autonomy

Is it possible to develop a person's capacity for autonomy? If so, how might this be done: for example, when bringing up children, at school or in the workplace?

There is, of course, much variation in the scope which people have to behave in the ways that they would like. Being in prison, for example, closes quite a few doors in more senses than one. And, in many other circumstances too, people's scope for autonomy may well be restricted. We may have to do a job we detest in order to provide for our family, for example, or not be able to act as we would like so as to avoid hurting another's feelings. But in almost all circumstances, and even where we are subject to physical disability or constraints, we can still exert autonomy in our thoughts and attitudes, as Leonard (in Window 1.2 in Chapter 1) demonstrated so well. The Austrian therapist Victor Frankl was himself incarcerated in a German concentration camp and observed that, even there, some prisoners were able to 'preserve a vestige of spiritual freedom, of independence of mind, even in such terrible conditions of psychic and physical stress' (Frankl, 1959, p. 103). His notion of the 'will to meaning' indicates our power to choose how we will interpret experience.

It was the capacity to initiate thoughts, in fact, which finally convinced William James that 'free-will' was no illusion. In his notebook of 1870, he wrote:

I think that yesterday was a crisis in my life. I finished the first part of Renouvier's second 'Essais' and see no reason why his definition of Free Will – 'the sustaining of thought *because I choose to* when I might have other thoughts' – need be the definition of an illusion. At any rate, I will assume for the present – until next year – that it is no illusion. My first act of free-will shall be to believe in free-will ... I will go a step further with my will, not only act with it, but believe as well; believe in my individual reality and creative power.

(James, 1920, pp. 147–8)

James's words here remind us of the significance of what we *believe* we are for the way in which we live. In this respect, there is a self-fulfilling quality about human experience. The first step towards developing one's capacity for autonomy is to believe that one has it. (Incidentally, this raises the interesting point that, because psychology is concerned with statements about why we behave in the way that we do, it cannot remain morally neutral. One of the criticisms which has been made of experimental psychology (see, for example, Heather, 1976) is that it tends to constrain our freedom by presenting us with a determinist account of human behaviour.)

As suggested in the quotation from Rollo May in section 7.1, the extent to which we exercise personal autonomy would seem to rest also on awareness of factors influencing our behaviour and experience. Once we become alerted to these, we have greater scope to counteract their effects and to initiate different patterns if desired. Thus, 'liberation' movements like gay and women's groups often place emphasis on 'consciousness-raising' about how society influences us. Psychology would seem well-placed to play a potentially important role here by throwing light on possible ways in which we are constructed and influenced by biological, developmental and social forces. It can also help us increase the scope of our autonomy by alerting us to new potentials and possibilities in ways of experiencing, and of relating to others.

The analysis of the experience of autonomy made earlier suggested that to act autonomously involves not just reflection on and choice between alternatives, but committing oneself to act on one's choice. In some cultures, particular attention has been paid to this aspect. In Japan, for example, one function of the martial arts and their accompanying exercises is to increase the capacity for self-control of body and mind and hence for acting as one chooses to do.

In a rather different way, a concern with cultivating autonomy can be found in the USA. It is presumed in the conventional notion that anyone is capable of bringing about what they desire (even to become President!), and encouraged in a host of popular self-help books with titles like *Pulling Your Own Strings* (Dyer, 1978) and *Awakening the Giant Within* (Robbins, 1992).

Most of psychology, in contrast to such examples, has been extremely wary about the notion of will. Both experimental psychology and psychoanalysis almost totally disregard it. The reason for this, of course, is that the concept makes no sense within the determinist paradigm within which both operate. Two notable exceptions to this trend have been Roberto Assagioli and the psychoanalyst Otto Rank. Rank (1936) made a useful analysis of the nature of *will*, distinguishing between negative or *counterwill* (opposing the demands made on one), *positive will* (bringing about what one has accepted from others as appropriate), and *creative will* (bringing about what one autonomously wants): he considers that these unfold in turn in the course of development. Assagioli was originally a psychoanalyst but later founded psychosynthesis – a therapeutic approach aimed at developing the intellectual, emotional, physical and spiritual potential of a person into a harmonious whole. One of Assagioli's books, *The Act of Will* (1974) explores the different facets of our experience of willing and making choices. A contribution he makes is to broaden the concept of will well beyond the Victorian notion of 'strong will'. Rather, he sees it as the active, creative process at the heart of the experience of self. His book also contains ideas and exercises for increasing the capacity to exercise autonomy. It is worth looking at this book if you want to pursue this topic for your own interest.

> Think back to Chapter 3, and the material there on Seligman's work on learned helplessness (section 5.2) and, in particular, Langer and Rodin's experiment which emphasized the significance of a sense of being in control for mental and physical health (section 5.1). How do these studies relate to the discussion here of the idea of cultivating autonomy?

But however we conceive of autonomy and its cultivation, a fundamental problem remains: that of *groundlessness*. If we are responsible for the choices we make and if there are no guidelines other than our own deliberations, on what kind of basis can we choose? Unless autonomous action is to be merely random or capricious (which, on the basis of the analysis presented here, it is not), it requires some sense of direction premised on values and beliefs. This brings us to our third existential issue – the need for *meaningfulness*.

Creating actions

ACTIVITY 4.15

1   Think of something you would like to do but would not ordinarily do (e.g. going to a museum, taking a taxi instead of a bus, holding a party, giving a present to someone).

2   Imagine yourself doing this.

3   Do it. Be aware that you have chosen to do it and have created an action which otherwise would not have happened.

4   You might like to repeat the exercise with other things you would like to do. (Or, alternatively, try not doing something you would usually do and modify the rest of the exercise accordingly.) Try incorporating a more conscious sense of creative autonomy into your everyday life.

Review of section 7

- We experience being able to choose (albeit a 'situated freedom').

- Choice or autonomy involves reflection on alternatives, commitment to one, and taking responsibility for that choice. One way of thinking of autonomy is as analogous to language, with its openness and capacity to generate novelty within a structured framework.

- Choice is an existential issue in that it confronts us with responsibility for creating the future. People may seek to avoid the responsibility of choice through various defences.

- There are cultural and individual difference in the focus on and exercise of autonomy. People may learn to develop their capacity to exercise autonomy.

- One reason for psychology's traditional disregard of the notion of autonomy is because it is incompatible with its determinist orientation.

- Psychologists concerned with ideas like autonomy and will include James, Rank and Assagioli.

8 Meaningfulness

ACTIVITY 4.16   Spend at least ten minutes thinking about the meaning of your life. What would you say you live for? What principles guide your actions? What do you regard as the point of your existence?

Reflect too on the nature of such questions. What kinds of answers are possible?

'Meaningfulness' is about finding (or searching for) meaning in reality as we experience it: in particular, having a sense of its relevance – what it is for, what it is 'about'. It implies a feeling of *engagement* or involvement with living and an awareness of having a value orientation (i.e. feeling that certain things matter).

A life which is deficient in meaningfulness is one which is experienced as lacking point, purpose and vitality; living is merely 'going through the motions'. Such *meaninglessness* is exemplified in classical mythology by the fate of Sisyphus, who was condemned forever to repeatedly roll a rock up a hill only to watch it come tumbling down again.

Lack of meaning in our lives is not something which may be immediately obvious. It may manifest itself only in a generalized apathy and lack of involvement in what we experience or do. But at moments when, for whatever reason, we reflect on the pattern of our lives, they may suddenly seem empty. In his book *Existential Psychotherapy*, Yalom (1980) includes a suicide note which vividly illustrates such an awareness:

> Imagine a happy group of morons who are engaged in work. They are carrying bricks in an open field. As soon as they have stacked all the bricks at one end of the field, they proceed to transport them to the opposite end. This continues without stop and everyday of every year they are busy doing the same thing. One day one of the morons stops long enough to ask himself what he is doing. He wonders what purpose there is in carrying the bricks. And from that instant on he is not quite as content with his occupation as he had been before.
>
> I am the moron who wonders why he is carrying the bricks.
>
> *(Yalom, 1980, p. 419)*

The significance of meaning in life is that it generates a sense of vitality and of meaningful engagement as opposed to passivity, withdrawal and alienation.

8.1   Sources of meaning

What then are the origins of a sense of meaningfulness? This question takes us to chapters both before and after this one in this book. One source of meaningfulness (in the sense of finding purpose or value in particular actions or experiences) is in bodily needs. When you are starving, or in peril for your life, what constitutes value direction or meaningfulness is not in doubt: it is to eat or to find safety. The need to find a meaning in existence is not an issue, because meaningfulness is provided in such cases by biological need. And, as Chapter 2 argued in discussing sociobiological explanations of sexual behaviour, there may also be predispositions to behave in particular ways (so that for the person concerned such actions matter and are meaningful) that may well have been shaped by evolution.

But humans are not only biological beings. We are also symbolic beings, capable of learning, assimilating and attributing meanings. Early childhood, in particular, provides a potent source of meaning in the forgotten or half-remembered experiences whose residues lie in our memory or unconscious and yet can help determine our feelings about what matters in life. Chapter 6 on the psychodynamic perspective will explore this aspect.

Meaningfulness, as well as being dependent on biological needs and childhood experience, is also culturally constructed. Thus, it can be as important to eat the 'right' kinds of food prepared in the 'right' way as it is to eat at all. Cultural values serve to give meaning and direction which often have no relation to individual physical survival and may indeed be in opposition to it (as demonstrated by those many times when people have chosen or have been persuaded to die for their beliefs). Cultural conventions as sources of meaning and direction can retain all the potency of biological needs. (As one example, in a plane crash in the Andes, a number of the survivors refused to eat the flesh of their dead companions even though not to do so meant certain death from starvation (Read, 1974)). In traditional societies, cultural values and conventions are able to retain their potency as a source of meaningfulness. The framework they provide is accepted by others in the same community and, like biological imperatives, it takes on a quality of 'givenness', of being the unquestioned 'way things are'.

8.2   The problem of meaning in contemporary society

The advent of more complex forms of social organization (in particular, technological society) undermines the sense of meaning and direction provided by these biological and cultural sources. On one level, it reduces the pressure of biological need. Life in western industrial societies rarely if ever needs to become a matter of finding enough food to survive. It serves also to break up the coherence of shared, culturally constructed frames of reference. In part, this comes about through the means it provides for vastly increased communication through broadcasting, literature of all kinds and travel. We are flooded with a plethora of alternative belief and value systems. Coherence is also undermined by the multiple worlds which are part of life experience in modern society. Not only does each of us inhabit a number of settings (e.g. work, home, etc.) where beliefs and purposes may differ, but the fact that we can escape from one into another also reduces the potency of the influence of any one (see Luckman, 1975).

A further factor in modern society which contributes to undermining an all-embracing framework of meaning in life is the development of scientific thought. The essence of the scientific approach is to question and enquire into the validity of established views. One effect of this in everyday life has been to raise doubts about many of the assertions made by the religions and ideologies on which traditional beliefs and values depend. Science's own attempt to exclude values from its operations has also had the effect of reducing the salience of values in secular world views built upon its foundations. Science (including experimental psychology) explains but makes no attempt to provide guidance or direction in the choices we confront in daily existence.

So how does a person in the modern world find ways of giving direction and meaning to his or her life? For a happy few, religious experience continues to provide a source of faith and inspiration – a way of making sense of life and deciding on priorities in action and experience. A major function of religions is to offer principles of moral guidance together with ways of making sense of reality which serve both to justify and give coherence to the moralities they espouse.

Where such certainty is no longer possible, what then? Even in societies as complex as our own, meanings and meaningfulness are also subject to cultural construction. They emerge out of interactions with others, relationships, and through participation in the shared enterprises of our culture. (This will be the theme of the following chapter.) One common pattern in contemporary society would seem to be that values (meaningfulness) become centred on aspects of people's daily lives, such as family, leisure, work and material comforts. This is certainly what Cottrell (1979) found in an intensive interview study of a sample of middle-class people in the UK. Apart from a general concern with contentment among the older interviewees and some signs of a romantic vision of a 'back-to-the-land good life', there seemed to be little concern with overarching values and ways of making sense of reality of the kind offered by religion. Nor was there much evidence of anguish over this. Most of the non-religious respondents seemed quite content to get on with whatever immediate projects they were engaged in without worrying too much about the need to make sense of it all. Although in a few cases political ideology had to some extent come to serve as a functional equivalent to religion, her conclusion was that, for the general run of her interviewees, 'no new religions were being born', nor were they felt to be necessary. (The concluding chapter in this book will return to this issue of meaning for people in contemporary society.)

Cottrell's study was limited both in the number (34) and type (professional) of her subjects. How far her findings can be generalized remains open to question. In any case, an existentialist might well consider that the participants in Cottrell's study were merely manifesting 'forgetfulness' and failing to live authentically with real awareness of their existential situation. In other words, although there may have been engagement with life (in having purpose, projects, etc.), this was unreflective involvement.

Interestingly, studies which have attempted to chart the way people develop and change through life (e.g. Levinson et al., 1978) suggest that a more reflexive need for deeper or superordinate meaning, which more fully acknowledges the nature of the human condition, asserts itself insistently only at particular stages in a person's life. It may be prompted by increasing age (e.g. the so-called 'mid-life crisis'), or the changes which come about through time (e.g. children leaving home), or it may arise in the wake of crises such as unemployment or divorce. People who have lived much of their lives content with *ad hoc* projects may suddenly awaken to a powerful desire to find a deeper, more all-embracing meaning to their lives. In his *Confession*, Leo Tolstoy vividly describes such an awakening in his own life:

> ... something very strange started happening to me. ... I began experiencing moments of bewilderment ... always taking the same form. On these occasions, when life came to a standstill, the same questions always arose:

> ... why do I live? Why do I wish for anything, or do anything? Or expressed another way: is there any meaning in my life that will not be annihilated by the inevitability of death which awaits me?

> *(Tolstoy, 1987, pp. 29–35)*

8.3   The search for meaning

Such questions pose a curious paradox. On one hand, they seem to demand an answer of a definitive kind – some firm sense of meaning which can provide a necessary basis for a fully authentic, engaged and vital existence. But reflection suggests that, once you get beyond the need for survival, there *is* no one definitive meaning to life. Or at least, the grounds for such answers cannot be provided by rational means. For the meanings we live by are created by the particular constellation of circumstances and experience which happens to mark our particular existence. From the standpoint of existential psychological analysis, there exists no meaning other than that created by ourselves as biological, social and experiencing beings. It is worth noting all three of these adjectives, for all three aspects would seem to be involved in whatever meanings life comes to possess. So finding meaningfulness in life comes down to the pragmatic issue of choosing a particular way of relating to the world that works for us, knowing that there will be consequences to our choice: we can, for example, go for short-term gratification or for long-term satisfaction. The problem is, how do we choose?

Yalom (1980) has made some attempt to classify the kinds of secular meaningfulness which people have sought in the face of such a paradox. There are those concerned essentially with self-gratification or development: *hedonism* is one example, where meaning is found in pleasure, the view that 'life is a gift, take it, unwrap it, appreciate it, use it, and enjoy it' (Brennecke and Amick, 1975, pp. 9-10). Another is *self-actualization* – the attempt to 'fulfil one's potential' by freeing oneself and trusting in one's intuitive wisdom to develop towards a sense of 'fuller being'. Meaning can also be found in *creativity,* not necessarily expressed only in some form of art but also in a general delight in bringing things into being and in relating to life in an imaginative and spontaneous way. There are also those solutions which transcend the self: *altruism* – finding meaning in serving others and trying to leave the world a better place (the road incidentally which Tolstoy was to take), and *dedication to a cause.* Yalom points out that these various forms of personal meaning are not mutually exclusive. In particular, different ones may be embraced at different stages in one's life. The psychologist who has perhaps been most concerned with the problem of meaning, Victor Frankl (1969), has suggested a somewhat different classification. Meaningfulness may be sought, he asserts, not just through *creativity* and the *experience of beauty* but also through *fortitude* – the capacity to face up to adversity and to find meaning in doing so.

To conclude this cursory survey of ways of searching for meaning, it might be worth mentioning an approach to life found among many Zen Buddhists. For this could perhaps be regarded as confronting the paradox which lies at the heart of any search for meaning. It is to regard all attempts to seek meaning in life as ultimately futile, whether this be through pleasure, creativity, altruism or dedication to a cause. But, by seeking to be fully conscious of immediate ongoing experience and what is happening for one at the moment, awareness in itself provides all the meaning required. This attitude is reflected in many Japanese haiku poems which capture the essence of an experience at a moment in time:

> Spring rain:
> Soaking on the roof
> A child's rag ball.
>
> *(Buson, 1964)*

There are no simple solutions to the paradox of how we find and create meaningfulness, arguably one of the most formidable problems of our time. But as Kurtz has pointed out, at its root lies 'not the epistemological demand for proof of life's value – but the quest for psychological stimulus and motivational appeal. What is at issue here is whether we can find within life experience its own reward' (Kurtz, 1974, p. 92). The issue then becomes one of inspiration as well as understanding. If psychology is to facilitate human potentials rather than merely preserve the status quo, it is an issue with which it must surely be concerned.

Have there been times in your life when you have experienced a particular desire to find a sense of meaning?

Does Yalom's classification of ways of finding meaning make sense in terms of your experience? Which of his categories is most significant for you? Are there others which you think might have been included?

Review of section 8

- Meaningfulness is about feeling engaged with living.

- Meaningfulness may derive from biological needs, experience of life (especially in childhood) and participation in the practices and beliefs of society.

- Because of its complexity, multiplicity and the influence of rational, scientific ways of thinking, contemporary society poses especial problems for its members in finding meaningfulness.

- The need for deeper, reflexive meaning may emerge at particular times in life.

- Secular meaningfulness may be found in hedonism, self-actualization, creativity, altruism and dedication to a cause (Yalom); the experience of beauty and fortitude as well as creativity (Frankl); and also in being fully mindful and aware.

9   Summary and conclusion

This chapter has presented an experiential perspective drawing on phenomenological, existential and humanistic psychologies. This perspective is based on a model of the person which emphasizes the centrality of *subjective experience* and that a person is an *intentional agent* who has the capacity to *reflect* on and to be aware of his or her own experience and situations.

In Part 1, four studies (of James, Csikszentmihalyi, Donaldson and Kelly) were presented which served to differentiate aspects of experience. A theme also developed there was the idea that subjective experience is intentional or generative. This is contained in Kelly's idea of 'constructive alternativism', and was explored further with the analogy of consciousness as metaphor and a discussion of the ways in which fantasy and imagination can involve 'inner directed' change in how we think and feel.

The existential approach emerges from and represents an extension of the phenomenological perspective. An important aspect of subjective experience is the ability to be aware both of being aware and of oneself as an existing person. This generates certain existential dilemmas or issues. Three of these were selected for discussion in Part 2: *time* – we are aware that we exist now but that at some time in the future we will not; *choice* – we are aware of our power of choice and that we ourselves play a part in determining the shape of our future experience and therefore the kinds of person we become; *meaningfulness* – we are also confronted with the problem of how to create some sense of direction or meaningfulness upon which to ground the experience and enterprise of living.

Although these three existential needs were focused on separately, it is apparent from the discussion that they are intrinsically *interlinked*. Our *choices* are linked with *time*, for example, for they have played their part in constructing our past and help to shape our future. Whatever *meaning* we attribute to our lives plays a part in determining what we choose. In such ways, the different aspects of the experience of self are interrelated and interwoven in the fabric of our personal lives and reflect the kinds of person we are.

For the existentialist, existential needs are seen as fundamental to and arising out of the conditions of human existence. That does not mean that there will not be *cultural variations* in awareness of these needs. But these are seen as resulting because the conditions of some societies facilitate reflexivity (and hence existential awareness) in their members more than others do. There is, in any case, so much in common in the life experience of people in any culture: we all live, relate to others, have some sense of self-awareness, die. Could there be any culture or historical time in which some individuals, at least, did not question the meaning of their lives, and had not some awareness of living in time, of the need to confront death and the prospect of non-being, and of their power to choose?

It is worth noting also that within any culture there will be *individual differences* in reflexivity. For some people in any society, existential awareness plays little part. We have seen too how different existential needs may become salient at different points in life. A growing child may have little awareness of time and existential issues, but the construction of identity is likely to become a central problem during adolescence, and the need for meaning and confronting finiteness may be more typical of middle and later life. But such variations between cultures and individuals are about differences in degree of reflexiveness. Even if we may not always be aware of them, existentialists would argue, existential issues confront us all.

In keeping with the model of the person presented, much of the method used in this chapter involved appeal to how *you* experience *your* world. It invited you to try what are perhaps new ways of reflecting on your experience. It even suggested personal experiments which might serve to extend your awareness about aspects of your experience. The goal here has been not only one of 'understanding about'; it has also been concerned with opening up and changing awareness – the ways in which you feel about yourself and existence. Facilitating change in awareness may also, of course, produce change in ways of living. In this respect, we might describe the goal of experiential psychology as 'agentic' (producing change) as well as phenomenological (concerned with understanding the nature of experience).

Experiential psychology in particular tries to do this by:

1   Heightening awareness of the nature of our experience.

2   Alerting us to the nature of the human condition.

3   Stimulating our reflexiveness: our awareness of ourselves and the ways in which we live our lives.

4   Facilitating our agency, heightening our awareness of our power to create our lives.

Thus, the experiential perspective is as much about inspiration as understanding. It is also what we might call a 'psychology of becoming', in that it is not just about the nature of self but about what the self might become.

Further reading

If you are interested in reading further about the kinds of analyses and approaches to the study of experience that were discussed in Part 1, then you should look at: Csikszentmihalyi, M. (1992) *Flow: The Psychology of Happiness,* London, Rider Press; or Donaldson, M. (1992) *Human Minds: An Exploration,* Harmondsworth, Allen Lane. For following up William James, a good place to begin is James, W. (1961) *Psychology: The Briefer Course* (ed. by G. Allport), New York, Harper and Row (first published in 1892). For a good introduction to Kelly, see Burr, V. and Butt, T. (1992) *Invitation to Personal Construct Psychology,* London, Whurr; or Bannister, D. and Fransella, F. (1971) *Inquiring Man: The Theory of Personal Constructs,* Harmondsworth, Penguin Books.

Ortony, A. (1979) *Metaphor and Thought,* Cambridge, Cambridge University Press still provides (despite its age) an excellent source of informed discussions about the nature and role of metaphor in psychology (though some of these are quite technical). Jaynes, J. (1990) *The Origin of Consciousness in the Breakdown of the Bicameral Mind* (2nd edn), London, Allen Lane, which is also referred to in the section on metaphor and consciousness, is controversial and speculative in much of its content but very stimulating.

For a readable introduction to phenomenological psychology, see Becker C.S. (1992) *Living and Relating: An Introduction to Phenomenology,* London, Sage. A more heavyweight but excellent book is Yalom, I.D. (1980) *Existential Psychotherapy,* New York, Basic Books. For background on the philosophical origins of phenomenological and existential approaches in psychology, look at May, R. (1983) *The Discovery of Being: Writings in Existential Psychology,* London, W.W. Norton. A useful source book here is Friedman, M. (ed.) (1964) *The Worlds of Existentialism: A Critical Reader,* New York, Random House.

An excellent 'pop-psychology' book on using the mind to produce change is Robbins, A. (1992) *Awakening the Giant Within,* New York, Simon and Schuster. Assagioli, R. (1974) *The Act of Will,* London, Wildwood, is also recommended.

If you are interested in the issue of meaningfulness, then have a look at Baumeister, R. (1991) *Meanings in Life,* New York, Guilford Press.

The books of Erich Fromm (e.g. *Man for Himself*, 1947, and *Fear of Freedom*, 1960, London, Routledge and Kegan Paul) also provide very readable analyses which bear on some of the issues discussed in Part 2.

The *Journal of Humanistic Psychology* and the *Journal of Consciousness Studies* are good sources for relevant articles.

References

Assagioli, R. (1974) *The Act of Will*, London, Wildwood House.

Becker, C.S. (1987) 'Friendship between women: a phenomenological study of best friends', *Journal of Phenomenological Psychology*, vol. 18, no. 1, pp.59–72.

Bergson, H. (1965) 'The possible and the real', in Browning, D. (ed.) *Philosophers of Process*, New York, Random House.

Black, M. (1979) 'More about metaphor', in Ortony, A. (ed.).

Boyd, R. (1979) 'Metaphor and theory change: what is "metaphor" a metaphor for?', in Ortony, A. (ed.).

Brennecke, J, and Amick, R. (1975) *The Struggle for Significance* (2nd edn), Beverly Hills, Clencoe Press.

Buson, Y. (1964) 'Spring rain', in *The Penguin Book of Japanese Verse* (trans. by G. Bownas and A. Thwaite), Harmondsworth, Penguin Books.

Campbell (1973) *Myths to Live By*, New York, Bantam Books.

Connolly, R. (1982) 'Sleeping partners', in *Observer Magazine*, February.

Cottle, T. J. and Klineberg, S.L. (1974) *The Present of Things Future*, London, Collier Macmillan.

Cottrell, M. (1979) 'Invisible religion and the middle class', unpublished paper, Linacre College, Oxford.

Csikszentmihalyi, M. (1992) *Flow: The Psychology of Happiness,* London, Rider Press.

Csikszentmihalyi, M. and Csikszentmihalyi, I.S. (eds) (1988) *Optimal Experience: Psychological Studies of Flow in Consciousness,* New York, Cambridge University Press.

Csikszentmihalyi, M. and Rochberg-Halton, E. (1981) *The Meaning of Things*, Cambridge, Cambridge University Press.

Dallos, R. (1991) *Family Belief Systems, Therapy and Change*, Buckingham, Open University Press.

Dallos, R. (1996) 'Creating relationships: patterns of actions and beliefs', in Miell, D. and Dallos, R. (eds) *Social Interaction and Personal Relationships,* London, Sage/ The Open University (Book 2 in this series).

Dennett, D. (1991) *Consciousness Explained,* New York, Little Brown.

Donaldson, M. (1992) *Human Minds: An Exploration,* Harmondsworth, Allen Lane.

Duck, S. (1973) *Personal Relationships and Personal Constructs: A Study of Friendship Formation*, London, Wiley.

Duck, S. (1982) 'The commonality corollary: two individuals in search of agreement', in Mancuso, J. and Adams-Webber, J. (eds) *The Construing Person*, Elmsford, NY, Pergamon.

Dyer, W. (1978) *Pulling Your Own Strings,* New York, Frunk and Wagnalls.

Eliot, T.S. (1974) *Collected Poems, 1909–1962*, London, Faber.

Erikson, E.H. (1950) *Childhood and Society,* New York, Norton. (Reprinted in 1977 by Triad/Paladin.)

Erikson, E.H. (1980) *Identity and the Life Cycle*, New York, International Universities Press.

Fischer, C.T. and Wertz, F. (1979) 'Empirical phenomenological analyses of being criminally victimized', in Giorgi, A., Knowles, R. and Smith, D.L. (eds) *Duquesne Studies in Phenomenological Psychology*, Pittsburgh, Duquesne University Press.

Flanagan, O. (1992) *Consciousness Reconsidered*, Cambridge, Mass., MIT Press.

Frankl, V.E. (1959) *Man's Search for Meaning: An Introduction to Logotherapy,* Boston, Beacon Press.

Frankl, V.E. (1969) *The Will to Meaning*, New York, New American Library.

Friday, N. (1976) *My Secret Garden,* London, Virago.

Friedman W. (1990) *About Time: Inventing the Fourth Dimension,* Cambridge, Mass., MIT Press.

Fromm, E. (1960) *Fear of Freedom,* London, Routledge and Kegan Paul.

Fontana, D. (1993) *How to Manage Time,* Leicester, British Psychological Society.

Fryer, D.M. and Payne, R.L. (1984) 'Proactive behaviour in the unemployed: findings and implications', *Leisure Studies,* vol. 3, pp. 273–95.

Giorgi, A., Fischer, W.F. and von Eckartsberg, R. (eds) (1971) *Duquesne Studies in Phenomenological Psychology*, Pittsburgh, Duquesne University Press.

Hariton, E.B. and Singer, J.L. (1974) 'Women's fantasies during sexual intercourse: normative and theoretical implications', *Journal of Consulting and Clinical Psychology*, vol. 42, no. 3, pp. 313–22.

Heather, N. (1976) *Radical Perspectives in Psychology,* London, Methuen.

Heidegger, M. (1962) *Being and Time,* New York, Harper and Row.

Hinkle, D.N. (1965) *The Change of Personal Constructs from the Viewpoint of a Theory of Implications*, unpublished Ph.D. thesis, Ohio State University.

Jahoda, M. (1982) *Employment and Unemployment*, Cambridge, Cambridge University Press.

James, W. (1920) *The Letters of William James* (ed. by H. James), London, Longmans Green and Co.

James, W. (1950) *The Principles of Psychology,* Vol. 1, New York, Dover. (First published in 1890.)

James, W. (1960) *The Varieties of Religious Experience,* London, Collins. (First published in 1892.)

Jaynes, J. (1990) *The Origin of Consciousness in the Breakdown of the Bicameral Mind* (2nd edn), London, Allen Lane.

Johnson-Laird, P. (1988) *The Computer and the Mind*, Cambridge, Mass., Harvard University Press.

Joubert, C.E. (1983) 'Subjective acceleration of time: death, anxiety and sex differences', *Perceptual and Motor Skills,* vol. 57, pp. 49–50.

Khayyám, Omar (1974) *The Rubáiyát* (trans. by E. Fitzgerald), London, Royal College of Art.

Keenan, B. (1992) *An Evil Cradling*, London, Vintage (Random House).

Kelly, G.A. (1955) *The Psychology of Personal Constructs,* Vols 1 and 2, New York, Norton.

Kelly, G.A. (1970) 'A brief introduction to personal construct theory', in Bannister, D. (ed.) *Perspectives in Personal Construct Theory*, London, Academic Press.

Kelly, G.A. (1979) 'Humanistic methodology in psychological research', in Maher, B. (ed.) *Clinical Psychology and Personality: The Selected Papers of George Kelly*, New York, Krieger.

Kelly, G.A. (1980) 'The psychology of optimal man', in Landfield, A.W. and Leitner, L.M. (eds) *Personal Construct Psychology: Psychotherapy and Personality*, London, Wiley.

Kierkegaard, S. (1957) *The Concept of Dread* (trans. by W. Lowrie), Princeton, Princeton University Press.

Kurtz, P. (1974) *The Fullness of Life*, New York, Horizon Press.

Lakein, A. (1984) *How to Get Control of Your Time and Your Life,* Aldershot, Gower.

Lakoff, G. and Johnson, M. (1980) *Metaphors We Live By,* Chicago, University of Chicago Press.

Levinson, D.D. et al. (1978) *The Seasons of a Man's Life*, New York, Wiley.

Luckman, B. (1975) 'The small life-worlds of modern man', in Brown, H. and Stevens, R. (eds) *Social Behaviour and Experience: Multiple Perspectives,* London, Hodder and Stoughton.

May, R. (1958) 'Contributions of existential psychotherapy', in May, R., Angel, E. and Ellenberger, H.F. (eds) *Existence*, New York, Basic Books.

May, R. (1967) *Psychology and the Human Dilemma*, Princeton, Van Nostrand.

May, R. (1969) *Love and Will*, London, Souvenir Press.

May, R. (1983) *The Discovery of Being: Writings in Existential Psychology*, London, W.W. Norton.

Mbiti, J. (1969) *African Religions and Philosophy*, London, Heinemann.

Noyes, R. (1981) 'Attitude change following near-death experiences', *Psychiatry,* vol. 43, no. 3, pp. 234–41.

Ortony, A. (ed.) (1979) *Metaphor and Thought*, Cambridge, Cambridge University Press.

Payne, B. (1974) *Getting There Without Drugs*, London, Wildwood House.

Rahilly, D.A. (1993) 'A phenomenological analysis of authentic experience', *Journal of Humanistic Psychology,* vol. 33, no. 2, pp. 49–71.

Rank, O. (1936) *Truth and Reality,* New York, Alfred A. Knopf.

Read, P.P. (1974) *Alive,* London, Alison Press (with Secker and Warburg).

Register, L.M. and Henley T.B. (1992) 'The phenomenology of intimacy', *Journal of Social and Personal Relationships,* vol. 9, no. 4, pp. 467–81.

Robbins, A. (1992) *Awakening the Giant Within,* New York, Simon and Schuster.

Roethke, T. (1968) *Collected Poems,* London, Faber.

Rumelhart, D.E. (1979) 'Some problems with the notion of literal meanings', in Ortony, A. (ed.).

Saint Augustine (1961) *Confessions* (trans. by R.S. Pine-Coffin), Harmondsworth, Penguin Books.

Schmitt, A. (1976) *Dialogue with Death,* Lincoln, Virginia, Chosen Books.

Serge, D. (1970) *Men in Prison,* London, Gollancz.

Servan-Schreiber, J.-L. (1989) *The Art of Time* (trans by F. Philip), London, Bloomsbury.

Singer, J.L. (1981) *Daydreaming and Fantasy,* Oxford, Oxford University Press.

Stevens, R. (1990) 'Humanistic psychology', in Roth, I. (ed.) *Introduction to Psychology,* Vol. 1, Hove, Lawrence Erlbaum/The Open University.

The Open University (1976) D305 *Social Psychology,* Block 9, *Man's Experience of the World,* Milton Keynes, The Open University.

Thomas, D. (1952) *Selected Poems 1934–1952,* London, Dent.

Tololyan, K. (1989) 'Narrative culture and the motivation of the terrorist', in Shotter, J. and Gergen, K. (eds) *Texts of Identity,* London, Sage.

Tolstoy, L. (1987) *A Confession* (trans. by J. Kentish), Harmondsworth, Penguin Books.

Yalom, I.D. (1980) *Existential Psychotherapy,* New York, Basic Books.

Yeats, W.B. (1961) *Essays and Introductions,* London, Macmillan.

Reflections

Contrasting methodologies

Methodologically, this chapter represents a turning point in the book. The approach presented here contrasts with that of Chapters 2 and 3. There, the focus was on explanations and, in particular, using the method of experimentation to establish cause-effect links. Chapter 3 showed how experimental research depended on operationalizing the ways in which people experience their worlds: that is, reducing them to observable responses which can be measured. The experiential perspective argues, however, that the full richness of our experience of the world cannot be effectively rendered into such 'operational' form but must be accepted as a qualitative subject-matter and treated on its own terms. In this it is united with other perspectives such as social constructionism (see the next chapter) and psychoanalysis (see Chapter 6). These perspectives all assert that *meanings are the essential subject-matter of psychology.* For them, the enterprise of psychology is a 'hermeneutic' one, designed to differentiate meanings and explore their forms and origins, rather than a 'nomothetic' one of trying to establish universal laws explaining behaviour. Instead of experiments designed to establish cause-effect relationships, we find qualitative analyses of experience (such as those of James, Csikszentmihalyi etc.), or other qualitative and analytic methods (more of which you will meet in the next two chapters) designed to help us to gain understanding of how and why people experience their world and act as they do.

The study of meanings and subjective experience as a qualitative subject, however, has its problems, for how can the analyses offered be evaluated? One way which was suggested in this chapter is to compare an account with your own experience. Does the account help to make sense of this? Note that this is not necessarily just a matter of testing it against what you already know. One function of phenomenological analysis, for example, is to *illuminate* experience; in other words, to make you more able to reflect on some aspect that you might have been vaguely aware of before. As was suggested in evaluating the work of Jaynes, accounts may also be assessed in terms of their plausibility: do they help us to make better or more satisfying sense of the phenomenon in question? Analyses can also be regarded as 'tools to think with'. Thus, they can get us thinking about the issue or area in a different kind of way: as might happen, for example, when you start to think about consciousness as like a metaphor rather than like a computer. However, although these are possible criteria for evaluating qualitative accounts, they cannot be applied in the precise way one might test an experimental hypothesis.

It must be remembered that the progress of understanding rests not only on evaluating the understandings we have but on generating those understandings in the first place: in other words, creating new insights into our experience and new ways of conceptualizing and thinking about it. Experimental psychology by its very nature emphasizes the testing of ideas. Qualitative psychology focused on meanings is more about the generation of ideas and describing and exploring what is going on and why.

Autonomy and determinism

The issue of autonomy and determinism (a key philosophical issue underpinning approaches to psychology) has already been commented on in the Reflections sections following the two previous chapters, but it is thrown into further relief here. For, as Chapter 4 makes clear, the idea of the person as an intentional, purposive agent is central to the experiential perspective's model of the person. And choice features as a key existential issue which we confront in our experience of being. It might seem that the determinist position which is implied by a natural science approach would be in direct opposition to such assumptions. So it is worth contrasting the treatment of agency here with that in the previous two chapters.

In Chapter 2, for example, it was suggested that because people experience being able to choose does not necessarily presuppose that they have autonomy in what they do. The discussion of alcoholism, for example, and also sociobiology, implied that behaviour is determined, at least in part, by genetic predispositions. Is it legitimate then to postulate (as existentialists do) that people have the capacity for autonomous choice? Interestingly, the author of Chapter 2 left this as an open question. Such determining influences, he suggested, might be thought of simply as bias rather than total determination. And genes might be regarded as coding for a nervous system in humans which makes autonomous action possible. As we noted earlier (see section 7.1), the existentialist position also acknowledges limiting influences, in that freedom is regarded as 'situated'. Biological, cultural and situational factors may all constrain and shape the options available to us, even though the individual may generate an autonomous response within these conditions.

Perhaps a useful analogy here might be the playing of a jazz pianist. The performance will be influenced by past learning and hearing other musicians play, by genetic and other factors which determine the skill of the pianist. It will also be influenced by the pre-established musical structures which make up the tune being played. And yet a good pianist can produce a pattern of sound which is not only quite individual and unique but at the same time it is so personally distinctive that a listening connoisseur could recognize who is playing after but two bars.

In Chapter 3, the importance of choice was also emphasized, especially in Langer and Rodin's study in an old people's home which made clear how important it is, for both mental and physical health, to allow people scope for exercising autonomy. And Petersen et al.'s attempts to set up 'optimism institutes' to encourage a more effective attributional style (see Chapter 3, section 5.3) is not dissimilar to the efforts of psychologists such as Assagioli to facilitate people's awareness of their ability to exercise autonomy (see Chapter 4, section 7.4).

The assumption of determinism (underlying, for example, psychology's use of experimentation) was imported, of course, from the scientific study of the natural world where a determinist perspective would seem to be an appropriate basis for explanation. How far that works when applied to the person in a social world (in whom autonomy may well be considered an intrinsic feature) is very much a matter for debate. It is certainly interesting that, even where a scientific methodology has been adopted as in Chapters 2 and 3, the understanding yielded still seems to suggest that autonomy is an important feature to take into account.

Kinds of psychology

Once we assume that people are intentional agents and that what they do will be affected by what they believe, then (as was noted in the Reflections section at the end of Chapter 3) the possibility arises that psychological research and theorizing may serve to affect the subject-matter it studies (i.e. people). In this way, it may have a self-fulfilling quality. If the importance of autonomy is emphasized, for example, then people may come to exercise it more and be given more opportunity to do so. This suggests a further criterion to be applied in assessing an approach: what consequences follow from it, not just in terms of the influence it may have on people, but also on what psychologists do? So, for the determinist psychologist, the task will be essentially to explain (perhaps also to attempt to predict or even control). But for a psychologist who accepts that people can be autonomous, the goal may well be not only to understand but also to facilitate that autonomy: thus, as was made clear, one aim of Chapter 4 is to help to stimulate reflection on your own experience of life.

I noted above that the contrasting methodologies we find in the chapters in this book would seem to reflect two rather different broad approaches to psychology. On the one hand, there is psychology as a natural science where psychologists are concerned with operationalizing and explaining in terms of cause-effect laws. On the other, there is psychology as a personal or social science where psychologists are concerned with differentiating or interpreting how and why we experience and act in the ways that we do. The assumption that people can be autonomous might lead us to suggest a third kind of psychology. This is psychology as what we might call a 'moral science' (using that term in its broadest sense to focus on what people choose to do and think). This is psychology concerned, as the existential approach is, not so much with why we are as we are but with the process of self-creation, with what we will become and how we will experience and act in the future. Psychology's role here is not only to raise consciousness about what influences help to make us what we are, but also to facilitate reflexiveness or 'mindfulness' through stimulating personal reflection about the process of living life.

You will have noticed that, in this chapter, poems and literary illustrations were used for this purpose of stimulating awareness. Their use may have prompted you to wonder about the relationship between literature and psychology. Examples from literature can provide useful expressions of the meanings which constitute the world of human experience. Nevertheless, literature is different from psychology. For the focus even of hermeneutic approaches in psychology is on research into psychological life and systematically differentiating, analysing and theorizing about this.

The next chapter continues the hermeneutic emphasis. It also focuses on the meanings which constitute being a person in a social world but, in particular, it goes on to look at where these come from. And it argues that they derive from the practices and relationships which make up social life.

CHAPTER 5

THE DISTRIBUTED SELF: A SOCIAL CONSTRUCTIONIST PERSPECTIVE

by Margaret Wetherell and Janet Maybin

Contents

1 Introduction

The previous chapters in this book have offered three quite different perspectives on the nature of the person in the social world. The biologist, the experimental social psychologist and the experiential psychologist all have a different 'take' on what it means to be a 'person', they understand 'the social world' in subtly different ways, and each draws on different research traditions to understand the relationship between the two.

Despite these differences, all three also share something in common. They tend to begin with the characteristics of the person (biological attributes, aspects of information processing, or features of consciousness) and work outwards from that point. This approach is sometimes called *psychological social psychology*. The alternative strategy, which we will adopt in this chapter, reverses this direction and could be called *sociological social psychology*. What answers do we find to questions about the nature of the self if we begin with the social context? How do culture, history and society shape the psychology of the individual?

This chapter will argue that, in a profound sense, the self is *socially constructed*. The exploration of this theme will take us across the globe from Japan to the Southern Sudan, from studies of children growing up in South Baltimore to a classroom in Milton Keynes in the UK. Section 2 of the chapter will try to clarify the claims involved in social constructionism. The following three sections will explore how these claims are put into practice in research on cross-cultural psychology, discourse analysis and children's language development.

Aims of Chapter 5

The aims of the chapter are:

- To introduce the social constructionist view of the self as continually shaped and reshaped through interactions with others and involvement in social and cultural activities.

- To present the idea that language is not a transparent medium for conveying thought, but actually constructs the world and the self in the course of its use.

- To investigate how children become social beings and the role of language, particularly narrative, in this process.

2   Establishing the argument

2.1   Attributes of personhood

Take a look at the list of assumptions below about the nature of the person. These assumptions are ones which many people in countries such as the UK and the USA would see as simply obvious or true, although they may also want to add items or qualify our list. As you read, consider the extent to which these premises may also have underpinned the research described in previous chapters of this volume:

1   A person is someone with a self-contained mind and consciousness; a unique individual who is separate and distinct from other people.

2   Each individual has one personality or a consistent set of traits, characteristics, preferences and abilities which sum up that person's true nature and which could be described and measured.

3   People own their thoughts and feelings. These are private, self-generated and organized within the inner self. Thoughts, feelings and internal states can, however, be expressed publicly through language, actions and through other symbolic means. Although people sometimes might struggle to find the right terms, their words reflect more or less accurately their internal states.

4   People, in these ways, are the centre and source of their experience. Individuals initiate action and try to realize themselves (their plans, beliefs, desires) in the world.

Summarizing these points, we end up with this description of the self – separate, self-contained, independent, consistent, unitary, and private. This list suggests a strong separation between 'the self' and 'the social world'. The premises above emphasize the privacy of the mind, our independence, and our autonomy as agents acting in the world.

In this view, the social context might 'impinge' upon or 'influence' the self rather like a snooker or billiard ball might collide with another ball, changing their directions momentarily; but this influence is seen as occurring between two already constituted and contained entities. Like the snooker ball, people are assumed to be roughly the same kind of thing in different situations, to have a unity and coherence. And, just as we see a snooker ball as an object whose characteristics could be described once and for all, the assumptions above suggest that people are open to description in the same way.

It is difficult to map the common-sense concepts above on to the academic psychological theories considered in previous chapters in any precise way. But there does seem to be some overlap, particularly with the experiential approach in Chapter 4. Although no one 'true' self is presumed and social influences are also acknowledged there, the experiential approach to the person does seem to assume that people are relatively independent of each other and self-contained, and it is these features which are seen as guaranteeing our autonomy. Much of the research cited in Chapter 4 certainly assumes that to find out about the self we should focus on the private and subjective world of individuals, their thoughts and the flow of experience inside their heads. If you remember, Chapter 4, section 2.1 discussed William James's conception of consciousness as always personal and therefore essentially private. Similarly, the design of many of the experimental studies described in Chapter 3 seems to assume that, in essence, people are the centre and source of their experience and thus their individual attributions and reactions in experimental settings are an appropriate focus for investigations of the person in the social world. In contrast, however, the biological perspective of Chapter 2 disavowed too strong an emphasis on the independent individual ('Our bodies are locked into inextricable complex interactions with other people; we affect and are affected by them'), while the cross-cultural research discussed in Chapter 3 on the relationship between cognitive style and cultural frameworks also questioned the independent and self-contained nature of the individual.

The perspective developed in this chapter develops from these last points. Social constructionists (cf. Bruner, 1990; Gergen, 1985, Harré, 1983; Shotter, 1993) argue for a merged view of 'the person' and 'their social context' where the boundaries of one cannot easily be separated from the boundaries of the other. The person, consciousness, mind and the self are seen as social through and through. As a consequence, it makes little sense to ask what is determined from the 'inside' and what is determined from the 'outside'.

Our physical bodies, separated from each other in space, social constructionists suggest, mislead us into taking a similarly 'separatist' view of our psychologies. But are our thoughts and feelings in a private locker to which only we hold the key? Social constructionists argue that, although we have a strong sense of an enclosed, private and self-contained world inside our heads, it would be more accurate to describe this internal place as a line momentarily and arbitrarily drawn around pieces of the public world. Certain chains of association, strings of dialogues, self-conceptions and operations on these have become incorporated within the person and then tend to be treated as personal property, as the life of 'my mind' rather than 'your mind'.

Many psychologists assume that the best view of the self is obtained when the social context is 'switched off' so that influences from other people do not complicate the picture. For social constructionists, the social world – social history, current social practices, social structures and social divisions, the patterning of everyday conversations and social interactions – should be *at the heart of* psychological investigations. The self, in this approach, is not an object to be described once and for all but is taken to be a continuously changing and fluid history of relationships (Gergen, 1991, 1994). Jerome Bruner captures this point nicely when he argues that the self has to be seen as *distributed*, not localized as is the snooker ball, but continually spreading, changing, grouping and regrouping across a relational and social field. Bruner argues (following

Perkins, 1990) that the self is best understood not as a pure and enduring core but as 'the sum and swarm of participations in social life' (1990, p. 107).

> Think of people's work, their children, their friendships, their writing, letters, marriages, diaries, and daily communications. These are part of them, they define who they are, and yet they exist in other mediums, distributing people well beyond the boundaries of their physical bodies. Where would you ask your biographer to look to find out about your existence?

If we accept this line of argument, we can see that identity becomes multifaceted, not singular or unitary as many conventional views suggest. There are a number of contextual selves, the people we are in different relational settings. To be sure, there must always be limits and constraints on this multiplicity. But our descriptions of people's identities will need to register the contradictions between their personalities, responses and actions in different situations. We will need to be sensitive to people's various involvements in social life, and the possible distributions of self across social contexts, in and outside bodies.

ACTIVITY 5.1

We shall return to these difficult and abstract points many times in the course of this chapter. At this stage you might like to note down the list of words below, as well as the term 'distributed self'. Try to locate these terms which summarize key aspects of personhood from a social constructionist perspective as you read the sections which follow, writing your own definitions and descriptions of their reference:

emergent
contextual
discursive
multiple
relational
mutual

The brief summary of social constructionist assumptions in section 2.1 may also have stimulated some questions, perhaps in relation to the arguments and topics raised in previous chapters, which you could also note at this point: questions such as – What about individual differences?; Is personality just a matter of social influences?; Where is individual choice and the capacity for reflexivity in all of this?; and so on.

2.2   The social self illustrated

To get some further purchase on the view of the person and the social context emerging here, we want now to illustrate this argument in some detail. The example we have chosen comes from anthropology. Anthropological work is useful for social psychology because sharing in the anthropologist's experience of living in a different culture forces a reconsideration of our most cherished understandings of what it means to be a person. This is a personal account from Dorinne Kondo, concerning her work in Japan. A Japanese-American born and raised in the USA, Kondo found her immersion in Japanese culture both disturbing and challenging.

ACTIVITY 5.2   At this point, you should read Reading A, 'On being a conceptual anomaly', which you will find at the end of this chapter. In what ways does Kondo's description of her experience contradict the four conventional premises about the nature of persons described at the beginning of section 2.1? What *new* ideas or information does this description add to your developing understanding of the nature of the self gained from the previous chapters of this volume?

Kondo's account is relevant to our developing understanding in two ways. First, her descriptions begin to indicate how Japanese senses of self might differ from more familiar views of the self found in the UK. This is vital evidence for the *social construction* of the self, and we shall consider this and other cross-cultural research in more detail in the next section. Secondly, and more importantly for now, Kondo's account makes us think about the general questions raised in section 2.1, such as: What does it mean to be a person?; What are the effects of the social situation?; To what extent are people independent and autonomous?

Kondo is describing a process of socialization and the process of learning a new cultural curriculum. Her sense of dislocation is a usual experience for anthropologists working in the field but more intense in this case because, as a Japanese-American, Kondo *looked* the part to her Japanese audience but could not be categorized as 'one of us', at least at first. For the social psychologist, what is fascinating in this account is the intertwining of the self and the social context and the merger of Kondo's inner world with her outer world. Kondo's experiences tell us a great deal about the process of social incorporation which happens continually in *all* our everyday lives (not just in Japan) but which has become so routine that it is difficult to perceive and pick out.

Kondo is being trained in new sets of behaviours and routines, such as the tea ceremony or other meal-time rituals. Through innumerable small-scale interactions, rewards and punishments, she learns what to do and say. But it is not just her external behaviour or the social mask which she presents to the outside world which is being redirected. As Kondo makes clear, she is also acquiring new patterns of thought, new internal monologues, self-descriptions, and new positionings of self in relation to other people. Acting, the 'outer' performance, cannot be easily distinguished from the 'inner' feeling. Indeed, this is what Kondo finds so disturbing – her body (posture, movement), mental states and attitudes seamlessly evolve together, recognized at the point when she catches her image unawares in the butcher's display case.

What is very evident in Kondo's account is the communal nature of social life and the *mutual* nature of social interaction (Still and Good, 1992). One cannot become socialized by oneself. The process is *relational* ('the sum and swarm of social participations'). Kondo gives the impression that the moulding of her Japanese self can be seen as a conspiracy or collaboration. Indeed, her experience and the experience of others around her was of situations of *joint action*, initially made uncomfortable by Kondo's cultural incompetence. Joint action (cf. Shotter, 1993) simultaneously positions all the participants, both oneself *and* the other person. The identities emerge in the interaction – in the 'in between space'. These features are characteristic of all coordinated social activity in Japan, Scotland, Hertfordshire, Canada – wherever people interact.

Consider the tea ceremony, for example, or the meal-time rituals Kondo describes. These social interactions assigned identities to all the participants. One can only define oneself as a certain kind of participant, a certain kind of person, because of the other person's contribution to, and definition within, the situation. No wonder Kondo's interlocutors were so keen to 'gently but insistently' guide her into 'properly Japanese [i.e. culturally recognizable] behaviour' and were sometimes impatient. Their sense of self and personhood also were at stake in these exchanges.

The tea ceremony

Japanese family having a meal together

A new picture of the psychological field is emerging here. As Figure 5.1 shows, any sharp demarcation between self and other is becoming more difficult to maintain, as is the notion of an independent and autonomous self. To talk of the person as 'jointly constructed', however, is not to imply that all are equal in these exchanges. As Kondo stresses, power is implicated here, too, and there are inequalities in the rights different people acquire or are awarded to structure the shape of joint actions. You might want to consider, for example, the gender dimensions of Kondo's experiences in the tea ceremony and meal-time rituals. (This theme is taken up in much more detail in Miell and Dallos (eds), 1996, and Wetherell (ed.), 1996.)

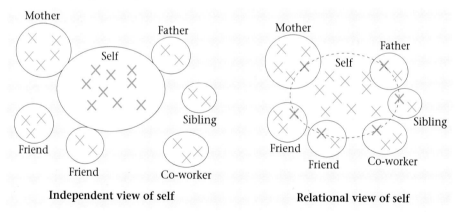

Figure 5.1 *Independent and relational views of the self (Source: based on Markus and Kitayama, 1991, p. 226)*

Kondo's new Japanese self, like the self of the growing child, is best described as *emergent*. The person is not fully-formed at the beginning, or completed at any point, but is continually constituted. Furthermore, as Kondo makes clear, there is not one self emerging but *multiple* and sometimes contradictory configurations. For Kondo, the multiplication is painful because of her many socializations: American woman, academic and researcher, Japanese woman, and so on. For the adult, new social identities must co-exist with old social identities, and sometimes these are in tension with each other. For the child, of course, the identities which emerge initially from this process are simply 'me', no other kind of self is known, and these preliminary senses of self are crucial for establishing a sense of continuity over time as new material integrates with old.

Kondo argues, on the basis of her research, that multiplicity is a fact of life for the ordinary Japanese cultural subject and for nearly everyone living in complex modern social worlds. In any highly differentiated industrial society such as Japan or the UK, movement across different sites, from home to work, for example, embroils the person in different social contexts and thus different identity possibilities – such as daughter, guest, neighbour, student, confectionery worker. Each of these communities has its own claims and its own identity pathways.

Some of the constraints on multiplicity are also evident in Kondo's account. Opportunities to take on different subjectivities (i.e. to experience oneself as a different kind of person) are combined with blocks to the spread of choices. People cannot choose to realize themselves in any way they fancy. Identities must be plausible in light of what has gone before; in relation, that is, to the collective history of previous responses and reactions. Without that plausibility, individuals cannot be recognized as 'themselves' or recognized as behaving in meaningful ways. The collection of identities which makes up the person must not be too fragmented; it must show some consistency and the person must show some reflexivity (see Chapter 4) or self-awareness of how they appear to others. Otherwise the person is in danger of being seen, literally, as eccentric, if not mad.

Multiplicity is largely a case of broad themes and variations. From Kondo's account there seems to be a broad theme that she and we can recognize as the 'Japanese self', or perhaps (sub-dividing a little) the 'Japanese woman's self'. Other multiplicities emerge from these regularities. It is also the case that, from diversity, tension and from the clash of identities within the person, change emerges as people negotiate their way among many possibilities, assimilating and resisting as they go.

ACTIVITY 5.3

If 'migrant' is defined broadly, then most of us could be said to be migrants. We have nearly all moved from town to town, from village to city or vice versa, sometimes from country to country, and certainly from community to community, job to job, or from primary school to secondary school within our home district as we have aged. What can you recall of the first days or weeks after you had moved into a new social world? How did you become 'socialized' and 're-socialized' in each case?

Most of us are familiar, too, with the situation of communicating with people from different backgrounds. You could evaluate Kondo's account in light of your experiences of this process.

Finally, Kondo's account is helpful in clarifying the nature of the social context which intertwines with personhood. The social psychological field in which people emerge is characterized by complexes of *meanings* and *practices*, to use Bruner's (1990) terms. In Kondo's case, 'meanings' included Japanese representations of what it is to be a reasonable and unremarkable human being, definitions about what is normal and natural, the resources of language, symbols, stories and ways of talking. The term 'practices' refers to the habitual and regular modes of life found in a society. In Kondo's case, the field of social practices included rituals concerning presenting oneself in public, the daily routines of people in the Shitamachi district of Tokyo and their methods for working with systems of mutual obligations.

The layout of the physical space (ecology and the physical environment) is as important here as the social nuances and, indeed, it is difficult to separate one from the other. Kondo describes, for example, how Japanese practices concerned with maintaining privacy are intimately bound up with material factors, architecture, space, money, the division of labour between men and women and between different categories of kin and workers. Meanings and social practices key into other aspects of the social context such as the institutions found in different societies (education systems, religions, the military), social structures and social divisions, such as those demarcating social class or kinship systems.

Kondo's account shows that meanings or symbolic and linguistic activities are not just cerebral, a matter of learning definitions in dictionaries, or knowledge which might be gained from etiquette books. They are always embedded in conversations and social interactions. Indeed, this is the main point of contrast with the conception of culture found in cognitive social psychology and presented in Chapter 3. In the experimental approach, culture tends to be understood as knowledge held in people's heads – as explanatory schema, for example. Social constructionists, on the other hand, see culture as more fluid and open, concerning relationships, interactions and a matter of everyday activities which continually shift and change.

One leading social psychological theorist, Rom Harré (1979), has argued that, if there is a fundamental or most basic social psychological activity, then we would have to say that conversation and social interaction are the best candidates for this distinction. Harré suggests that a considerable part of our life consists of talking: conversations, dialogues, monologues, communal exchanges of view, arguing and gossiping. How far do you agree with this? What proportion of your waking hours do *not* involve any talk whatsoever?

This point about the centrality of meanings, talk and communication in the social psychological field can be summed up by saying that we are beginning to see that our identities are, in part, *discursive* products. Language, talk and discourse provide some important raw materials for the construction of the self, whether in Japan or in the UK. People are embedded in conversations and we constantly make sense of the world through narratives and stories (Sacks, 1992). The ways in which we talk and are talked about help make different kinds of self possible. As Geoffrey Beattie notes, 'conversation is without doubt the foundation stone of the social world – human beings learn to talk *in* it, find a mate *with* it, are socialized *through* it, rise in social hierarchy as a result *of* it, and, it is suggested, may even develop mental illness *because* of it' (quoted in Muhlhausler and Harré, 1990, p. 21). Even the person living on their own or the most solitary mystic sitting under a tree in rural India may well find their heads are full of past and possible future conversations. We shall return to this point about language, meanings and identity many times in this chapter.

In people's social worlds, the social and the economic, the material and the mental, the ecological and the cultural are interconnected so that to seek to clarify any one set of meanings and practices is to pull on a thread which unravels the whole nexus. Identity and personhood are thus *contextual*. They are located within, and defined by, the complexes of social activities which we summarize as Japanese culture or describe as the English, American, French or Russian ways of life.

Review of section 2

- The social constructionist perspective argues that conventional views of the person as self-contained, separate, independent and consistent across situations are misleading.

- Instead, from this perspective, consciousness and self emerge in fields of meanings and practices which are socially and culturally organized. The person is social through and through. The material which makes up the social environment is the same stuff which composes the mind.

- This intertwining of the self and the social context is most evident when someone such as an anthropologist learns another culture and when we look at people's experiences in strongly collectivist cultures such as Japan, but the processes involved are those which routinely structure all our daily lives.

3   Culture and psychology

Chapter 3 noted that people's attributional styles vary across cultures, and Kondo's experiences are a further example of these cross-cultural differences. The social constructionist perspective can be seen as following up the implications of these findings for understanding the relationship between the person and the social context. Social constructionists argue that the dependence of people's sense of self on their social and cultural situations means that we have to reconceptualize the nature of the individual. People are best described as distributed, emergent, contextual and so on, rather than as singular, independent, self-contained and self-generative. But is it really the case that people's psychologies are so strongly shaped by their social and cultural situations? Chapter 3 described some research on differences in cognitive style, but what about people's core experiences of personal identity and continuity? Surely 'under the skin' we feel much the same kind of emotions and have much the same basic psychologies?

3.1   'Personne' and 'moi'

The French anthropologist Marcel Mauss argued in a famous lecture in 1938 that one way of handling these questions (which are key ones for both social psychology and anthropology) is to make a distinction between what he called 'personne' and 'moi' (Mauss, 1985). 'Moi' refers to a person's sense of being conscious, of being a body in space. It could be seen as comprising the most basic features of people's psychology. 'Personne', on the other hand, refers to social concepts of what it means to be a person.

Mauss seemed to see 'moi' as a kind of world-wide sense of self, a biological given that might be present in every human (Allen, 1985). He pointed out that as far as he knew there has never been a tribe or human grouping which does not have some kind of term for I/me. And, 'there has never existed a human being who has not been aware, not only of his [sic] body, but also at the same time of his individuality, both spiritual and physical' (Mauss, 1985, p. 3). 'Personne', on the other hand, refers to something which is culturally specific. The concepts of the person which make up 'personne' are found in the central social institutions of a society, in kinship systems, in legal systems, in religion, in views of morality. 'Personne' refers to sets of ideas about what it means to be human, assumptions about how people should behave, about motivation, conduct, and the influences on the person.

Thinking back to Kondo's description of her experiences in Japan, we can see that concepts of 'personne' are evident in ceremonies and rituals such as the tea ceremony but also organize relationships within the family and understandings of what it means to be a good neighbour. What is unclear from Mauss's essay, however, are the borderlines of 'moi' and 'personne' and the lines of connection between the two. How do culturally variable notions of 'personne' affect a person's basic sense of self? Is 'moi' (the part of personhood Mauss saw as pan-human and universal) simply a sense of having a body which belongs to oneself? Is this basic aura of self-reference all that is shared? Does 'personne' extend to what we might call psychology in general – emotions, drives, motives, consciousness, phenomenologies and our internal and subjective life – the features of the self considered in Chapters 2, 3 and 4? What are the effects of cultural and historical variations on these aspects of our lives?

> You might like at this point to clarify your own initial views on the extent of cultural influences. Which aspects of people's psychology would you say might be socially constructed, reflecting 'personne', and which might relate to 'moi' – a pan-human sense of self? What about dreams, feelings, reactions to others, a sense of personal power, the flow of consciousness?

Later generations of psychological anthropologists and cross-cultural psychologists, following in Mauss's footsteps, have done much to elaborate the cultural foundations of human psychology, and, as we saw, some of this work was introduced in Chapter 3. In returning to this topic and developing it in more detail, we shall look again at the case of Japan, and then at aspects of 'personne' among the Dinka people of Southern Sudan, and, in section 3.3, at research on emotions.

3.2   Contrasting concepts of the person

Kondo argues that where 'personne' in Japanese culture differs from concepts of the person found in contemporary North American or British culture is in the assumption of the fundamental connectedness of human beings to each other and the centrality of social obligations in everyday life. As Kondo's landlady commented – 'The Japanese don't treat themselves as important do they? That is, they spend time doing things for the sake of maintaining good relationships, regardless of their "inner" feelings.' Two North American social psychologists, Markus and Kitayama (1991), argue that this interconnectedness is evident not just in the Japanese definition of 'self' (as *jibun* – meaning, 'one's share of the shared life space') but also in the emphasis placed on the control of personal desires, ambitions and preferences which might disturb the collective equilibrium. This blurring of 'self' and 'society' is particularly evident in the anecdotes, proverbs and clichés Japanese culture endorses:

> In America, 'the squeaky wheel gets the grease.' In Japan, 'the nail that stands out gets pounded down.' American parents who are trying to induce their children to eat their suppers are fond of saying 'think of the starving kids in Ethiopia, and appreciate how lucky you are to be different from them'. Japanese parents are likely to say 'Think about the farmer who worked so hard to produce this rice for you; if you

don't eat it, he will feel bad, for his efforts will have been in vain' ... A small Texas corporation seeking to elevate productivity told its employers to look in the mirror and say 'I'm beautiful' 100 times before coming to work each day. Employees of a Japanese supermarket that was recently opened in New Jersey were instructed to begin the day by holding hands and telling each other that 'he' or 'she is beautiful'.

(Markus and Kitayama, 1991, p. 224)

Japanese interconnectedness is similarly evident in the grammatical forms of the Japanese language (see Box 5.1). Social constructionists such as Muhlhausler and Harré (1990) argue that these points about grammar are psychologically as well as linguistically significant. The ways

---

BOX 5.1 Personal pronouns and self reference

According to Harré and Gillett (1994), the English and Japanese languages represent two extremes in the use of personal pronouns. English has very few pronominal devices (e.g. 'I', 'me', 'you', 'he', 'she', 'we'), whereas Japanese contains one of the most expansive pronominal systems so far found: 'The resources of Japanese are such that in a conversation between two Japanese people using pronouns and verb inflections something like 260 different social relations between them could be represented. Not all of these possibilities are actually used' (1994, p. 105).

Kondo notes that the way the English pronoun 'I' operates encourages a belief in a whole bounded subject who can move unchanged from situation to situation ('The "I" who wakes up in the morning is presumably the same "I" who goes to work, who talks to a boss, who takes care of the children, who goes to bed at night'; Kondo, 1990, p. 32). English allows its speakers to distinguish strongly between 'I' and the context. In comparison, Japanese speakers constantly register, as they talk, their shifting relationships and movement across the social scene, not just through the wide range of pronouns but through the choice of verb forms also. Kondo asks us to consider the four simplest possible ways of saying in Japanese 'to hold' or 'to carry':

> The base form, *motsu*, is relatively informal, a form you could use with friends. The 'medium polite' form, *mochimasu*, indicates more distance. It could, for example, indicate that you and the addressee are acquaintances but not good friends. When speaking to status superiors – teachers, bosses – you would probably select *omochi ni narimasu* to refer to the superior's actions. But to offer to carry your boss's bags, for instance you should use *omochi shimasu*, the humble form.
>
> *(Kondo, 1990, p. 31)*

in which people can position themselves in social interaction and conversation depend intimately on the patterns of self-reference which are possible in their language as well as other aspects of their social situation. Grammar and the pragmatics of everyday language use can highlight certain kinds of identity and social relationships. As Kondo notes, in Japanese, 'awareness of complex social positioning is an *inescapable* element of any utterance ... for it is *utterly impossible* to form a sentence without *also* commenting on the relationship between oneself and one's interlocutor' (1990, p. 31).

Markus and Kitayama argue, on the basis of their own and other's experimental research, that these emphases in local Japanese concepts of the person have a number of powerful psychological effects on perception of self in relation to others, on the cognitive processes associated with motivation, and on the experience of emotion: in other words, on aspects, often seen as pan-human and universal features of the self. As Mansur Lalljee noted in Chapter 3, Japanese students, when describing themselves, are much more likely than North American students to use terms which embed the self in activities or relationships with others. Japanese students describe themselves through what they do (e.g. 'I play tennis at weekends') rather than through a set of generalized, abstract, cross-situational traits (e.g. 'I am an optimistic person', 'I am a friendly person').

Similarly, North Americans, when asked in research studies to estimate how long their experience of different emotions lasts, report experiencing their emotions for longer than Japanese participants, and report experiencing, too, more bodily symptoms such as a lump in the throat. North Americans are more likely to attribute uniqueness to themselves and assume that they are better than most other people in terms of abilities which are important to them. Japanese, on the other hand, are more likely to display what Markus and Kitayama call a 'modesty' bias'. In these cases we can see how 'personne' structures basic psychological processes.

Comparison with Japan clarifies the individualistic emphasis in many western cultures such as the USA (the focus on individual achievement, individual expression, individual authenticity, autonomy and independence). Comparisons with yet other cultures highlight further aspects of varying concepts of the person, as Box 5.2 overleaf illustrates.

It is clear from Box 5.2 that Dinka understandings of the person are likely to produce a profoundly different sense of embodiment from Euro-American understandings. A dualism of body and mind with mental states separable from physical states does not seem to be part of Dinka ontology although the distinction is commonplace for English language speakers. Similarly, the notion of a strongly differentiated internal world is much less prevalent in Dinka culture.

Again, as in the case of Kondo's experiences, it is important to stress that these meanings (such as Dinka conceptions of 'breath' and 'heart') are not emerging in abstract but are tied to social practices such as streams of joint activities around the collection of food, forms of agriculture, the

---

BOX 5.2   Dinka representations of self

Godfrey Lienhardt, a British anthropologist, carried out fieldwork among the Dinka people of the Southern Sudan (Lienhardt, 1985). He contrasts their conception of the person with the English notion of 'self' in the following ways:

1   The Dinka did not use the English distinction between 'body' and 'soul'. When a person died, for instance, the Dinka saw the body as still essentially that person, in contrast to the English conception of a corpse as a mere shell from which the soul and 'personness' have departed. The Dinka did see the body as being animated by 'breath/life', but this was a physical rather than a spiritual concept; for example, it was seen as strongest in the vigorous and healthy, and weakest in the old and ill.

2   The Dinka did not share the English distinction between 'heart' and 'mind'; the word for heart, *'pwou'* could also be translated, depending on the context, as 'chest', 'mind', or 'intention'. Both intellectual and emotional states were described in relation to the heart. For example, *'My heart is there'* means 'I agree', *'heart loss'* means 'to lose control of oneself', to *'have the heart darken'* is to be startled, frightened or sorry. Commonly used expressions were *'sweet (or tasty) heart'* for 'happy' and *'bad heart'* for 'aggrieved'.

3   Where the English use the word 'self', the Dinka used *'gwop'* which also means 'body'. 'Myself' is literally 'I body', 'yourself' is 'you body' and so on. *'Sweet body'* means 'lucky', *'body afraid'* means 'shy, embarrassed or timid' and *'body heavy'* means 'sick'.

Lienhardt suggests that, in comparison with the fairly rigid distinctions in English between physical, moral, emotional and intellectual attributes, the Dinka language creates a less differentiated conception of the person. In contrast to the abstract notions of, for example, 'trust' or 'suspicion' in English, the Dinka relate personal attributes directly to the physical matrix of the human body.

---

distribution of resources, and kin systems for regulating sexuality and inheritance.

In addition, societies and cultures are made up of multiple institutions and systems of social practices which often develop contradictory understandings of the person. (Remember how Kondo's experiences produced a multiplication and complication of her identities, and thus her self, rather than a simple shift from one way of life to another.) This fragmentation is evident, too, in African societies such as the Dinka. It is important to avoid the assumption that people are 'cultural dopes', blandly reproducing just one dominant notion of the 'personne' or acting out one homogeneous cultural personality. Societies are best characterized as active and *changing* fields, with some predominant meanings, understandings of the self and practices, but also with lines of tension and conflict between different concepts of the person. These tensions may well be played out within the psyche of any one individual as well as between groups of people.

It is also important to stress that because human beings across the world share the same environmental pressures (to find food, to rear children), and deal with these using roughly similar body shapes and biologies, inevitably there will be similarities in the clumps of meanings and practices which evolve around these environmental pressures. To the extent that meanings and practices contain similar themes and deal with commensurate problems, then similar psychologies should also emerge. Through sharing our experiences and interpretations, using a common language, it is possible to compare, empathize and communicate.

What do the lines of evidence and claims reviewed in this section tell us about the relationship between 'personne' and 'moi'? This work, along with the experimental studies reviewed in Chapter 3, suggests that common-sense ideas of the person ('personne') found in a culture or society are likely to have important *practical* consequences, since they seem to go to the heart of how individuals 'naturally' regard themselves in the 'depths' of their consciousness. It might well be the case that all people everywhere have a sense of individuality, but the work we have been considering suggests that people's understanding of this individuality will be crucially influenced by their social milieu. We are beginning to see that the boundaries between 'personne' and 'moi' may be difficult to distinguish. A social constructionist would see this work as suggesting that experiential assumptions from introspection about fundamental features of the human psyche may only be a reflection of western sensibilities. The next section will continue this exploration of the relationship between culture and psychology, looking at the experience of emotion.

3.3   The social construction of emotional lives

Chapter 2 of this book looked at the biological aspects of emotional expression and suggested that there is a complex interaction between the physiology of emotion (e.g. the release of hormones), subjective feelings and the social influences present in the environment. Schachter and Singer's (1962) experiment in which subjects were injected with adrenalin and presented with different role models was used to illustrate this point. In this section we want to dwell in a bit more detail on this intertwining of feelings, culture and biology.

The psychological anthropologist Michelle Rosaldo (1984) takes a strong social constructionist position on emotions, arguing that: 'feelings are not substances to be discovered in our blood but social practices organized by stories that we both enact and tell. [Feelings] are structured by our forms of understanding' (1984, p. 143). What does Rosaldo mean by this? Feelings involve thoughts, they involve our immediate sense of who we are, our interpretations of our current projects which might be threatened, disrupted or furthered by the events to which we are

,responding. Feelings are thus bound up with the stories, myths and conventions of a culture which guide people on how to react in different circumstances. As a result, certain kinds of emotional expression and certain ways of understanding emotions become habitual and characteristic in a cultural group. This is what is meant by Rosaldo's suggestion that 'feelings are ... social practices' (see also Lutz, 1988).

Emotions which we distinguish in our culture as shame, love, rage, envy, resentment, guilt, joy, and so on, are closely connected to our immediate perceptions of self and our current activities. These perceptions of self in turn are linked to culturally variable conceptions of appropriate projects for people to undertake. Consider, for example, the different emotional lives possible in a society like North America, where many believe that it is desirable for emotions to be spontaneously expressed; where it is assumed that anger, for instance, builds up inside and must be let out before it can die down. Compare this with societies which Markus and Kitayama (1991) describe as interdependent, such as Japan, where what is valued in local communities is social harmony above individual expression.

Try to imagine living in a society such as Tahiti where anger, it seems, is greatly feared and avoided, or among the Utka Eskimos where, apparently, there is minimal talk of anger, or recognition of it as a feasible response. According to Markus and Kitayama, such people do not show any signs of outrage in situations where the average American or European would be 'boiling over'. When Utka witness such displays from foreigners, their terms for such events are better translated as 'childish' than 'angry' (although see Box 5.3 which looks at the problems involved in translating terms across cultures and the danger of overgeneralization and stereotyping). You might like to imagine, too, living among Maori people in Aotearoa (New Zealand in pre-colonial days) where strong emotions were frequently conceptualized as visitations from outside, rather than individually generated from the inside, governed instead by an unseen world of magical and supernatural powers and forces (Smith, 1981).

Among the Ilongot, studied by Rosaldo, it is believed that anger can be 'forgotten' and that an angry person can be 'paid for' their anger which then disappears. As Rosaldo points out, the disappearance of anger in this way, and the phenomenological experience involved, may be difficult to reconstruct if our common-sense understanding of anger is strongly focused on individual rights and individual boundaries, sees this emotion emerging as a result of 'frustration' or 'insult', and includes notions of 'venting' anger, concepts of revenge, and a generally 'volcanic' imagery aptly implicated in that image of 'boiling over' with rage.

The Ilongot identify an emotional state they call 'liget', associated with head-hunting practices and with masculinity, which in some ways resembles our 'anger' but which also has overtones of what we might call 'energy' or 'passion':

> Liget is a distinct possession of the male, and we in Western culture could scarcely imagine its expression among us. A young Ilongot possessed by liget might weep or sing or sulk. He might stop eating

certain foods, slash baskets, yell, spill water, or demonstrate irritation and distraction. And, when liget has reached its peak, he will be moved to slice the head from a neighbouring tribesman. Having taken a head, he feels his liget transformed and transforming. His resources of energy are increased, he feels passion for the opposite sex, and he acquires a deepened sense of knowledge.

(Gergen, 1991, p. 10)

As this description demonstrates, 'liget', like our notions of 'revenge' or 'romantic love', is a state in which thought and feelings become bound in with cultural practices and with cultural stories about what people should feel in certain situations. Thought and feeling are also bound up with the moral life of a culture and, as the emphasis on head slicing suggests, with the different values placed on human life. It is difficult to

---

BOX 5.3   Methodological issues in cross-cultural research

A major difficulty in investigating the cultural foundations of human psychology is the problem of translation. If we use English terms like 'love', 'pride', 'anger', these are redolent with particular theories about emotions and associated with particular kinds of events and relationships which may not map on to experience and meanings in the culture being studied. Similarly, since emotional experience is always embedded in cultural stories, the translation of a term from another culture into, for example 'anger', uproots the emotion from its cultural contexts and obscures differences (White, 1992). Many social constructionists would take what is termed a relativist position, and argue that emotions (and other aspects of personal and social life) can only really be understood in relation to their own cultural context. We cannot appreciate the significance of 'liget' for instance, unless we have a deep understanding of Ilongot culture. The challenge for the anthropologist, then, in researching and documenting another culture, is to remain true to the local meanings and experience, but communicate them in a comprehensible way to an outside audience.

How far forms of experience *can* be translated across cultures in this way is a matter of continuing debate among anthropologists. This is also a difficult issue for social constructionists, since it could be argued that for translation to be comprehensible at all there must be some shared understandings between human beings which transcend local cultural contexts and are therefore 'given' rather than 'constructed'. Another methodological issue for cross-cultural research is the danger, through focusing on differences between cultures, of producing over-generalized and stereotyped notions of, for instance, 'the Japanese mind' or 'the West', which obscure important differences within cultures, between people of different ages, gender or class for example. You may like to consider this issue in relation to the research we have been discussing in this chapter.

separate the feeling, and the psychology of that feeling, from this broader ethical and cultural context. It is in this sense that Rosaldo argues that we should look for the substance of the feelings in the complexes of meanings and practices which societies and cultures develop.

As Box 5.3 notes, a major problem in working out the contribution of social and cultural factors to the experience of emotion is deciding when an experience is 'really the same' and when it is 'actually different'. Some social psychologists (e.g. Ekman, 1971) would argue that people everywhere do have the same basic emotional reactions: it is simply that different groups learn varying ways of describing these universal emotions, learning to display some and repress others. A strongly social constructionist position, in contrast, would argue that local meanings and practices actually structure what is felt.

People within the same culture may well differ in their individual or personal constructions of emotions. Those social psychologists who stress cultural influences on emotion are happy to accept this level of individual variation but would want to link these personal constructions to social constructions and see how they arise from individuals' particular experiences of social relationships worked through their family histories. This topic will be taken up in more detail in section 5.3.

Review of section 3

- Research on cross-cultural variations in concepts of the self and in psychological responses suggests the importance of the social situation in constructing human psychology.

- Research on cross-cultural differences is beset with methodological problems of translation but there is ample evidence for considerable differences across cultures and societies such as Japan, North America, the UK and the Dinka of Southern Sudan in concepts and understandings of what it means to be a person ('personne').

- Social constructionists argue that such differences are also crucial for basic concepts of the self ('moi') and for personal human reactions such as emotions and thoughts. As a result, any universals in people's experiences of themselves are likely to be quite limited.

- A 'feeling' cannot be easily separated from 'thoughts' or from cultural and collective interpretations of appropriate behaviour. People understand themselves, other people, and their social and physical world through cultural stories or through meanings and practices which are usually multiple and contradictory.

4   Discursive psychology

As we have progressed, points about discourse and language have recurred several times. We noted, for example, the importance of pronouns in constructing cultural concepts of the self and the difficulties in translating psychological states across languages. We also referred earlier to the person as 'discursive' and argued that identity and sense of self are very much bound up with systems of meaning. In the remainder of this chapter, we want to look more closely at language and how it works as a medium linking culture and social life with the construction of the person. We will examine, first, the views of discourse analysts regarding the nature of language and communication (Edwards and Potter, 1992; Potter and Wetherell, 1987) and then, in section 5, the role of language and narrative in child development.

4.1   Discourse as social action

One way of studying language is to think of it as an abstract system of rules. Languages, for instance, consist of vocabulary and grammar: semantics and syntax. We could look at correct ways of speaking, ungrammatical forms and the ordered patterns which make up recognizable speech. We could see language as an autonomous and independent structure, a form of knowledge which can be codified in dictionaries and grammar textbooks. As David Graddol (1994) notes, if we take this 'structuralist' view, then we can see language as a kind of self-contained machine or mechanism made up of components (phonemes, sentences, clauses, adjectives, verbs) which go together in certain patterns to make the system work.

This notion of language as a 'machine' or abstract system has been helpful for certain purposes and has inspired a great deal of psycholinguistic research, most notably by Noam Chomsky (1965), into the nature of the underlying rules governing language use. As social psychologists, however, our interest is rather different and we need an alternative understanding of what language is and how it works. Discourse analysts stress that language is not just an abstract system of rules, it is also a *practical activity*. It is a form of social action in its own right, a process of communication. But how should we understand these communicative acts? Take a look at Figure 5.2 overleaf which presents one possible model.

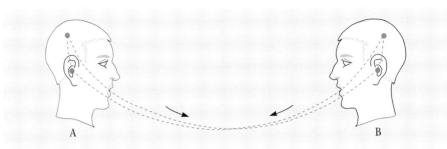

Figure 5.2 A model of communication (Source: based on Saussure, 1974, p. 11)

If we unpack this model we can see that language is conceptualized here mainly as a medium or 'transport system' (the arrows) which conveys messages from one mind to another mind. I have a thought which I want to communicate to you. I encode that thought in words, you then decode the words to find the thought. In this model of communication, people are assumed to be independent of language. They are pre-existent characters who *use* language. Language is the vehicle which carries the objects along as they are communicated, faithfully reflecting them from one mind to another. Expression is seen as an individual matter, with people struggling by themselves to find the right words. Crucially, too, images of communication such as Figure 5.2 encourage a strong distinction between talk and doing, between words and action. Words are used to describe and convey, action happens elsewhere and might be the subject of the communication.

But does language act as this kind of neutral or transparent medium? When we want to express ourselves and communicate, is it the case that we simply pick up language (the abstract system of rules) and go to work, encoding and decoding ideas in our minds, much as we might pick up a spade to dig the garden and then lay it down again when we have finished, with no further consequences? Related to this, language is often understood as a process of straightforward naming, where words are matched to things. Those things could be objects in the world such as trees, roads, gardens and grass, they could be actions and events, or they could be states inside the person such as thoughts, moods, beliefs, fantasies, and so on. But can we assume that language can be so neatly separated from what it describes?

Discourse analysts and social constructionist social psychologists question these assumptions about how language works. Indeed, as we shall see, their argument is that these assumptions obscure the social and collective basis of language and are contradicted also by the way people actually use words. As we move towards the study of *discourse* (the talk and texts of social life) and away from the study of abstract systems of rules, we become interested in the study of human linguistic practice and language as a form of social action. Our discussion begins to connect with some points made in Chapter 3 concerning the *pragmatic* aspects of language and communication (remember the cooperative principle and the politeness principle?). And we begin to see that communication is a form of social engagement which acts back on those communicating and constructs their nature. Language constructs both objects and people.

4.2   Building worlds and building selves

As a way of illustrating this alternative view of language and communication, take a look at Extract 5.1. This transcript comes from a videotape of a couple, Jenny and Larry, consulting with a family therapist, Sluzki.

Extract 5.1

Transcript conventions:

(-) = pause

( ) = transcription doubt

Sluzki: What kinds of problems were there?

Jenny: Uhm (-) again back to the you know what I said originally I think ya know just like this inability to communicate feeling like we were (-) living in in you know separate (-) houses and that we weren't really (-) working as a couple we weren't like a couple, I mean we really didn't have (-) a relationship so to speak I mean uhm I felt that if if things happened to Larry he couldn't talk to me about them

Sluzki: He didn't talk to you about it?

Jenny: No he's he's very introverted and an very ah private, very private person

Sluzki: Um hum

Jenny: And he (doesn't)

Sluzki: When things happen to you what?

Jenny: When things happen to me I mean now with therapy it's it's it's more (-) ah it's easier for me now t' to talk about things I want to talk about things (-) I mean my feelings are more on the surface and I have a need to

Larry: I think it's not therapy I think I think it's just her personality

Jenny: But therapy certainly brought a lot of that out

Larry: Could be

Jenny: I mean I feel more comfortable about talking about my feelings and expressing them

Larry: We're different in that way, she has a problem she likes to talk (-) about it or reiterate on it (-) a number of times a large number of times in my view

Sluzki: Yes that's a problem

Larry: And and I (-) so (-) on that issue (-) she's probably, if there is (-) an objective way to look at it, I think she's probably over does the talking about problems and I (-) tend to under (-) talk those

Sluzki: Uh hm

Larry: and I think the balance between us is (-) is ah about right

Sluzki: Um huh

(-)

Jenny: Well I don't know

(-)

Sluzki: Yeah:

Jenny: I'm not so sure that I overdo it though

(-)

Jenny: Because I talk to other people ya know about problems and they seem to have similar reactions you know when they have a problem they they seem to (-) talk to me about it just the way I talk to them about it so I mean if I'm comparing myself to other people that I know I don't feel like I'm overly reactive or anything like that

(-)

Jenny: I mean that again is very subjective

Sluzki: Absolutely

Jenny: Ya know

Sluzki: Yeah

(-)

Jenny: So (-) the way he views (-) uhm my (-) over-reaction or the way somebody else would look at it they might think that I'm even under-reacting to certain problems so it's again very subjective

Sluzki: Um hmm

(-)

Sluzki: Ah in addition to that this is an old discussion

Jenny: Uh huh

(-)

Sluzki: Yeah?

Jenny: An old one?

Larry: Yes

Jenny: Yeah yeah definitely an old one

Larry: You ob-obviously you

Jenny: Uh hum

Larry: don't believe that you overdo problems otherwise you

Jenny: Um huh

Larry: wouldn't do it I mean you think you handle

Jenny: Uh hum right

Larry: problems correctly and I think I do but what I'm saying is you obviously don't think you do it incorrectly otherwise you would change it, and I don't think I do it incorrectly otherwise I would change it but I think wha-what the

Sluzki: Yeah

Larry: prob-what's happening is ah (-) is that uhm we both have a different idea on what's the correct way to handle (-) problems that come up

(-)

Sluzki: Yeah

Larry: That's all

Sluzki: Uhm (-) one way or another you are involved in a in a very particular ritual ...

Source: adapted and simplified from Buttny, 1993, pp. 68–70

Verbatim transcripts such as Extract 5.1 are very different from our intuitions about speech and from our later recollections of conversations. We tend to think we speak rather like characters in a play but, as you can see, transcribed speech suggests that everyday talk is not at all like play dialogue. Utterances are regularly ungrammatical without eliciting comment, for instance.

Now read Extract 5.1 again and this time think about the assumption that language works as a neutral and unintrusive medium which merely matches words to things. Consider, too, whether the view of communication laid out in Figure 5.2 is the most useful description of what is going on here.

ACTIVITY 5.4

Three features of natural language use disrupt the assumption that language is a neutral and unintrusive medium. First, let us take the relationship between talking and doing. As John Austin (1962) pointed out in his theory of speech acts, *all utterances both state things and do things*. Consider, for example, Jenny's description early on in Extract 5.1 of Larry as 'very introverted and very private'. This is a statement with a specific meaning and sense but it is also an utterance which does something. In other words, this piece of talk also has to be seen as an *action*. Jenny's description of Larry does some important business in the negotiation about the couple's problem.

As Edwards and Potter (1992) argue, descriptions such as Jenny's account of Larry are frequently related to participants' concerns and interests – they use them to present their own case and to undermine another's talk or action. Indeed, we can see how Larry's later redescription of the problem as actually one of Jenny's making, due to her 'over talking', attempts to reconstitute the issue. His turn in the conversation is another action, again an utterance which both states and does something. The point to take from this is that we can begin to question the view that communication involves a relatively simple process of having an experience, encoding that into words, and then transmitting the description to another ear, or eye if the communication is read. Instead, in talking or writing, we are acting. Discourse always has an *action orientation*.

A second and closely related feature of discourse has been described by the sociologist Harold Garfinkel (1967). As we noted, one standard assumption is that language is neutral and self-effacing. There is the world and there are words to describe and faithfully record this world. Or, there are mental events (thoughts, moods, beliefs) and language transmits this internal reality. But is this what is happening in Jenny and Larry's conversation with their therapist? Their talk, like any talk or writing, is not merely about actions, events and situations, it is also a potent and *constitutive* part of those actions, events and situations.

In describing, Jenny and Larry, along with the therapist, are building a world, they are constituting their social reality, manufacturing and constructing their lives. Through this negotiation, their social world becomes populated with characters who acquire certain attributes, relationships become formulated as being of certain kinds, some forms of relating become defined as problematic and some as constructive and positive, and so on. In other words, social life is in no way separate from the words. Talk is not neutrally recording here; the words are constituting social and personal life.

The third point about language use concerns how meaning becomes defined and the importance of context. This has been described as the *indexical* property of discourse:

> The basic idea, derived from philosophy (Bar-Hillel, 1954) is a simple one. If one person says 'my stomach hurts' and then someone else utters the same sentence, although the sentences are the same, the reference is different. Different stomachs are indexed by the same

sentence. Or take 'it's a nice day' – this sentence could be used as a surprised description of sunshine or perhaps an ironic comment on further rain. In general, indexical expressions are expressions whose *meaning alters with their context of use* (Barnes and Law, 1976). ... [T]he vast majority of expressions used are indexical. That is their sense and reference are settled by looking at features of their context or occasions of use.

(Potter and Wetherell, 1987, p. 23)

This point is easy to illustrate with Extract 5.1. In fact, the real challenge would be to find a non-indexical expression. Take again, as an example, Jenny's characterization of Larry as an introverted and private person. Our understanding of this statement depends on the surrounding talk, as well as our own ideas about what introversion is, and what we hear Jenny trying to achieve with this utterance. The same characterization of Larry might be offered by Larry himself, his boss, his mother, or his best friend, and Larry's response in each case might be quite different because the statement would index something very different in each context. Larry might agree, offer further examples of his introversion, he might get angry, he might respond 'You are just saying that because ...', and so on. The *particular* meaning of any utterance is always determined by the context and by the network of surrounding talk and/or writing.

Unlike the assumption (discussed in section 4.1) that language reflects an already existing state of affairs where meaning is determined by the objects and events talk denotes, we can see how the constitutive and indexical properties of talk lead to very different conclusions. Meaning is a joint accomplishment. It is clear, too, as Edwards and Potter (1992) argue, that to build a world is to build a self and vice versa. This approach to language breaks down the idea that there are certain classes of utterances which refer to some set of events 'out there' in the world, and other classes of utterance (perhaps confessional or revelatory) which are interesting for what they tell us about self, motivation and cognition. In Extract 5.1, for instance, we can see how versions of the self and the world are mutually dependent. Larry talks about himself ('I tend to under talk'), he talks about Jenny ('I think it's not therapy, I think it's just her personality'), and he comes to a conclusion about their situation ('we both have a different idea on what is the correct way to handle problems that come up').

All of this talk is intertwined, in the sense that, to accomplish himself as a certain kind of person with a certain position in this negotiation, Larry has to characterize the situation as a certain kind of situation and Jenny, too, as a certain kind of person. Conversely, to succeed in presenting the situation as one of those kinds of situations rather than something perhaps more blameworthy or problematic, Larry has to construct and accept certain constructions of himself. To define oneself in talk is also to define the nature of social reality. And this double property of talk similarly undermines a view of language as an abstract independent system which can be used transparently, as a mere conveyance for thoughts and objects.

ACTIVITY 5.5

Discourse analysts argue that these features (action orientation, the constitutive nature of language, and indexicality) apply to all interaction, not just to talk in therapy. To test this out for yourself you could try tape-recording (if possible), or just listening to several different types of everyday talk, especially conversations involving accounts and explanations, self-descriptions and descriptions of other people. You could listen out, for example, for occasions on the radio or television when people (such as two politicians from different parties) are giving different versions of the same event. In these cases, the constitutive properties of talk and its action orientation can be very evident without detailed transcripts. How does each politician formulate the objects (policies, situations, people) they are discussing? What actions (blaming, praising, rationalizing) is their discourse designed to achieve? Are there any expressions, clichés, or terms such as 'free enterprise', 'community spirit', 'family values' used by both politicians? How do these convey a particular meaning (perhaps different in each case) because of the context of the surrounding talk – in other words, how far is their meaning indexically determined? Finally, what about identity – what kind of self is each speaker constructing?

Discourse analysis and its role in social psychological research are discussed further in Wetherell (ed.) (1996). As a final point, however, it is worth noting how these arguments extend beyond the purely interpersonal domain. Jenny and Larry are engaged in therapy, and this is a mode of discourse and form of life with some quite specific features. Compare it, for example, to politics and the political interview, or to religion and the discourse which might be found in the Catholic confessional, or to the conversational practices typically found between parents and children.

In fact, Extract 5.1 could be read in all these ways. It has some vaguely 'confessional' features, the accusation and counter-accusation are reminiscent of a politician on *Newsnight*, and so on. However, there are also important differences in background assumptions, in what is taken for granted and in the kinds of narrative characters (self- and other-descriptions, ways of building selves and worlds) which populate therapy compared with other forms of life such as religion or politics. Indexicality, again, is relevant here, since it is these broader social practices which also set the scene and define the context for interpreting meaning. Crucially, each 'scene of language' found in a form of life sets up different contexts in which power relations are played out through the selves and worlds they encourage. It is in these ways that we can see how the work on discourse considered in this section connects with the research on culture and psychology considered in section 3. Language is the medium of culture. This point will come more clearly into focus in section 5 when we look at how language intertwines with the socialization of children, playing a formative role in the construction of social beings.

Review of section 4

- One way of analysing communication is to see language as a neutral and transparent medium which conveys thoughts from one mind to another.

- Discourse analysts reject this assumption, pointing to three features of language use which suggest instead that language and discourse actively *construct* the world and the self. These features are (a) the action orientation of discourse, (b) its constitutive nature, and (c) indexicality.

- These properties of discourse give us a better understanding of the role language plays in the social and cultural construction of the person (described in sections 2 and 3), since to a large extent cultural influences are mediated through writing, talk and conversation.

5   The development of social beings

In this section, we want to look in more detail at social constructionist approaches to child development and at how people *actively* produce their social worlds. We have argued that people are social products, influenced by the culture and the complexes of meanings and practices which make up their social worlds, but how do children become social beings and what is the role of language in this process? Is this construction of the person an active or a passive process? Social constructionist approaches suggest that the business of being shaped as a person by others, and by the cultural environment, starts right from the earliest stages of life. This is not to deny that children are born with differences of temperament and differing mental propensities, but because these individual characteristics are developed, expressed and experienced through the child's participation in social relationships and activities, these characteristics are seen as acquiring meaning through social processes.

In the past, theories about children's socialization have tended to focus on how the 'outside' – cultural beliefs, values and so on – is brought to the 'inside' – the child's inner cognitive, emotional and imaginative development. But there has been an increasing interest in how children themselves become active agents in this process, affecting the course of their own development and construction of self. Language, long acknowledged as one of the most powerful agents of socialization, has proved a crucial area for exploring how this actually happens, as children use it to interact with others, represent and explore personal experience, and as a cognitive tool in inner thought. Language as both a publicly shared and privately utilized symbol system is the site where the individual and the social make and remake each other (Miller and Hoogstra, 1992, p. 83). Recent detailed research on the language practices of children and their carers in various cultures suggests that socialization is very much a dynamic and interactive process.

This changing conceptualization of socialization is related to a move from systematic views of culture and language, found, for example, in much social cognitive work on cultural concepts and schema (see Chapter 3), to the more dynamic and fluid notions emphasized in this chapter which stress that beliefs and meanings are negotiated continually through situated encounters and practices. If we see culture not as a static collection of beliefs and values which a child has to learn once and for all, but as the negotiation and provisional realization of beliefs and values through ongoing interactions and practices, then the child becomes an important agent, not just in his or her own social construction, but in the continuing construction of culture itself.

Think back to Kondo's experience in Japan. This illustrates quite clearly the idea of culture as something which is realized and enacted through activities and relationships rather than something which can be pinned down and labelled in abstract notions like 'the Japanese woman', or in charts of company hierarchies and kinship diagrams. Viewing culture as a process means that a newcomer like Kondo, or a young child, must be seen as to some extent affecting others, and affecting cultural practices, at the same time as they themselves are being socialized by them. Think, for instance, about how some people's values and beliefs are changed through the experience of rearing young children; and there are, of course, plenty of examples of societies where cultural practices have changed greatly through contact with outsiders.

We shall start our review of this work on social development by looking at ideas about language and socialization presented by two early key theorists, the American social philosopher, George Herbert Mead (1863–1931), and the Russian psychologist, Lev Vygotsky (1902–1936).

5.1   Mead and Vygotsky

For both Mead and Vygotsky, the direction of development is very definitely from the social to the individual, through language. Both saw language acquisition and interactions with others as crucial, and believed that thought consists essentially of internalized social dialogues. This would suggest that the way we remember events, or struggle with particular dilemmas, and plan future encounters, involves the internal running through of actual or imagined dialogues.

How far is this true for you? You might like to think about this in relation to what has been going through your head in the last ten or fifteen minutes? For some examples of internal dialogues, look back to Box 4.5 in Chapter 4 and Brian Keenan's account of his thoughts during his incarceration.

Processes of individual thought, then, for Mead and Vygotsky, reflect the outer social world, with all its encoded relationships, cultural values and knowledge beliefs. As we shall see, however, they each had rather different views about the nature of this outer social world and the individual's role within it, so there are corresponding differences in their conceptualization of the internal process of child development, and the relationship between the individual and the cultural environment.

Mead was particularly interested in how children acquire the ability to take on the perspectives of others, which he saw as fundamental both to social and moral development and to self-awareness. He suggested that there are three stages in the development of the child's self, each shaped by the roles and attitudes of others. In the 'preparatory stage' the young baby is motivated by basic biological drives and instincts, but gradually becomes used to particular sequences of behaviour and events (for example, that crying brings mother and food). From the beginning of the acquisition of language, children begin to learn the symbolic representations of the adult world, which then shape their own experience. Next, in the 'play stage', young children begin to try out the perspectives and attitudes of others, using their own experience of these attitudes as directed towards themselves (for example, they role-play an adult scolding, or a doctor examining). Finally, in the 'game stage' children begin to be able to organize a number of roles simultaneously in relation to themselves, and to appreciate interrelationships between the viewpoints of a variety of others.

As their social experience broadens, Mead believed that children reach a point where they can organize the combined attitudes and perspectives of people within the whole social group into a 'generalized other'. This becomes an important source of internalized social control; on moral issues, for instance, the child may be guided by taking on the perspective of the 'generalized other'. Mead represented thought as a dialogue between the 'I', the more spontaneous and intuitive aspects of the self, and the 'me', the internalized attitudes of others, as indicated in Box 5.4 overleaf.

BOX 5.4 The I/me dialogue

Let us suppose that a child finds herself in a situation where she can help herself to a large box of chocolates, without fear of detection. If she is tempted to take some chocolates, something like the following conversation might take place:

I	me
I would like some chocolate.	But they are not yours and Mummy said it's wrong to take things without asking.
So what! I want them.	You know it isn't right.
If I take them quickly, no one will know.	That's naughty.
There are lots of chocolates in the box; it won't matter if I just take a few.	Chocolates are bad for your teeth.

Of course, the actual process of conversing internally does not go on in terms of complete sentences or in terms of words alone. Mead depicts it as a kind of mental tug-of-war. The 'me' in the scheme represents internalized group standards, while the 'I' is less social, more individualistic.

(The Open University, 1984, p. 105)

Mead suggested that we are constantly seeking the realization of the 'I', which emerges most directly in artistic creativity, impulsive actions, or when the strength of emotions breaks down normal social sanctions. This distinction between the 'I' and the 'me' has some overlap with Mauss's distinction between the 'personne' and the 'moi' considered in section 3.1, but these are not identical concepts and cannot be compared directly, as they were designed for different tasks. Both Mead and Mauss were concerned with social influences on individual minds and both argued that our minds are penetrated by social and cultural practices. Whereas Mead used his distinction to label different aspects of our internal dialogues, Mauss was concerned, as an anthropologist, with labelling and understanding the concepts of the person found across a culture or society and their influence on people's beliefs and understandings of themselves. Some of these concepts ('personne') might be specific to a particular culture and society and some ('moi') might be universal, shared by all societies since they reflect common properties of human minds.

Although Mead considered that organizing the attitudes of the child's social group into a 'generalized other' marks the mature development of the self, he also acknowledged that the 'me' continues to be modified through dialogues with others and through our membership of new social groups during the course of our lives (for example if we join a political party or become parents). His insights about the way people revise their symbolic representations of the world and ideas about themselves through interaction suggest a dynamic view of the self, as the 'me' becomes reconstituted through new dialogues in different contexts. One of the main lines of research developed from Mead's work (known as 'symbolic interactionism') has focused on how meanings are negotiated within groups and social organizations of various kinds. Less attention has been paid to how these meanings are shaped by broader cultural and historical processes.

Vygotskian theory (published in the West from the 1960s; e.g. Vygotsky, 1962 and 1978) has a stronger focus on language itself, and a more dynamic conception of development and the social world. Vygotsky argued that when children internalize dialogues experienced within particular social practices, the words carry with them the social and cultural trappings of the contexts within which they have been experienced. These cultural meanings shape the ways language contributes to internal cognitive processes, and how it is used by children as a tool to help them solve tasks on subsequent occasions.

Vygotsky believed that children's conceptual development occurs first on the social level, through dialogue, before being internalized to become part of individual cognitive processes. He suggested that, through interaction, children are helped to extend themselves mentally across what he calls their 'zone of proximal development' (ZPD) – that is, the difference between what they could have achieved unaided, and what they are able to manage with the support of adults or more competent peers (Vygotsky, 1978). This may happen through a non-verbal action (for example, if an adult moves a piece in a puzzle, or rearranges blocks to help with a mathematical calculation); but usually this help occurs through dialogue, as the adult talks the child through the problem, or asks leading questions. Bruner (1985) suggests that the adult here supplies a kind of vicarious mental scaffolding until the child has grasped and internalized the new concept, in the same way as an iron scaffold might support a building during its construction, and then be removed on its completion.

Vygotsky and Bruner's ideas have been taken up by educationalists who argue that the 'scaffolding' provided by teacher-pupil dialogue is a centrally important part of teaching and learning. This approach is often contrasted with the more indirect role assigned to the teacher by Piaget, who believed that children should discover for themselves, within a learning environment organized by the teacher.

Because of the indexical properties of discourse which we discussed earlier, the way in which this scaffolding is done, formally or informally, is culturally shaped. In other words, children learn the context as well as the skill. If you remember, this proved problematical for Kondo when she became competent in preparing the Sakamotos' evening meal but found that the etiquette surrounding the serving of the meal carried messages about the position of women which she found very difficult to stomach. Thus, Cole (1985) terms the ZPD the point where 'culture and cognition create each other'. The very learning activities which form the basis for children's cognitive and conceptual development are those which induct them into particular cultural values and beliefs, and ways of organizing knowledge and experience.

Vygotsky argues that developing children use language as a tool to achieve tasks and change their environment, and are themselves mentally transformed in the process. Each new concept acquired transforms the simpler mental structures which were there before. Thus, although Vygotsky sees the child's cognitive development as strongly socially constructed, the child is also quite a powerful agent within this process, and there is a dynamic and dialectical (or back and forth) relationship between the various transformative changes within the child and its changing social and cultural environment.

Vygotsky's ideas have been used to support the more *distributed* notion of the self we introduced in section 2.1. If conceptual development occurs first in the process of social interaction, before being internalized, then the notion of a 'mind' sometimes seems to extend beyond the individual. For instance, problem solving may be a joint rather than an individual mental activity when a child is 'scaffolded' through a task by an adult or more able friend, and it is the collaborative 'mind' generated through the interaction which carries the learning edge. Similarly, groups of children playing or working together may jointly be able to solve a problem which no one child could have accomplished on its own. And at an everyday conversational level for children or adults, there are often instances of what has been called 'joint remembering', where individuals spark off each other's contributions to construct collaboratively a complete account.

ACTIVITY 5.6

In the extract below, a group of undergraduate students are recalling the feature film *ET*. Notice how Karen, Diane and John each contribute significantly to the joint recall:

Karen: well he goes to the fridge to get something to eat first doesn't he with the dog following him

Diane: yeh that's it

Karen: mm

Diane: and he finds him feeding the dog

John: and then and then he finds the beer

Diane: and then he finds the beer and what is it there's a link between

	⌈ Elliott and E.T. & ⌉
Karen:	Elliott's at school
John:	⌊ telepathic link ⌋

Diane: & that whatever happens to E.T. Elliott feels the same effects and E.T. got paralytic [*laughs*] and so E.T. is sort of going

Lesley: all a bit drunk

Tina: that's right I remember

Transcript convention:

[ ] = overlap between speakers

(Middleton and Edwards, 1990, p. 25)

To summarize, both Vygotsky and Mead treat human consciousness as constituted through language encountered in dialogues with others, and both see the young child as internalizing social beliefs and values through these dialogues which become part of individual thought. For Mead, this internalization comes about through the child taking on the attitudes of others via language and role-play, and he conceptualizes the basis of cognition as a covert dialogue between the 'I' and the 'me', both of which are aspects of the self. Vygotsky, on the other hand, sees the child as internalizing the real-life dialogues they have had with others and applying these to mental and practical problem solving. Because the internalized dialogues bring with them their social and cultural connotations, the language children use to think with is always heavily culturally and socially saturated.

Mead adopts a model of society often described as 'functionalist', according to which the pieces of society all fit together as an organic whole. He also adopts a rational view of individual development. Vygotsky, on the other hand, uses a Marxist model of continuing dialectical and transformative change in the social world, the child's internal development, and the relationship between them. His theory suggests that the self is continually in the process of being constructed and that the boundary between one mind and another can become blurred in the course of interaction.

BOX 5.5   Mead and Vygotsky

	Mead	*Vygotsky*
Social theory:	Normative, functionalist: society a harmonious continuing organic whole process	Marxist: society a historical dialectical process
Role of the child:	Rational social actor moulded by attitudes of others	Cognitively shaped through language practices; also an active participant in those practices
View of development:	Fairly orderly progression through additive developmental stages	Each new development transforms previous ones, and changes the child's environment
Key concepts:	Generalized other; 'I'/'me'; role-taking; symbolic interactionism	Language as a cognitive tool; cognition originating in social interaction; zone of proximal development

---

5.2   Acquiring communicative competence

A body of interesting recent work by psychological anthropologists focuses on the question of how children's participation in social practices is mediated through language in different cultures, and the consequences of this for their own individual development. In addition to using Vygotsky's ideas, another important strand in this work comes from research on communication within anthropology (Hymes, 1972) which has involved the documentation of a wide range of language practices and an examination of their function and meaning across a variety of different cultures. This work shows that children need to learn not just various aspects of the language system – grammar, phonology, and so on – but also how to become competent speakers within a particular cultural setting.

Children have to know when and how they should talk in different contexts and with different people, and how to interweave non-verbal gestures and body language in with speech. Equally importantly, they have to learn when and how to listen, and how to 'detect and interpret the unspoken assumptions that lie behind talk' (Miller and Hoogstra, 1992, p. 84). These kinds of communicative skills are crucial to cultural competence, and affect other people's attitudes and reactions towards us as particular kinds of people (rude, sensitive, witty, intelligent, and so on), which in turn shape our own experience of self. Remember how Kondo's competence in performing a formal greeting when she first met Mr Sakamoto made such a favourable impression on him; he called her a 'fine granddaughter' and she in her turn was encouraged to continue modifying her behaviour, so as to win the family's approval.

Kondo was fairly self-conscious about what was happening as she gradually acquired greater communicative competence, but how do children acquire these kinds of skills? Like Kondo, they learn ways of talking through observing and taking part in day-to-day social activities – this is how they come to realize whom should be spoken to with deference, which occasions are appropriate for telling rude jokes, when they are expected to keep quiet until spoken to. In addition, care-givers sometimes explicitly model for the child what he or she should say. In Britain and America this modelling tends to be limited to politeness routines like, 'Thank you for having me', or, 'Please may I leave the table', but in some cultures the care-giver models whole conversations for the infant. For instance, Kaluli mothers in Papua New Guinea tend to hold their babies looking outwards rather than facing themselves as western mothers do, and speak as if for the baby in 'dialogues' with older children and other family members. When the Kaluli mother pretends to be the baby, she adopts a high-pitched voice, but otherwise uses well-formed language and speaks in an appropriate way for the person the baby is supposed to be addressing. Very young Kaluli babies are not spoken to directly, and do not experience western type 'babytalk' or 'motherese' (the adoption of a particular voice pitch, tone and vocabulary when talking to young infants who are not expected to understand what is actually said). Instead, Kaluli babies learn very early on about ways of talking to a significant number of different people in the community, and they also learn the principle that it is up to them to modify their language when speaking to more senior others (just about everybody when you are a baby), and not the other way round (Ochs and Schieffelin, 1984).

5.3   Learning to express anger and aggression

In section 3.3 of this chapter, we argued that, although emotions might seem to come from the very core of the person and therefore be one of the most strongly individual aspects of the self, in fact feelings, self and the social context are all closely interconnected. The experience and expression of emotions such as love, shame, anger and guilt are culturally and socially shaped, above all through language. If you remember, we quoted Rosaldo's research into Ilongot stories and accounts of experience concerning the emotion called 'liget'.

Stories can play a powerful role in socialization, and we want to look now in some detail at an example of research which examines the influence of conversational stories on young children's emotional development, and on their construction of self. First, we want to focus on how the experience and expression of specific emotions may be shaped and influenced by dialogues and narratives between young children and their carers.

Miller and Sperry (1987) use data from their longitudinal study of communicative practices between 2–3-year-old white working-class girls and their mothers and other care-givers in South Baltimore to examine the expression of, and talk about, anger and aggression. The researchers had not planned to focus on these emotions, but they emerged as significant themes in the interviews when mothers spoke about their own histories and beliefs about child-rearing, and in the talk and activity during observation periods. Miller and Sperry became interested in how the children were developing their own ways of expressing and talking about anger, and they found two aspects of the children's language experience particularly significant: the mothers' accounts of personal experience related in their children's presence, and the mothers' verbal interventions in their children's activities. Both of these strongly reflected the mothers' own beliefs, child-rearing goals, and past experience.

Mothers' stories about how someone else had made them angry, or how they would have reacted in a specific situation were not censored in front of the children; for instance, one mother told the following story in front of her 2-year-old:

> This guy [who lives] in the back of us, the other night comin' in from work – they said they don't know why he did it – coming home from work he took a lead pipe and beat his wife all in the face and the head with it. Well, busted her eardrums. They had to sew several, the bottom of her chin and all up on her head. And he took and drug her from the living room, kicked her unconscious. And drug her from the living room into the kitchen and finally put her behind the refrigerator … I'm afraid I'd a had picked up somethin', the nearest thing that was to me and slammed him in the head with it before he'd a gotton me real good.

(Miller and Sperry, 1987, p. 11)

In most accounts (though not the one above), the aggression was recounted as conducted largely through dialogue – name-calling, threatening, insulting, accusing and arguing. For example, one mother recounted her reaction to a young woman in the street who had called her a big-nosed bitch: '"ARE YOU TALKIN' TO ME?" I says, "Well, you fat slob you … "' (Miller and Sperry, 1987, p. 13). These two examples are typical in their use of verbs of aggression and terms of abuse rather than an explicit description of feeling angry. Also, in these and other accounts, anger is always justified by linking it to a specific transgression; for example, a husband's violence, or a neighbour's insult.

These stories are part of the mothers' own ongoing construction of self, but they also provide an important aspect of the socializing context for their daughters. So what are young children learning through listening to such stories? Miller and Sperry suggest that the following messages are conveyed:

1   Life involves many events of anger and aggression, and it is important to stand up for yourself in these situations.

2   These events are fit topics for narrative talk and young children are not too sensitive to hear them.

3   One talks about anger mainly by recounting actions rather than describing feelings, and it is important to justify anger or aggression by reference to an instigating injury (that is, by implicit reference to social and moral standards; for instance, it is wrong to beat one's wife or gratuitously insult someone in the street).

In terms of interactive behaviour with their daughters, the mothers punished children who spontaneously displayed aggression towards a parent or another care-giver, but on the other hand would actually provoke their daughters into aggression through teasing and pretend fighting, which they saw as helping them learn to defend themselves. The children, therefore, had to learn to distinguish between justifiable anger (in self-defence), and unjustifiable (self-indulgent) anger. The way the mothers verbally intervened when children exhibited emotion in interactions either with adults or other children, by distracting, reprimanding, accepting or provoking the child's anger, seemed to communicate a particular set of rules about expressing anger and to be articulated in relation to two key terms, 'sissy' and 'spoiled':

1   When another child hurts or wrongs you, defend yourself (don't be a sissy).

2   But don't respond angrily or aggressively without reason (don't be spoiled).

3   When mother teases you and pretends to bully you, show you can stand up for yourself (don't be a sissy).

4   Otherwise, do not direct anger or aggression at your mother or other parent figure; comply with their standards (don't be spoiled).

The mothers told the researchers that they were particularly concerned that their daughters should not become 'sissy' or 'spoiled'. Both these terms were linked with displaying anger and aggression: a 'spoiled' child asserts herself and expresses anger when she should not; while a 'sissy' cannot defend herself adequately against the aggression of others. Miller and Sperry suggest that the mothers' attitudes towards their children's displays of anger and aggression were organized by cultural beliefs about issues of strength/weakness, maturity/immaturity, self-protection/self-indulgence and suppression/expression of feelings, in relation to child-rearing and mental health.

By the age of two and a half, all the children understood that they needed to justify their aggression by reference to another person's instigating act. Their use of accusations showed they recognized breaches in moral rules, and could use verbal protests, threats, insults and assertions. One child had started elaborating accusations into narratives of anger and aggression.

The way young girls in South Baltimore learn through teasing to be assertive and how to defend themselves reflects particular cultural values. It contrasts, for instance, with practices among the Utka Eskimos, considered in section 3.3, where negative feelings are strongly disapproved of, and children are encouraged to respond to teasing by ignoring it or laughing. We might expect these children to develop different interpersonal and intrapersonal strategies for coping with attacks to the self, with the South Baltimore children relying more on tools of retaliation, and the Utka children on tools for maintaining equanimity (Miller and Hoogstra, 1992).

It could be argued that what children are learning here is not how to feel, but rather the social rules for *displaying* feelings. Social constructionists, however, would claim that the talk and interaction involved in learning these rules affect children's actual individual experience of feelings, and influence their emotional development in specific, culturally shaped ways.

5.4   Narrative, dialogue and the emerging self

We have mentioned the importance of stories told by care-givers about their own experience, in front of young children. Narrative is one of the most widely used ways of creating, interpreting and presenting images of the self within face-to-face interaction. Bruner (1986) suggests that it is the major way in which we account for our actions and the events around us, and that 'our sensitivity to narrative provides the major link between our own sense of self and our sense of others in the social world around us' (p. 69). Of course, as in Jenny and Larry's dialogue in section 4.2, we never simply relate events 'neutrally', but slant them in a particular way to highlight how they affect us, or portray us in a particular light. In addition, conversational narratives provide an important sense of self-continuity – a self that maintains a certain integrity throughout the events that are recounted. In their stories, discussed in section 5.3 above, the mothers from South Baltimore portrayed themselves as particular kinds of people, communicated values about desirable personal attributes, and demonstrated culturally approved ways of self-presentation. There are also narrative practices which involve the young child more directly: stories told about the child in its presence, stories told by the child in which the care-giver intervenes, and stories told to and with other children.

Research suggests that the stories children tell are an important site not just for representing the self in a particular way, but also for actually exploring and negotiating significant aspects of the self in relation to growing up in a particular culture. In addition, children compare themselves with others, and try out other people's perspectives, through their informal, conversational, narrative accounts.

Read the extract below about 'being a brave person'. How well does this account illustrate the key aspects of the social constructionist perspective listed in Activity 5.1 at the end of section 2.1?

> Five year old Melissa and eight year old Jenny jointly described a family trip to the fair in which Jenny compared her own actions with Melissa's: 'She was on this very scary ride that I wouldn't go on', and Melissa added, 'I was on um this real scary ride'. During the next nineteen conversational turns the ride was described in detail and then Jenny reiterated her fear, 'I was too afraid [to go on the ride]', and Melissa responded, 'You know what, Jenny? Jason [her older brother's friend] was too "fraid, scared"'. Finally, Melissa made an explicit, within-turn comparison of herself and Jason, 'He was too scared to go on the dragon and I did'.
>
> *(adapted from Miller et al., 1992, p. 63)*

In this co-narration, Melissa is defined as brave through being compared with two older children, Jenny and Jason. Rather than appearing in one initial statement, however, the definition is collaborative and ongoing, as Melissa takes on Jenny's perspective and offers it back, extended, through two further comparisons. Melissa now has some grounds for describing herself which emerge in the course of the narrative account she and Jenny develop for their actions. This account illustrates Mead's idea of children taking on another person's perspective and applying it to themselves, through dialogue, and it also shows how the sense of self (Melissa) is *emergent* (through the collaborative story), *contextual* (she is brave at the fair – possibly not in another context), *discursive* (the bravery is established through the story), *relational* (she's brave in relation to Jenny and Jason), and *mutual* (her bravery is corroborated by Jenny).

Melissa here seems to take on Jenny's perspective on her actions in a fairly unproblematical way; but story-telling also gives opportunities for children to question and resist other people's evaluations of their actions, as the examples in Box 5.6 overleaf, from conversations between 10-year-olds talking in a classroom in Milton Keynes, demonstrate.

BOX 5.6 Swearing and going to Clayson

Swearing

Julie is talking to Kirsty while working on a display in the classroom. They have been discussing their anxiety about the amount of swearing on the tape-recordings of their informal talk collected by a researcher:

Julie: Children aren't meant to swear.

Kirsty: If people swear at them, they can swear back.

[...]

Julie: I swore at my mum the other day because she started, she hit me.

Kirsty: What did you do?

Julie: I swore at my mum, I says 'I'm packing my cases and I don't care what you say' and she goes 'Ooh?' and (I go) 'yea!'. I'm really cheeky to my mother.

(Maybin, 1993, pp. 143–4)

Going to Clayson

The class are drawing pictures as part of follow-up work to their teacher's reading from *The Silver Sword*. Their teacher has just announced that pupils will be getting their school reports to take home at the end of the week. Mr Clayson is the headteacher of the school:

John: Since I started at this school I've only been to see Mr Clayson once.

Laura: Neither have I.

Julie: (gasps) I've been there about ten times ... always going to Clayson every single day. Wack, wack, wack because she's been a good girl! I normally go there because I say I've been involved, when I'm not. I stick up for my other friends.

John: I know, you're trying to get your nose in and things.

Julie: I'm not, I'm sticking up for my friends and I say that I was doing it as well.

(Maybin, 1993, p. 139)

In the first extract, Julie starts with a statement which Mead would probably see as representing the 'generalized other' – she even refers to herself in the third person, 'children aren't meant to swear', with her use of the particularly emphatic term 'meant' suggesting a firm social rule. But Kirsty refutes this by invoking a different kind of rule – if somebody does something to you, then there is nothing wrong with reciprocating.

Julie then uses a short anecdote to explore these two apparently conflict-ing rules in the context of a specific situation, which raises additional issues about resisting authority and about her own relationship with her mother (both of these themes resonate for Kirsty with echoes from other anecdotes told by Julie on previous occasions). Through the medium of the anecdote Julie appears to be arguing, on the one hand, that she was justified in swearing, because her mother hit her, but, on the other hand, that she is still 'really cheeky'. The evaluation of her actions is left ambiguous, as it is in the second extract 'Going to Clayson'.

Here Julie subverts the public and institutional significance of being sent to the headteacher through joking that she goes there every day, caricaturing what happens (corporal punishment was not used in the school), and inverting the normal relationship between behaviour and punishment. There is a conflict here between school values and peer-group values, and she suggests that loyalty to one's friends should take precedence over honesty, as defined in school terms. Punishment in her case constitutes a martyrdom to friendship rather than a just response to bad behaviour. This meaning is however itself subverted by John, who claims that Julie's actions should not be interpreted as loyalty, but as nosiness. The issue is never resolved and, as in many other conversa-tions, a number of possible meanings are carried forwards, any of which may be drawn on in future dialogues.

We can see here again the collaborative, provisional and contextual negotiation of the person, and the conflicting and unresolved evalua-tions of an individual's actions. Through conversational anecdotes such as these, children are using language to try out, negotiate and question cultural meanings focusing around relationships, institutions and social practices, while at the same time exploring possible, and at times con-flicting, identities. There is another good example of this, from Margaret Donaldson's work, in section 2.3 of Chapter 4.

One of the ways children do this is through taking on other people's voices, either directly as if they were their own, or through re-enacted dialogues in anecdotes, as Julie does in the first extract ('I says "I'm pack-ing my cases …" and she goes "Ooh?"'). In anecdotes and other reported dialogue these voices are produced and managed by the narrators to con-struct events in a particular manner, and to present and try out particular speaking subjects for themselves. Thus, Julie presents herself as assertive and defiant in the anecdote about swearing, through the dialogue she sets up between herself and her mother. You may remember how, in the ther-apy session extract discussed in section 4.2, Jenny also presented herself as a particular kind of person, and justified the way she talked about feelings and personal problems by referring to her conversations with others.

The construction of particular kinds of speaking subjects in Julie's anec-dote, and the relationships between them and with voices and themes in other anecdotes, enable Julie and her friend Kirsty to explore and reflect on their own ambiguous and changing positioning within dialogues with adults, as they move from childhood into adolescence. The apparent inconsistency in evaluative perspective between Julie's different utterances is explained if we see the speaking subject here not as a consistent 'self' expressed within individual utterances, but rather as being provisionally constructed through the dialogic relationship between the different voices she invokes.

The Russian theorist, Bakhtin (1981), who worked in the 1920s and 1930s during the same time-period as Vygotsky, argues that thought is internalized dialogue, and that language forms and themes are internalized from dialogues to become inner speech. Our efforts to understand people, relationships and situations, or to resolve moral dilemmas, may be played out internally through the taking on and managing of voices in constructed inner dialogues, rather than through the more simple dialogue between the 'I' and the 'me' envisaged by Mead. Since, for Bakhtin, utterances and texts in the outer world are a site of struggle, and are populated with the voices of others, then an inner consciousness made up of dialogues will itself be dialogic, multi-voiced, and fragmented.

The inner dialogue (Source: The Guardian, *28 May 1994)*

5.5 Language and power relations

We saw in section 5.3 how the way mothers talk to and about their children is shaped by particular cultural beliefs concerning strength and weakness, self-protection and self-indulgence, and the negative associations of being a 'sissy' or 'spoiled'. The language we use orders and evaluates knowledge and experience in relation to deeply held beliefs and values, and the particular ways in which languages (or 'discourses') do this tend to become dominant in specific social contexts. The social theorist Michel Foucault suggests that certain areas of social life are shaped by powerful discourses; for example, the organization of health care is heavily influenced by the discourse of medical science (though some might argue that, with the current changes in Britain, this is being overtaken by a discourse of market relations).

In addition to ordering and evaluating knowledge and experience, different discourses position people in different ways, with varying degrees of power. For instance, you might feel more (or less) powerfully positioned as a 'client' than as a 'patient'. Children acquiring language in a particular cultural setting find themselves being inserted into particular discourses, where their position is an important aspect of their evolving self. For instance, research in Britain and in the USA has shown that parents interact and talk differently with their daughters and sons, from a very early age. However, as some of the anecdotes discussed in section 5.4 above demonstrate, children are not totally compliant in taking on cultural attitudes and values, but are involved in complex struggles, reflecting changing relations of power with others and their efforts to understand and construct cultural meanings.

The transition from childhood into adolescence is of course a time of considerable change in relations with other people, but in an important sense children are positioned in particular relations of power, and manoeuvre to increase their own power, right from the point of their first entry into language. As they get older, children become more adept at switching and negotiating between discourses in order to try to achieve more powerful positions. But notice that broader aspects of power relations in society such as gender are still an important factor, as the example in Box 5.7, from the developmental psychologist Valerie Walkerdine, demonstrates.

BOX 5.7   Doctors and nurses

The children in a nursery class have been playing doctors and nurses and the nursery nurse supervising them has encouraged the little girl 'nurses' to help the boy 'doctors'. One girl, Jane, goes into the Wendy House where she pretends to make tea for the patients. Derek, one of the 'doctors', follows her in:

Jane: You gotta go quickly

Derek: Why?

Jane: 'Cos you're going to work

Derek: But I'm being a doctor

Jane: Well, you've got to go to work doctor' cos you've got to go to hospital and so do I. You don't like cabbage, do you? (he shakes his head) ... Well you haven't got cabbage then. I'm goin to hospital. If you tidy up this room be sure and tell me.

Source: Walkerdine, 1981, p. 20

In taking control of the tea-making Jane creates a more powerful position for herself than that of servicing doctors, but she produces an even more decisive shift in her relation to Derek by switching to a home-managing discourse which positions him as a little boy or dependent husband. Jane's taking on of roles here is not just to do with learning different perspectives of significant others in the adult world, but is motivated by a desire for control, exercised through culturally specific, gendered social interactions symbolically expressed through language. Ironically, she achieves this control through taking up an assertive position within a discourse which itself implies women's subordination.

Review of section 5

- The development of children as social beings is a two-way process: children are inducted through language into particular social and cultural processes, but at the same time they are important agents in their own social construction, and in the ongoing construction of culture itself.

- A substantial part of children's cognitive and emotional development is mediated through language practices experienced in particular cultural settings. Learning a language, learning through language and becoming a particular person are all closely interrelated.

- Exposure to and participation in ways of telling stories helps children develop tools for communicating and evaluating who they are, for assessing other people's evaluations of them, and establishing personal continuity across time and space. Narratives may contain messages about appropriate behaviour and ways of conducting relationships, but can also be used by children to explore, negotiate or resist a variety of beliefs and values, and to represent themselves in different ways.

- Children are, right from the start, negotiating power relations through the dialogues in which they are involved, and which position them in particular ways. This positioning is an important aspect of the emerging social person.

6   Conclusion

This chapter has now gone full circle. We began, in sections 2 and 3, with culture and the meanings and practices which make up the social context, and, in section 5, we saw how children work with and incorporate these meanings and practices. The important role which language and discourse play in the construction of the person, connecting the adult and the child with their social and cultural context, has also been a central theme. We have tried in this chapter to emphasize the ways in which people are a product of their social and cultural context, but this does not mean that people are merely 'social dopes', passive victims of their social circumstances. The social constructionist perspective on the person, as we have seen, stresses joint action, dialogue, debate, conversation, conflict and discussion, both between and within people as they try to reconcile the diverse 'voices' or internal dialogues which make up their mental lives. Social life provides us with multiple influences, multiple selves, and with the tools both to engage with others as well as resist and change our social and cultural heritage.

Reading A
On being a conceptual anomaly

D. Kondo

Source: Kondo, D. (1990) *Crafting Selves: Power, Gender and Discourses of Identity in a Japanese Workplace*, Chicago, University of Chicago Press, pp. 9, 11–24.

When I first made my acquaintance with this Tokyo neighbourhood, the air was still warm and humid, awaiting the cleansing winds and rains of the September typhoons. I had come to study the relationship of kinship and economics in family-owned enterprises. [...] By the time I left Japan, during Taikan, the coldest days of the winter season, it had been twenty-six months since I first arrived, and the problematic of kinship and economics had come to pivot around precisely what I perceived to be even more basic cultural assumptions: how *selfhood* is constructed in the arenas of company and family. [...]

As a Japanese American, I created a conceptual dilemma for the Japanese I encountered. For them, I was a living oxymoron, someone who was both Japanese and not Japanese. Their puzzlement was all the greater since most Japanese people I knew seemed to adhere to an eminently biological definition of Japaneseness. Race, language, and culture are intertwined, so much so that any challenge to this firmly entrenched conceptual schema – a white person who speaks flawlessly idiomatic and unaccented Japanese, or a person of Japanese ancestry who cannot – meets with what generously could be described as unpleasant reactions. White people are treated as repulsive and unnatural – *hen na gaijin*, strange foreigners – the better their Japanese becomes, while Japanese Americans and others of Japanese ancestry born overseas are faced with exasperation and disbelief. How can someone who is racially Japanese lack 'cultural competence'? During my first few months in Tokyo, many tried to resolve this paradox by asking which of my parents was 'really' American.

Indeed, it is a minor miracle that those first months did not lead to an acute case of agoraphobia, for I knew that once I set foot outside the door, someone somewhere (a taxi driver? a salesperson? a bank clerk?) would greet one of my linguistic mistakes with an astonished 'Eh?' I became all too familiar with the series of expressions that would flicker over those faces: bewilderment, incredulity, embarrassment, even anger, at having to deal with this odd person who looked Japanese and therefore human, but who must be retarded, deranged, or – equally undesirable in Japanese eyes – Chinese or Korean. Defensively, I would mull over the mistake-of-the-day. I mean, how was I to know that in order to 'fillet a fish' you had to cut it 'in three pieces'? Or that opening a bank account required so much specialized terminology? Courses in literary Japanese at Harvard hadn't done much to prepare me for the realities of everyday life in Tokyo. Gritting my teeth in determination as I groaned inwardly, I would force myself out of the house each morning.

For me, and apparently for the people around me, this was a stressful time, when expectations were flouted, when we had to strain to make sense of one another. [...] For my informants, it was clear that coping with this anomalous creature was difficult, for here was someone who looked like a real human being, but who simply failed to perform according to expectation. They, too, had every reason to make me over in their image, to guide me, gently but insistently, into properly Japanese behavior, so that the discrepancy between my appearance and my cultural competence would not be so painfully evident. I posed a challenge to their senses of identity. How could someone who *looked* Japanese not *be* Japanese? In my cultural ineptitude, I represented for the people who met me the chaos of meaninglessness. [...]

My guarantor, an older woman who, among her many activities, was a teacher of flower arranging, introduced me to many families who owned businesses in the ward of Tokyo where I had chosen to do my research. One of her former students and fellow flower arranging teachers, Mrs Sakamoto, agreed to take me in as a guest over the summer [...] During my stay with the Sakamotos, I did my best to conform to what I thought their expectations of a guest/daughter might be. This in turn seemed to please them and reinforced my tendency to behave in terms of what I perceived to be my Japanese persona.

My initial encounter with the head of the household epitomizes this mirroring and reinforcement of behavior. Mr Sakamoto had been on a business trip on the day I moved in, and he returned the following evening, just as his wife, daughter, and I sat down to the evening meal. As soon as he stepped in the door, I immediately switched from an informal posture, seated on the *zabuton* (seat cushion) to a formal greeting posture, *seiza*-style (kneeling on the floor) and bowed low, hands on the floor. Mr Sakamoto responded in kind (being older, male, and head of the household, he did not have to bow as deeply as I did), and we exchanged the requisite polite formulae, I requesting his benevolence, and he welcoming me to their family. Later, he told me how happy and impressed he had been with this act of proper etiquette on my part. 'Today's young people in Japan,' he said, 'no longer show such respect. Your grandfather must have been a fine man to raise such a fine granddaughter.' Of course, his statements can hardly be accepted at face value. They may well indicate his relief that I seemed to know something of proper Japanese behavior, and hence would not be a complete nuisance to them; it was also his way of making me feel at home. What is important to note is the way this statement was used to elicit proper Japanese behavior in future encounters. And his strategy worked. I was left with a warm, positive feeling toward the Sakamoto family, armed with an incentive to behave in a Japanese way, for clearly these were the expectations and the desires of the people who had taken me in and who were so generously sharing their lives with me.

[...]

At first, then, as a Japanese American I made sense to those around me as a none-too-felicitous combination of racial categories. As fieldwork progressed, however, and my linguistic and cultural skills improved, my informants seemed best able to understand me by placing me in meaningful cultural roles: daughter, guest, young woman, student, prodigal Japanese who had finally seen the light and come home. Most people preferred to treat me as a Japanese – sometimes an incomplete or unconventional Japanese, but a Japanese nonetheless. [...]

My physical characteristics led my friends and co-workers to emphasize my identity as Japanese, sometimes even against my own intentions and desires. Over time, my increasingly 'Japanese' behavior served temporarily to resolve their crises of meaning and to confirm their assumptions about their own identities. That I, too, came to participate enthusiastically in this recasting of the self is a testimonial to their success in acting upon me.

Conflict and fragmentation of self

Using these ready-made molds may have reduced the dissonance in my informants' minds, but it served only to increase the dissonance in my own. What occurred in the field was a kind of fragmenting of identity into what I then labeled Japanese and American pieces, so that the different elements, instead of fitting together to form at least the illusion of a seamless and coherent [...] whole strained against one another. The war was not really – or only – between Japanese and American elements, however. Perhaps it had even more to do with the position of researcher versus one of daughter and guest. In one position, my goal had to be the pursuit of knowledge, where decisive action, independence, and mastery were held in high esteem. In another, independence and mastery of one's own fate were out of the question; rather, being a daughter meant duties, responsibilities, and *inter*dependence.

The more I adjusted to my Japanese daughter's role, the keener the conflicts became. Most of those conflicts had to do with expectations surrounding gender, and, more specifically, my position as a young woman. Certainly, in exchange for the care the Sakamotos showed me, I was happy to help out in whatever way I could. I tried to do some housecleaning and laundry, and I took over the shopping and cooking for Mr Sakamoto when Mrs Sakamoto was at one of the children's association meetings, her flower arranging classes, or meetings of ward committees on juvenile delinquency. The cooking did not offend me in and of itself; in fact, I was glad for the opportunity to learn how to make simple Japanese cuisine, and Mr Sakamoto put up with my sometimes appalling culinary mistakes and limited menus with great aplomb. I remember one particularly awful night when I couldn't find the makings for soup broth, and Mr Sakamoto was fed '*miso* soup' that was little more than *miso* dissolved in hot water. He managed to down the tasteless broth with good grace – and the trace of a smile on his lips. (Of course, it is also true that although he was himself capable of simple cooking, he would not set foot in the kitchen if there were a woman in the house.) Months after I moved out, whenever he saw me he would say with a sparkle in his eye and a hint of nostalgic wistfulness in his voice, 'I miss Dōrin-san's salad and sautéed beef,' one of the 'Western' menus I used to serve up with numbing regularity. No, the cooking was not the problem.

The problem was, in fact, the etiquette surrounding the serving of food that produced the most profound conflicts for me as an American woman. The head of the household is usually served first and receives the finest delicacies; men – even the sweetest, nicest ones – ask for a second helping of rice by merely holding out their rice bowls to the woman nearest the rice cooker, and maybe, just maybe, uttering a grunt of thanks in return for her pains. I could never get used to this practice, try as I might. Still, I tried to carry out my duties uncomplainingly, in what I hope was reasonably good humor. But I was none too happy about these things 'inside.' Other restrictions began to chafe, especially restrictions on my movement. I had to be in at a certain hour, despite my 'adult' age. Yet I understood the family's responsibility for me as their guest and quasi-daughter, so I tried to abide by their regulations, hiding my irritation as best I could.

This fundamental ambivalence was heightened by isolation and dependency [...] this dependency and isolation increased my susceptibility to identifying with my Japanese role. By this time I saw little of American friends in Tokyo, for it was difficult to be with people who had so little inkling of how ordinary Japanese people lived. My informants and I consequently had every reason to conspire to recreate my identity as Japanese. Precisely because of my dependency and my made-to-order role, I was allowed – or rather, *forced* – to abandon the position of observer. Errors, linguistic or cultural, were dealt with impatiently or with a startled look that seemed to say, 'Oh yes, you are American after all.' On the other hand, appropriately Japanese behaviors were rewarded with warm, positive reactions or with comments such as 'You're more Japanese than the Japanese.' Even more frequently, correct behavior was simply accepted as a matter of course. *Naturally* I would understand, *naturally* I would behave correctly, for they presumed me to be, *au fond*, Japanese.

Identity can imply unity or fusion, but for me what occurred was a fragmentation of the self. This fragmentation was encouraged by my own participation in Japanese life and by the actions of my friends and acquaintances. At its most extreme point, I became 'the Other' in my own mind, where the identity I had known in another context simply collapsed. The success of our conspiracy to recreate me as Japanese reached its climax one August afternoon.

It was typical summer weather for Tokyo, 'like a steam bath' as the saying goes, so hot the leaves were drooping limply from the trees surrounding the Sakamotos' house. Mrs Sakamoto and her married daughter, Takemi, were at the doctor's with Takemi's son, so Mr Sakamoto and I were busy tending young Kaori-chan, Takemi-san's young daughter. Mr Sakamoto quickly tired of his grandfatherly role, leaving me to entertain Kaori-chan. Promptly at four p.m., the hour when most Japanese house-wives do their shopping for the evening meal, I lifted the baby into her stroller and pushed her along ahead of me as I inspected the fish, selected the freshest looking vegetables, and mentally planned the meal for the evening. As I glanced into the shiny metal surface of the butch-er's display case, I noticed someone who looked terribly familiar: a typical young housewife, clad in slip-on sandals and the loose, cotton shift called 'home wear' (*hōmu wea*), a woman walking with a charac-teristically Japanese bend to the knees and a sliding of the feet. Suddenly I clutched the handle of the stroller to steady myself as a wave of dizzi-ness washed over me, for I realized I had caught a glimpse of nothing less than my own reflection. Fear that perhaps I would never emerge from this world into which I was immersed, inserted itself into my mind and stubbornly refused to leave, until I resolved to move into a new apartment, to distance myself from my Japanese home and my Japanese existence.

[...]

'Epiphany' and a shift in the problem

This moment of collapse [of identity] was followed by a distancing process. I returned to the United States for a month, and upon returning to Japan, I moved into the apartment promised me, next door to Hatanaka-san, my landlady and friend from the tea ceremony class. This arrangement turned out to be ideal, for I could enjoy the best of both worlds: the warmth of belonging to a family and the (semi) privacy of my own space. I immersed myself in research, finding contacts through Hatanaka-san. In fact, I ended up working in businesses owned by two of her grade school classmates: a hairdressing salon owned by Yokoyama-sensei, and the Satō confectionery factory [...]

I have written 'collapse of identity' and 'distancing process'. But the dis-tancing was only relative, for the same pressures were there, both inter-nal and external, the pressures to be unobtrusively Japanese. In most cases my informants still guided me into these roles and at times refused to let me escape them. In moving to a different neighbourhood and away from the Sakamotos, I had simply exchanged the role of daughter for other culturally meaningful positions – those of guest, neighbor, wor-ker, young woman – that demanded participation and involvement.

Indeed, the shift in the focus of my study lay precisely in this participa-tion. As time wore on, it seemed to me that the relationship of kinship and economics in these family-owned firms – the problem I had initially set out to study – was always filtered through an emphasis on personal relationships. An awareness of this person-centered universe impressed itself upon me in myriad ways. Certainly anyone who lives in this Shitamachi (downtown) district cannot help but be aware of the constant presence of others. In my neighbourhood, the houses were so densely packed that the walls almost touched. Though I lived in my own apartment, I shared a wall with Akemi-chan, Mrs Hatanaka's daughter, and we would try to be solicitous of each other's daily routines: I was especially careful to refrain from typing when she was practicing the piano. Whenever I opened my back window to air my *futon* or to hang up my clothes to dry, I inevitably ended up conversing with the gracious, elderly woman next door, who was always out tending her garden. 'Cold, isn't it?' 'Beautiful morning.' 'They say it's going to rain again.' 'Today feels like another scorcher.' As the seasons passed, we exchanged the conventional yet somehow comfortable and comforting greetings about the weather, before branching off into other topics of mutual interest. [...]

Minute details of everyday life also attracted people's attention. I was able to smell the cooking from the two houses nearest me, and I am certain that others could take note of my daily menu. No visitor could pass unnoticed. I could easily have kept, had I chosen to do so, a highly accurate accounting of the comings and goings from the Hatanakas and at least two other houses near mine. And the Hatanakas never failed to comment on the appearance of each of my visitors. [...]

It may seem that I am describing a society where everyone meddles in everyone else's business, where privacy is breached at every turn. This is, indeed, one of the stereotypes of this Shitamachi, or downtown area, that I often heard from people who lived in the Uptown, or Yamanote, section of Tokyo. Yet I should not neglect to convey the sensitivity and care that so often animated social life in my neighbourhood. The Hatanakas, for instance, were especially solicitous. After a hard day at work, I could almost always count on a tap on the door, and the cheery Mrs Hatanaka would be there, bearing some wonderful concoction – more often than not, a delicious, hot meal. [...]

The demands and obligations of Japanese social life came to assume increasing importance in my life. [...] I felt bound by chains of obligation to my sponsors, my relatives, my friends, and my co-workers, and though I appreciated their concern for me and realized my responsibility to return the kindnesses they had shown me, I simply did not have enough hours in the day to accommodate all of them.

The situation came to a climax one day when I received a phone call from a local teacher who had arranged a number of interviews for me. He began with '*Jitsu wa ...*' (actually ...) a phrase that almost always precedes the asking of a favour. My antennae went up, sensing danger. Well, said he, there was a student of his who would love to learn English conversation, and well, he would like to bring her over to meet me the following evening. Since he had been of so much help to me, I knew I could not refuse and still be considered a decent human being, so I agreed. But I was in a foul mood the entire evening. I complained bitterly to my landlady, who sympathetically agreed that the *sensei* should have been more mindful of the fact that I was so pressed, but she confirmed that I had no choice but to comply. She explained that the *sensei* had been happy to give of his time to help me, and by the same token he considered it natural to make requests of others, who should be equally giving of themselves, their 'inner' feelings notwithstanding. '*Nihonjin wa ne*' she mused, '*jibun o taisetsu ni shinai no, ne.*' (The Japanese don't treat themselves as important do they? That is, they spend time doing things for the sake of maintaining good relationships, regardless of their 'inner' feelings.) I gazed at her in amazement, for her statement struck me with incredible force. Not only did it perfectly capture my own feelings of being bound by social obligation, living my life for others, it also indicated to me a profoundly different way of thinking about the relationship between selves and the social world. Persons seemed to be constituted in and through social relations and obligations to others. Selves and society did not seem to be separate entities; rather, the boundaries were blurred. This realization, coming as it did through intense participation in social life, led me to shift my research problem from kinship and economics to what seemed to be an even more fundamental assumption: how personhood was defined in a Japanese context [...]

In fact, my decision about when to leave Japan was linked to this re-writing of identity. The final months of fieldwork are generally the best and most productive: the months of laying groundwork pay off in the increasing intimacy and comfort in your relationships and in the depth of the insights you are able to reach. This fact made me ever more reluctant to say that my research was 'finished.' I kept extending my stay at the factory; it became something of a joke, as the older women would tease me about my parents, whose 'neck must be sooooo long,' the expression one uses to describe someone who is waiting impatiently. 'You must have found a boyfriend,' they would tell me, or, laughing, they might suggest, 'Why not find a nice Japanese boy and settle down here?' I laughed with them, but I continued to stay on as research became more and more productive, until one event convinced me that the time to depart was near. At a tea ceremony class, I performed a basic 'thin tea' ceremony flawlessly, without need for prompting or correction of my movements. My teacher said in tones of approval, 'You know, when you first started, I was so worried. The way you moved, the way you walked, was so clumsy! But now, you're just like an *ojōsan*, a nice young lady.' Part of me was inordinately pleased that my awkward, exaggerated Western movements had *finally* been replaced by the disciplined grace that makes the tea ceremony so seemingly natural and beautiful to watch. But another voice cried out in considerable alarm, 'Let me escape before I'm completely transformed!' And not too many weeks later, leave I did.

Further reading

For a comprehensive yet accessible overview of the social constructionist argument in psychology, it is worth reading Bruner, J. (1990) *Acts of Meaning*, Cambridge, Mass., Harvard University Press. Bruner describes his approach as 'cultural psychology' but he covers much of the same ground as social constructionism.

The edited collection by Schwartz, T., White, G. and Lutz, C. (1992) *New Directions in Psychological Anthropology*, Cambridge, Cambridge University Press, gives a feel for contemporary developments in the study of culture and psychology, although it is quite dense.

If you are interested in following up work on discourse analysis, then you could look at Potter, J. and Wetherell, M. (1987) *Discourse and Social Psychology*, London, Sage. If you want further background on the trends in developmental psychology discussed in section 5, then probably the best place to start is with Vygotsky's (1978) classic text *Mind in Society: The Development of Higher Psychological Processes*, Cambridge, Mass., Harvard University Press.

References

Allen, N.J. (1985) 'The category of the person: a reading of Mauss's last essay', in Carrithers, M., Collins, S. and Lukes, S. (eds) *The Category of the Person*, Cambridge, Cambridge University Press.

Austin, J. (1962) *How to Do Things with Words*, London, Oxford University Press.

Bakhtin, M. (1981) 'Discourse in the novel', in Holquist, M. (ed.) *The Dialogic Imagination* (trans. by C. Emerson and M. Holquist), Austin, University of Texas Press.

Bar-Hillel, Y. (1954) 'Indexical expressions', *Mind*, vol. 63, pp. 359–79.

Barnes, B. and Law, J. (1976) 'Whatever should be done with indexical expressions?', *Theory and Society*, vol. 3, pp. 223–37.

Bruner, J. (1985) 'Vygotsky: a historical and conceptual perspective', in Wertsch, J.V. (ed.) *Culture, Communication and Cognition: Vygotskian Perspectives*, Cambridge, Cambridge University Press.

Bruner, J. (1986) *Actual Minds, Possible Worlds*, Cambridge, Mass., Harvard University Press

Bruner, J. (1990) *Acts of Meaning*, Cambridge, Mass., Harvard University Press.

Buttny, R. (1993) *Social Accountability in Communication*, London, Sage.

Chomsky, N. (1965) *Aspects of a Theory of Syntax*, The Hague, Mouton.

Cole, M. (1985) 'The zone of proximal development: where culture and cognition create each other', in Wertsch, J.V. (ed.) (1985) *Culture, Communication and Cognition: Vygotskian Perspectives*, Cambridge, Cambridge University Press.

Edwards, D. and Potter, J. (1992) *Discursive Psychology*, London, Sage.

Ekman, P. (1971) 'Universals and cultural differences in facial expressions of emotion', in Cole, J.K. (ed.) *Nebraska Symposium on Motivation*, Nebraska, University of Nebraska Press.

Garfinkel, H. (1967) *Studies in Ethnomethodology*, Englewood Cliffs, Prentice Hall.

Gergen, K. (1985) 'The social constructionist movement in modern psychology', *American Psychologist*, vol. 40, pp. 266–75.

Gergen, K. (1991) *The Saturated Self*, New York, Basic Books.

Gergen, K. (1994) *Toward Transformation in Social Knowledge* (2nd edn), London, Sage.

Graddol, D. (1994) 'Three models of language description', in Graddol, D. and Boyd-Barrett, O. (eds) *Media Texts: Authors and Readers*, Clevedon, Multilingual Matters/The Open University.

Harré, R. (1979) *Social Being: A Theory for Individual Psychology*, Oxford, Blackwell.

Harré, R. (1983) *Personal Being*, Oxford, Blackwell.

Harré, R. and Gillett, G. (1994) *The Discursive Mind*, Thousand Oaks, Sage.

Hymes, D. (1972) 'On communication competence', in Pride, J. and Holmes, J. (eds) *Sociolinguistics*, Harmondsworth, Penguin Books.

Kondo, D. (1990) *Crafting Selves: Power, Gender and Discourses of Identity in a Japanese Workplace,* Chicago, University of Chicago Press.

Lienhardt, G. (1985) 'Self: public and private. Some African representations', in Carrithers, M., Collins, S. and Lukes, S. (eds) *The Category of the Person*, Cambridge, Cambridge University Press.

Lutz, C. (1988) *Unnatural Emotions: Everyday Sentiments on a Micronesian Atoll and Their Challenge to Western Theory,* Chicago, University of Chicago Press.

Markus, H. and Kitayama, S. (1991) 'Culture and the self: implications for cognition, emotion and motivation', *Psychological Review*, vol. 98, pp. 224–54.

Mauss, M. (1985) 'A category of the human mind: the notion of person; the notion of self', in Carrithers, M., Collins, S. and Lukes, S. (eds) *The Category of the Person*, Cambridge, Cambridge University Press.

Maybin, J. (1993) 'Children's voices: talk, knowledge and identity', in Graddol, D., Maybin, J., and Stierer, B. (eds) *Researching Language and Literacy in Social Context*, Clevedon, Multilingual Matters/The Open University.

Middleton, D. and Edwards, D. (1990) *Collective Remembering*, London, Sage.

Miell, D. and Dallos, R. (eds) (1996) *Social Interaction and Personal Relationships*, London, Sage/The Open University (Book 2 in this series).

Miller, P.J. and Hoogstra, L. (1992) 'Language as tool in the socialization and apprehension of cultural meanings', in Schwartz, T., White, G. and Lutz C. (eds) *New Directions in Psychological Anthropology*, Cambridge, Cambridge University Press.

Miller, P.J. and Sperry, L.L. (1987) 'The socialization of anger and aggression', *Merrill Palmer Quarterly,* vol. 33, pp. 1–31.

Miller, P.J., Mintz, J., Hoogstra, L., Fung, H. and Potts, R. (1992) 'The narrated self: young children's construction of self in relation to others in conversational stories of personal experience', *Merrill Palmer Quarterly*, vol. 38, pp. 45–67.

Muhlhausler, P. and Harré, R. (1990) *Pronouns and People*, Oxford, Blackwell.

Ochs, E. and Schieffelin, B. (1984) 'Language acquisition and socialization: three developmental stories and their implications', in Schweder, R.A. and LeVine, R.A. (eds) *Culture Theory: Essays on Mind, Self and Emotion*, Cambridge, Cambridge University Press.

Perkins, D.N. (1990) 'Person plus: a distributed view of thinking and learning', paper delivered at the Symposium on Distributed Learning at the Annual Meeting of the AERA, Boston, 18 April.

Potter, J. and Wetherell, M. (1987) *Discourse and Social Psychology*, London, Sage.

Rosaldo, M. (1984) 'Toward an anthropology of self and feeling', in Schweder, R.A. and LeVine, R.A. (eds) *Culture Theory: Essays on Mind, Self, and Emotion*, Cambridge, Cambridge University Press.

Sacks, H. (1992) *Lectures on Conversation*, Vols I and II, Oxford, Blackwell.

Saussure, F. De (1974) *Course in General Linguistics*, London, Fontana.

Schacter, S. and Singer, J.E. (1962) 'Cognitive, social and physiological determinants of emotional state', *Psychological Review*, vol. 69, pp. 379–99.

Shotter, J. (1993) *The Cultural Politics of Everyday Life*, Buckingham, Open University Press.

Smith, J. (1981) 'Self and experience in Maori culture', in Heelas, P. and Lock, A. (eds) *Indigenous Psychologies*, London, Academic Press.

Still, A. and Good, J. (1992) 'Mutualism in the human sciences: towards the implementation of a theory', *Journal for the Theory of Social Behaviour*, vol. 22, pp. 105–28.

The Open University (1984) D307 *Social Psychology: Development, Experience and Behaviour in a Social World*, Unit 4, *Perspectives on Socialization*, Milton Keynes, The Open University.

Vygotsky, L. (1962) *Thought and Language,* Cambridge, MIT Press and Wiley.

Vygotsky, L. (1978) *Mind in Society: The Development of Higher Psychological Processes,* Cambridge, Mass., Harvard University Press.

Walkerdine, V. (1981) 'Sex, power and pedagogy', *Screen Education,* no. 38, pp. 14–24.

Wetherell, M. (ed.) (1996) *Identities, Groups and Social Issues*, London, Sage/The Open University (Book 3 in this series).

White, G.M. (1992) 'Ethnopsychology', in Schwartz, T., White, G.M. and Lutz, C. (eds) *New Directions in Psychological Anthropology*, Cambridge, Cambridge University Press.

Reflections

This chapter has presented a social constructionist perspective: that we are intrinsically a product of the social world: that the ways in which we think and feel, as well as the ways in which we relate to each other, have been created out of the social practices and modes of conceptualization of the culture in which we live and have been raised. It has illustrated this by showing how the meanings we attribute to ourselves, each other and the world are inseparable from the discourses in which we engage, and emerge out of the dialogic process of language development.

Relation between theory and method

Methodologically, this chapter has been similar in approach to the preceding one. The evidence drawn upon in developing the arguments has come primarily from qualitative rather than quantitative research, including detailed ethnographic work with different groups of people, studies of transcripts, and from observations and sometimes participant observation. There have been few examples of the kind of experimental work presented in Chapter 3. It is worth noting here how theory and method go hand in hand. If we take, for instance, a view of language as linked to context and regard discourse as action-orientated, if we see social interaction as a process of negotiation and joint action, and culture as fluid and open, then it becomes problematic to try to control the context through setting up situations in a laboratory. From a social constructionist point of view, the interesting material is removed when variables are controlled in this way.

The social construction of personal experience

The emphasis on construction in this chapter continues and extends the focus in Chapters 3 and 4 on people's need to make sense: to interpret and explain the world they experience. What the authors of this chapter have tried to demonstrate, however, are the strong links between *personal constructions* and *social constructions*. This applies, they claim, even to private events of deep personal significance such as emotions of grief, rage, love, and so on. How we understand such feelings, construct them, and make sense of circumstances which evoke them has a great deal to do with the social worlds in which we move. The production of meaning, Wetherell and Maybin argue, is a public process and, since we make sense of our experience in terms of such meanings, social process will guide phenomenology or the nature of our experience.

An interesting point which arises from this position is, if all ideas are socially constructed, what is the status of social constructionist theory itself as a claim to knowledge? Is the theory itself also socially constructed or can it stand outside the process of construction? This is a complex issue. Generally, social constructionists do not claim to be immune to the processes they describe in others. As Kenneth Gergen (1973) commented, social psychology is a form of history. At the moment, at this period in our history, social constructionist ideas resonate with the concerns of 'postmodern' societies, but ideas about people and society will change as people and societies change. In the social constructionist view, this relativism and the historical nature of social psychology does not mean that these theories should not be asserted as part of the social process of argument and negotiation of meaning.

Conflicting accounts

The emphasis that what we experience as well as how we express ourselves are inherently socially constructed is, of course, a core point of issue between this and the perspectives presented in the earlier chapters in this book. The biological perspective of Chapter 2, for example, would see the experience of particular emotional feelings, as well as some of the facial expressions that accompany them, as being genetically based. In this chapter, however, we saw how social constructionists such as Rosaldo claim that even the most basic emotional feelings are intertwined with social conventions and practice. Further, although social constructionists argue that people are actively engaged in building their social worlds (and sometimes resisting social influence), they are also sceptical about the experiential position expressed in Chapter 4 that people have a capacity for autonomy and choice. In the social constructionist view, it is difficult for people to think past their collective intellectual histories; our choices are always grounded in the social materials which are available. Indeed, this perspective would see the idea of autonomy (especially the highly individual-centered version of freedom found in some parts of Euro-American societies) as itself socially and culturally mediated. Social constructionists would contrast, for example, what they see as the *interdependent* concept of the person found in societies such as Japan with the *independent* concept assumed by existentialists.

While such examples would seem to indicate fundamental incompatibility of views, comparisons between the perpectives are not necessarily straightforward. On the one hand, as we saw in this chapter, social constructionists do not view people as passive pawns: they do allow a role for individuals in actively shaping their lives. One the other hand, neither the biological and experiential perspectives (nor indeed the experimental approach), as we saw in the earlier chapters, seek to deny the influence of social factors. And there is no reason why some degree of social construction should necessarily be incompatible with their positions. Ekman (1971), on the basis of extensive cross-cultural research, has presented an interesting theory of emotion which relates to both biological and social constructionist positions and might be seen as a bridge between them. He claims that while basic emotional feelings and expressions may be biologically determined, the rules which elicit or inhibit such displays of emotion may vary from culture to culture. So whereas the form of expression and feelings attached to grief may be universal, by whom they are displayed and the conditions under which they are elicited will be subject to cultural conventions. (But whether, of course, as a result of the meanings attached by this cultural process, we are still dealing with the same emotion from culture to culture is a matter of debate.)

The existentialist notion of 'situated freedom' also acknowledges social process as among those factors which help to shape the choices we make. And experientialists do not deny that there are cultural variations in both concerns with autonomy and the degree to which it is exercised. But, as with Ekman's position in relation to the expression of emotion, they see such differences as arising from the degree of facilitation or inhibition of such concerns which different cultures apply. Thus, they would question how deep the apparent cultural differences between, say, Japanese interdependence and the Euro-American emphasis on the individual really go.

If social constructionists view other perspectives as paying insufficient attention to the significance of social construction, they in turn can be accused of being slow to recognize any universalities in human conduct, and any limitations and constraints imposed by the biological foundations of human life. Where the social constructionist perspective is weakest is probably in detailed examinations and explanations of individual differences. In many respects such differences are outside the scope of its theorizing. For the causes of these differences, it is necessary to look at, say, the biological perspective or go to the next chapter which offers a psychodynamic account. The concluding chapter will return to this tricky issue of the relationship between perspectives.

Problems of interpretation

Such disputes highlight one of the core problems with interpretative and analytic approaches. Very often the evidence used can be interpreted in different ways and it is difficult to choose between these interpretations. For example, the dualism of body and mind that we find in Euro-American culture is seen by social constructionists as the result of social history. (They might consider, for example, that the doctrines of Christianity may well have played an important role in generating dualistic notions.) However, an alternative experiential interpretation might be that the dualistic notion which is found in contemporary culture merely reflects core phenomenological reality rather than any social construction (and Christianity represents one expression of this). We do experience ourselves as a mind within a body, the experientialist perspective would assert: this is a fundamental property of a self-aware human being. If we accept Lienhardt's findings with the Dinka as valid, however, it is unclear how these experiences would be assimilated or interpreted by such a position.

As is acknowledged in Chapter 5, when it comes to drawing conclusions from studies of cultures other than our own, problems of interpretation become particularly acute. It is because of such difficulties, of course, that experimental social psychologists are wary of interpretative approaches and stress the need to restrict study to variables which can be operationalized. But it is debatable whether the experimental approach is any less subject to disputes over interpretations as to what experimental data signify. In any case, as we have seen, both experiential psychologists and social constructionists unite in arguing that to preclude meanings (and meanings presuppose interpretation) is to eliminate the very essence of the subject-matter of psychology. Without interpretation of some kind, it is impossible to understand the self.

We turn now to the final perspective to be presented in this book – the psychodynamic approach. This also is built on interpretative method. But it shifts the focus of interest to individual differences. It sees the origins of these in unconscious feelings. And its concerns go beyond discourse and the dialogic processes of language and concept acquisition to the emotional strata laid down in the earliest years of a person's life.

References

Ekman, P. (1971) 'Universals and cultural differences in facial expressions of emotion', in Cole, J.K. (ed.) *Nebraska Symposium on Motivation,* Nebraska, University of Nebraska Press.

Gergen, K. (1973) 'Social psychology as history', *Journal of Personality and Social Psychology,* vol. 26, pp. 309–20.

CHAPTER 6

THE DEFENSIVE SELF: A PSYCHODYNAMIC PERSPECTIVE

by Kerry Thomas

Contents

1   Introduction

This chapter uses the ideas and evidence of practising psychoanalysts to think about how we become the people we are.

The psychodynamic tradition began in the world of neurology, psychiatry, paediatrics and the clinical science of the consulting room, and its ideas are not commonly found at the centre of academic psychology. This chapter sets out to do something new. It treats psychodynamics essentially as *social* psychology. I shall recast psychodynamics as a form of enquiry and understanding that is primarily concerned with the psychological and social development of the person and the creation of selfhood in a social world.

What can psychodynamics offer to social psychology? We shall find that psychodynamics has a unique set of concepts, a language, and a method – psychoanalysis – for studying subjective experience. It has theories about what drives social life. It can describe and explore the *processes* by which the social world 'gets inside' to create us as essentially social beings. Through psychoanalysis it can also explore the *content* of our internal worlds. By content I mean the particular ways in which each of us makes sense of the external world and then represents it symbolically, inside, creating our own psychic realities and ultimately our selfhood. In psychodynamics, the presence and influence of the 'other' is constant and profound, whether in the reality of the external world or in our internal worlds. Psychodynamics will be presented as a tool to examine the way individuals construe and internalize the social world and are constituted by it.

The basic assumptions of psychodynamics are outlined in section 2 of the chapter. We shall discover that, from the psychodynamic viewpoint, things are not as they seem; that much of what we take for granted about ourselves, about social life and society may need to be re-thought.

In section 3, three psychodynamic approaches are examined in more detail: the theories of Freud, Klein and the British object relations school. Each approach makes different assumptions about what drives social life, and has different views about the organization of the mind and the construction of selfhood. The three approaches, however, are united in the emphasis they place on the avoidance of anxiety through mobilization of psychological defences, some of which are built into the structure of the mind early in development.

Section 4 explores the nature of the self and experiences of selfhood. We shall see that psychodynamics suggests that our experiences of our selves may not be so complete, so smooth, so unitary, so real or so agentic as we think. And that 'self' itself may be a defensive structure which protects a sense of wholeness.

Why am I using the term 'psychodynamic' rather than the more usual term 'psychoanalytic'? The term 'psychoanalytic', strictly, refers to the work of Freud, his theories and clinical psychoanalysis, although it usually encompasses those who have refined or extended his ideas. By using 'psychodynamic', a different and generic word, I am emphasizing that a great deal has changed in theory and practice, both in parallel with Freud and since his time. Some of the developments have questioned or abandoned fundamental Freudian assumptions; and some of the disputes constitute the very issues that we need to address here, such as 'what drives social life?'.

Most of you will know something about Freud. His psychoanalytic concepts are now commonplace in ordinary life and ordinary language. But this is not going to be a chapter about Freud — you won't find even a mention of the Oedipus complex until section 3.1. Pause here and remind yourself what you already know about psychodynamics, or psychoanalysis. Make a list of concepts and key words. In this list you will almost certainly have some of my main themes, but there will probably be others that you will miss. Keep the list near you as you continue with the chapter and see how much of your list is covered as the arguments unfold.

ACTIVITY 6.1

How does the psychodynamic perspective relate to the other approaches in this book? Because psychodynamics provides a comprehensive account of subjective experience, in some respects it overlaps with other perspectives. It has many of the same concerns, such as interactions of innate and environmental influences, the importance of language, how selfhood is constructed and tussles between determining forces and agency. But sometimes psychodynamics suggests something quite different and incompatible, because it makes different assumptions about the nature of the person and uses very different methods of enquiry. Although psychodynamics has always tried to find generalizations about psychological processes, such as Freud's scheme for the psychosexual stages of development, the data have come from the consulting room and are the behaviours and, more importantly, the words and meanings of *individuals*.

The most obvious conflict with previous chapters concerns the status of consciousness. In psychodynamics, consciousness itself is seen as a problem. Conscious awareness is assumed to be partial, just the tip of an iceberg, and a biased version of the totality of what we 'know' and have experienced. Much that is meaningful and most that is motivating is hidden in the unconscious. By suggesting that there is another layer of subjective experience, we *could* think of psychodynamics as just extending other viewpoints. But this is not the case. There is a real clash here because, according to psychodynamics, consciousness, rational thought and agency are largely subjugated to the main driving force — the dynamic, determining unconscious.

In some cases psychodynamics *does* extend or elaborate on ideas in earlier chapters. For example, biology is central to psychodynamics; the focus is always the mind and body *together*. In psychodynamics, embodiment is the subjective experience of having a body, living in it and through it and adapting psychologically as it grows and ages; the raw data of psychodynamics are the kinds of feelings and thoughts and turmoil concerning bodily sensations and emotions that are talked about in the consulting room – anxiety, anger, euphoria, psychosomatic symptoms, masturbatory fantasies, sexual desire and so on.

Sometimes psychodynamics 'goes behind' what is discussed in other perspectives, offering a different kind of explanation for similar findings. You may remember, for example, that Chapter 3 began with a game of dice. The players were insisting that if they said or did certain things they would have an effect on the outcome of the throw – a kind of 'magical thinking'. The cognitive perspective of Chapter 3 conceives of the person as a creature who tries to represent accurately, understand rationally, problematize and exert control over the environment. But if you look more closely at the discussion in that chapter you will find that a lot of the human effort – the motivation – is directed not towards 'real' control but towards a *feeling of having control*. This may require a kind of 'irrationality' – the distorting of information about the external world or about ourselves. Chapter 3 provides evidence of such distortions or biases, leading to the 'fundamental attribution error'. In psychodynamic terms, these are defence mechanisms: the dice players' rituals would be described as an omnipotent defence against the vagaries of dice and the world more generally.

The idea of psychological defences is central to all schools of psychodynamics and is one of the main themes of this chapter. According to psychodynamics, we are organisms who structure our lives defensively, to avoid anxiety. Anxiety is not only a painful bodily sensation, but can interrupt thoughts and intentions leading to disorganization of moment-to-moment behaviour. When extreme, anxiety can lead to feelings of disintegration and threaten the sense of being a whole person. This chapter is organized around the concept of a defensive self. Until recently the term 'self' has been avoided in most psychodynamic theories; but all psychodynamic viewpoints share the notion that our central identity, whether we call it ego or self, has to be constantly defended against anxiety in order to limit disruption and maintain a *sense* of unity.

In common with much of this book and with Chapter 5 in particular, psychodynamics is concerned with *how*, *when* and *to what end* we construct our internal, symbolic representations of the external world. As in the social constructionist viewpoint of the previous chapter, no assumption is made that external, objective realities are 'printed' accurately (or even inaccurately) on to pre-existing individuals. In contrast to Chapter 5, in this chapter the emphasis is individualistic, on the idiosyncrasies of each person's psychic reality rather than commonalities of 'reality' as social constructions, created and maintained in social networks.

The psychodynamic perspective also differs from the social constructionist view in emphasizing the importance of the earliest years of life
for the development of the self. Our internal worlds and our psychic
realities *are* our selves. Selfhood is deeply influenced by other people.
Much of the self is seen as *constituted* from internal representations of
other people and relationships – whole people, aspects of people and,
most importantly, the ways they relate to us and to each other. Basic to
psychodynamics, therefore, is the idea that the structure and content of
our selves are constructed during the vital years of babyhood and childhood through interaction with primary carers. This micro-social context
is seen as the link between individuals and society.

According to psychodynamics, each of us exists within our own psychic
reality; our own unique internal representations of the world are biased
or constructed to serve particular, personal ends. In our internal worlds,
our psychic reality is the only reality there is – and it can lead to denials
or exaggerations, idealizations, or any other kind of 'magical thinking'.
In psychodynamics, demarcations between reality and fantasy are
difficult to make or maintain. Much of the stuff of psychodynamic
understanding is either conscious fantasy or unconscious phantasy
(denoted as unconscious by the different spelling). One of the main features of psychodynamics and the process of psychoanalysis is the idea
that 'real' external reality, varieties of internal symbolic representations
of reality, conscious fantasies, unconscious phantasies and memories are
constantly entangled in our subjective experience and thus in the way
we act in the world. This standpoint is very different from the other
chapters in the book.

Aims of Chapter 6

The aims of this chapter are:

- To use psychodynamic theories and the evidence of
  practising psychoanalysts as a form of social psychology
  – in order to think about how we become the people we
  are, how the social world gets inside us and constitutes
  our selves.

- To outline the underlying assumptions common to most
  psychodynamic theories.

- To describe three psychodynamic accounts which have
  different assumptions about (1) what drives social life,
  and (2) what influences the forms in which the external
  world is represented in internal worlds to constitute
  psychic reality and selfhood.

- To demonstrate the central role of defence mechanisms
  in the early structuring of the mind.

- To use psychodynamic insights to think about the self.

2   Basic psychodynamic assumptions

According to the psychodynamic perspective, 'things are not as they seem'. In Euro-American societies, at least, most people assume that humans have access to their own beliefs and mental states most of the time. Most people believe that we can, and do, think through our intentions and actions, seeking truths and making rational decisions in a real and accessible world, that we are 'centred egos' in control of our thoughts, feelings and behaviours. We believe that in our social lives people usually communicate their knowledge and their intentions accurately (and honestly) to others in the service of their individual or joint goals. The psychodynamic approach undermines much of this.

2.1   Unconscious motivation

Basic assumption: Human behaviour and consciousness are largely determined by unconscious motives.

The unique contribution of psychodynamics, in all its versions, lies in its most basic assumption: that the structure, content and dynamics of the psyche are not necessarily available to consciousness. According to psychodynamics, human behaviour is largely determined by primitive motives which originate in the unconscious, and remain so deeply buried that we have no access to them, although we can sometimes gain partial access with the help of psychoanalysis. Because the unconscious is thought of as the source of motivation, it is called the *dynamic unconscious*. Unconscious motives are frequently in direct conflict with conscious thoughts and intentions.

A further assumption, that of psychological determinism, states that virtually all our behaviour is motivated and goal-directed and no behaviours (or almost none) are random or accidental. This is further complicated by the principle of over-determination. According to this, several different motives and causes can, and usually do, give rise to a particular feeling, thought or behaviour.

These assumptions are very much at odds with other psychological versions of individual experience, behaviour and the accepted dynamics of social life. In psychodynamic theories, it is the dynamic unconscious which is in control most of the time, playing out a drama in which the narrative is beyond awareness and the enactments are beyond the conscious control of the experiencing subject. It follows that our ordinary accounts, to ourselves and others (including psychologists) of what we do, what we feel and what happens to us are at best limited and most of the time are likely to be inaccurate.

If the unconscious is out of consciousness, then how can it ever be known? The unconscious is unknowable by the experiencing subject, but its existence and nature can be indirectly tested by other people.

It is, in most respects, like any other hypothetical construct; and hypothetical constructs are commonplace in psychology and other forms of scientific endeavour. What this means is that the unconscious will always be a hypothesis but one that can be tested in a variety of ways; and until it is disproved or rejected as no longer useful, it can be retained.

However, the unconscious is particularly problematic in one sense: its manifestations will be confusing, disguised and contradictory.

BOX 6.1   Clinical evidence: what is psychodynamic theory based upon?

A common criticism of psychoanalysis has been that the theory is based on Freud's work with a very small sample of patients – western, middle-class, neurotic women. How can their subjective experiences and the processes observed during their analyses count as the basis for a theory of people in general?

This issue of Freud's small and 'pathological' sample has long been irrelevant. During Freud's own time, many other analysts worked with people who had a range of clinical difficulties. Jung, who was a psychiatrist, analysed people with much more serious conditions – schizophrenia and other kinds of psychotic disorder. Jung's work with psychotic patients was one of the sources of insights into subjective experiences of fragmentation and breakdown of the self. In much less florid forms, the experience of fragmentation and impending loss of self is now thought of as more normally distributed in the population. We shall return to this idea in section 4 of the chapter. Klein introduced psychoanalysis of children – a very different source of subjective experience and one which cannot rely on verbal accounts alone. Recently, Sinason (1992) has shown that it is possible to work psychoanalytically with adults and children who have severe learning difficulties.

The notion that psychoanalytic data derive only from pathology is dated. Jung was one of the first to work with people who had no clinical reason for analysis – they were usually people in mid-life who wanted to extend their self-knowledge and gain access to their creativity. Jung was also the originator of the idea that analysts themselves must be analysed. This is now a requirement of all rigorous psychoanalytic trainings and has produced a vast amount of material on the internal worlds and subjective experience of people who would not be thought of as clinical cases.

There are other, more valid, criticisms of clinical psychoanalytic data. For example, these data are collected by (and usually described and presented by) single observers (the particular analyst) who can neither be entirely objective nor uninvolved; and specific cases cannot be replicated. These criteria, however, are requirements of a particular kind of science (as indicated in Chapters 2 and 3). In Chapters 4 and 5 we saw that accounts of subjective experience and

---

'texts' of lives are 'there to be interpreted'. It is not a matter of the truth of an account but of understanding an account in its own terms, and case by case, since no two lives are ever the same: the validity of the data is not questioned. The same can be said of psychoanalytic case material. What the patient says and does are data to be interpreted. The interpretations can be challenged, of course, as can relations between the data and particular aspects of theory.

The psychoanalytic setting as a source of data has particular features. Psychoanalysts are trained for many years to be observers of others and of themselves. Through their self-knowledge they can reflect upon, but not engage with, the communicative efforts of the patient in the intimate twosome of the consulting room. In this way, analysts' own biases are minimized. But, paradoxically, an essential part of their work is using themselves – their emotional and bodily reactions (such as tenseness, sleepiness, etc.) to what the patient brings into the session – as tools with which to understand the patient's inner experience. Ultimately, however, analysts are participants. This is because their verbal interventions – their interpretations to patients – are intended to bring about change in the patients' internal worlds and influence their subjective experience. Intervention followed by close observation of change is, of course, a kind of experiment, an experiment with its own kind of validity, limited usually to the particular case and rarely similar enough to other cases to have validity in terms of the criteria of traditional science.

(What goes on in the consulting room, the kinds of data available, the use of the relationship between analyst and patient – known as the transference and countertransference – to promote understanding and change are discussed in Thomas, 1996.)

2.2   Irrationality and defence mechanisms

Basic assumption: Consciousness and our internal versions of the world are systematically distorted so as to avoid anxiety.

The assumption of unconscious motivation has another subversive impli-cation. Our conscious versions of what is going on are not randomly mistaken, but *distorted in systematic ways*. Our biases and mistakes have a syntax of their own which serves unconscious motives. According to psy-chodynamics, we are not rational truth-seekers attempting to model the world in as accurate a way as we can. Rather, we are defended creatures who distort reality because we cannot bear the psychological pain of the truth. We construct versions of the world that compromise between enough accuracy for physical survival and enough distortion to reduce the psychological pain of existence to bearable levels. For each of us, this is our psychic reality.

We might prefer to rephrase this kind of irrationality as 'rationally goal-directed with respect to unconscious motives'. But often our irrationality is indeed maladaptive and sometimes it is perverse; that is, self-damaging in a wider or longer term view. These failures in defence systems lead to the kinds of psychological problems that psychoanalysis tries to address.

According to psychodynamic theorists, defence mechanisms such as repression, denial and projection are part of *normal* psychological processing. However, they are largely unconscious – we are not usually aware that we are defending or how we are defending. If we did know what we were doing, much of the defence would be undermined and truths about reality, conflict and anxiety would return to consciousness. In this view, any observations of behaviour or attempts to understand subjective experience must find ways to infer the operation of defence mechanisms, and thus must always be prepared to look for unconscious motives and the sources of apparent irrationalities.

What are we defending against? Like all animals, we try to avoid physical pain. But, the evolution of consciousness has created the possibility of psychic pain – a great part of which is anxiety. *Objective anxiety* is generated by real events that are actually happening; *signal anxiety* is an alerting mechanism. Signal anxiety can be occasioned by conscious thoughts, images, memories etc.; that is, by revisiting conscious internal representations of past traumas or expectations, or by fantasies of future physical pain and lesser frustrations. These representations might also be stimulated by current external events. Signal anxiety can also be aroused directly, without conscious thoughts or images, by unconscious phantasies (meaningful 'connections' or 'ideas' in the unconscious). Anxiety may also be elicited by repressed (i.e. unconscious) internal conflicts. We also defend against consciousness of past, present and future emotional states such as rage, loss, loneliness and despair. Some of these kinds of psychic pain are clearly to do with the social world. They can be occasioned by the influence and actions of the important 'others' that we relate to, or by our fantasies about these other people. Anxieties and pain can also be the result of the demands and sanctions of society (sometimes called moral anxiety). Some anxieties are to do with existential truths about the human condition – meaninglessness and the inevitability of death. One of the most profound sources of anxiety concerns a sense of impending loss of identity, or fragmentation and loss of self.

Since these kinds of anxiety (other than objective anxiety) are the result of psychological processes rather than external danger, they are often collectively known as *neurotic anxiety*. They might be thought of as irrational, but anxiety has a rational function: it is part of an early-warning system of threats of disequilibrium in the ego or threats to the sense of wholeness of the self. These so-called irrational anxieties can be thought of as 'inwardly directed vigilance' (Rycroft, 1968). Thus, anxiety is the first step in the defensive process that protects the ego, ensuring a sense of integrity, continuity, robustness and mastery. It is not primarily concerned with physical survival but with psychological survival.

2.3   Internal worlds and the developmental focus

Basic assumptions: Internal versions of the external world form very early in life. They are not one-to-one mappings of the external world, nor of experience in it, but are emotionally charged constructions. Internalized versions of other people and relationships are central features of internal worlds. Living in such internal worlds confers on experiencing subjects their own versions of reality known in psychodynamics as their psychic reality.

Internal worlds are created, from birth (and perhaps even during intra-uterine life) from internalizations – *introjections* – of the external world. Internal worlds are based on a mixture of innate propensities of some kind or another, and direct experience of the external world. At first, this direct experience of the world is pre-verbal, often highly emotional. Much of this early experience takes place 'in tandem' with another human being, the primary carer, and consists of interchanges of sounds, looks and feelings. Later, direct experience of the world is elaborated through language. Internal worlds have both content and structure – they are organized. As they begin to develop, both their content and organization will filter and colour infants' 'passive' experiences of the external world. Quite soon, internal worlds also actively impose direction and constraint upon intentions and behaviour in the external world and also guide understandings and meanings of further experiences. Thus, the earliest weeks and months of life are crucially important. Different psychodynamic approaches put differing emphases on the respective roles of nature and nurture in this process of construction. Section 3 of the chapter will explore these differences.

Psychodynamic accounts differ from most other accounts of learning and socialization in two important ways. First, psychodynamics conceives of internal worlds that are largely unconscious. They are not temporarily out of awareness, as in most cognitive approaches; they are, in part, permanently out of awareness – but nevertheless motivating. Secondly, internal worlds are furnished not only with belief and knowledge structures in the abstract, but peopled with *internal objects*. In psychodynamics, 'object' is a term used to stand for 'other person' or occasionally some other definable aspect of the world, drawing a distinction between other people (objects) and the subject, the experiencing 'I'. The thesis is that a large part of what is taken in and remains most salient is in the form of holistic versions of important people from the external world.

Versions of other people are 'taken in' (introjected) whole, in parts (part-objects) and *in their relationships* with the experiencing subject and others. It is thought that these internal objects and internal object relations are the most crucial furnishings of internal worlds; and it is through these introjects that the infant and small child learn about the complexities of the social world. It follows that psychodynamics, compared with most other psychological approaches, places far more importance upon the earliest interactions with other people. It is the *minutiae* of responsive-ness, overall feeling tone, emotional states, power relations (and the internal worlds) of other people, especially mothers and fathers or other early carers, that are by far the most important environmental influences on the shaping of infants' internal worlds and their developing versions of psychic reality.

> There is a similarity here to the idea of incorporating dialogues, found in the developmental theories of Mead and Vygotsky. But in psychodynamics these internalizations are much earlier in life and are established before the child has the benefit of much in the way of language. Nevertheless, there are parallels – the processes Mead and Vygotsky describe also involve a rather mysterious business of 'taking in' chunks of 'knowing' and 'feeling', via some kind of identification with another person, which become internal thoughts.

Internal objects and internal object relations provide not only templates for ways of relating but also the raw material of selfhood. Introjections of other people can be identified with and made part of one's self. Some such identifications may be momentary, or relatively short-term, or they may be permanent. In this view, selfhood is built up from long-term, relatively stable identifications with internal objects and their ways of relating. Again, this fundamental psychodynamic notion gives great weight to early and very early experience of the micro-social world which is translated into internal worlds and becomes the source of self. Psychodynamics also assumes that introjects of intimate, and less inti-mate, relationships carry 'loaded' messages about broader patterns of social relations. Thus, it is our earliest, *pre-verbal* encounters with people that provide the raw material for reproducing the social order: forms of gender behaviour, patterns of equality and inequality, dominance and submission.

Compared with other psychological perspectives, psychodynamics con-sistently places much more importance on pre-verbal and non-verbal modes of communication. It also emphasizes emotions, early forms of thinking and the persistence and the survival into adulthood of infantile (primitive) and highly charged forms of internal representation. From a psychodynamic viewpoint, therefore, any consideration of the impact of society on individuals has to take account of the fact that, by the time language arrives, most of the influential events have already happened and most of the structure of the mind is already laid down. Language will elaborate experience but, according to many psychodynamic the-orists, language, in particular for the purposes of relating to others, is an impoverished medium whose precision in factual domains fails to make up for the loss of more primitive kinds of communication. The way language influences people and 'makes things happen' may well depend less on the words than the emotional charge they carry, and on the *way they are used* – ways which tap into more primitive and unconscious processes.

2.4   The experiencing subject

Basic assumption: Experiencing subjects, each with his or her own psychic reality, are at the centre of the stage. Individuals' idiosyncratic meaning systems, constructions, memories, fantasies, unconscious phantasies and dreams are the raw data of psychodynamic theories and clinical psychoanalysis. Paradoxically, much that is and has been 'experienced' by the experiencing subject is unconscious and not directly accessible.

Freud began as a scientist in the traditional manner, attempting to find general laws about psychodynamic processes that apply to everyone. Freudian theory, for example, contains 'laws' about psychosexual developmental stages, and also about the impact of infant care regimes on ensuing patterns of personality.

However, as Freud developed his theory – working with patients, their symptoms and verbal accounts of their remembered histories and current lives – he moved away from his own scientific, biological training. It became clear that psychoanalysis, and psychodynamic theory more generally, must be essentially concerned with the details of the symbolic worlds that are internal and unique to individuals.

Frosh, a psychologist who integrates academic psychology and psychodynamics, believes that psychodynamics is alone in being able to provide a discourse which is

> finely attuned to the nuances of subjectivity … [can] grapple with psychological phenomena which are more extensive than those of consciously willed acts, a language that can reveal the unappreciated connections between what we experience and what it is we are. A language, therefore, of the unconscious – of impulses, anxieties, wishes and contradictory desires that are structured and re-structured by our immersion in the social order … In psychoanalysis, it is the subjectivity of the individual which is the centre of concern, a subjectivity given not just by what can be easily expressed as a consciously available 'I', but also by·obscure and· contradictory segments of a hidden self.
>
> *(Frosh, 1991, p. 1)*

It is a fundamental assumption of the psychodynamic perspective that individuals each have their own idiosyncratic representations of the world – their own intricately developed meaning systems. These meaning systems include assumptions about other people and relationships, characteristic ways of thinking, forms of imagery, fantasies, unconscious phantasies and dreams. Individuals have their own 'tongues' or 'idiolects'; that is, their own vocabularies and ways of using language, and their own language of symbolism in the widest sense. It is individuals' subjective experience, in its full symbolic complexity, together with their own life-stories and their overall construction of a self, that are the raw data of psychodynamic explorations. But this is problematic in several ways.

Given the role of the unconscious in psychodynamic theory, it follows that people's conscious accounts of their subjective experience must, by definition, always be partial: *access to subjective experience* is therefore problematic. Accounts are likely to be contradictory, changeable, and they may be designed to deceive (unconsciously) or to disguise unpalatable, anxiety-producing features of the inner or outer world. Not only will unconscious meanings, images and feelings be hidden (that is, be absent from consciousness and consciously constructed accounts), but unconscious motives may also disguise and distort what *is* apparently available. Sometimes the workings of the unconscious leak through into verbal communications (and overt behaviour) in the form of 'slips of the tongue', lapses of memory and the other 'mistakes' of everyday life that Freud used as one of his starting points for investigating the unconscious.

This view of subjective experience as essentially partial and disguised provides the main point of contrast with the idea of the 'reflexive self' put forward in Chapter 4. According to the psychodynamic version of subjective experience, the value of reflection on one's own experience is severely limited. Psychoanalysis claims to extend the capacity for reflection, to some extent, with the help and intervention of another person.

A further problem is the *interpretation of subjective experience*. A fundamental assumption of psychodynamics is that, in the special and privileged setting of psychoanalytic sessions, analysts are able to treat verbal accounts of subjective experience together with observations of overt behaviours *as if they are texts to be deciphered and interpreted*. Psychoanalysts try to look through the words of the communications to the meanings that lie behind, to discover the patient's own language of symbolism, fantasies, dreams and constructions of meaning, and the richness of *what it is like to be* the patient. This is a process of becoming familiar with the patient's inner world and psychic reality whilst remaining sufficiently separate to 'look through and behind' the verbal accounts, to watch for systematic patterns, and in various other ways infer unconscious motives and meanings.

A common misconception of the psychoanalytic process is that the analyst is trying to find out the 'truths' about what happened to the patient in the past – 'historical truths'. The raw data of psychoanalysis are much more tentative and 'constructionist' than this. These data include free associations about past and present life; current happenings and feelings; old memories, fantasies, dreams; and the variety of relationships with the analyst that emerge over time as replays of the past (transferences) and as evocations of hidden voices in the analysand's inner world. The status of understandings of these data is closer to 'narrative truth' – the largely negotiated story of the analysand's life and selfhood. This view of psychoanalysis is consistent with the idea that meanings are 'made' rather than discovered.

Language is the primary medium for describing and communicating inner experiences and is the psychoanalyst's main route to patients' consciousness and their unconscious. But language is not always sufficient for the task. Feelings and images often seem to be beyond or apart from language. And there may well be individual variation in this experience of the inadequacy of language. Psychodynamic theories suggest that feelings or images of experiences that cannot be expressed in language may reflect experiences that pre-date language. Difficulties in expressing a feeling or experience in language may also be a defence against a painful memory. *Language can hinder communication* and thus the understanding by another of subjective experience. Language can convey to the listener a quite different message from what is consciously intended. Sometimes this will be a manifestation of unconscious processes (such as a defence), but it may also be because there is no perfect mapping of language on to concepts and things.

Finally, we need to remember that language is not a transparent medium. When we learn language we do not take in a neutral set of tools with which to name (in a simple one-to-one mapping) and then express subjective experience that already exists. Chapter 5 showed how language can actually create meanings. Taking this one step further, as language is learned and elaborated throughout life, it brings the social world with all its messages (in terms of emotions, value judgements, power relations and much else) right into the centre of the internal word of the person – *language becomes a constituent of the self.*

Review of section 2

The fundamental assumptions of the psychodynamic perspective that are central to this chapter are:

- Human behaviour and conscious awareness are largely determined by unconscious motives.

- Our conscious experience and internal versions of the world are systematically distorted so as to avoid anxiety. Defences are built into the structure of our minds from a very early age.

- Internal representations of the external world begin to form very early in life, before the acquisition of language. These internal worlds are not one-to-one mappings of the external world or of our experience in it. They are constructions which often exist in several versions. They are often charged with powerful emotions.

- Individuals' idiosyncratic meaning systems, constructions, memories, fantasies, unconscious phantasies and dreams are the raw data of psychodynamic theories and clinical psychoanalysis.

- A large component of internal worlds are introjected versions of other people and relationships, known as internal objects and internal object relations. As objects and object relations are introjected they carry with them pre-verbal social 'messages' about values, gender and power relations. It is largely from these internal figures and relationships, and our identifications with them, that selfhood is constructed.

- Psychodynamics provides a set of concepts and a language for exploring individuals' idiosyncratic meaning systems – conscious and unconscious.

3   Psychodynamics and the origins of social life and selfhood

This section will examine how three different versions of psychodynamics approach a cluster of questions about the origins of social life and selfhood.

ACTIVITY 6.2

What kinds of question might we need to consider about our socialness (or sociality)? Use what follows below as a guide. Think about what your answers would be and any other questions you could add. You might want to return to this activity at the beginning of section 4, or perhaps when you have completed the chapter, and you can then see if your questions and answers have changed or been elaborated.

How do we become social? How does our socialness (our sociality) 'get inside' us? When does this happen? What kinds of process might be involved? What part does language play? Can we be social beings before we have language?

Are we separate individuals first and foremost, who gradually take on a veneer of sociality through immersion in the social world? Or do we only become our selves *as* we become social? In other words, do we have recognizable 'selves' which progressively become socialized? Or is our selfhood essentially social?

Are we programmed to relate to others from the beginning? What drives this relating? Do our first experiences of having biological needs satisfied (or not) in the social world shape us into creatures that seek out others as means to our gratifications? Or do you think something else is going on?

Sociality requires both a drive and a capacity to engage in social life, and it is likely that the prerequisites of sociality will already be in place when we are born. An inherited tendency to become social and to relate might be based on biological drives which have social implications (attachment, or sexuality and reproduction, for instance). This idea underlies the Freudian approach, which is based on the drive for sexual pleasure and tension-reduction *via other people*.

There is now a great deal of evidence that humans have an innate capacity for engaging in social life – blueprints that ensure that we can communicate from the earliest weeks of life, and that we can learn language easily (see Mehler and Dupoux, 1994; Stern, 1985; and Trevarthen, 1993). There is also some evidence that relating and relatedness are built-in goals in themselves, that we relate to others for the pleasure of intimacy in itself and the delight of developing our symbolic capacities. This idea underlies object relations versions of psychodynamics, which will be discussed in section 3.3.

Our sociality is made up of the 'content' of our selves which largely originates in the social world – knowledge, beliefs, values, relationships and language. But it is also possible that we are born with innate structures that serve as *prototypes* for the content and organization of our sociality. Some of the unconscious phantasies we shall meet in the work of Klein (section 3.2) are quite close to this idea.

The psychodynamic perspective provides a language for describing what drives social life and for describing the very earliest introjective processes through which the content of sociality is established. These processes take place in the context of social life – the taking in of versions of other people and relationships. According to psychodynamics, these introjects form the structure and the content of internal worlds and shape the psychic realities that constitute our selves. But different versions of psychodynamics give different answers to the question 'how and when do we absorb the content of the social world?'. This section will outline (1) Freudian, (2) Kleinian, and (3) 'object relations' explanations of sociality. We shall find that the particular assumptions of these three approaches lead to rather different kinds of selfhood.

The three viewpoints have fundamentally different positions on what motivates the earliest forms of relating and thus the beginnings of sociality. Two are *instinct theories*, the classical Freudian and classical Kleinian approaches. In both, the basic assumption is that people (infants, children and adults) are primarily motivated by biological drives to seek others as a means to drive reduction – consummation of some kind. The third approach, the British object relations school, includes several different accounts; these are not instinct theories (or not primarily instinct theories) but instead emphasize 'relating with others' as the basic human motivation.

The three viewpoints differ in the weight they give to innate determinants. Instinct theories stress the unfolding psychosexual stages and the 'driven' quality of infants' activity patterns in search of biological drive reduction. They also give different weights to the influence on internal worlds of *actual* early interactions with the world and *real* people (real interpersonal influence) compared with the intrapsychic influences of innate drive states and/or innate prototypes and unconscious phantasies. The three viewpoints also differ in their accounts of the 'gap' between what is outside and what gets represented inside us. From all this it follows that the three viewpoints have different models of the structure of people's internal worlds, of what drives and moulds the creation of meanings, and of the *kind of self* that we can become.

Although there is some evidence for each of the three viewpoints, there is not enough evidence of a kind which would enable one to select between them, and no attempt will be made to choose which is the 'real' truth. The differences between the theories will be used to generate questions and to think about the *possible* origins and constituents of social life and the self.

The theoretical accounts are set out in Boxes 6.2, 6.3, 6,4, and 6.5. The language of all these theories is typically psychodynamic. They offer emotionally polarized accounts of mental states, which are essentially 'primitive' and often destructive – the kinds of ideas that many of us try to ignore, or project well away from ourselves into outgroups and 'real' war zones. They do not use the discourse of 'scientific' psychology. Because of this possible unfamiliarity, one strategy might be to read the accounts in Boxes 6.2 to 6.5 first, in sequence, and then to read the comparison and discussion in the main text, returning to the accounts in the boxes for a second time.

3.1   Freud: instinct as the driving force

Freudian psychodynamics is an instinct theory: individuals are seen as driven by biologically-based desires (the pleasure principle) and in particular their sexual drive. These desires are already present in the small child and their consummation is the motivating force for relating with others. The fundamental conflict within individuals is between the drive for pleasure, first directly experienced with the mother, and the constraints put upon this drive by society, first directly experienced in the form of the mother, and then the father, the family and society. Being socialized into the family and into society is seen as largely to do with finding the means to curb these desires so that ordinary, unexciting and survival-oriented life can proceed – the reality principle. Becoming an adult requires leaving behind exquisite infantile pleasures and renouncing desire in order to adapt to reality – the triumph of the reality principle over the pleasure principle.

BOX 6.2   A Freudian account of the origins of the internal world

Freud used a model of the mind that contained three metaphorical structures: the id, the ego and the superego. The *id*, entirely unconscious, comprises the instinctual forces; a developing child has to learn to harness this energy to master the external world and the realities of survival. For example, the child has to learn to delay sensual gratification in the service of a longer term plan – in which gratification may well still figure, if in a different or sublimated guise. Conflict resolution and compromise is the task of the *ego*. In Freudian psychodynamics, during healthy development the ego increases in strength. The ego is thought of as the centre of the person, its function being to maintain equilibrium between the desires of the id, the realities of the external world and the demands of society and its culture which are eventually internalized in the form of the *superego*.

Victory of the reality principle is achieved by the ego, bolstered by a crucial ego defence mechanism: the repression of desire into the cellar-like unconscious. Here, prohibited desires do not disappear but remain forever. They are a source of energy and conflict, but energy has to be expended to keep them repressed. Their attempts to reappear arouse anxieties, which in turn have to be defended against. Thus, the underlying relation between the individual and the micro-social world (and society more generally) is one of compliance, painful compromise and ego defence.

Freud said that the ego is first and foremost a body ego: drives originate in the physical body. They have a source of energy and a goal – some form of consummatory behaviour, which either provides pleasure or removes some discomfort, tension or pain. Human development is seen as the passage through a succession of stages, each governed by the unfolding of particular patterns of behaviour which are components of fully-fledged instinctual behaviours. Freud focused on the development of sexuality. Here the source of energy is called the libido and the goals are sexual pleasures of some kind or another or the reduction of sexual tension. Drives also need objects – other people – who help the subject to achieve the consummatory goal. In an adult, the object of sexual drive is likely to be another person; in an infant, it might be a part-object such as the mother's breast.

By including the need for an object in his conception of instinct, Freud acknowledged the potential influence of other people, and aspects of the environment, as important mediators of satisfaction for pleasure-seeking individuals; but other people are seen as secondary to drive satisfaction. Their function – actual, or desired, or withheld – varies according to the psychosexual development of the subject. In the Freudian model, infantile sexuality is associated with the sequential emergence of erogenous zones in the body. This begins with the mouth, from birth, and the potential gratification of feeding and sucking; then follow the urethral and anal zones, the gratification of elimination, and the tussles over control – self-control versus control demanded by parents. According to Freud, at around the age of 5 years, sexual excitements become focused on the 'phallic' organs (clitoris/penis) and, simultaneously, sexual feelings begin to be associated with the body and attention of the parent of the opposite sex.

What then follows are the classical Freudian triangular rivalries with parents, disruption in the family, and the major conflictual construct of psychoanalysis – the Oedipus complex. Social taboos, threat of punishment, and children's mistaken beliefs about their developing bodies lead to a fear of castration (boys) and fear and anger at already having been castrated (girls). Freud believed that defensive identification with a parental figure, usually the father, then follows. A version of the father is internalized as a moral force representing the constraints and potential retributions of society – and sexual desires are repressed. Freud used this internalization of the father as the source of gender modelling, based on fear, for boys. But he never found a satisfactory alternative to explain girls' gender modelling.

The product of internalization is the superego – an internal judgmental parent. In Freudian theory, this internal figure is essentially male and based on the father. This part of the theory has caught the imagination of social theorists because it allows for internalization of 'the law of the father' (i.e. the rules of the establishment in a *patriarchal* society).

> Note that the reality principle is about surviving in the external world. It does not necessarily mean that internal representations have to be, or are, exact replicas of an external reality – but rather that sufficient 'reality' must be represented to ensure survival.

The Freudian approach describes an internal world which has a relatively simple structure. In the unconscious are all the instinctual drives and the source of energy, the libido, collectively known as the id. The ego (the 'I') is partly conscious and partly unconscious. It maintains and regulates the main psychological functions (called 'secondary processes') such as perception and attention, and has the task of adapting to the external world, controlling the primitive desires and the irrational and timeless unconscious phantasies of the id (these 'primary processes' are often manifest in dreams).

In classical Freudian theory, there is one major figure in the internal world, one internal object – the superego. This is essentially an introject of the father, and is not in place until a relatively late age, somewhere between 3 and 5 years old. The father is introjected by boys through a defensive identification. This is explained as 'becoming the father' along with his strength of character, sexuality, gender behaviours, etc., in order not to be punished by him – specifically in order not to be castrated by him (in phantasy) as retribution for a boy's sexual desire for his mother.

For girls, the process contains yet more twists and turns, since girls have to identify with their mothers to take in gender roles, but they also have to introject father to provide a 'moral sense'. The details of this are less important than the overall argument. What we are concerned with is the *gap* between children's experience of their mothers and fathers and the nature of the parental introject. In Freudian theory, external, real parents are seen as represented internally in distorted ways *because they are seen as the objects of sexual desires*. This is a major tenet of Freudian theory: reality is distorted by sexual drives. Children's unconscious phantasies and conscious fantasies create the distortions and, according to Freud, these processes are universal and only partly affected by children's actual experiences:

> … From this perspective the sexual instinct is not simply a striving, an impulse, a desire, but the vehicle by which human beings create meaning. In other words, Freud did not simply propose that the sexual instinct be thought of as generating sexual wishes and impulses … [but] that human beings interpret all perceptions in terms of sexual meanings, thereby *creating* experience.
>
> *(Ogden, 1986, p.19)*

Freud originally believed that his disturbed patients, male and female, had been subjected to real seduction and abuse. He later believed that some of these patients were recounting, and sometimes enacting in the transference, phantasy relationships and phantasy traumas which were distortions of real objects and real situations created by drive states. He did not reject the possibility that some of his patients had been seduced, or abused in other ways. But his shift of emphasis to the notion that internal worlds are at least to some extent built on unconscious phantasy and fantasy opened the door to his elaboration of drive theory and laid the foundations of psychoanalysis. Some analysts now think that he grossly underemphasized the number of people who are actually abused and the impact of this abuse (see Masson, 1984).

The id, ego and superego have remained in most post-Freudian theories. They continue to represent conflict between the biological individual and the social order. The social order is already represented in the minds and expressed in the language and behaviour of parents, and is internalized *defensively* by the child. In healthy development, internal conflict peaks at the age of 5 years, and then is resolved. The version of selfhood that follows is a compliant individual whose internal world is built around sexual meanings but who has, nevertheless, subdued biology; conflict and fragmentation caused by desires are repressed so as to reach a reality-oriented experience of unity in a monolithic, moral and objective world. The internalized parent keeps alive a sense of certainty and authority – albeit through the threat of moral anxiety, guilt and punishment. This internalized parental figure, together with a strong ego, holds the self together.

3.2 Klein: a theory of instincts and internal object relations

Klein always thought of herself as a Freudian; but she worked with children as well as adults and this led to a substantially different theory. Klein's evidence came from her psychoanalysis of small children, in regular, contained settings, with standardized play material and small figures of animals and people. In this setting, free play took the place of free associations in adults. She found that the content of children's play and verbal comments, the kind of language they used *and their relationship with her* revealed their unconscious phantasies, conscious fantasies and the kinds of 'theories' they had about what the world is like, especially their perceptions of significant others and the relationships of the latter with the child and with each other.

Klein's psychoanalytic material showed that the inner worlds of children as young as 2 years old are already populated with terrifying, punishing versions of parental figures. She concluded, on the basis of her clinical work with disturbed children, that, well before the age 4 to 5 years, children experience the kinds of emotions that are associated with sexual love and three-person relationships: jealously, envy and rage and the prototypical Oedipal situation. She also concluded that much of what is represented in children's internal worlds *is not directly the result of actual experiences.*

Although Klein moved a long way from Freud theoretically, she remained an instinct theorist. She believed that internal worlds are the outcome of drives, and that they are *essentially defensive*, constructed to protect infants and small children from the intense negative emotions associated with their unfulfilled desires, lost pleasures, envy, jealousy, Oedipal rivalries and sexuality. But whereas Freud thought that universal processes lead to painful Oedipal conflict and the defensive introjection of the superego at around the age of 4 to 5 years, Klein saw evidence of this kind of internalization as early as the second year of life. She also saw evidence that early introjects consisted of *many* punishing, frightening superego figures, mothers as well as fathers and others, all of whom induce guilt and persecutory anxiety.

Again like Freud, Klein believed that what directs the formation of internal worlds and the creation of meaning is essentially *innate and intrapsychic.* She believed that children's internal worlds of exaggeratedly idealized and persecutory objects are *not* representations of children's real experiences with their real parents and carers. According to Klein and Kleinians, the polarized categories of internal objects (supportive versus threatening; nourishing versus withholding; good versus bad, etc.) are determined by the unfolding of innate unconscious phantasies.

BOX 6.3   A Kleinian account of the origins of the internal world

Klein retained most of the main constructs of Freudian theory, including psychosexual development and the Oedipus complex, although she thought that most of these stages should be placed much earlier in life. She put much more emphasis on the negative aspects of biological drives leading to powerful, destructive emotions like hate and envy.

In Kleinian theory, a baby is thought to be born with two conflicting instinctual impulses, to love and to hate. Using the process of unconscious phantasy and driven by love and hate, the baby creates its own world of internal objects which approximate to the people around the baby, but only in a very crude and emotionally polarized form. They are primarily *intrapsychic* creations and at first these internal objects are *part-objects*. 'Part-object' is a Kleinian term used to emphasize the idea that the other person is experienced not as a whole person but as the source of a function – a bodily function, or as that body part of the other (usually the breast) which has afforded the baby satisfaction or frustration. Another way to think of this is to regard what gets represented internally as versions of the ways in which other people relate to the baby. Klein would claim that the mother first appears in the baby's mind as two part-objects – an exaggeratedly good breast and an exaggeratedly bad breast. The good breast is an introjection of all the good features of a satisfying, comfortable feed together with all the associated emotions and physical sensations of contact with the mother – an idealized object of desire. The bad breast is an introjection of all the bad features of a too-long-waited-for, screaming-with-hunger-cramps, unsatisfying feed with its associated bodily sensations and emotions of frustration, pain and rage – an object of hate and fear and persecutory feelings. (Klein said that all this held equally for bottle-fed babies.)

Klein's psychoanalytic work with small children convinced her that, from the very beginning of life, infants are subject to terrible anxieties and that the rudimentary ego has to protect itself by various defence mechanisms. For example, unconscious phantasies of an idealized breast, amplified perhaps by good experiences of feeding, create a good internal part-object. When the baby is alone and getting hungry, this good, satisfying breast can be 'held on to' or hallucinated as comfort or wish-fulfilment. In order to prevent the rage provoked by the bad, frustrating breast (an innate, unconscious negative that is amplified by inevitable, ordinary frustrations) from 'contaminating' the good breast and arousing anxiety, the baby's infantile ego protects itself by using the defence mechanism of *splitting*. The two part-objects are kept separate, and any early attempt to recognize that they are parts of the same 'whole' object evokes considerable anxiety. The baby's hate and anger directed towards the bad internal object is got rid of by *projection* on to the external world. Once this happens, the bad feelings seem to be coming not from within but from some outside agent, and the baby feels persecutory anxiety.

This description of the inner world of an infant might give an impression of something approaching a state of paranoia, and Klein called this early mental state of infants the *paranoid-schizoid position*. Through this work of Klein it is now accepted by many psycho-dynamic theorists and analysts that mental states akin to this occur from time to time in normal adult life, and that difficulties during the infantile paranoid-schizoid position can lead to pathological schizoid states in later life in some individuals. The term 'position' is used rather than 'stage' because, although the positions are encountered and 'passed through' rather like a developmental stage in infancy, they can be and are returned to at various times in the normal course of ordinary life. Thus, they are not stages that healthy individuals deal with and surmount once and for all in childhood. In this respect they differ from the concept of stages that Freud used.

Gradually the infant's internal world becomes more complex, with real experiences of real people; and eventually, at around the age of 6 months, part-objects begin to be recognized as parts of whole objects – mothers, fathers and siblings, etc. The baby learns that satisfying and frustrating experiences can come from the same person. Now the infant begins to recognize some of the disparity between its internal objects and what is 'out there'. Then there is a new conflict: between love for the mother and guilt resulting from rages and destructive impulses towards her frustrating aspects. The infant then experiences ambivalence. If infants can identify strongly enough with the internal good object (the internalized good mother) then they will feel that they can 'repair' the damage they may have done to her in their frustration. This is a crucial point in Klein's work and is called the *depressive position*. The anxiety arising from this conflict is called depressive anxiety – quiet, sad withdrawal.

The depressive position is seen as an essential part of a normal infant's development. As soon as the baby knows its mother is one whole person, then it has to be able to deal with the anxiety and feeling of loss when she is away; and a feeling of guilt that it has driven her away and perhaps destroyed her with its rage. As time passes, and with the repeated experience that the mother does come back, the baby learns to hold on to his or her internal good object and thus deal with separation without being overcome by feelings of inner chaos and persecution.

The depressive position, like the paranoid-schizoid position, can be returned to in later life as the result of an integration of defensive splits. An example might be accepting that another person (or life event) is not 'all good' or 'all bad' but an *uncomfortable* mixture of the two. In Kleinian theory, the depressive position, compared with the paranoid-schizoid position, is a more mature and more *realistic* stance in the external world.

Unconscious phantasies have been described as something between an instinct and a thought and have been called the 'unthought known'. The content of these phantasies is symbolic and the symbolism is (can only be) in terms of the infant's own body, bodily sensations, and basic functions, and the bodies and bodily functions of the adults that are close – essentially the mother, but the father too. In other words, symbolic activity arises from the very stuff of the infant's earliest experiences of the world outside its mind but is structured by primitive, innate meaning systems:

> My hypothesis is that the infant has an innate unconscious awareness of the existence of the mother. We know that young animals turn at once to the mother and find their food from her. The human animal is not different in that respect, and this instinctual knowledge is the basis for the infant's primal relation to its mother.
>
> (Klein, 1959, p.248)

Phantasy-based internal worlds, where internal object relating occurs between polarized and highly emotive versions of 'external' others, lead to painful and essentially fragmented subjective experience. The anxiety aroused by this elicits primitive defence mechanisms in infants and small children. These defences, such as splitting and projection, come into effect much earlier in life than the ego defences described by Freud. The Kleinian view of the self is more conflictive and fragmented than that of Freud.

The crucial points for the argument here are that, according to Klein, the earliest structuring of the mind is motivated and shaped (distorted) by the infant's innate sexual drives and powerful emotional states. The meaning systems and psychic reality that are created are defensive, enabling the infant to obtain gratification whilst avoiding anxiety and intense negative emotions such as hate, envy and jealousy. Although the child acts on the basis of a psychic reality that has been largely created irrespective of the actual external world, these actions *in* the world will, inevitably, have an impact on real relationships. And some modification of the internal world will follow.

3.3   Object relations: theories of emotional nurturance and intersubjectivity

The British object relations theorists differ from Freud and Klein in their basic assumption that *people are not pleasure-seekers but are people-seekers*; that relating is not a means to drive reduction but is a goal in itself. They questioned the central role of drives and some (e.g. Fairbairn) rejected instinct theory completely. Being attached to others, confirmed by others, communicating and relating are seen as primary motivations. In evolutionary terms, this can be thought of as the manifest advantage of a set of motivations that ensured physical safety and enough proximity with others over long enough periods to develop systems of symbolic representation including language and complex forms of social life. Although often influenced by Klein, object relations theorists differ from Klein in concluding, on the evidence of their own psychoanalytic work, that internal worlds are formed as the result of the infant's earliest experiences of *real relating with real people*. In the history of psychodynamics, the object relations theorists were unique in making the move from a one-person or *intrapsychic psychology* (as in the work of Freud and Klein) to a two-person or *interpersonal psychology*.

Most object relations theorists (like Klein but unlike Freud) believe that there is a rudimentary ego (or self) from birth. In the Freudian view (and that of one object relations theorist, Winnicott), at the beginning of life infants experience a kind of undifferentiated 'fused' state between themselves and their mothers. The infant exists in an objectless world infused with what Freud called primary narcissism – a kind of self love – as opposed to object love. In contrast, according to Klein and most of the object relations theorists, object relating starts at birth.

In object relations theory, infants and children are seen as essentially 'innocent' and dependent on a nurturing environment of real others. The successes and failures of that environment and the capacities of the carers are the source of infants' internal worlds, their psychic reality and their health or their pathology: '… there is no "instinctual sin" if the caretaking objects relate appropriately to the infant's needs' (Grotstein, 1994, p.113). This shift in psychoanalytic theory towards the importance of real experiences with real people has considerable implications for social psychology. It places the emphasis on the actual micro-social environment as a determinant of sociality and self. Whereas, in Freudian and Kleinian theories, what the child actually encounters is less important for its psychic reality than the 'distortions' created by intrapsychic drives, object relations psychoanalysts work with what is closer to a trauma model. Internal worlds are representations of what is outside, but what is outside is far too often deficient and damaging; what we become is profoundly influenced by failures of the environment, both at the level of interactions and care with primary carers and at the level of societal failures.

In providing an alternative to the Freudian and Kleinian emphasis on phantasy as the source of internal worlds, the object relations approach suggests that phantasy versions of objects and object relations *may follow defensively* from real trauma:

> … infants employ phantasy secondarily to alter the painfulness of and thus tolerate the experience of reality. This burying or alteration of intolerable reality … can be seen as the quintessential paradigm both for child abuse and molestation specifically and for post-traumatic stress disorder generally.
>
> (Grotstein, 1994, p.135)

BOX 6.4 Winnicott: the 'true self' needs a 'good enough' environment

Winnicott was a paediatrician as well as a psychoanalyst. His evidence came from psychoanalysis with adults, and from his clinical work with infants *in the company of their mothers*. Much of his theoretical work was focused on the mother-infant unit. Winnicott believed that at first the infant has no sense of difference from the mother – that there is a merging of the two. Winnicott's best known quote is: 'There is no such thing as a baby … if you set out to describe a baby, you will find that you are describing a *baby and someone*. A baby cannot exist alone, but is essentially part of a relationship' (Winnicott, 1947). Out of this oneness the infant's self begins to differentiate. The mother, in what he called a state of 'primary maternal preoccupation', provides a 'facilitating environment' for this process. The attunement of her responses with the infant's experience reinforces the infant's omnipotent creativity, providing a sense of trust, a belief in the goodness of the world and eventually a capacity to be alone and a capacity to play. According to Winnicott, it is playing, first with the mother, then alone but in the mother's presence, and later playing alone, undisturbed by needs for instinctual gratification, that is the source of development of the self and all creative activity:

> Playing is a form of doing, but of a special kind, in which there is an interplay of personal psychic reality and the experience of the control of actual objects. The appropriate responsiveness of the mother allows her to become a subjective object and, with further good interaction, an objectively perceived object; and the self differentiates as a result of the essential role of play.
>
> *(Sutherland, 1980, p.838)*

Providing that there is sufficient attunement between mother and infant, the infant's 'true self' will emerge from activities in the 'transitional space'. These are intersubjective activities in which, at first, the infant is not differentiated from mother, but then gradually separates *that which is self* from *that which is not self*, and then from *that which is other*.

In Winnicott's writing, the burden of the importance of fit between mother and infant is slightly mitigated by his insistence that ordinary mothering is usually 'good enough'. The mother's task is actively to present the world, with its inevitable frustrations, to the infant 'in manageable chunks', allowing the infant to maintain omnipotent illusions until it can, in her opinion, deal with reality and with disillusionment. According to Winnicott, mothers don't have to be perfect – good enough is about right. If mothers are too good, the infant is not stimulated to phantasize or fantasize, to replace mother (or replace the momentarily unavailable breast) when she is not there. If everything is too present and too perfect, the infant has no reason to hallucinate what it needs and thus learn to think. When the mother is not good enough, when attunement is faulty and the external environment impinges too much and/or too soon, the infant's 'true self' may be protected by the development of a defensive 'false self'. We shall return to this in section 4.

The object relations perspective of Winnicott suggests a particular role for phantasy and defence in the internalization of the world. According to Winnicott, healthy psychological development requires and depends upon a maternally-sponsored *illusion,* a deliberately presented distortion of the world. Only by this means can an infant develop a capacity to think, to play and to emerge as a self. Thus, psychic development depends upon a crucial phase in which 'real' reality is inappropriate and even damaging. Disillusionment has to be introduced gradually so that it can be assimilated by the self without danger of disintegration. The origins of the self, therefore, lie in defence, unreality and creative illusion.

Fairbairn, one of the first British object relations analysts, moved right away from Freud and instinct theory although, paradoxically, he was strongly influenced by Klein (Fairbairn, 1990). According to Fairbairn, what humans seek is emotional contact with other people. Fairbairn based his theory on two points: first, children need to feel loved, initially by the primary carer (usually mother) and then by other members of the family or close group; secondly, but just as important, children need to feel that their own love is received and valued. In Fairbairn's view, when these two conditions are not met, the developing psyche will be harmed. The failure of carers and the social environment to meet these two conditions is considered to be traumatic, leading to withdrawal and to ego splits; that is, to a fragmentation of the self. In extreme instances, the result is withdrawal to the extent that real relationships in the real world are replaced by relating in fantasy (and phantasy). When this happens it provides a sense of control, because relating is primarily with internal objects rather than with real people.

Fairbairn's ideas about *normal* psychic development initially grew out of his work with the dreams of schizoid patients. Fairbairn was one of the first to identify the pathological 'schizoid personality'. Such people are usually withdrawn, isolated, have low affect and are fearful of intimacy. The term schizoid refers to the divisions or splits in their personality. However, he also pointed out that schizoid features and schizoid-like experiences of alienation are quite common features of personality in general. He suggested that the fragmentation of parts of the self in early childhood is defensive but is part of normal development and will follow from relatively ordinary environmental frustrations, or common traumas such as separation from a mother who is hospitalized – as well as being the outcome of more dramatic sources of damage. Fairbairn believed that a rudimentary, fragile ego is present from birth, but is liable to split or fragment for defensive reasons so that *each part operates with a different reality.* Schizoid features in many of us can lead to quite different experiences of self at different times, or in different situations. The internal world (or, in Fairbairn's terminology, the *endopsychic structure*) that Fairbairn described is based on such defensive splits in the ego.

BOX 6.5   Fairbairn: a fragmented self

Fairbairn's model of the inner world has similarities to Klein's multiple internal objects and internal object relations, but there are significant differences. He believed that the primary motivation in development is relating with real external objects; but *what is internalized is essentially the disappointing, frustrating aspects of such real relationships*. The point he was making was that, insofar as real relating is satisfactory, then internalization and the creation of internal objects and internal object relations is unnecessary. This, of course, means that the internal world for Fairbairn is bound to be a painful and sad place, peopled with disappointments.

In Fairbairn's model, the infant or small child introjects two painful versions of its relationship with mother (or the primary carer). First, there is the 'rejecting mother' (called the antilibidinal object). This becomes attached to a part of the child's ego which identifies with the rejection and becomes the 'internal saboteur' (called the antilibidinal ego). Secondly, there is the exciting, potentially loving and gratifying but actually frustrating mother (called the libidinal object). This is attached to a fragment of the child's ego which encompasses the loving, needy part (called the libidinal ego). These two disappointing ego and object pairs, defensively internalized for control, have now brought the external mixture of excitement/ rejection and gratification/frustration into the internal world. Now the pain and conflict are inside and necessitate another defensive move. The two painful ego-plus-object pairs are isolated from the central core of the ego (self); they are split off to leave the central core of the conscious ego (self) attached to an idealized and safely desexualized version of the original object (the mother).

Fairbairn further proposed that the internal saboteur (the antilibidinal ego) is particularly powerful because of its attachment to the rejecting parts of the internal mother, and that it joins up with the central ego (self) in further hostile repression of the needy, and thus dangerous, libidinal ego.

Implicit in Fairbairn's theory is the idea that most infants and small children create this kind of defensive internal structure to protect themselves from the quite ordinary failings of their carers and families, as well as instances where carers have more serious pathology. Fairbairn believed that these early structural splits in the infant's psyche are not necessarily pathological. An infant can move on to a less rigidly split endopsychic structure providing that later developmental stages ameliorate rather than reinforce the splits. But if the Oedipal stage and adolescence are also problematic, then the splits becomes pathologically rigid – the structure of the schizoid personality.

Fairbairn's theory, like other versions of object relations theory, describes a developmental process in which a distortion of the world protects the self. In this case there is a paradox because parts of the self itself are 'distorted' (made bad), in order to make the external world more bearable. Grotstein (1994, p. 115) has described the process as a 'laundering' of the image of the carer, *at the child's own expense*. It is at the child's expense because the child achieves the laundering by creating badness within itself. The formation of the endopsychic structure and the laundering is adaptive because it enables the dependent child to experience, in phantasy, some sense of control over the other people that, despite disappointment, it still needs. The child cannot integrate its needy part and feels itself to be unlovable; it feels endlessly criticized by the internal saboteur, which is experienced as a source of rejection and self-attack coming from within, picking and criticizing and felt to be autonomous and not under ego control. The child also feels that its own capacity to love is bad – bad because it was never validated. This has been linked to recent infant research by Murray (1992) and Trevarthen (1991) which demonstrates how infants withdraw from interactions and appear to 'give up' after experiences of malattunement.

Fairbairn's version of the internal world provides an explanation for the way in which some children and adults repeatedly try to relate with others who will inevitably disappoint them in some way – called the 'allure of the bad object' (Armstrong-Perlman, 1991). The irrational repetition continually confirms the closed system of the endopsychic structure, avoiding the need for a complete restructuring – which would be even more anxiety-provoking.

Other object relations analysts have raised the stakes by stressing that humans have a need not just for relating but for an intense form of intimacy which may even be a prerequisite for infants to thrive. This relatedness is both biological and sensual, and when it fails the infant experiences malattunement. Bowlby, another object relations analyst, studied attachment behaviours such as crying, cooing, trailing after mother, and clinging. He came to think of attachment as based on biological predispositions and stamped in by reinforcement, but also as motivated by the pleasure of being physically close to another. It is possible that the residues of a biological drive for attachment – to ensure physical safety – have become elaborated in humans into something approaching a need for intimacy – for emotional intensity – which continues to underpin object relating in later life. Rayner, a contemporary psychoanalyst, has put this point more strongly. He suggests that early intimacy with parents, especially the mother

> … when working well, seems likely to have its own form or emotional patterning of delight – even perhaps its own experience of primitive beauty or something close to it. Loss of the assurance of such an experience constitutes a trauma … the individual thenceforward searches in one way or another for his lost intimacy or its substitutes.
>
> *(Rayner, 1991, p. 24)*

The idea that intimacy with another is so important from infancy onward goes beyond attachment to a need for conditions in which intersubjectivity can grow and be sustained, providing further opportunities for the creation and development of symbolic systems, the modelling of other people's minds and, by these means, the development and deepening of sociality.

Review of section 3

Psychodynamic accounts differ in their explanations of how and when we become social and the kinds of selfhood we achieve:

- Freudian and Kleinian accounts are instinct theories in which social life and relating are motivated by biological drives. Other people and relationships are largely the means to biological ends. Object relations theories place more emphasis on 'people as people-seekers' rather than 'seekers of pleasure' and of drive reduction.

- Freudian, and especially Kleinian, accounts emphasize innate drives and unconscious prototypes of relating as determining the creation of internal worlds and meaning systems. Object relations theorists emphasize actual experiences in relationships as the source of internal worlds and psychic reality.

- The Freudian internal world is a relatively simple structure in which the gap between external reality and internal representations is a function of sexual drives which distort external 'realities' and create experience. The major defensive feature is the repression of desires into the unconscious.

- The Freudian model of selfhood is compliant and guilty. It is the outcome of subdued biology, and desires that are defensively repressed into the unconscious.

- Kleinian internal worlds are densely populated from early in life with emotionally polarized versions of people encountered in the external world. These representations are the result of innate drives and unconscious phantasies rather than experiences with real others. Defences of splitting and projection are mobilized from birth.

- The Kleinian model of selfhood is potentially fragmented. There is a tendency to move between the sad, ambivalent reality of the depressive position and the persecutory anxiety and dissociations of the paranoid-schizoid position. In this latter state, internal chaos and anxiety are projected into the external world, affecting perceptions and relating.

- Object relations theorists believe that relating is what drives social life. Internal worlds and selfhood are made up of internalized versions of others and relationships. Defensive distortions in internal worlds protect the infant/child from painful reality.

4   Psychodynamics and selfhood

This section will use some of the psychodynamic insights about the origins and constituents of self described in section 3 to explore the nature of the self and to think about how we actually experience our selves.

The self and related terms are concepts that are notoriously difficult to define and, until relatively recently, psychoanalysis has avoided the use of the term self. Much of what are ordinarily thought of as functions of the self are discussed under the heading of ego and ego functions. In very simple terms, the self is a metaphorical psychological structure that encompasses and organizes many of the processes and functions of mental life. To do this, it must have at least some degree of stability. Even with this simple idea of the self, there are at least two paradoxes to think about; a good starting point is Frosh's description of why psychodynamics provides an indispensable and different angle on the self.

The first paradox is that the self is both an object of knowledge (self-knowledge and more general theoretical knowledge) *and* the experienced centre – the 'I' – of the consciously experiencing subject: 'I look out at the world from the vantage-point of my own self ... "I" am my self, but I can know myself by reflection and observation ...' (Frosh, 1991, p. 2).

The second paradox is that, although I am my self and closer to myself than anyone else can be, this very embeddedness prevents me from fully knowing myself. Frosh argues that dialogue with another person is necessary in order for me to know myself – to see my self from the vantage-point of another (this approach is similar to that of Mead.) The need for an 'other' to know one's self would, I think, hold true even without the idea of the dynamic unconscious. But if we now include the basic psychodynamic assumption that much of what we are is hidden and can only reach conscious experience in partial, contradictory and disguised forms, then the vantage-point of the other becomes even more important and rather different from what Mead envisaged. Once we take the unconscious into account, the other (the analyst) requires some additional and specialized skills. The analyst can get access of an indirect kind to my inner self: '... the analyst hears what I say, sees what I do, and can make a judgement about the nature of the structure from which these things arise. Thus the analyst can only *reason* my self into being; she or he can never observe it directly; I, on the other hand, am too close to it to see it all' (Frosh, 1991, pp. 2–3; my emphasis).

4.1   Subjective experience of selfhood is incomplete

Earlier chapters have assumed that we have access to our selves, that we can talk about our selves and give accounts of what we are and why we do what we do. But many thinkers and writers have described searches for hidden parts of the self. For example, Teilhard de Chardin, the modern religious mystic, wrote:

> I took the lamp and, leaving the zone of everyday occupations and relationships where everything seems clear, I went down into my inmost self, to the deep abyss whence I feel dimly that my power of action emanates. But as I moved further and further away from the conventional certainties by which social life is superficially illuminated, I became aware that I was losing contact with myself. At each step of the descent a new person was disclosed within me of whose name I was no longer sure, and who no longer obeyed me. And when I had to stop my exploration because the path faded from beneath my steps, I found a bottomless abyss at my feet.
>
> *(Teilhard de Chardin, 1957, pp. 76–7)*

Psychodynamic theories assume that much of the self is hidden and our subjective experience of selfhood is partial. What we can experience directly is not only the 'tip of an iceberg' but may be disguised by unconscious motives and defences. The closest we can get to an overall picture of ourselves is through the eyes and ears of another person. This other person, if an appropriately trained psychoanalyst, can look through and then behind the changeable accounts we provide from day to day and situation to situation, keep track of our moods, try to piece together the bits and search for an underlying structure, a self, that might generate our experiences. This structure will always be hypothetical, a construction. Although its 'truth' cannot be tested in a traditional scientific way, it can be tested against our emotional reactions to it, whether or not it provides something that is meaningful, perhaps something that enables us to change a little.

In what ways have psychodynamic theories explained the inaccessible aspects of selfhood? Much of what makes up our selves comes into consciousness out of the unconscious id but then has to be repressed in accord with internalized rules of conduct and societal taboos. This is the classical Freudian idea of a metaphorical 'horizontal' divide between consciousness and that which is pushed down into the unconscious. But there are other psychodynamic versions of how and why our experience of our selves is partial. Winnicott, for example, suggested that, under certain conditions in infancy, the 'true self' has to be hidden permanently, deep in the unconscious, and protected by a conscious, compliant version of the self called the 'false self' (Winnicott, 1960). Winnicott believed that a false self takes over when the true self is so impinged upon and intruded upon by the preconceptions and demands of the infant's principal carer that it cannot develop.

Other psychodynamic explanations for the partial nature of the experience of selfhood are in terms of 'vertical' splits in consciousness (rather than repression down into the unconscious), so that some parts of the self and some versions of reality are accessible at a particular time whilst others are split off and inaccessible. For example, the object relations psychoanalyst Kernberg describes patients diagnosed as having 'borderline' conditions (borderline between neurotic and psychotic). These patients, although disturbed in some respects, nevertheless manage to continue with ordinary life:

> ... there may exist ... contradictory manifestations of the patient of such an impressive nature that one comes to feel that there is a compartmentalization of the entire psychic life of the patient ... [a] patient appeared to be lying 'impulsively' at times: at other times he gave the impression of feeling guilty or ashamed of lying, and insisted that lying was no longer a problem for him and angrily accused other people (the therapist) of lying. What was striking was the complete separation of the times the 'impulsive' lying occurred, from the times the patient remembered the lying but would feel no longer emotionally connected with it ...

> While the patients were conscious of these several contradictions in their behaviour, they would still alternate between opposite strivings with a bland denial of the implications of this contradiction, and they would also show what appeared to be from the outside a striking lack of concern over this compartmentalization of their mind ... what we might call mutual denial of independent sectors of the psychic life.

> (Kernberg, 1986, pp. 351–2)

> ... I inferred that what we have called splitting of the ego in this case served an essential function of protecting the patient against anxiety.

> (ibid., 1986, p. 350)

If our subjective experience of selfhood is incomplete, which of our partial experiences of self is real? This is particularly relevant when we talk about vertical splits in the experience of self. We find that demarcations between those people who are completely in command of 'reality' and those who are not begin to break down. Such questions resonate with the ideas already discussed in this chapter: we all struggle to create an internal version of reality that equips us to deal reasonably effectively and not too anxiously with the external world, without it necessarily being an accurate internal replication of the world. In some areas of functioning, especially in our relationships with important others, we put considerable effort into constructing adaptive phantasies, fantasies or narratives.

How can we now think about being 'out of touch with reality' – a phrase that is used as a simple definition of a psychotic state? Most people agree that there *is* an extreme condition of psychosis, but also that individuals who have some degree of 'borderline psychosis' can function well in many or most areas of their lives. Many Jungian analysts and modern psychoanalysts, especially Kleinians and object relations theorists, believe that many of us have encapsulated 'psychotic areas' in our selves which can come to light in extreme situations or in particular kinds of intense, interpersonal relationships. By 'encapsulated' I mean split off so that it doesn't affect or communicate with other segments of the mind. An encapsulated or split off fragment of self is not open to comparison with other versions of reality – it cannot be reality-tested. Sometimes these vertical splits lead to what are called dissociated states (see Box 6.6).

BOX 6.6   *Reconstructing memory*

Examples such as that of Kernberg's 'borderline' patient raise questions about other kinds of dissociated states. Currently, a great deal is being written and said about the connection between specific traumas, such as sexual abuse in childhood, and apparent loss of memory of the event – either on the part of the victim or the perpetrator. This could refer to repressed memories, or to memories and emotional states that are split off, or dissociated from consciousness. The difference between repression and dissociated states is far from clear; and just as confusing is the evidence about whether or not lost memories or dissociated states can be suddenly recovered during therapy.

Many analysts have had experience of patients, neither questioned nor guided, who have apparently recovered painful memories and/or painful emotional states. But it is also true that 'memories' can be created during therapies, during hypnosis *and during ordinary conversations in ordinary relationships*. Again, we are re-entering the area of constructions of internal worlds. Internal worlds are constructed and then continuously reconstructed. Where do memories begin and end? Every time we talk to someone, tell something or even think about an event or emotional state that happened in the past, it is reconstructed in the present context, or unknowingly elaborated by other thoughts (Fonagy, 1994; Conway, 1995; Conway et al., 1995). Reconstruction can occur when ideas are in 'working memory' (i.e. when they are conscious and consciously being worked with); but it is likely that reconstructions also occur out of awareness (i.e. unconsciously). The process of 'reality' reconstruction is in many respects the same as that of fantasizing (or, if unconscious, phantasizing). The notion of *historical truth* disappears behind that of *narrative truth*.

We tend to assume that the parts of the self that we *do* know about are the more important parts. But the parts that are inaccessible may be of more value, as in the case of Winnicott's inaccessible 'true self'. Jung, in particular, was wary of the power and rationality that we now attribute to conscious processes. He believed that consciousness is frequently over-estimated at the expense of 'older' wisdom that is present in all of us in the unconscious.

4.2   One self or many

One of the most basic assumptions about the self, in the West, is that we each have *a* self – a single self that is bounded, lives inside us and is relatively enduring. But this notion seems to be at odds with much of what we experience, in ourselves and others. Perhaps we need to rethink this idea of a unitary self – a process that began in Chapter 5 with the 'distributed self'. We have seen that several psychodynamic accounts have suggested that a consistent and unitary self cannot be assumed. For example, built into all psychodynamic theories is the idea that our self-hood *changes* as we develop and age; this is especially true of Jung's work. Another example is the notion that we may have 'many selves': there is a resurgence of interest in 'multiple personalities'. And this has less pathological parallels in the Jungian idea of many selves which together make up the 'self':

> In the psychology of our unconscious there are typical figures that have a definite life of their own.
>
> All this is explained by the fact that the so-called unity of conscious-ness is an illusion. It is really a wish-dream. We like to think that we are one; but we are not, most decidedly not … Complexes are autonomous groups of associations that have a tendency to move by themselves, to live a life of their own apart from our intentions. I hold that our personal unconscious, as well as the collective unconscious, consists of an indefinite, because unknown, number of complexes or fragmentary personalities.
>
> *(Jung, 1935, p. 81)*

Jung believed that complexes are 'an agglomeration of associations … sometimes of a traumatic character, sometimes simply of a painful and highly toned character' (Jung, 1935, p. 79). He reported experimental studies and interpreted the clusters of exaggerated responses to certain words as evidence of unconscious emotional responses revealing uncon-scious autonomous complexes.

Perhaps we *do* have many selves despite the continuing fiction that we each have but one. Perhaps the self is fragmentary by its very nature. Subjective experiences of selfhood, the observations of writers, and psy-chodynamic theories based on clinical observations, all suggest that self-hood may be a matter of *constructing a single reality by which to live,* but that we do this *despite* our experience of several or many realities – several selves. Why is it so important to maintain the idea of one self? Perhaps it is because it can be operationally difficult and emotionally painful to have selves that conflict.

Each of the psychodynamic accounts in section 3 outlines *a self that is potentially divided*. In Freudian psychodynamics, conflict centres on sub-dued desires that are repressed, with a lasting sense of loss. The Freudian ego, the centralized, organizing capacity to process information, resolve conflicts, make compromises and deal with the reality principle, is what holds together the embattled parts of the inner world (Freud, 1940). In Freudian psychoanalytic discourse, a great deal of psychic energy and defensive manoeuvring is given over to this task of subduing conflict *in order to maintain a sense of unity* and a relatively unambivalent orientation to the world, with a degree of consistency over time.

Object relations psychoanalysts and Kleinians place more emphasis on the complexity of the internal structures, and from this follows the possibility of continuing internal conflict and fragmentation. Object relations theories also describe selves that are made up of other people and relationships, introjected and identified with, usually during childhood. Identification is something we all think we know about, probably because we all experience it all the time. Nevertheless, it is a mysterious and compulsive process which is not understood:

> … suddenly a man who was walking a yard or two in front of me slipped off the edge of the pavement. I immediately righted myself, just as if I were about to stumble into the street … I became aware of how when we are not on guard we mirror the movements we perceive in others … the reflex evocation in the observer of the behaviour and feelings of the person observed, an automatic process linked with perception and quite distinct from conscious imitation.
>
> *(Sandler, 1993, p. 1101)*

The object relations view of selfhood as constituted through introjections followed by identifications, some fleeting (primary identifications) and some more lasting or permanent (secondary identifications), is conducive to thinking about ourselves as *a series of selves*. It suggests many voices, some loud and clear, some quiet but insistent, voices that speak out with conflicting demands, inconsistent emotions, at different times and in different places and, especially, in different current relationships. Insofar as our selves are made up of introjected relationships and dialogues between our inner voices, we continuously experience, internally, the conflicts inherent in these relationships.

Both Mead and Vygotsky have suggested that selves are the result of interactions and symbolic interactions between the infant/child and other people. The child together with the 'other' (parents, carers, peers, teachers) jointly create the substance of the child's self through the medium of symbolic systems – language and play and 'taking the role of others'.

In Mead's work, the basic argument is that language, play and games (symbolic forms of interaction), through role-taking and modelling others' minds (individuals and generalized others), develop the capacity for using symbols and for reflecting upon and developing the self. These skills, in turn, elaborate interactions with others in an increasingly complex way, based on shared meanings about the world and people's intentions and behaviour. Vygotsky suggested that children are social before they are individuals – that their thought-processes and cognitive development depend upon the internalization of the dialogues they encounter in the social world (see Chapter 5, especially section 5.1).

The idea that we experience our selves as made up of other people and their voices and relationships not only questions the assumption of a unitary self, but it also begins to undermine the common assumption that each of us has a self that is bounded. Chapter 5 described a 'distributed self' that is continuously created *between* people, in ordinary interactions and conversations, rather than being bounded and inside each of us. Those versions of psychodynamics that see the self as constituted out of internalized others and relationships encompass the possibility of a more fluid self and a self that gets 'mixed up' with others – at least some of the time:

> The boundaries between self and not-self, between the self representation and the representation of the object, should not be regarded as set in concrete ... it is appropriate to speak of a boundary-setting function ... which normally comes into operation extremely quickly to differentiate self from other – in this context a function of disidentification, of saying '*No, it is not me, it is the other.*' I want to emphasize the speed and force with which unconscious boundary-setting can normally take place, but I should like to stress equally how quickly it can fade when we are not paying full attention to what is happening. When we watch an acrobat, and tense our bodies in a way which reflects the movements of the acrobat, we have temporarily suspended the boundary between the self representation and the representation of the object being observed, with a resulting lack of distinction between self and object; self and object representations are temporarily the same. The self–object boundary can be reimposed extremely quickly, but it would seem likely that there is a constant unconscious fluctuation in the degree and intensity to which this boundary is put in place, and it is this fluctuation which may permit the unconscious process of recurrent primary identification to take place. The bridge provided by such primary identification may, incidentally, be the pathway towards certain forms of learning ...
>
> *(Sandler, 1993, p. 1103)*

This quotation suggests two positions on the bounded self. First, it implies that permeability between people happens, via identifications, but that it is to be guarded against – an implicit endorsement of the value of bounded self. But, secondly, it also suggests that mix-ups based on identifications may be an important way of learning. Confusions or mix-ups of self with another are commonplace, although often we are not conscious of what is happening. Perhaps, in adult life, they are most salient in intense relationships, such as 'being in love'. Mix-ups occur under stress, in the therapeutic setting, in regressions, and also in pathological states. They can be seen in dreams, where the storyline mixes up the characters. Such mix-ups are known as *projective identifications*. In infancy, projective identifications – between infants and primary carers – are thought to be a primitive form of communication and the means by which intersubjectivity is created. In psychodynamics, this has become known as 'normal' communicative projective identification.

Trying out *being* the other, momentarily or for longer periods, permits a crossover between knowledge of self and knowledge of the other. It leads to an exchange of experience, meaning and sometimes capabilities, and to a shared knowledge of subjective states. Projective identification is also the process by which people can create something new 'in the space between them' – the intersubjective space between two minds. Language may be part of the process, but, in psychodynamic theory, projective identification does not necessarily need words, it can be a completely non-verbal process, enabling complex communication between mother and infant.

People seem to vary the extent to which they 'live in projection'. This might be the extent to which a person maintains long-term projective identifications with a particular other. When this happens the person unconsciously talks about the other as if talking about themselves. Without being aware of what is happening, the person gets upset when something unpleasant happens to the other and feels good when the other is happy. In psychodynamic theory, when an adult lives in projection, even when 'in love', it is a state from which one expects and even hopes they will emerge.

'Living in projection' might also refer to the frequency and fluidity of identifications between a person and various others – perhaps those in the workplace, or in other salient groups to which they belong. In this sense, some people seem to have relatively permeable boundaries between themselves and others, quite a lot of the time. They are very engaged with and interpenetrated by the lives of others. My own experience with patients is that this happens more often with those who have been brought up in large families, especially when they are one of the younger siblings. Even if they have long left their original families, it can feel as if their internal worlds are still full of the 'swarm of participations' (see Chapter 5, section 2.1) from their sibling group. Freud wrote most clearly about identification as a process in the context of groups (Freud, 1921). (For further discussion of identification and projective identification in relationships, see Thomas, 1996; for discussion of identification and projective identification in groups, see Morgan and Thomas, 1996) This way of thinking about the unboundedness of the self, in particular environments, is suggestive of the Japanese 'interpenetrating ways of living' described in the previous chapter. In the Reading by Kondo, social life was portrayed as interpenetrating in several senses – close living conditions, lack of privacy, ubiquitous social rituals and the norm of continuous comparison and reflexiveness about relating.

The examples discussed in this section suggest that our common assumptions about the unity and the boundedness of the self may be an illusion, a construction. Section 4.3 will argue that the unitary, bounded self can be thought of as a construction which has the function of a defence mechanism. This defensive construction preserves a sense of being autonomous and centred and thus promotes action in the present. In the longer term, this constructed self provides a centre for narratives – for stories which make sense of what happens in our lives over time.

Narratives of our selves over long periods of time show that we can tolerate the idea of changes in self. In our narratives, these changes in self are not only possible but quite commonplace. They are woven into stories with 'explanations' about how each change came about. Cause-and-effect explanations involve ordinary and unexpected life events and *usually involve the influence of new relationships*. In object relations terms, these new relationships provide more raw materials for the self, for further introjections and identifications, or they reawaken introjections of earlier relationships that have not been identified with.

The early development of self and the possibility of change in selfhood is part of all psychodynamic accounts. In object relations terms, the lifelong motivation to relate, together with a degree of continuing permeability to others and to relationships, is the source of change and growth of the self. But this drive to continue relating and introjecting exists in tension with the need to preserve a familiar, safe and unitary sense of self.

> There is a dialectic here between the 'closed system' of defensive sameness and the 'open system' of self-growth through relating and expanding the self. A healthy self can risk losing sameness for a while in order to expand by introjections and new identifications before returning to some degree of unity. These 'open system' ideas of the self are set out in a recent collection of papers by Sutherland (see Scharff, 1994). They are not new, however, since the idea of a self that exists from birth and unconsciously drives the individual to expand selfhood is a central part of the work of Jung. Jung did not describe this in terms of a drive to relate, or in terms of relationships and introjections, but he did conceptualize the self as a whole as an open system, comprising complexes and sub-personalities that can be integrated into the expanding self. Fordham, a Jungian analyst, has shown how, in infancy and throughout life, we oscillate between states of integration and de-integration (not disintegration). During de-integration, wholeness is sacrificed for short periods (or even momentarily) in the service of expansion followed by re-integration. Nevertheless, the capacity to regain wholeness is crucial and the self itself has to be defended (Fordham, 1974, 1985).

4.3   'Self as a defence' and 'defences of the self': holding the fragments together

Why is it important (at least in western culture) to maintain a sense of a unitary self? Disunity, or worse, fragmentation, is a state that we neither want to experience, nor think about. Defensive manoeuvres re-establish a sense of wholeness, if only in the short term, and promote an unequivo-cal and survival-directed orientation to the external world. It may be that the unitary self – our identity – is a defensive *construction* whose function it is to provide a sense of continuity. The paradox is that, once this self is constructed, it seems to be so important to our well-being that it must itself be protected.

Psychodynamic theories describe various defensive manouvres that maintain a sense of unity. Anxiety forewarns us about potential conflict from repressed desires, or powerful emotions, or inconsistent ideas; that is, it warns of impending disruption. Defences then come into operation which act so as to maintain or restore a sense of unity. Conflicts may be repressed into the unconscious, or a sense of disunity may be avoided by splitting, or by dissociations – separating the warring parts so that they are not conscious at the same time. In Kleinian theory, inconsistent feel-ings may be split from each other and the 'bad' emotional states and 'bad' parts of the self may then be projected outwards into the external world and 'got rid of' into other people. In this way, the good parts are kept inside, generating a feeling of wholeness.

There are other manoeuvres that essentially boost ego strength or bolster a fragmenting identity. These bolstering mechanisms can strengthen the sense of a unitary self *either from the inside or from outside*. In Freudian theory, a healthy, strong ego maintains unity from within. The ego works in conjunction with the superego, which can be thought of as a moral code that is inside and that helps to hold the self together: a strict superego figure will be used to keep the 'self in line'. Some people may bolster their sense of self by not only being strict on themselves (perhaps being workaholics) but perhaps also by being strict with, or heavily criti-cal of, other people. The mechanism here is thought to be that the weak, disintegrating self is projected out on to others or on to society and then 'whipped' into place 'out there'. This example is of a defence that uses projection outward *and* uses external sources of support for the self.

This kind of defensive holding together of the self can be seen in some forms of extreme religious behaviour; and in those who end-lessly proselytize against the evils of … whatever … TV violence and sex, and so on. The defence works three ways to maintain unity: it provides a rigid internal moral code; and an external 'cause' which transcends the self; and it externalizes the 'breakdown' of unity (breakdown of law and order?). Perhaps this accounts for some of the dramatic cases of public figures who get caught out doing just the sort of 'bad' things that they spend their public lives trying to eradicate.

People often deal with a fragmented sense of reality and broken up experiences of self by attempting some inner quest (as Freud and Jung did in their self-analyses, and as many mystics have done), or by turning to other people for help in the form of therapy. Psychoanalysis itself pro-vides a way of holding the self together. It helps the individual to find meaning in seemingly senseless and chaotic experiences and behaviours

– weaving together meanings into a coherent whole. In this way, the self becomes a centre for narratives. Many forms of psychodynamic therapy, with their acknowledgement of the role of phantasy (and fantasy) in the formation of early and continuing internal worlds, function by helping the patient to construct and accept versions of the self put together into a plausible narrative of the self and of the experiences that constitute it. A common misunderstanding about psychodynamic psychotherapy is that it seeks historical truth (i.e. absolutes about the past), but much of what happens during psychoanalysis amounts to a negotiated and worked-through mutual reconstruction.

A sense of unitary selfhood can also be bolstered from outside by adopting the unifying traditions of religion, family, political causes and ideologies in general. Freud thought that religious beliefs and feelings accommodated a continuing need for dependence on a strong father-figure – an external source of help and guidance which, even in adulthood, could maintain a sense of wholeness and independence: 'The ordinary man cannot imagine this Providence in any other form but that of a greatly exalted father, for only such a one could understand the needs of the sons of men, or be softened by their prayers and placated by the signs of their remorse' (Freud, 1930, p. 23).

Sometimes the need for external support leads an individual to be so absorbed into an ideology or fundamentalist belief system that it seems as if the self is being highjacked or replaced by an external structure. At least part of the mechanism here involves identification, often with a particularly charismatic figure. Freud (1921) describes how ego strength can be boosted through identifications in group settings. In groups, identifications (like all primitive processes) can be especially powerful, in part because the group makes the individual feel childlike, reviving early emotions and dependencies. (This topic is discussed in Morgan and Thomas, 1996.)

The initial development of ego strength in infancy requires an appropriate degree of ego defence: the ego needs to be protected by having the world presented in a limited form. Winnicott's concepts of 'the facilitating maternal environment' and 'good enough mothering' are concerned with the presentation of the world to the infant in manageable chunks that are by no means an accurate or full reflection of the reality of the world. Later, as ego strength develops, the child can be gently disillusioned. Lacanian psychoanalytic theory also emphasizes the fictional and provisional nature of early simplified images of the world and the self. Lacan uses the idea of a 'mirror phase' in early childhood when the child creates a self by identifying with an 'image of the self' reflected by the mother. Temporarily, this promotes a sense of coherent ego, a relief from the subjective experience of conflicting desires and impulses. But the reflection is deceptive, a view from outside which smoothes away the fragmentation. As language develops, the child realizes the extent of conflicts and contradictions that were not seen in the 'mirror' provided by the mother. The child is left with a sense of loss (Lacan, 1949).

In adulthood, in a rather similar way, a unitary self can be bolstered by maintaining a constrained and rigid orientation to the world. This is a defence that has been called 'intolerance of ambiguity' and it often co-exists with a cognitive style – across most areas of life – that attempts to control or eliminate uncertainties and imposes rigid categories on the world, distorting information to this end. Intake of information is limited, complexities avoided and metaphor ignored or concretized. What follows is a controlling and often irrational orientation, in which the external world is mentally converted into something strong, simple and absolute which can then be taken in to provide an illusory ego strength and an illusory sense of agency. This defensive system is often associated with stereotyped attitudes and racial prejudice.

In a classic study of social psychology, Adorno et al. (1950) used a psychodynamic framework to explain how some adults come to be highly prejudiced, anti-Semitic and potentially fascistic. They found in their sample that these traits co-existed with a history of a certain type of child-rearing environment, and a particular kind of personality. This came to be known as the *authoritarian personality*. Their psychodynamic explanation rests on the hypothesis of a set of defensive manoeuvres.

Adorno et al. found that their racist and potentially fascist subjects tended to come from families where a great deal of weight was placed on authority, rigid discipline and conditional affection – conditional upon obedience and conformity. The underlying internalized object relations were those of dominance and submission, introjected from a micro-social environment which generated fear, and anger that could not be safely expressed. In adulthood, these subjects have a characteristic cognitive style, which follows from defences rather like those described above: a sense of weakness inside is compensated for by attempts to find strengths and absolutes in the outside world. These adults are authority-dependent, and find comfort in identifying with the submissive side of the dominance-submission pattern of their childhood relationship with parental authority. But their own aggression is projected outward on to an outgroup; in this case a racial minority. If the aggression is not projected it will disrupt the sense of unity of the self. The aggrandisement that might follow from membership of social groups supporting racism still further bolsters the weak ego.

Of course, this is not the whole story of racial prejudice and fascism. Certain societal conditions must also exist that permit or encourage the projection of hatred and rage. (This topic and the work of Adorno et al. are discussed in Wetherell, 1996.)

4.4   Selfhood: universal or situated?

Psychodynamic theories set out to find universal explanations of the mind and the self, even though they have been based on observations of western social practices, family structures and child-rearing patterns. How can these provide universal explanations?

We have seen how psychodynamic theories are embodied, from the out-set. And it may be this that provides a valid universal basis for the the-ories, on which cultural and other local variations can build. Embodiment includes innate temperamental features of humanness and the biologically defined sequence of interacting drives and development. It includes powerful physical experiences that are common to everyone – the pain of being hungry, of being unwell, of having sore skin, being cold, hot, frightened, and feeling alone and not held. These are experiences that infants, children and adults will have irrespective of cul-ture and the specific kind of caring that is the local norm.

Freud's classical psychoanalysis was presented as a universal theory, with claims about the universality of its central tenets. How can this be valid in view of the centrality of the Oedipus complex – a construct that depends vitally on specific family structures and kinship patterns? This question has long been disputed. Other versions of psychodynamics play down the importance of Oedipal conflict, to varying degrees. For many psychodynamic theorists, the 'problem' is no longer the sudden aware-ness at the age of 4 or 5 years of a sexual triangle between child, mother and father, but the universal problem that infants face when their intense feeding-based experience of relating to one other person is intruded upon by the intimate demands of another – usually the mother's sexual partner. In most psychodynamic theories now, the move from dyadic concerns to triangles begins much earlier in life. Also, in a slightly different form, it is met even earlier with siblings and sibling rivalry.

The theories that focus on the mother-infant feeding couple have firmer biological grounds for universality. This is because they emphasize early experiences of relating, primitive emotions of jealousy and envy, the bio-logical givens of early physical experiences of hunger, pain, etc., and the physical dependence of the infant on one or few carers. From this would follow, universally, a relational space in which emotions can be reliably communicated and validated – leading to the first stages of intersubjec-tivity (Trevarthen, 1993). Other biological universals also play an impor-tant part in psychodynamic accounts – the experience of physical and sexual development, ageing and death, although again these will be socially constructed, locally, in different ways.

The social constructionist view of the self is that we will each be a product of our historical time, culture and subculture. We will create and re-create ourselves, but always within the limits and opportunities, materials, technologies, myths and social realities at our disposal. In this view, there will be a great deal of variation in the overall nature and constituents of selves; *but there will also be different local assumptions about what self is*. Not only might self be different in form and content in different times and countries and cultures, but the *theories* we produce about the self will change; they too will be a product of time and culture.

In the present chapter, the different psychodynamic accounts are all products of western thinking and culture, but there is evidence of historical change. Over time, from Freud to the present, there is a movement towards conceptualizing the self as more fluid and constructed, a self that is created in very early interactions with other people. There is an increasing acceptance of sub-selves that are evoked to some extent by situations and especially by particular relationships. Some object relations accounts describe a potential fluidity of self, constructed and reconstructed *in the course of relationships* through evocations of past identifications and introjections of new ones.

If we look closely at the psychodynamic accounts given in this chapter, we shall find that each one makes different assumptions about selfhood, makes value judgements about social practices, suggests different relations between individual and society, and then constructs a different 'model' of what a person *should* be. What, in each account, constitutes a healthy self? What is seen as the *successful* entry of the child into the social world? What is the implied relation in each account between internal worlds and the external world? It has been said that Freud championed the fathers, Klein championed the mothers, and the object relations theorists champion children (Grotstein and Rinsley, 1994, p. 10). How might these different starting points affect accounts of the relation between selfhood and the social order?

4.4.1 Freud: compliant selfhood in a patriarchy

In the classical Freudian view, children become social beings as and when they learn to repress their instinctual drives, forego satisfactions and internalize a superego figure in the guise (usually) of a punitive father. The child develops ego strength and establishes a morality as the result of internal struggles, repression, anxiety, ego defences to bolster the efficiency of the ego, and eventually a 'coming to terms' with the demands of the reality principle.

This is a compliance model of the relationship between individual and society. There is an assumption that an objective external reality exists to be incorporated, but that the form in which it becomes represented internally is distorted by the child's drives, particularly its sexual drives. Because of this fundamental mismatch between external reality and its demands, and the drive-distorted phantasies of the internal world, the individual cannot be in harmony with the external world and remains essentially 'guilty', struggling to achieve a working compromise between innate, chaotic desires and a punitive 'law of the fathers'.

4.4.2 Klein: fragmented selfhood oscillating between paranoia and ambivalence

Freud's theory was conceived in the context of a patriarchy, of which he was certainly a part. The Kleinian contribution marks a small move towards matriarchy. Now the focus is infancy and early childhood. We find a model of the individual who, almost irrespective of the actual social world, is driven from birth by destructive blueprints – unconscious phantasies – that release innate envy and hate. The intensely emotional and polarized versions of reality that infants/children create are thought of as so persecutory that psychological defences have to be mobilized from infancy. And these mechanisms of splitting, and projection of internal phantasies outward, remove the infant/child still further from the reality of the external world.

In Kleinian theory, the child enters the 'real' social world only when it is able to address its ambivalence (love and hate) and integrate the splits of the paranoid-schizoid position. The effort to become social centres on achieving the sadness of the depressive position. The depressive position requires a realization of the destructiveness of the internal world, and toleration of the pain associated with emotional complexities and uncertainties of the external world, particularly other people. In Klein's theory, the healthy child gradually achieves some consolidation of the depressive position. But oscillation between the depressive position and the experience of fragmentation – paranoid splits in the ego and persecutory anxiety – remains an intermittent feature of our adult experience of selfhood.

What are the implications of the Kleinian approach for relations between the individual and society? From her Freudian training, Klein took the idea of the punitive superego, but she brought it into children's consciousness much earlier in life. Superego figures – in the plural – are not so clearly paternal. Frightening maternal figures appear as well, to control not only sexual urges but innate hate, aggression, jealousy and envy. In the depressive position, the infant, or adult, has to take responsibility for having created an internal world of 'phantoms', internal objects which have taken the place of and been confused with the real objects (people), leading to certain kinds of relating in the external world: 'The advantage of her scheme is that it gives the infant/patient a sense of ownership of his [sic] own autobiographical scenario, a sense of being the creator of his own history by phantasmally organizing it' (Grotstein, 1994, p. 135).

The force of the Kleinian position is that human destructiveness and the potential for fragmentation can only be partially contained; it will be defensively projected out into the world, increasing paranoia and affecting social life and the formation of social structures. The chaos within the self appears in the external world. Insofar as Klein rejected classical Freudian theory, she replaced the 'guilty' socialized individual, still struggling with repressed desires, with a person who, on reaching the depressive position, feels both guilty and sad. The sadness is due to the damage caused by primitive emotions, and the damage caused by the 'false' internal world and its implied allegations about others.

4.4.3 Object relations theories: selfhood created out of others and relationships

Object relations theories have a different position. Self and sociality are seen as much more influenced by the outside world as it is actually experienced. Object relations theories reject or reduce the influence of biological drives, replacing them with a need for other people *per se*; and they give centre stage to the *dependent* child and its entitlement. Patriarchy versus matriarchy is replaced with a view of children as 'entitled to consideration in their own right'. Children are seen as having some kind of organizing self from birth *and* as having the capacity to see (only too clearly) the reality into which they have been born. The model is one of individuals who, in their dependent state of *needing* these objects, first have to internalize the realities of the external world and *then* distort them in order to survive the pain of real malattunement, or neglect or abuse. Once the process of internalization is under way, defence mechanisms, phantasies and splits come into action.

The object relations model of the individual in society places a considerable burden on those who care for infants, giving them responsibility for children's healthy psychological development and for their selfhood. This highlights the dependence of the child on adults, not just for physical survival but for the structure as well as content of its mind, and for the integrity of its self. But the object relations model is also potentially optimistic because it focuses on the social environment as facilitating growth and development and the holding together of ego fragments. It allows for a benign view of the role of the social world, especially direct interactions in small family groups which, in evolutionary terms, have provided an environmental niche for massive elaboration of our symbolic capacities. Modern versions of object relations theory suggest that motivation to maintain close emotional bonds with significant others provides opportunities to internalize other people and their relationships as the constituents of our selves and as templates for our ways of relating throughout life.

These three theoretical models of the self and of the subjective experience of selfhood are very different from each other. However, the idea that self is a theoretical construct that changes with historical and cultural locations means that we might consider the relevance of these psychodynamic accounts for contemporary cultures and current experiences of selfhood.

4.5   Postmodern self: empty or saturated?

What model of the self might we construct now, late in the twentieth century, and facing the beginning of the next millennium? How *do* we experience our selves in times characterized by very rapid change and disruption in the external world, when communities are fragmented, religious beliefs and other ideologies are undermined, and distantly conceived multimedia communications are continuous and unavoidable influences on our realities. What can the psychodynamic perspective contribute to the idea of the 'postmodern self?'

'Postmodern' refers to a time-period when the honeymoon with 'modernity' – science, technological progress and social freedoms – is over. The postmodern self describes the selfhood that many people seem to be experiencing now, at least in the West: a mixture of disillusionment, boredom, confusion, and celebration.

Saul Bellow has described the contemporary scene, putting the words into the mouth of one of his fictional characters:

> ... It's the disposition of autonomy and detachment, a kind of sovereignty we're all schooled in. The sovereignty of atoms – that is, of human beings who see themselves as atoms of intelligent separateness. But all that has been said over and over. Like, how schizoid the modern personality is. The atrophy of feelings. The whole bit. There's what's-his-name Fairbairn. And Jung before him comparing the civilised psyche to a tapeworm. Identical segments, on and on. Crazy and also boring, forever and ever. This goes back to the first axiom of nihilism – the highest values losing their value.
>
> *(Bellow, 1982, p. 259)*

Here Bellow is drawing attention to the separateness, unconnectedness and cut-offness of schizoid states and of current selfhood. Bellow focuses on the sameness and meaninglessness and boredom.

In another account, Frosh focuses on the other side of the coin – the excitement and fear of constant change and the intrusiveness of novelty:

> ... contradiction, fluidity, multiplicity ... the real turmoil in the outside world is mirrored internally, as it must be if there is any link between the two orders. If the self is constructed through relations with stable objects and dependable people, then it must be unsettled when these objects keep disappearing, to be replaced by new, exciting but equally disposable alternatives ... Postmodernism ... denies that there is any depth of significance in these processes, but nevertheless celebrates the merry-go-round excitements of perpetual plurality ... modern states of mind and forms of selfhood, then, are forged in the context of instability of a cataclysmic kind ... opening the way to pathologically defensive states and to a fluid and generative creativity ... certainties of self can slip away ... closing down may bring a sense of security and knowing who one is but at the price of continuously having to ward off the assaults of the new ... [Postmodernism] is characterized by uncertainty, rapidity of change and kaleidoscopic juxtapositions of objects, people and events ... finding our uncertain way through these uncertainties is a prime task for contemporary existence ...
>
> *(Frosh, 1991, pp.6–7)*

Frosh has linked these kinds of experiences to contemporary forms of psychopathology. If selfhood varies across time and culture, then we might expect pathologies to vary also. This is not a new idea. For example, conversion hysteria which was common in Freud's time is now very rare. Although it is difficult to separate the prevalence of a disorder from increased interest, or even from a kind of resonance between the spirit of the times and certain configurations of symptoms, Frosh (1991) suggests that certain pathologies of self are the direct result of postmodern life. In particular, Frosh and many others have suggested that the 'narcissistic' disorders of aggrandisement of the self may be one of the characteristic pathologies of our time. These follow not from simple overevaluation of the self but as a compensation for early damage to the self. Paradoxically, narcissistic personalities are desperately bolstering a weak and fragmenting self. That self also has to be protected from real relating and denies dependencies.

Another pathology thought to be of our time is the schizoid personality, described by Fairbairn (see section 3.3) and alluded to in the Bellow quotation. The schizoid personality is typically withdrawn, affectless and incapable of maintaining intimacy. Another contemporary pathology is the borderline psychotic condition, such as that described in the quotation from Kernberg in section 4.1 above. Borderline patients often struggle to maintain coherence in their selves against forces of excessive splitting of aspects of reality. It may be that their selves have already begun to collapse.

Other observers of the contemporary self have coined more memorable and less pathological terms for 'the way we are' now. Two of these are the 'empty self' and the 'saturated self'.

Cushman believes that, currently in the West, the most influential version of the self is one that:

> ... experiences a significant absence of community, tradition, and shared meaning. It experiences these social absences and their consequences 'interiorly' as a lack of personal conviction and worth, and it embodies the absences as a chronic, undifferentiated emotional hunger ... [and] thus yearns to acquire and consume as an unconscious way of compensation for what it has lost: it is empty.

> Over the course of the twentieth century it has become apparent ... that Americans have slowly changed from a Victorian people who had a deeply felt need to save money and restrict their sexual and aggressive impulses ... [to] become a people who have a deeply felt need to spend money and indulge their impulses.

> ... the current self is constructed as empty, and as a result the state controls its population not by restricting the impulses of its citizens, as in Victorian times, but by creating and manipulating their wish to be smoothed, organized and made cohesive by momentarily filling them up.

> *(Cushman, 1990, p. 600)*

This view uses a psychodynamic metaphor; it describes the breakdown of what is essentially a Freudian version of self followed by a movement into a more regressed state of infantile dependence and hunger and a need to be filled up.

On the other hand, Gergen's 'saturated self' is not empty, but too full. Gergen agrees with Cushman that we have lost much of the traditional community that we used to have. But rather than being empty, Gergen argues, we are overfilled with new and often technological manifestations of social life, such as television, video, newspapers, telephones, travel, junk mail and so on. These forms of communication and *indirect* interaction are commonplace for most people in technological societies. But they are manifestations of a massive and deep social change. Although technologies remove us from much 'real' engagement with social life, paradoxically they increase the possibilities for a kind of engagement and influence – at a distance:

> The change is essentially one that immerses us ever more deeply in the social world, and exposes us more and more to the opinions, values, and life-styles of others …

> What I call the technologies of social saturation are central to the contemporary erasure of individual self. … There is a populating of the self, reflecting the infusion of partial identities through social saturation. … one begins to experience the vertigo of unlimited multiplicity.

> (Gergen, 1991, p. 49)

Gergen's saturated self mirrors the current external world. But it also represents an extreme version of internal worlds as described by object relations theory. By this I mean that it describes an overuse, or an abuse, of normal introjective and identificatory processes. The contemporary environment for minds is characterized by a combination of both intrusiveness and lack of boundaries: technological symbolic systems of a high level of complexity, which create rapidly changing 'virtual relating' and 'virtual communities', penetrate, often unwanted, into our physical and mental space. The ordinary human mechanisms for learning about other people, the world and creating versions of ourselves are overloaded and confused.

It is a world in which we exist in a state of introjective overload and rapidly changing identifications and disidentifications. And much of this is through 'virtual' social practices and encounters. We are constantly exposed to and bombarded by all kinds of virtual communications – these get right into our lives. We are surrounded by partial interactions, abbreviated images of other lives, incomplete narratives; but we engage with them and introject their objects and object relations, their loaded messages. We get addicted to 'soaps', identifying with the characters, following their stories as if they were part of our own lives – and thus we live in projection instead of in our selves.

It seems as if external fragmentation is being mirrored internally. Or is it that our experience of internal fragmentation, our increased awareness of the 'bits and pieces' that make us up and that now seem difficult to make into a unified and motivating whole, is really the nature of the mind? Is this the way we are when stripped of our traditional means of externally bolstering our selves – when external systems of community, law, oppression, belief, faith, idealization and hope disappear?

Review of section 4

- The self is a construct that is used to account for organization of much of mental life. It is both a theoretical construct and something we experience. We can know about the self as the object of theories and as the object of our ordinary self-knowledge. But it is also experienced as the centre of being and agency.

- According to psychodynamics, our experience of self can only be partial since much is out of reach, either repressed into the unconscious or compartmentalized by the defence of splitting.

- Introjection and identification are the processes by which the self is created. It is through the introjection of other people and relationships that the social world gets inside and constitutes the self.

- Identificatory processes suggest that the self may not be bounded but permeable and fluid. The self may be more open to mix-ups between people and influences from other people than is commonly assumed in western cultures.

- Subjective experiences of internal conflict, contradictions and fragmentation are defended against by removing disunity from consciousness using the mechanisms of repression, splitting and dissociation and the bolstering of the self, from inside and outside. These defences maintain a unitary centre for action. It is possible that the 'self' is itself a defensive illusion.

- Forms of self (in terms of both structure and content) and pathologies of self vary across cultures and history. The forms of selfhood that appear both influence and are influenced by contemporary and local assumptions, and by formal theories about the self.

- Psychodynamic theories have been cast as universal – and this seems to depend largely on their basis in embodiment. In other respects, psychodynamic accounts reflect cultural assumptions. They arrive at different conceptions of the self and what constitutes a mature and healthy self.

- Object relations theory can explain the contemporary, postmodern self in terms of intrusive overload of processes of introjection and identification.

Further reading

This chapter has treated psychodynamic theories as a form of social psychology; Frosh is another author who attempts this. You will find that his work is written at a higher level, and covers a wide range of issues. His books compare the contributions of academic psychology and psychodynamic theory over a variety of topics including sociality and identity. See Frosh, S. (1989) *Psychoanalysis and Psychology,* London, Macmillan, and Frosh, S. (1991) *Identity Crisis: Modernity, Psychoanalysis and the Self,* London, Macmillan.

You may prefer to focus first on psychodynamic ideas. In this case, an important book to read is Symington, N. (1986) *The Analytic Experience*, London, Free Association Books. It is beautifully written and easy to digest – everyone's favourite. A good pairing with this would be Stern, D. (1985) *The Interpersonal World of the Infant,* New York, Basic Books. This book is unique and widely quoted. It combines modern developmental psychology with psychoanalytic ideas.

If you are particularly interested in developmental psychology, from a psychodynamic point of view, you might like to read psychoanalytic accounts of infant observations: Miller, L., Rustin, M., Rustin, M. and Shuttleworth, J. (1989) *Closely Observed Infants,* London, Duckworth; and Piontelli, A. (1985) *Backwards in Time,* London, Clunie Press. Another book which starts from a developmental perspective is Klein, J. (1987) *Our Need for Others and its Roots in Infancy*, London, Tavistock Publications. This covers several different psychodynamic accounts. The first part of this book 'rewrites' psychology and could easily be skipped. Start with Part Two.

There are two other excellent books on psychoanalytic theories, especially object relations theories – although they are less accessible than Symington: Rayner, E. (1991) *The Independent Mind in British Psychoanalysis*, London, Free Association Books, and Ogden, T.H. (1986) *The Matrix of Mind*, Northdale, NJ, and London, Jason Aronson Inc.

If you have a special interest in the work of Melanie Klein try: Segal, H. (1986) *Introduction to the Work of Melanie Klein*, London, Hogarth Press, or Mitchell, J. (1986) T*he Selected Melanie Klein*, Harmondsworth, Penguin Books – in that order.

There are several dictionaries that might be helpful. The most basic of these is Rycroft, C. (1968) *A Critical Dictionary of Psychoanalysis*, Harmondsworth, Penguin Books. A more advanced psychoanalytic dictionary is Laplanche, J. and Pontalis, J.B. (1988) *The Language of Psychoanalysis*, London, Karnac Books. There is also a specialized Kleinian dictionary: Hinshelwood, R.D. (1991) *A Dictionary of Kleinian Thought*, London, Free Association Books.

References

Adorno, T.W., Frenkel-Brunswik, E., Levinson, D.J. and Sanford, R.N. (1950) *The Authoritarian Personality*, New York, Harper and Row.

Armstrong-Perlman, E.G. (1991) 'The allure of the bad object', *Free Associations*, vol. 2, pp. 343–56.

Bellow, S. (1982) *The Dean's December*, New York, Penguin Books.

Conway, M.A. (1995) 'Autobiographical knowledge and autobiographical memories', in Rubin, D.C. (ed.) *Remembering Our Past: Studies in Autobiographical Memory*, Cambridge, Cambridge University Press.

Conway, M.A., Collins, A.F., Gathercole, S.E. and Anderson, S.J. (1996) 'True and false autobiographical memories of everyday events: a diary study', *Journal of Experimental Psychology: General* (in press).

Cushman, P. (1990) 'Why the self is empty: toward a historically situated psychology', *American Psychologist*, vol. 45, no. 5, pp. 599–611.

Fairbairn, W.R.D. (1990) *Psychoanalytic Studies of the Personality*, London and New York, Tavistock/Routledge.

Fonagy, P. (1994) 'A psychoanalytic understanding of memory and reconstruction', *Psychotherapy Section Newsletter*, no. 16, England, The British Psychological Society.

Fordham, M. (1974) 'Defences of the self', *Journal of Analytical Psychology*, vol. 19, pp. 192–9.

Fordham, M. (1985) *Explorations into the Self*, London, Academic Press.

Freud, S. (1921) 'Group psychology and the analysis of the ego', in Strachey, J. (ed.) (1955) *Standard Edition*, vol. 18, London, Hogarth Press and the Institute of Psycho-Analysis.

Freud, S. (1930) *Civilization and its Discontents* (trans. by J. Riviere), London, Hogarth Press and the Institute of Psycho-Analysis.

Freud, S. (1940) 'An outline of psychoanalysis', in Strachey, J. (ed.) (1964) *Standard Edition*, vol. 23, London, Hogarth Press and the Institute of Psycho-Analysis.

Frosh, S. (1991) *Identity Crisis: Modernity, Psychoanalysis and the Self*, London, Macmillan.

Gergen, K.J. (1991) *The Saturated Self: Dilemmas of Identity in Contemporary Life*, New York, Basic Books.

Grotstein, J.S. (1994) 'Notes on Fairbairn's metapsychology', in Grotstein, J.S. and Rinsley, D.B. (eds).

Grotstein, J.S. and Rinsley, D.B. (eds) (1994) *Fairbairn and the Origins of Object Relations*, London, Free Association Books.

Jung, C.G. (1935) *Tavistock Lectures, Lecture 3*, London, Routledge and Kegan Paul.

Kernberg, O. (1986) 'Structural derivatives of object relationships', in Buckley, P. (ed.) *Essential Papers on Object Relations*, New York, New York University Press.

Klein, M. (1959) 'Our adult world and its roots in infancy', in Klein, M. (1993) *Collected Works*, vol. III, *Envy, Gratitude and Other Works*, London, Karnac Books.

Lacan, J. (1949) 'The mirror stage as formative of the function of the I as revealed in psychoanalytic experience', in Lacan, J. (1977) *Ecrits: A Selection*, London, Tavistock Publications.

Masson, J.M. (1984) *The Assault on Truth: Freud's Suppression of the Seduction Theory*, New York, Farrar, Straus, Giroux.

Mehler, J. and Dupoux, E. (1994) *What Infants Know*, Oxford, Blackwell.

Miell, D. and Dallos, R. (eds) (1996) *Social Interaction and Personal Relationships*, London, Sage/The Open University (Book 2 in this series).

Morgan, H. and Thomas, K. (1996) 'A psychodynamic perspective on group processes', in Wetherell, M. (ed.).

Murray, L. (1992) 'The impact of postnatal depression on infant development', *Journal of Child Psychology and Psychiatry*, vol. 33, pp. 543–61.

Ogden, T.H. (1986) *The Matrix of Mind*, Northdale, NJ, and London, Jason Aronson Inc.

Rayner, E. (1991) *The Independent Mind in British Psychoanalysis*, London, Free Association Books.

Rycroft, C. (1968) *A Critical Dictionary of Psychoanalysis*, Harmondsworth, Penguin Books.

Sandler, J. (1993) 'On communication from patient to analyst: not everything is projective identification', *International Journal of Psycho-Analysis*, vol. 74, pp. 1097–1107.

Scharff, J.S. (1994) *The Autonomous Self: The Work of John D. Sutherland*, Northdale, NJ, and London, Jason Aronson Inc.

Sinason, V. (1992) *Mental Handicap and the Human Condition*, London, Free Association Books.

Stern, D. (1985) *The Interpersonal World of the Infant*, New York, Basic Books.

Sutherland, J.D. (1980) 'The British object relations theorists: Balint, Winnicott, Fairbairn, Guntrop', *Journal of American Psychoanalytical Association*, vol. 28, pp. 829–60.

Teilhard de Chardin, P. (1957) *Le Milieu Divin*, London, Fontana.

Thomas, K. (1996) 'The psychodynamics of relating', in Miell, D. and Dallos, R. (eds).

Trevarthen, C. (1991) 'The other in the infant mind', paper and videotape presented at The Psychic Life of the Infant: Origins of Human Identity Conference, sponsored by the University of Massachusetts at Amhurst.

Trevarthen, C. (1993) 'The function of emotions in early infant communication', in Nadel, J. and Camaioni, KL. (eds) *New Perspectives in Early Communicative Development*, London, Routledge.

Wetherell, M. (1996) 'Group conflict and the social psychology of racism', in Wetherell, M. (ed.).

Wetherell, M. (ed.) (1996) *Identities, Groups and Social Issues*, London, Sage/The Open University (Book 3 in this series).

Winnicott, D.W. (1947) 'Further thoughts on babies as persons', in Winnicott, D.W. (1964) *The Child, the Family and the Outside World*, Harmondsworth, Penguin Books.

Winnicott, D.W. (1960) 'Ego distortion in terms of true and false self', in Winnicott, D.W. (1985) *The Maturational Processes and the Facilitating Environment*, London, Hogarth Press.

Reflections

This chapter has presented a psychodynamic perspective on the self which shows the development of psychodynamic ideas since their first expression in the work of Freud. It reveals a movement away from a medical, scientific orientation towards the more constructionist approach of current psychodynamic thinking. In Freud's time, the early psychoanalytic explorations of mind and experience were driven by a search for 'truths' about the biology of the mind, and generalizable truths about psychological distortions of the reality of the external world. But, as Freud began to stress the importance of conscious fantasy and unconscious phantasy in the formation of people's psychic reality, the relationship between internal versions of reality and 'real' external reality has become controversial. This chapter shows how, as post-Freudian psychodynamics has shifted towards a constructionist position, the distinction between a 'constructed' internal world and a 'real' external world melts away.

The chapter makes an original contribution by showing how post-Freudian developments in theory, particularly those of the object relations psychoanalysts, can inform our ideas about the socially constructed nature of the self. Object relations views of the self are presented as largely compatible with the social constructionist perspective. There are points of difference, as the author makes clear: the psychodynamic approach still places the critical origins of adult experience *very* early in childhood, often prior to the development of language. But both perspectives question the idea of a unitary self, and of fixed boundaries between self and others. The view of self which emerges from this chapter is multiple, and peopled by the voices of others, particularly the significant others of our early life.

Relationships between the perspectives

In this chapter, which presents the last of our five perspectives, contrasts are made between the psychodynamic position and the other perspectives that have been presented earlier. Although there are considerable areas of overlap between the domains addressed, the psychodynamic perspective often treats these in very different ways from the other four approaches. The psychodynamic perspective starts, for instance, with the presumption of the importance of the biological (as with the concept of id), particularly in the case of instinct theorists such as Freud and Klein. However, this is done only in the most general way by reference to particular drives such as sex and aggression. It is quite different from the treatment of the biological basis of the self in Chapter 2 where reference is made to causal explanations (in terms, for example, of genetic or hormonal influences) and to functional ones based on the notion of evolutionary development. This is not to say that the two approaches are inconsistent, but Chapter 2 places more specific emphasis on biological factors and spells out the processes through which they take effect.

Similarly, although it is made clear in Chapter 6 that the psychodynamic perspective works with the subjective experience of the person, this contrasts with the experiential perspective presented in Chapter 4, because the psychodynamic perspective sees phenomenological realities as representing underlying unconscious meanings and feelings, often in limited and distorted versions, rather than as being of intrinsic interest in their own right. Likewise, psychoanalysts would consider that the cognitive-experimental approach treats the interpretations that people make of the world around them in too unproblematic a fashion. While this perspective acknowledges the influence of cognitive biases, in the psychodynamic view it does not take into account the distortions of unconscious motivations. In response, both experiential and cognitive-experimental perspectives raise serious doubts about the validity of the theoretical concepts and assumptions on which the interpretations of psychoanalysts are based.

It is worth observing that, historically, the development of psychoanalysis has come about largely independently of mainstream psychology. However, this is not to say that psychodynamic ideas have lacked influence. Chapter 6 mentions the authoritarian personality study which combined psychodynamic thinking with the attitude-scaling techniques of social psychology. In the mid-twentieth century, a number of social learning theorists tried to use some psychoanalytic ideas expressed in their own terms, especially with reference to the processes of socialization. There have also been numerous attempts by psychologists and others to test isolated psychodynamic ideas through experimental and anthropological studies. More recently, with the shift in social and developmental psychology away from experimental techniques, and the shift in psychodynamic theory away from instinct models, the stage has perhaps been set for greater mutual assimilation than we have hitherto seen: this has already borne fruit in studies of child development by psychologists who have been inspired by psychodynamic ideas.

The question of evidence

As the author of the chapter points out, although psychodynamics inevitably rests on interpretation, this has to be true of any approach (including experiential and social constructionist perspectives) which takes meanings or the ways in which people experience and make sense of their worlds as its central subject-matter. However, although all interpretation involves some form of construction or 'going beyond the evidence given', psychodynamic interpretation would seem to have to go 'further beyond the evidence' than the others do precisely because it is concerned to elicit unconscious meanings which are difficult to access. Psychoanalysts claim that their training (including their own training analysis which alerts them to the potential distortions arising from their own countertransference) uniquely fits them to do this. However, the sceptic might regard such training as more akin to a process of socialization into a particular way of thinking about and relating to the material of their patients' lives. Questions might also be raised about the nature of the clients who generate the evidence on which the theories have been based. They do not constitute a representative sample of the more general population. Most of the children treated by Melanie Klein, for example, were referred by their parents because of problem behaviour. Can we assume that the aggressive phantasies and splitting she found during their analyses are necessarily typical of children as a whole? And with adults, can we necessarily assume, as psychoanalysts do, that the examples of ego splitting observed in their patients are illustrative of normal experience?

Analysts deny the validity of such doubts and emphasize the wide variety of people who enter psychoanalysis these days. Analysts would argue that phantasies and splitting can be observed generally – for example, in children's play, adults' dreams and in the everyday defensive behaviour of ordinary people. They believe, as the chapter makes clear, that analysts are uniquely placed in their exposure to the intimate thoughts and feelings of a variety of patients. This, together with the skills acquired through their training to observe and reflect on their own experience of their patients, provides the basis for the theoretical propositions they assert.

Realism and constructionism

Underlying the perspectives presented in this book has been the difficult philosophical issue of the nature and status of reality. Is it something which exists in some form quite apart from the way we make sense of it? Is our task to find out about it as best we can? This would be the position, for example, of the biological perspective. The underlying bases of behaviour and experience which are focused on include tangible physiological processes, genes and hormones: the task of the biological perspective is, through experiment and observation, to find out how these operate. This realist position would also seem to apply, at least to some extent, to the cognitive-experimental perspective of Chapter 3, as indicated by the research methods it advocates.

The social constructionist perspective of Chapter 5 presents an alternative position. There, the explicit assumption is that realities are constructed by the particular social practices and interactions in which we engage. Psychological experience and the meanings we attribute to the world are necessarily constructions rather than simple representations or approximations to a 'real' reality which exists outside of the human mind and apart from human practices.

Both Chapter 4 on the experientialist perspective and Chapter 6 on psychodynamics seem to move between realist and more constructionist positions. In the Freudian view, for example, the way the world 'really' is is *distorted* by sexual drives to create the psychic realities of our internal worlds. But a constructionist position is expressed in the assertion that the self changes with historical and cultural locations. This mixture of emphases on what is real *and* on what is constructed is increasingly part of psychodynamic thinking, and this chapter has demonstrated a trend from a realist to a more constructionist view. There are analysts who, in their clinical work, pursue phantasy-driven distortions of encounters with the 'real' world, whilst others think of all accounts of the self and psychic processes as constructions, some being more adaptive and useful to a person than others. The former viewpoint is evident in the classical notion of psychoanalysis as *historical reconstruction*. Here, the aim of therapy is conceived of as recovering experiences which 'really' happened in the past in order to unravel the distortions of process which, in interaction with sexual drives, these experiences now impose. However, at present, psychodynamic therapy is more likely to be seen in a constructionist way – indeed, as a form of *narrative reconstruction*. The aim here is to seek for interpretations that offer a more satisfactory account of the way things are (in the sense that they allow psychological movement forward) rather than purporting necessarily to be an account of what actually happened.

Determinism and autonomy

There is also something of a paradoxical mixture in the psychodynamic position on autonomy and determinism. On the one hand, psychodynamic thinking and psychoanalytic technique are premised on the assumption of psychic determinism. On the other, the processes of psychoanalysis and psychoanalytic psychotherapy assume some possibility for change. The crux of this paradox is that, in the psychodynamic view, change and personal growth come about only through the observations and verbal interventions of another person (the analyst). In these terms, psychodynamic therapy could be regarded as a form of scaffolding, as this term was used in Chapter 5, to enhance the reflexiveness of the client, and to empower him or her to expand consciousness and construct more satisfying modes of living and relating.

Section 4 of Chapter 6 introduced questions about the nature of the self in the modern world, a theme which will be taken up in the next and final chapter. This will look back over the perspectives which have been presented in this book and reflect on the general issues they raise for our understanding of the self.

CHAPTER 7:

THE SELF IN THE MODERN WORLD: DRAWING TOGETHER THE THREADS

by Richard Stevens and Margaret Wetherell

Contents

1 Introduction

The final section of Chapter 6 raised the question of the nature of the self in the modern world from a psychodynamic viewpoint. We want to begin this concluding chapter by taking up this topic in more general terms. As the previous chapter asked, 'What model of the self might we construct now, late in the twentieth century, and facing the beginning of the next millennium?' (p. 326). We don't have any new answers to offer in this final chapter but we believe that the perspectives developed in this book provide a map and guide for the future. They present the accumulated wisdom of social psychology in this area, but they also reflect important strands in the response of Euro-American cultures to broad questions about the nature and meaning of life. One of the main aims of this chapter is thus to review the perspectives, placing them side by side, not only as an aid to study, but as a reminder of what has been achieved in making sense of the nature of the self as we move towards and into the next millennium.

The different perspectives considered in this book provide, not only a range of intellectual frameworks for speculating about the psychological consequences of modern and/or postmodern life (theorists differ as to whether we have entered some kind of postmodern age), but also a set of premises about method. Will our path into the next millennium be eased by rigorous research measuring the observable consequences of social changes, or by more interpretative and open-ended investigations tracing the multiple connections between people and their social worlds? The diversity of the perspectives and the methods they advocate raises questions about the kinds of knowledge claims involved and about the ways in which the perspectives interrelate which we will also try to address in the chapter.

Aims of Chapter 7

The aims of this chapter are:

- To explore, through discussing the nature of the modern self, some of its features and dilemmas.

- To review the perspectives presented in the previous chapters.

- To consider the relationship between the perspectives. Are they complementary, in conflict, in parallel or in some other form of relationship with each other?

2 The self in the modern world

Chapter 6 introduced the notion of the modern self or postmodern self, but why talk about a *modern* self in the first place? Does not the sense of self transcend culture, history and society? The impact of culture on our sense of self was a theme which was initiated in Chapter 3 (see, for example, the study by Cousins, 1989, comparing the identity concepts of Japanese and Americans) and developed in Chapter 5 (remember the Kondo reading and also the discussion of Lienhardt's (1985) research on Dinka concepts of the mind/body relation). Most researchers now accept that the concern with individuality which characterizes what M. Brewster Smith (1994) usefully refers to as 'Euro-American' identity has emerged from particular historical circumstances in the development of these societies, and that it contrasts with the collectivist style that tends to be more common in other parts of the world (see, for example, Triandis et al., 1993). It has also been argued that this shift to a focus on individuality has been one of the factors that led to the development of psychology. As Smith (1994) has expressed it:

> Modern versions of selfhood took shape in the intellectual context of the Enlightenment and the Romantic movement (Taylor, 1989) and the social context of capitalism and the industrial and political revolutions of the eighteenth and nineteenth centuries (Baumeister, 1986). The cultural focus during the present century on the autonomous, self-contained individual with a rich conscious and even unconscious inner life may be partly responsible for the plurality and proliferation of psychology as a science and profession and of personality and clinical psychology among its subfields.
>
> (Smith, 1994, p. 406)

2.1 The self as a source of meaning

Several commentators have argued that one of the principal distinguishing features of modern Euro-American societies is that the self has become a source of meaning and value in itself (this theme was noted, too, in Chapter 6). One early analysis of the effects of contemporary society on consciousness argued, for example, that because we now live our lives in many contexts, and are never totally immersed in just one context, a strong sense of individual or personal identity is encouraged (Berger et al., 1974). People who live in or move between more than one setting are likely to be the most aware of having an individual sense of self. How far mobility in itself is instrumental in generating a conscious sense of self, however, is open to question. There are certainly people with an acute sense of self-awareness who have led circumscribed and sedentary lives (for example, a writer such as Emily Dickinson). Nevertheless, it would seem that, as older institutions such as religion and familiar forms of communal organization break down, more and more emphasis is placed on the person and personal identity as the touchstone for meaning in life. Uniqueness and the fulfilment of individual potential become central values displacing previous emphases on conformity to established ethical and social principles and awareness of one's social position in a hierarchy.

This process, however, has been understood in different ways. The last chapter, for instance, contrasted Bellow's despair with Frosh's emphasis on the exciting aspects of uncertainty, and the 'empty self' was contrasted with 'the saturated self'. Baumeister (1991), whose work we shall look at in more detail in this section, takes a relatively positive line on the changes which characterize modern times. He bases his argument on his theory that people find meaning in life by attempting to satisfy four needs. These are:

- *Purpose (or rather being purposive):* This involves having particular goals. Baumeister sees purpose as taking the form of either intrinsic 'fulfilments' which are satisfying in themselves (such as the pleasures of listening to music or playing football) or extrinsic ones aimed at achieving desired, future states.

- *Value:* This refers to the desire to justify what we do, to endow it with legitimacy.

- *Efficacy:* This need is satisfied by performing particular acts or by the understanding we feel we possess.

- *Self-worth:* This is derived from a person's sense of confidence in what he or she does and believes.

In relation to the need for efficacy, you may remember, from Chapter 4, Csikszentmihalyi's finding that 'flow' experience results from activities that are neither too easy nor too hard (in other words where the experience of control or skill is likely to be optimal).

In Chapter 3, section 1.3, discussion of work by Strickland et al. (1966) and by Langer (1983) suggested that people tend to believe that they have more control than they do. Such optimistic illusions play an important part in maintaining both their sense of efficacy and self-worth.

Baumeister examines the ways in which modern society is organized around these bases of meaning. Euro-American cultures offer an abundance of *goals* (associated with work, personal activities, projects and relationships). Because they offer scope to engage in many kinds of activity, there is much potential (even if it may not always be achieved) for experiencing *efficacy* also. And, because many different kinds of comparison can be made between people, there is considerable scope in modern Euro-American societies for ensuring a sense of *self-worth* or self-esteem (more, for example, than in a historical period or culture with more limited and fixed status hierarchies).

How far do you agree with Baumeister's assessment of the potential of Euro-American societies to meet these needs? How do social class, material disadvantage, or social inequalities, for example, affect people in relation to the goals offered in Euro-American cultures?

The critical problem for people in modern society, Baumeister argues, is society's inability to offer a firm *value* base. Because of the demise of religion and tradition, there is no longer consensus as to what constitutes good and evil. Baumeister asserts that, today, value is now sought in the *personal sphere,* in, for example, achievement at work, in relationships and, in particular, in the development of self. In Baumeister's view, self or identity becomes particularly significant as a source of meaning because our sense of self-worth and our sense of efficacy also depend on the way we think about our self.

Baumeister considers that other aspects of life have become subordinated to the development and creation of identity. The value of work, for example, comes to reside more in its potential for defining the kind of person we are, rather than in pursuing it for its own sake, as a source of income or survival, or even for achieving a sense of efficacy or self-worth. Relationships too become an important part of the creation of identity, and intimacy a means of facilitating reflexive awareness. The effect of all this is that, in the modern world, the enhancement of identity in itself becomes a value base, a moral ground (see Box 7.1 overleaf). If work or a relationship ceases to be fulfilling or conducive to the development of self, this is considered to be justification in itself for moving on.

As Taylor (1992) has cogently pointed out, one consequence of having the self as a value base is inevitably a *moral relativism*. People accept that everybody, like themselves, has the right to espouse whatever values they choose. While such relativism may at times appear to result from an inability to make moral distinctions, in fact it is, as Taylor emphasizes, deliberately asserted by the modern person as a moral position.

BOX 7.1 The ageing self

If the self is the primary source of meaning for people in contemporary society, it follows that death must constitute a major threat. For to die is then to negate the source of meaning itself. Lasch (1978) has argued that, in the 'culture of narcissism' (which is his characterization of modern society), ageing must also present a major problem; for to grow old undermines the skills and qualities on which the flowering of identity may depend.

How far do you agree with this idea?

It might be argued that Lasch's view overemphasizes dependence on others for validation of self. Although, for some persons, self-worth is highly dependent on how people in general seem to view them, for others it rests much more on self-assessment or on the regard only of 'kindred spirits'. Lasch's view of the problem of ageing also assumes an ageist position that denies acknowledgement of the qualities of older people. As Laslett (1989) has made clear, there is no reason why the meaningful construction of personal identity should not continue until very late in life, perhaps to the point of death, although it may gradually come to take a somewhat different form. In his conception of the eight ages of man, Erikson has suggested that the final stage of life revolves round the polarity of 'integrity', which he regards as accepting one's life as it is ('as the accidental coincidence of but one life cycle with but one segment of history'), as opposed to the 'despair' of continuing to try to make your life other than it is. Out of the interplay between integrity and despair may emerge the fruits of our final years – the quality of wisdom (1950, p. 241).

2.2   Identity projects

The sociologist Anthony Giddens (1991) also accepts that the particular feature of the 'late modern' age (the term he uses to designate the present time in which we live) is the loosening of the patterning of lives which might be found in more traditional societies. Late modernity has become what he calls a time of high 'reflexivity'. Giddens defines 'self-identity' as 'the self as reflexively understood by the person in terms of her or his biography' (1991, p. 53). His idea that, in late modern society, identity has become a 'reflexive project' is consistent with Baumeister's view discussed in section 2.1 that the construction of self is increasingly being turned to as a source of interest and meaning. Today, 'each of us ... lives a biography reflexively organized in terms of flows of social and psychological information about possible ways of life ... "How shall I live?" has to be answered in day-to-day decisions about how to behave, what to wear and what to eat and many other things ...' (ibid., p. 14). Giddens points out the increasing importance to our lives in late modern society of what he calls *abstract expert systems* such as psychotherapy. But he does not necessarily regard the increasing use of counselling and psychotherapy as due to increased anxiety levels in late modern society, nor as simply a therapeutic resort for a saturated or empty self; he sees them rather as a further expression of the reflexivity of the self.

BOX 7.2   Identity projects

The Oxford philosopher and social psychologist Rom Harré (1983) has similarly used the term 'identity projects' to refer to efforts to achieve self-directed development and expression of self. Such identity projects may take the form of the pursuit of fame or status or recognition of some kind. Or they may be concerned with more personal aspects of ourselves and the way we think about ourselves regardless of others' opinions. This may involve developing our potentials to create and to relate to others, or enriching our experience and understanding (cf. Maslow's (1973) idea of self-actualization).

In a world of alternative life-style options, Giddens argues, *life-planning* assumes special importance: 'Life plans are the substantial content of the reflexively organized trajectory of the self. Life-planning is a means of preparing a course of future actions mobilized in terms of the self's biography' (1991, p. 85). We construct our lives as part of the project of creating our identity. He argues that this is not limited to the affluent. It is true of everybody in late modern society, however poor or restricted their lives may be. We are '... virtually obliged to explore novel modes of activity, with regard to ... children, sexual relations and friendships. Such an exploration, although it might not be discursively articulated as such, implies a reflexive shaping of self-identity' (ibid., p. 86). This poses at least two problems:

1   To pursue reflexive life projects in a context of poverty and deprivation, Giddens asserts, can make the task '... an almost insupportable burden, a source of despair rather than self-enrichment' (p. 86).

2   Another problem in late modern society is the trivialization of the construction of identity through consumerism. Giddens quotes Bauman: 'Individual needs of personal autonomy, self-definition, authentic life or personal perfection are all translated into the need to possess, and consume, market-offered goods' (Bauman, 1989, p. 189). Identity projects become translated into the pursuit and purchase of the latest fashion, listening to trendy music, creating the ideal home.

What are your views on the following questions?

Does poverty necessarily make the task of reflexively creating the self 'an insupportable burden'?

In late modern society, are identity projects necessarily trivialized by consumerism?

Is life-planning an issue for everyone?

ACTIVITY 7.1   Spend a few moments jotting down notes on the identity projects in your life. What are they? What do they involve? Are they directed at social recognition, changing your physical appearance, increasing your sense of self-worth or efficacy, at self-actualization, or some other goal?

If you are above the age of fifty, do you feel that life holds as much, if not more, scope for identity projects than it held before?

2.3   The saturated self

Like Giddens and Baumeister, Kenneth Gergen (1991), whose concept of 'the saturated self' was introduced in the last chapter, sees the self firmly rooted in the conditions of contemporary society. As a result of the greater complexity of society and new technologies for communication and travel, we are becoming increasingly saturated with 'the voices of humankind'. Newspapers, television and video-recorders, radio, easy long-distance travel, computer communications, junk mail and even answerphones engulf us with a plethora of images and information and the views and opinions of others. Gergen's illustrations of 'random moments from contemporary life' include:

> You find your mailbag stuffed with correspondence – advertisements for local events, catalogues from mail-order houses, political announcements, offers for special prizes, bills, and, just maybe, a letter …

> You try to arrange a meeting with a business colleague in New York. She is attending a meeting in Caracas. When she returns next week you will be in Memphis. When all attempts to arrange a mutually convenient meeting place fail, you settle for a long-distance phone meeting in the evening.

> *(Gergen, 1991, p. 48)*

Most of the technologies on which this information explosion is based have emerged only in the last twenty or so years and Gergen believes that their impact in postmodern society will lead to changes in our consciousness.

ACTIVITY 7.2

If you are in any doubt what saturation refers to, switch on the radio, flick through the channels on your TV, or pick up a newspaper. Note how they present a constant stream of information, going from one thing to another, opinions and the reporting of fact, from news of tragedy to triviality, from commercials to sports, without a moment's pause.

Social saturation changes our consciousness, Gergen believes, because it results in the fragmentation of both our self-conceptions and relationships. It produces what he calls the condition of 'multiphrenia', a 'new constellation of feelings and sensibilities, a new pattern of self-consciousness involving the splitting of the individual into a multiplicity of self-investments' (ibid., pp. 73–4). Critical to Gergen's argument is the proposal that:

> … social saturation brings with it a general loss in our assumption of true and knowable selves. As we absorb multiple voices, we find that each 'truth' is relativized by our simultaneous consciousness of compelling alternatives. We come to be aware that each truth about ourselves is a construction of the moment, true only for a given time and within certain relationships.
>
> *(ibid., p. 16)*

Gergen links this new consciousness with the postmodernist movement in contemporary literary criticism. This views language as 'dominated by ideological investments, its usage governed by social convention, and its content guided by literary style'. In this view, language does not express an underlying reality; it creates this in itself.

In relation to this conception of language, you may remember the views of discourse analysts discussed in section 4 of Chapter 5 and the notion of discourse as action-orientated and constitutive of social life.

Gergen extends this notion of the construction of social realities through language to the self:

> With the spread of postmodern consciousness, we see the demise of personal definition, reason, authority, commitment, trust, the sense of authenticity, sincerity, belief in leadership, depth of feeling, and faith in progress. In their stead, an open slate emerges on which persons may inscribe, erase, and rewrite their identities as the ever-shifting, ever-expanding, and incoherent network of relationships invites or permits.
>
> *(ibid., p. 228)*

For Gergen, in this postmodern world 'life itself may become a form of play, in which one transforms ventures into adventures, purpose into performance, and desire into drama' (ibid., p. 193). And he sees its bright as well as its negative sides. For him, the way to the future is in a move from individualism to 'relational realities' and the life of community; and also in what he calls the 'free play of being' which involves 'experimentation with being, risk, and absurdity' (ibid., pp. 248–9). In therapy, for example, he argues that the goal should be to play with different ways of thinking about the self: for one kind of story about the self will work in some contexts or relationships but not at all in others. The postmodern therapy advocated by Gergen would open clients up to a multiplicity of possible personal narratives to free them from the limiting constructions imposed on them in their past.

Gergen contrasts postmodern consciousness with earlier romantic and modernist conceptions of the self. In the former, depth of feeling, purpose, passion and commitment were paramount. Key notions here were the importance of authenticity and sincerity. An individual's duty, as it was for romantic poets such as Coleridge and Wordsworth, was to work out the nature of their experience, to feel passionately, and act coherently on this basis. In modernist movements, in contrast, reason, morality and the assumption of our ability to progress were stressed. These kinds of views were held, for example, by scientists and social reformers who saw their actions as contributing to the march of human progress, increased control and knowledge, and who saw these as the goals on which a life should be based. Both romantic and modernist views are premised on the assumption of an underlying stability of being, in contrast to postmodern consciousness which emphasizes fragmentation and uncertainty about absolute values. For Gergen, a critical issue in contemporary life is that while, as a culture, we are entering into postmodern consciousness, as individuals we nevertheless continue to live our lives with romantic and modernist images of self. While these may be voices that we adopt on occasion in the free play of being, neither is consistent, he considers, with the uncertainties of the postmodern world.

To what extent do you agree with Gergen's analysis of the postmodern condition? These kinds of diagnoses have become fashionable in recent years and, given the complexity of society, history and social change, they are difficult to evaluate. What has changed and how change should be evaluated are matters of intense debate in sociology, psychology, social theory and cultural studies. A key question is whether you find these interpretations of modern life useful for making sense of the changes in your own life, perhaps in comparison to the lives of your parents or grandparents? To what extent has your life become multiphrenic? How fragmented are the value bases you use to guide your decisions? Do you feel a loss of authenticity, of depth of feelings and of faith in progress? Do you consider that you can, as Gergen suggests, 'inscribe, erase, and rewrite [your] identities as the ever-shifting, ever-expanding, and incoherent network of [your] relationships invites or permits'? Or are there stable, immutable features in your sense of personal being? You may prefer the visions of life Gergen describes as modernist or romantic, but do beliefs in real experience, passion and progress still fit with the kind of society in which you live?

Is there a new postmodern self for the new postmodern society? (Source: The Guardian)

It is important to question whether analyses of the postmodern condition are pertinent to the majority of people in European and American societies. As we implied earlier, in discussing Baumeister's analysis, we may certainly throw at Gergen that most denigrating criticism in the formidable armoury of the social sciences: is not his analysis simply a product of his class background? As Smith (1994) rather dryly comments, 'Gergen's examples suggest that he may be unduly focused on the experiences of the academic and corporate jet set to which he belongs' (pp. 407–8). Smith questions how relevant such conceptions of saturated, empty or fragmented selves are to the concerns of 'children growing up in central city poverty and in fractured families, of HIV-infected people around the world facing the prospect of AIDS, of impoverished multitudes crowding against immigration barriers and sometimes leaking through them' (ibid., p. 406). He argues that 'it is the experience of the Euro-American élite that is evoked when we apply the label "postmodern" to our present predicament' (ibid., p. 406). Other commentators argue that, while the diagnoses of the postmodern condition or late modern age offered by authors such as Gergen and Baumeister are accurate, more attention needs to be paid to power relations in society which suggest that people's experiences of modern conditions in different social groups, and across the globe, will be uneven (Sampson, 1993; Haraway, 1990). Questions can also be raised about whether the particular practices that Gergen emphasizes – technological developments in communication and travel – are necessarily the most formative ones for many people in contemporary society.

Although Giddens, Baumeister and Gergen conceive of the self in contemporary society in slightly different ways, use different terminology (postmodern, modern, late modern age), and emphasize different aspects of contemporary experience, all agree that there has been a shift in Euro-American societies from a more constricted, stable and coherent existence to cultures characterized by uncertainty and change. All note the emergence of individualism and the increased emphasis on the self as a source of meaning. What are the implications of these analyses of the modern self?

Giddens argues that one important political consequence is reflected in the movement from what he calls emancipatory politics to life politics. Emancipatory politics was based on the traditional questions of justice, participation and equality; while life politics refers to questions about 'how we should live': questions which, although they may now be explored on a political and global level, have their source in concepts like personal growth and self-actualization. Recent social movements such as feminism and the development of environmental pressure groups thus combine emancipatory themes with broader questions about lifestyle and desirable forms of identity:

> Feminism can more properly be regarded as opening up the sphere of life politics – although emancipatory concerns remain fundamental to women's movements. Feminism, at least in its contemporary form, has been more or less obliged to give priority to the question of self-identity. 'Women who want more than family life', it has been aptly remarked, 'make the personal political with every step they take away from home'. In so far as women increasingly 'take the step' outside, they contribute to processes of emancipation. Yet feminists soon came to see that, for the emancipated woman, questions of identity became of pre-eminent importance.
>
> *(Giddens, 1991, p. 216)*

What do these developments suggest about one possible role for psychology in the future?

There are also moral and ethical implications of these changes in identity. As Taylor has pointed out, the word 'authentic' has come to refer to the idea that the 'self' is the source of value, and that to be authentic means getting in touch with the 'true' self. However, its existential meaning refers not to this but to acknowledging the experiential realities and conditions of our existence – in particular, that we are capable of choice and changing the way things are, and can play some part in creating who we are. And, as Taylor goes on to assert:

> ... in articulating this ideal over the last two centuries, Western culture has identified one of the important potentialities of human life. Like other facets of modern individualism – for instance, that which calls on us to work out our own opinions and beliefs for ourselves – authenticity points us towards a more self-responsible form of life. It allows us to live (potentially) a fuller and more differentiated life, because more fully appropriated as our own. ... at its best authenticity allows a richer mode of existence ...
>
> *(Taylor, 1991, p. 74)*

Claims about the modern self also raise epistemological issues – issues about the status of knowledge claims – and these become particularly salient as we come to the end of this book and begin to think about the relationship between the diverse perspectives we have been considering. If you remember, Gergen argues that, 'With the spread of postmodern consciousness, we see the demise of ... faith in progress' (1991, p. 228). In this view, science and the concepts through which we might try to understand the modern self become relativized. In the face of such a postmodern challenge, however, Smith argues that, 'the crux of the matter is whether it is still possible to retain some toehold to sustain the old human struggle toward truth, goodness, and beauty as meaningful ideals' (1994, p. 409). Arguing from a 'modernist' (rather than a postmodern) position, Smith maintains that 'truth claims cannot be reduced to rhetoric and politics, even when we become more alert to the role of rhetoric and politics in our would-be scientific discourse' (ibid., p. 409).

> Are there truths about the self that we can strive for in social psychology? Are there fundamental psychological processes which we may hope to discover? Or is it, as Gergen asserts, that in postmodern times 'the very concept of an "authentic" self with knowable characteristics recedes from view. The fully saturated self becomes no self at all' (Gergen, 1991, p. 7). We would like you to keep these questions in mind as we proceed.

In further evaluating the work of Giddens, Baumeister and Gergen, you might like to look back now at each of the perspectives presented in previous chapters, review their main characteristics and consider if and how they might relate to the ideas about the modern self presented by these three theorists. In essence, they are making assertions about the nature of consciousness and experience in modern societies, and these psychological claims are as open to debate as the sociological aspects of their theories. In Chapter 6, for example, questions were raised about whether the multiphrenic or fragmented modern self is so new – does this conception simply describe the essentially split and defended nature of the mind described in Chapter 6? Giddens, Gergen and, to some extent, Baumeister see identity as defined by historical, social and cultural conditions, and in this respect their work meshes with social constructionist arguments presented in Chapter 5. But are the experiences of the modern self described above the mere products of changes in Euro-American culture? How might the experiential perspective described in Chapter 4 react to this point? Is it rather the case, as existentialists might well retort, that the conditions of late modern society have merely thrown into relief the fundamental groundlessness of our existence and our own existential role in constructing ourselves? Do they merely reveal to us the basic elements of the human condition? What other kinds of critique do you think might be levelled at these analyses from the standpoint of the perspectives you have encountered in this volume? Could you describe these as critiques from romantic or modernist conceptions of self?

ACTIVITY 7.3

---

3 Perspectives in review

This section will review the main characteristics of the perspectives, the types of method and understanding they involve, and the contexts in which they developed, in the light of these discussions of the modern self. In this process, we shall come back to some of the points raised in Activity 7.3 above.

3.1 The biological perspective

Chapter 2 considered how the study of biology might help our under-standing of the self. It drew on a wide range of biological research including ideas about the influence of genes and hormones on behaviour and the relevance of an evolutionary perspective for understanding social behaviour (as well as for understanding the origins of our physical characteristics). Chapter 2 looked at the implications which studies of brain malfunction (for example, studies of blindsight and split brains) might have for our understanding of personal being. It also looked at the contribution of a biological perspective to understanding addiction, a behaviour pattern with profound personal and social implications.

The origins of the *biological perspective* are self-evident. It is based on research and ideas in sciences such as physiology and ethology (the study of animals in their natural environments). In effect, it treats the person in the social world as an example of just another species in its habitat (albeit one with rather special attributes). At the *functional* level, it utilizes concepts and principles from evolutionary theory and, at the *causal* level, it is concerned with the physiological processes that underlie behaviour and experience.

What intellectual frameworks does this perspective provide for under-standing the nature of the modern self and what tools for analysis? The message is a mixed one. On the one hand, a biological perspective emphasizes *continuity* in some aspects of basic psychological functioning and the *universal* nature of these aspects as opposed to the kinds of diver-sity and cultural influences celebrated by the social constructionist per-spective, for example. A biological perspective also notes our dependence on a functioning brain (if that brain is damaged then some kinds of social action are entirely ruled out) and the vulnerability (to disease or accident, for example) of the embodied self in whatever culture or period we reside. When considering these inbuilt aspects and possibilities, bio-logical research questions whether social practices determine all that we are and can become. Sociobiology presents perhaps the strongest form of this argument. Sociobiologists would argue that there are certain con-stancies or parameters in being human (such as our genetic inheritance) which can remain largely unaffected by the culture in which we live. There are certain features of the way we behave and relate to others which are not simply abandoned as a result of the changing social context. Here, then, we find strong reservations as to whether radically new modes of self can come into existence without biological, evolutionary change.

On the other hand, Chapter 2 also emphasized the ways in which our bodies and our social circumstances intertwine. A major focus of the chapter was the subtle and complex two-way interaction between biological and social processes. This interaction was illustrated by studies of emotional arousal (e.g. Schachter and Singer, 1962), pain, and heart disease (e.g. Williams, 1989). Remember, too, the brief discussion of depression? Research on consciousness described in the chapter emphasized the *flexibility* generated by our nervous systems, and their social responsiveness. One of the striking features of the synaptic organization of the brain and nervous system is its plasticity: 'as well as being a highly complex structure capable of an almost infinite array of electrical and chemical activity, the brain possesses the powerful attribute of mental plasticity; it can make and break nerve connections over a period of intellectual training – anything from remembering a route home to learning a Mozart symphony' (Connor, 1995). The strength of connections and their nature are thus established through *experience* from conception onwards, and from this plasticity emerges the possibility of social evolution and multiple ways of being in the social world. From this point of view, Gergen's notion of the multiphrenic self or Giddens's notion of the reflexive self characteristic of the late modern age are as biologically plausible as the more integrated and grounded identities thought to characterize 'pre-modern' periods.

In an important sense, our ideas about what it means to be human will guide biological research. If identity is defined through concepts of agency and self-awareness, then studies of consciousness can consider how those properties might have evolved. Different perspectives on the self could suggest different foci of attention for biological investigations. It is interesting to ponder on what a biology of consciousness proceeding from a psychodynamic or social constructionist account of self and identity might look like, for example. What underlying processes would be looked for in this case? Unfortunately, the biological perspective and the embodied nature of our experience are often neglected in courses in social psychology. Partly this is due to the tendency to compartmentalize different areas of research so that those with skills in physiology rarely study social theory and vice versa, and partly it is because of the assumption that consideration of biology is marginal to understanding social psychological aspects of people because these are primarily an expression of social and symbolic processes.

The methodology emphasized in Chapter 2 was that of the natural sciences. This type of approach is often called 'positivistic'. Positivism in psychology tends to assume realism – that there is a world of behaviour out there which can be accurately described. Its method is to try to specify knowledge about human behaviour in what is regarded as a scientific form; in other words, basing it only on investigations which employ measurement and, if possible, experiments. As we look at the challenges for social psychology in the future, this approach reminds us of the powerful technologies of investigation developed in the past. As such, the biological researcher is perhaps more likely to side with Smith's arguments in section 2 above, and with the continued search for truth rather than with Gergen's relativistic and postmodern view of the demise of faith in scientific progress towards authentic knowledge.

3.2   The cognitive experimentalist perspective

The author of Chapter 3 makes it clear that, while 'the term "an experimentalist perspective" applies easily enough to the contents of this chapter', the range of methods in the studies drawn on is not confined to experiments. He defines the key characteristics of this experimentalist approach as an emphasis 'on measurement, on reliability and on objectivity. As in the other sciences, the goals include establishing generalizations and making predictions' (see Chapter 3, section 1, pp. 92–3). When the goal of the experimental social psychologist is to establish fundamental laws about the ways in which we behave (like laws in the natural sciences such as gravity), then this perspective is often described as taking a *nomothetic* approach.

Chapter 3 made clear the value of experiments for understanding the ways in which people make sense of and relate to the social world. It also illustrated the value of experiments in developing and refining hypotheses. Experimentation and the nomothetic approach are based on particular assumptions about epistemology and the nature of the person. These styles of investigation assume, for example, that the analysis of causes is the best mode of explanation in social psychology and, to some extent, they presume the existence of an underlying 'reality' to investigate. Working from these assumptions, experimentation usually requires the operationalization of the subject-matter being dealt with (i.e. specifying it in observable or measurable form).

There is an immediate contrast to Chapter 2, in that the experimentalist perspective is defined essentially in terms of its methodological approach. In biology, this would be taken for granted: there is little or no dispute about adopting the methods of natural science. In the case of psychology, however, alternative methodological approaches are possible. Making clear which one is being used is one way to define a perspective. In Chapter 3, the focus of interest is on how we make sense of other people, ourselves and the social world around us (in the context of this perspective, this is usually called *social cognition*). And as we saw in the subsequent chapters, this is a topic that can be and is approached in a range of very different ways.

The use of an experimentalist perspective in social psychology is, of course, by no means confined to work on attribution and cognitive style. For example, experiments on social interaction are discussed in Miell and Dallos (eds) (1996), and experiments on groups are discussed in

Wetherell (ed.) (1996), especially in Chapter 1 by Brown. In fact, the experimentalist approach has been (and probably still is) the prevailing perspective used in social psychology, especially in the USA.

So what kinds of generalizations has experimentalist work on the interpreting self produced? One example mentioned in Chapter 3 is the prototype explanation of the ways in which we categorize events in the social world. Experiments (see, for example, Lalljee et al., 1993, in section 2.3 of Chapter 3) provide supporting evidence of the importance of this way of organizing information and its centrality in the process of interpretation. We are shown that such understanding has useful applications. Knowing that people interpret their own behaviour in this particular manner makes it possible, for example, to design procedures to help patients suffering from panic attacks (see the work of Clark and colleagues discussed in Chapter 3, section 2.4.2). The effectiveness of such interventions can then be established by further experiments.

> Can you remember the cognitive-behaviour therapy that Clark used to help patients suffering from panic attacks? If not, you might like to refer back to Chapter 3, section 2.4.2.

Another example of a generalization produced by experimental work on cognitive processes involved in interpretation is what has been called the fundamental attribution error. As Lalljee puts it, 'People frequently see outcomes as caused by the person rather than the context or situation in which they occur' (section 3.1, p.106). Experiments are used here not only to establish this effect but to explore the conditions under which it holds. Thus, it is less likely to apply in explaining our own behaviour (especially if this has had negative consequences, a phenomenon known as 'self-serving attributions'). Again, the work of Seligman on learned helplessness shows how this kind of understanding can have practical value and be of help in treating some patients suffering from depression.

> Do you remember how attribution style may be related to depression? Can you remember the kind of treatment that was used in cases of this kind?

Chapter 3 emphasized the importance of taking social factors and cultural context into account in understanding both the ways in which we conceptualize ourselves and the ways in which we explain the actions of others. The studies of cultural influence cited here were not strictly experiments but they nevertheless included measures or categories of some kind. They show how, by methods such as categorizing subjects into groups and comparing these groups (as, for example, in Van den Heuvel's (1992) study of Moroccan and Dutch children living in Amsterdam), an experimentalist approach can be brought to bear even in research on cultures and on the psychological effects of recent social changes.

If we think about the characteristics of the modern self in light of this perspective, we again obtain a mixed message. On the one hand, this approach points to potential regularities in the way people interact with and interpret their social world which result from fixed features of the information-processing system, such as categorization. These perennial features of the interpretative process suggest a solidity and continuity to human reactions in the face of rapid change. On the other hand, the discussion of cultural influences on cognitive style suggests that there is enormous flexibility here, too. Future research in this area is likely to place even more emphasis on understanding changes in cognitive style which arise as a consequence of new information technologies, new forms of work, and new relationships with machines such as the computer.

3.3   The experiential perspective

The humanistic perspective in psychology was very much a reaction in the mid-twentieth century to the dominance of the experimentalist paradigm in psychology. Those who began it (such as Rogers, Maslow and Kelly) argued that the experimentalist's emphasis on what could be perceived and measured could not capture the richness of human experience. They considered too that the abstract generalizations produced by experimental method were too far removed from the psychological realities of everyday life. Experimental methods also limit the kinds of behaviour that can be studied. Drawing their inspiration from phenomenology and existentialism, humanistic psychologists saw much more value for psychology in focusing on the actual experience of people. As we noted, the *experiential* perspective is the label created in Chapter 4 for a hybrid of these related approaches – phenomenological, existential and humanistic psychology. The origins of the experiential perspective, then, are very different from those of the experimentalist perspective. They are more closely related to philosophy and literature, and to counselling and experiential groups than to the natural sciences. These might be considered to be appropriate origins, for the focus here shifts from measurement and hypothesis-testing to qualitative consideration of meanings: to what people experience rather than that which can be observed by others. It is a shift also from a third-person to a first-person perspective.

While this perspective is clearly topic-based – on subjective experience and reflexive awareness – the very use of those terms implies a qualitative approach. In fact, as we noted, three kinds of method were drawn on in Chapter 4. The first was phenomenological analysis of different aspects of experience. A second approach used was to attempt to conceptualize the nature of the way in which we experience the world (e.g. drawing on concepts such as *personal constructs* or *metaphor*). The third approach was to try to stimulate the reflexive awareness of the reader about existential aspects of experience.

Can you recall two studies discussed in Chapter 4 which involved phenomenological analyses of different aspects of experience?

Which existential issues were focused on in Chapter 4?

Note that work on the nature of identity in modern and postmodern societies reviewed in section 2 above also develops a strong phenomenological focus. In effect, authors such as Giddens and Gergen are developing arguments about how recent social changes might have affected our experience of ourselves, of others and of social life. What are the main changes they recognize? How do they describe the phenomenology of modern life? It is, of course, difficult to conduct thought experiments across history, but which aspects of our experience do you think might be open to change in this way and which feel to you to be fundamental and more resistant to change?

The experiential perspective is premised on two assumptions which it attempted to demonstrate both by rational analysis and appeal to experience. One is that subjective experience (conscious awareness, fantasy and imagination, etc.) in itself has the capacity not only to represent but to generate. Through reflection and thought, the author argued, can come about change and novelty. The other assumption is that the human capacity for reflection on our experience (reflexiveness) can also play an important role in generating what we think, feel, do and become.

In this way, the experiential perspective is asserting that we have some capacity to create the kind of person we become. However, in addition to the idea of *personal construction,* the existential approach assumes that there are certain features of human existence (e.g. finiteness, the capacity for choice) which are fundamental and apply to everybody (even though we may choose to ignore them). This view would suggest that, despite social changes in recent years, these fundamental aspects of being human are carried from the past into the future giving a robust basis for ethical, political and moral life. An important concept in this work is the notion of *situated freedom.* People are undoubtedly influenced by their social circumstances, but within and through these they are also free to organize and construct their lives as they see fit.

The experiential perspective would question the radical malleability assumed in some discussions of the self in modern society and would ask whether changes in technology can have such a major effect on consciousness. The experiential position sees considerable commonality of experience between the selves of different times and cultures: is the ecstatic experience of the modern disco dancer, it might ask, so far removed from the feelings created in the distant past by celebrations around an ancient fire? While it accepts that there may be cultural differences in degree of emphasis on existential concerns, it points out that death and the need to choose confront us all. (Faced with the problem of the saturated self, one choice open to us is, of course, to reduce the saturation we encounter by resisting the trivia of newspapers, portable phones and TV!).

Given the model of the person it presents, with notions such as autonomy and growth, as well as its origins in both philosophy and experiential work with people, it is perhaps not surprising that the main thrust of this perspective has been more in applied areas such as counselling and organizational psychology than in scientific research. Like the biological perspective, it has traditionally featured far less in academic social psychology than its experimental or social constructionist counterparts.

3.4   The social constructionist perspective

The social constructionist perspective presented in Chapter 5 moved the site of debate from personal constructions to social constructions. For the social constructionist, the context is much more than an 'influence'. Rather, social process and practices are given a central role in constituting people's experience and actions. This perspective argues that the boundaries of the person and the social context cannot be easily separated from each other: 'The person, consciousness, mind and the self are seen as social through and through' (section 2.1, p. 222).

Can you remember what is meant by the notion of the self as discursive? How did Vygotsky characterize the relationship between the child and the social context?

This perspective marks a shift from a *psychological social psychology* where the focus is on the individual (biological attributes, aspects of consciousness, processes of interpretation) to a *sociological social psychology* where the focus is on the social processes which construct the individual. The authors argued that, 'in a profound sense, the self is *socially constructed*' (section 1, p. 220). They went on to demonstrate how social construction operates by examining, first, the cultural basis of self-understanding. Remember, for example, the contrasts between Japanese and North American self-descriptions discussed by Markus and Kitayama? The importance of language and discourse in the cultural shaping of the individual was highlighted. It was argued that language and discourse construct social and individual realities. Research, for example on narratives of anger and aggression in a South Baltimore community, demonstrates the context and mores which children internalize as they become social beings. The work of Mead and Vygotsky, as well as modern discourse analysis, focuses our attention on the dialogic processes involved in both conversations and learning language, and on how joint and mutual constructions emerge dialectically in the process of interactions.

The claims of this perspective encourage a debate with many of the assumptions made by the other perspectives. For example, where the focus of the other perspectives assumes an 'individual', the social constructionist approach calls into question the notion of a consistent, self-contained person implied by this concept, replacing it with the idea of the distributed self which regards a person as made up by all the different kinds of interactions he or she engages in, by the 'sum and swarm of participations in social life' (section 2.1, p. 223).

Like the experiential perspective, the social constructionist approach also questions the usefulness and validity of experimentalists' attempts to find abstract generalizations about human behaviour. It raises doubts, however, about the idea of a self-contained and private world of subjective experience assumed by the experientialist, and is interested in the social history of talk about existential needs rather than seeing these as fundamental aspects of human existence. While biological psychologists may tend to place more stress on the universal nature of processes underlying, say, emotional expression, there are some important points of continuity with the biological perspective as developed in Chapter 2. Social constructionists examine, for example, the way in which bodily experience will be interpreted by the persons concerned and thus how interactions between the social and the biological might proceed.

Perhaps more than any other perspective, the social constructionist perspective encourages the kinds of doubts raised by Gergen and other postmodern theorists about the possibility of true knowledge independent of people's social and cultural positions. If the mind is formed through the incorporation of the social, as this approach suggests, then our attempts to make sense of social life, whether these are academic or lay, will reflect our social, cultural and historical situation. Gergen, who has been a prominent figure in the development of social constructionist thought in social psychology, has argued that social psychology is inevitably a form of history. In other words, in this view there are only situated knowledges.

3.5 The psychodynamic perspective

Chapter 6 dealt with a variety of psychodynamic approaches and demonstrated some of the ways in which psychodynamic thinking has developed since the pioneering work of Freud. But all of these approaches have one central theme: 'The unique contribution of psychodynamics, in all its versions, lies in its basic assumption: that the structure, content and dynamics of the psyche are not necessarily available to consciousness' (section 2.1, p. 286). Furthermore, the picture of the self which psychodynamics presents is fundamentally fragmented and in conflict. Indeed, the chapter suggests that the experience of a unitary, cohesive self is merely a defence.

Can you remember the four assumptions on which, Chapter 6 argues, all psychodynamic theories are based?

Who were the main psychodynamic theorists who were featured in this chapter and what were the main points of difference between them?

If social constructionism invites radical rethinking about the nature of personal experience and social life, then so too does the psychodynamic perspective. The origins which are regarded as crucial in this case are not so much the practices and interactions of the wider social contexts but specific relationships with carers and others, particularly in terms of the way these are experienced emotionally by the infant.

In contrast to the experimental approach, the emphasis in the psychodynamic approach is on defensive manoeuvres and emotions rather than the rationality of inference and attribution. This flavour, too, is carried over to ways of thinking about the self in the modern world. Remember the pathologies of modern life identified by psychodynamic theorists, such as narcissistic disorder and the schizoid personality?

In contrast to the experientialist's emphasis on conscious awareness and personal autonomy, the stress is on dynamic unconscious processes and defences against anxiety. With notions like defensive distortion, psychodynamic theorists claim that the phenomena of observed behaviour and thoughts and feelings as experienced cannot be taken at face value. We must look for their underlying, not manifest, meaning. This can only be done, they assert, with the help of interpretative psychodynamic techniques and concepts. There is concern with means for achieving personal change, but this is seen as coming through effort and understanding in opening up closed and defensive meaning systems rather than through facilitating reflexive awareness.

Although the focus here is on the unconscious residues of emotional experiences of childhood, developments in psychodynamic theorizing which are presented in Chapter 6, such as object relations theories, are very much *social* theories. As we have seen, it is the quality (or deprivation) of early relationships that are regarded as providing the basis for the adult's experience of self. This emerges from and through the emotional interplay of early relationships. Like the social constructionist position, the psychodynamic perspective casts doubt on the idea of a coherent self by placing emphasis on the complexity of internal structures of the self and on the possibility of internal conflict and fragmentation. This emphasis gives a different twist to Gergen's notion of the modern fragmented or multiphrenic self, since the micro-social world of infant experience is seen as having much more impact on the self than does social and technological change.

Again, the psychodynamic perspective would seem to cast doubt on the wisdom of depending on either observed behaviour or conscious experience (as the experimentalist and experiential perspectives respectively propose). This approach introduces new methods and topics into social psychology. The importance of delving behind free associations is discussed, for example, as well as the importance of interpreting transference, dreams and children's play. The difficulties of interpreting unconscious meanings and defensive processes which are not readily accessible are highlighted.

The core problem with material which involves interpretation of any kind is in finding ways of assessing its value or usefulness. A variety of criteria for assessment have been suggested in the preceding chapters, including plausibility, seeming consistency with available evidence, logical coherence, the use to which the interpretation can be put, and appeal to experience. None of these, however, in the experimentalist's view, offers quite the same possibility for consensus as is the case with experimental

results. Nevertheless, psychodynamic (and experiential and social constructionist researchers) would argue that, in spite of such limitations,
some kind of interpretative approach is essential because to understand
the person in a social world requires getting to grips in some way with
the web of meanings that constitutes personal life and social worlds.

ACTIVITY 7.4

At some stage you may wish to review each of the perspectives in the
preceding chapters and make notes on which factors they emphasize as
producing *personal and social change*. For the perspectives are not just
intellectual frameworks, but viewpoints with crucial moral and political
ramifications. As well as being academic productions or exercises in
scholarship, they have a personal significance as we try to make sense of our
lives.

One feature, for example, of almost all social psychological theories is that they
can impact on us, their subject-matter, by changing the ways in which we view
ourselves and hence the ways in which we act. As Chapter 2 illustrated,
whether alcoholism is conceived of as a disease or as a reasonable way of
adapting to difficult circumstances can have implications for the self-concept
and behaviour of alcoholics, as well as affecting the way in which they will be
regarded by others.

The position of each perspective should be considered in terms of the degree
to which it regards personal and social change as possible and what
it considers to be the key processes by means of which change can come
about.

4   The relationship between perspectives

It is important to realize that the idea of *perspectives* is itself a construction that we are using to distinguish some of the different kinds of
approach you can find in psychology. We believe that the five particular
perspectives included in this book are a useful categorization of different
ways of looking at and trying to understand the self. They enable us to
appreciate the very different ways of making sense of social behaviour
which you can find in social psychology. They also help, as we saw in
the last section, to draw attention to significant differences in methodology and epistemology (forms of understanding) which are encountered.
However, not all theories or approaches in social psychology fit neatly
into one or other of these perspectives, and the theories and research
covered in this book could have been aligned and contrasted in different
ways.

Presenting the five perspectives in order may have made it seem like a gradual progression to more enlightened views. Such an impression may have been intensified by the assertion that the last two chapters imply radical rethinking of assumptions made by other perspectives. However, such a progression is not intended. The earlier perspectives, had they appeared later in the sequence, could equally well have questioned the premises of the others. We have seen examples of how, in some cases, one perspective has represented a reaction to perceived limitations of another. It is useful generally to see each of the perspectives in the context of its historical or intellectual origins.

In this section, the focus is on the question of how *the different perspectives interrelate*. We have seen how varied the perspectives are, operating with different assumptions, with different concepts and methods, and presenting different pictures of the relation between the person and the social world. How then should we make sense of this diversity?

4.1 Towards complex descriptions

While accepting that the perspectives look differently at the self and social life, one way of regarding them is to see them as complementary, as revealing different facets of our complex subject-matter. Thus, a fruitful way of proceeding is to begin working on syntheses and dialogues between these approaches. As we saw in the discussion of alcoholism in Chapter 2, a simple biological or any other kind of explanation just does not suffice on its own. We need to take into account not just possible genetic factors but also the social situation, personality factors, and ways in which the person thinks about him or herself.

If we combine, for example, our experience that we can change and create ourselves (as emphasized by the experiential perspective) with awareness of the constraints on who we can become (stressed by social constructionist and psychodynamic perspectives), we throw into relief the potentially tragic dimension of the experience of self.

Again, if we combine the notion from social constructionism and psychodynamics that we are constituted by different 'voices' with the experiential idea that we have self-awareness and choice, this leads to a conception of self as 'a cast of characters who are acting out a dramatic narrative, the unfolding plot that guides them being the generator of our concept of self' (Bruner, 1995). While both genes and one's historical epoch perform crucial functions as 'editors' and 'playwrights', they do not predetermine our unfolding selves. Rather, it is more like a play where the players get caught up in the action and improvise as they go. In other words, we are guided in our improvising and choice of different characters in different situations by the narratives we construct ourselves about the particular kinds of self we deem ourselves to be.

What happens if we try to apply all of the different understandings offered by our perspectives to one person or problem? This might be in order to make sense of one person's life history – the central decisions, relationships and trajectories that make up a life. Or perhaps it is a therapeutic issue – a question of counselling someone unsure of their future and wishing to make sense of their past. Perhaps it is an exercise in prediction – given a child raised in this social context, with these parents, with these opportunities and these limits, this temperament and biological constitution, what will be the result? Perhaps it is a problem in human relations, in management, in educational psychology, in group work, and so on. How do we produce a good description, a description on which one can move forward, from the different understandings presented in this book?

Let us take a more detailed example – how might psychologists understand depression and work with depressed people? We could begin with the *experiential* approach. Here is a set of concepts and methods orientated precisely to this issue of producing good descriptions of people's phenomenological states, introspecting on a moment-to-moment basis, recording constructs, choices, the order, framework, flow and disorder of a mind. We could also explore if the feelings of depression seemed related to concerns with existential issues – the prospect of death, for example, or a sense of meaninglessness or confusion and uncertainty over choices to be made. The existential aspect of this approach would encourage us to appeal to the self-awareness of the person concerned to confront such questions and perhaps to change his or her usual style of response and thus the feelings this creates. We might also usefully apply attribution theory and *experimental research* on cognitive style. Does this person, for example, suffer from the sequential cognitive and information-processing biases described as 'learned helplessness'? Is there a regularity here in attributional style and, if so, what are the consequences of any such regularities? If we found evidence that there was a tendency to explain negative events in terms of internal, stable and global causes (the pattern associated with depression), we could then use cognitive therapy to try to produce change in style of attribution. We might ask questions too about the amount of control in life situations which the person perceives him or herself to possess. We could then go on to consider the contribution of the *psychodynamic* theorist. What defensive manoeuvres can we recognize in the phenomenological record and the cognitive profile? What pattern of object relations in early childhood might have led to the emotional feelings now being experienced? Are there features in the person's current situation or relationships that may be stirring unconscious memories of these early experiences? In such cases, it would be the catalyst of psychodynamic therapy that would need to be applied. *Social constructionist* theorists consulted for their views might look for clues in the socially constructed nature of this person's identity. Is this a woman or is it a man? Ethnicity, culture, class, and community – how do these interpenetrate to produce this set of internal narratives and these particular shifting voices of the mind? Are they likely to lead to feelings of depression because they imply conflict or powerlessness perhaps? Solutions here may require changing the immediate social or political context. *Biologically-oriented psychologists,* in their turn, would bring to bear what is known about the biochemical and neural reactions implicated in the states of mind we recognize as depression, such as cortisol level. Biochemical interventions in the form of taking drugs may be recommended as a support at least.

It is not that these approaches are all necessarily relevant to any one individual case of depression, but rather that one or more may be involved, and that the fullest understanding of what is going on is likely to come from taking into account the understandings offered by all. Thus, Kelly (1955) regards theories or perspectives as having a *focus of convenience* (that is, what they deal with best) and a *range of convenience* (implying that some aspects may be outside their scope). It therefore makes sense to interrelate the different foci and ranges that each offers. In other words, there is a great richness here and potential for many interconnections, conversations and joint investigations. The danger of laying out perspectives one after the other is that this potential for cross-fertilization is minimized and underplayed. Synthesis, the search for relationships, and the complementary basis of the perspectives is one answer to diversity, since all the perspectives agree that multiple influences are involved in human conduct, and these will include biology, early development, cognitive processes, reflexive awareness and agency, and relationships and social influences.

4.2   Working with 'non-negotiables'

Although such interrelated or complex approaches might seem to hold much promise, in practice communication and attempts at shared understanding between the different perspectives in social psychology (and in psychology more generally) have often been limited. One reason for this is that, in the context of professional communication, any account will be implicitly evaluated in terms of the assumptions held by the intellectual community concerned. Only certain kinds of method (for example, experimental evidence or psychodynamic interpretation) will be deemed acceptable. Other forms of understanding not conforming to the pattern favoured may be quite simply dismissed out of hand.

Another problem is that conversations between theorists and the investigation of complex interactions are also likely to throw up a number of 'non-negotiables' or points of possibly irreconcilable dispute between perspectives.

ACTIVITY 7.5   Before proceeding, make a list of some of these likely non-negotiables or points of conflict between perspectives.

An obvious one which occurs to us concerns the existence of the dynamic unconscious or the idea that people's emotions, intentions, desires and actions are determined by habitual states of mind which are inaccessible to reflection. For the existential writer, Jean-Paul Sartre, whose existential philosophy is related to the experiential perspective outlined in Chapter 4, the notion of a determining unconscious was something to be resisted. Why? Because such a notion challenges the idea of individual autonomy and responsibility and the claims developed in Chapter 4 for 'situated freedom'. Sartre argued that when people fail to recognize their responsibility and capacity for change and self-creation, they are acting in 'bad faith' or inauthentically. The concept of a dynamic and determining unconscious, however, suggests that the idea of personal autonomy based on self-awareness may be illusory.

The social constructionist theorist shares the psychodynamic researcher's scepticism about the degree to which we can be aware of ourselves, but for different reasons. Chapter 5 suggested that another reason why we might not properly understand ourselves is because it is often difficult to obtain a broader perspective on the social and cultural conditions structuring our understandings. The children studied in South Baltimore, for example, come to take certain ways of expressing anger for granted, as 'normal behaviour', as a result of their socialization. Research on the Utka suggested a very different organization of the emotions. The possibility of the social construction of our mental lives suggests also the possibility of constructions of the self which are influenced by ideologies connected to broader power relations in society of which we may know little.

Although the biologist and the experimental social psychologist may have remained silent while this dispute was going on, biology has an important contribution to make to discussions of the unconscious through research on the biological processes governing the organization of attention and memory. And work on categorization and attribution also has important implications for the possibilities of accurate self-knowledge.

What, for instance, does the existence of regular attributional styles or biases in the perception of others suggest about the transparency of consciousness and the possibility of self-knowledge? (Remember the Duncan (1976) experiment which was discussed in Chapter 3, section 2.1, p. 97.)

One reason for this silence might have been despair at the introduction of a concept with such an apparently unscientific basis. Can the dynamic unconscious be observed? Can it be translated into measurable events? The experimental psychologist Eysenck (1985), for example, has been scathing about what he sees as the entirely speculative and hypothetical assumption of a dynamic unconscious. Debates over method and what is admissible evidence clearly have the potential to highlight a number of other 'non-negotiables'.

Other points of dispute which spring to mind concern the importance of early childhood in constructing adult personality. Is life-history really determined in those early years and what aspects are fixed? How important is language? In addition, there is the question of where the limits of biological and social influences are to be placed. Sociobiology extends the biological sphere quite a distance into social action; social constructionists prefer instead biological approaches which stress the malleability of the human mind because of the role this allows for symbolic and cultural processes in the construction and definition of mental states.

Faced with such 'non-negotiables' (and others you may have thought of such as different positions on autonomy and determinism), what can be done? What stances can researchers take up in relation to differences of this kind? These questions raise issues about the status of knowledge claims and questions about truth and the nature of the real. Two possible contrasting strategies can be highlighted among the many complex treatments of this issue to be found in social science and philosophy.

First, disputes between perspectives and the existence of competing accounts could be seen as an empirical problem – that is, as discrepancies which can be tackled by further research to establish the truth and the nature of what is really the case. For instance, we could see debates about the role of genetic inheritance or the existence of a dynamic unconscious as setting up contradictory hypotheses where it might be possible to perform a crucial experiment or conduct some other piece of decisive research so that one hypothesis could be rejected. And, even if no single crucial experiment is possible, we could still see these as problems which will be solved in due course as different kinds of evidence accumulate and theories develop.

One of the problems in evaluating ideas and research in this way is that the criteria and evaluative strategy to be used are likely to be different depending on the perspective you take. Where a biologist may appeal to tangible measures of physiological processes, a social constructionist may draw on an analysis of ideology and its influence. While an experimentalist may rely on the results of experiments, a phenomenological approach may involve appeal to experience.

A second stance on diversity therefore emphasizes the constructed nature of reality. Perspectives, in this view, are like stories or world views. They mediate our perceptions of reality. There is no access to reality independent of our concepts and theories: in which case, disputes are a serious matter – since they concern what might prove to be incompatible world views where there are few shared criteria for arbitration. All we can do in this situation is to try to persuade each other through argument and further research which clarifies or highlights the debates. Change will come in time (though not necessarily for the better) through the elaboration of new world views and new paradigms for scientific debate, rather than through decisive empirical solutions.

Gergen takes this position and rejects the idea that any knowledge can represent some fundamental or once and for all understanding of reality. In his view, perspectives in psychology should be seen as 'entries in the discursive practices of the world' (1991, p. 103), optional forms of discourse needing to be evaluated alongside other discourses like literature, politics or the views of people in the street. Conversation and dialogue between them are necessary and will be continual. He argues, in fact, that in this context the social psychologist has an ethical and political duty to make a contribution to the arguments found in democratic societies by asserting his or her position. Brewster Smith, on the other hand, is not inclined to relinquish so easily the search for some form of truth. He sees in the post-modern stance 'an ingredient of resentful envy' of the status the natural sciences have achieved. And while he accepts that 'we must include in our scope the realm of meanings and values that distinguish human science from the other sciences', he also argues that 'we abdicate any distinctive or useful role as a science and profession if we give up either the aims and strategies of science toward approximating an ideal of truth' (Smith, 1994, p. 411).

5   Conclusion

We will leave you to form your own views on the different perspectives presented in this book and the relationship between them. Section 2 ended with a set of questions (see page 351) about whether there are truths about the self that we can strive for in social psychology. Are you persuaded that there are such things or have you come to question the nature of truth in itself?

We hope that the discussion of these issues has stimulated your thinking about the self. For this book, and the series of which it is a part, has been written in the spirit of what Jerome Bruner has called 'open-mindedness'. By this he refers to:

> a willingness to construe knowledge and values from multiple perspectives without loss of commitment to one's own values. ... It demands that we be conscious of how we come to our knowledge and as conscious as we can be about the values that lead us to our perspectives. It asks that we be accountable for how and what we know. But it does not insist that there is only one way of constructing meaning, or one right way. It is based upon values that, I believe, fit it best to deal with the changes and disruptions that have become so much a feature of modern life.
>
> *(Bruner, 1990, p. 30)*

Further reading

See Roy Baumeister's *Meanings of Life* (1991) for an excellent discussion of issues about finding meaning in contemporary life.

Kenneth Gergen in his book *The Saturated Self: Dilemmas of Identity in Contemporary Life* (1991), which has already been extensively referred to in the chapter, offers an articulate and provocative analysis of the effects of postmodern society upon consciousness and the self.

Anthony Giddens's *Modernity and Self-Identity: Self and Society in the Late Modern Age* (1991) presents an interesting and in some ways different analysis from Gergen of the psychological impact of present-day society.

M. Brewster Smith launches a spirited counter-attack on postmodernist analyses, and comments on both Gergen's and Giddens's ideas in an article in *American Psychologist* called 'Selfhood at risk: postmodern perils and the perils of post-modernism' (1994, May, pp. 405–11).

References

Bauman, Z. (1989) *Legislators and Interpreters,* Cambridge, Polity Press.

Baumeister, R.F. (1986) *Identity: Cultural Change and the Struggle for Self,* New York, Oxford University Press.

Baumeister, R.F. (1991) *Meanings of Life,* New York, The Guilford Press.

Berger, P.L., Berger, B. and Kellner, H. (1974) *The Homeless Mind,* Harmondsworth, Penguin Books.

Brown, H. (1996) 'Themes in experimental research on groups from the 1930s to the 1990s', in Wetherell, M. (ed.) *Identities, Groups and Social Issues,* London, Sage/ The Open University (Book 3 in this series).

Bruner, J. (1990) *Acts of Meaning,* Cambridge, Mass., Harvard University Press.

Bruner, J. (1995) personal communication.

Connor, S. (1995) 'Landmarks of the mind', *Independent on Sunday,* 28 May 1995.

Cousins, S.D. (1989) 'Culture and self-perception in Japan and the United States', *Journal of Personality and Social Psychology,* vol. 56, pp. 124–31.

Duncan, B.L. (1976) 'Differential social perception and attribution of intergroup violence: testing the lower limits of stereotyping of blacks', *Journal of Personality and Social Psychology,* vol. 34, pp. 590–8.

Erikson, E.H. (1950) *Childhood and Society,* New York, Norton. (Reprinted in paperback (1977) by Triad/Paladin.)

Eysenck, H.J. (1985) *The Decline and Fall of the Freudian Empire,* Harmondsworth, Viking.

Gergen, K.J. (1991) *The Saturated Self: Dilemmas of Identity in Contempora~* New York, Basic Books.

Giddens, A. (1991) *Modernity and Self-Identity: Self and Society in the Late Modern Age*, Cambridge, Polity Press.

Haraway, D. (1990) 'A manifesto for cyborgs: science, technology and socialist feminism in the 1980s', in Nicholson, L.J. (ed.) *Feminism/Post-modernism,* New York, Routledge.

Harré, R. (1983) *Personal Being*, Oxford, Blackwell.

Kelly, G.A. (1955) *The Psychology of Personal Constructs,* New York, Norton.

Lalljee, M., Lamb, R. and Carnibella, G. (1993) 'Lay prototypes of illness: their content use', *Psychology and Health*, vol. 8, pp. 33–49.

Langer, E.J. (1983) *The Psychology of Control*, Beverly Hills, Sage.

Lasch, C. (1978) *The Culture of Narcissism*, New York, Norton.

Laslett, P. (1989) *A Fresh Map of Life: The Emergence of the Third Age*, London, Weidenfeld and Nicolson.

Lienhardt, G. (1985) 'Self: public and private. Some African representations', in Carrithers, M., Collins, S. and Lukes, S. (eds) *The Category of the Person,* Cambridge, Cambridge University Press.

Maslow, A.H. (1973) *The Farther Reaches of Human Nature,* Harmondsworth, Penguin Books.

Miell, D. and Dallos, R. (eds) (1996) *Social Interaction and Personal Relationships*, London, Sage/The Open University (Book 2 in this series).

Sampson, E.E. (1993) *Celebrating the Other: A Dialogic Account of Human Nature*, New York, Harvester Wheatsheaf.

Schachter, S. and Singer, J.E. (1962) 'Cognitive, social and physiological determinants of emotional state', *Psychological Review*, vol. 69, pp. 379–99.

Smith, M.B. (1994) 'Selfhood at risk: postmodern perils and the perils of postmodernism', *American Psychologist*, May, pp. 405–11.

Strickland, L.H., Lewicki, R.J. and Katz, A.M. (1966) 'Temporal orientation and perceived control as determinants of risk-taking', *Journal of Experimental Social Psychology, vol.* 2, pp. 143–51.

Taylor, C. (1989) *Sources of the Self: The Making of the Modern Identity,* Cambridge, Cambridge University Press.

Taylor, C. (1991) *The Ethics of Authenticity,* Cambridge, Mass., Cambridge University Press.

Triandis, H.C, Betancourt, H., Iwav, S., Leung, K., Salazar, J. M., Setiadi, B., Sinha, J.B.P., Touzard, H. and Zaleski, Z . (1993) 'An eticemic analysis of individualism and collectivism', *Journal of Cross-Cultural Psychology*, vol. 24, pp. 366–83.

Van den Heuvel, H. (1992) *Us and Them: The Influence of Ethnicity and Gender on Stereotypes, Attitudes and Explanations of Behaviour,* Amsterdam, University of Amsterdam.

Wetherell, M. (ed.) (1996) *Identities, Groups and Social Issues*, London, Sage/The Open University (Book 3 in this series).

Williams, R. (1989) *The Trusting Heart*, New York, The Free Press.

Index

Acknowledgements

Grateful acknowledgement is made to the following sources for permission to reproduce material in this book:

CHAPTER 1: Sacks, O. (1973) *Awakenings*, pp. 240–56, Gerald Duckworth and Company Ltd, Copyright © 1973, 1976 by Oliver Sacks; Barthes, R. (1975) *Roland Barthes*, trans. R. Howard, Macmillan, London and Basingstoke, reprinted by permission of Editions du Seuil.

CHAPTER 2: *Figures:* Figure 2.3 (a) and (b): Halliday, T. (ed.) (1992) SD206 *Biology: Brain and Behaviour*, Book 3, *The Senses and Communication*, Figures 5.21 and 5.22, The Open University; Figure 2.6(a): Sperry, R.W. (1964) 'The great cerebral commissure', *Scientific American*, January 1964, p. 49. Copyright © 1964 by Scientific American, Inc. All rights reserved; Figure 2.6(b): Springer, S. and Deutsch, G. (1989) *Left Brain, Right Brain*. Copyright © 1989 by Sally P. Springer and George Deutsch. Used with permission of W. H. Freeman and Company.

CHAPTER 3: *Text:* Extract 3.1: Langer, E.J. and Rodin, J. (1976) 'The effects of choice and enhanced personal responsibility for the aged: a field experiment in an institutional setting', *Journal of Personality and Social Psychology*, vol. 34, no. 2, pp. 191–8. Copyright © 1976 by the American Psychological Association. Reprinted with permission. *Figure:* Figure 3.1: reprinted from *Behaviour, Research and Therapy*, vol. 24, Clark, D.M., 'A cognitive approach to panic', p. 463, Copyright © 1986, with kind permission from Elsevier Sciences Limited, The Boulevard, Langford Lane, Kidlington OX5 1GB, UK. *Tables:* Table 3.1: Duncan, B.L. (1976) 'Major category frequencies by harm-doer/victim race pairings' from 'Differential social perception and attribution of intergroup violence: testing the lower limits of stereotyping of blacks', *Journal of Personality and Social Psychology*, vol. 34, no. 4, p. 595. Copyright © 1976 by the American Psychological Association. Adapted with permission; Table 3.2: Smith, P.B. and Bond, M.H. (1993) 'Hofstede's four dimensions of culture-related values', *Social Psychology Across Cultures*, p. 39, Harvester Wheatsheaf. Used by permission of the publisher, Prentice Hall/A Division of Simon & Schuster.

CHAPTER 5: *Text:* Buttny, R. (1993) *Social Accountability in Communication*, Sage Publications Ltd, © Richard Buttny 1993; Reading A: Kondo, D. (1990) *Crafting Selves: Power, Gender and Discourses of Identity in a Japanese Workplace*, The University of Chicago Press, © 1990 by The University of Chicago. All rights reserved. *Figures:* Figure 5.1: Markus, H.R. and Kitayama, S. (1991) 'Culture and the self: implications for cognition, emotion and motivation', *Psychological Review*, vol. 98, no. 2, p. 226, Copyright © 1991 by the American Psychological Association Inc. Reprinted with permission; Figure 5.2: Saussure, F. De (1959) *Course in General Linguistics*, © 1959 Philosophical Library, New York. *Photographs:* pp. 225 and 226: Pictures Colour Library. *Cartoon:* p. 262: *The Guardian*, 28 May 1994, © Steven Appleby.

CHAPTER 7: *Cartoon:* p. 349: *The Guardian*, © Steven Appleby.

COVER ILLUSTRATION: Kasimir Malevich, *Sportsmen*, c.1928–32, oil on canvas, 142 × 164 cm., State Russian Museum, St Petersburg.